VOLUME 5

LATIN

AMERICAN

URBAN

RESEARCH

LATIN AMERICAN URBAN RESEARCH

This series is published in cooperation with

The Center for International Studies, Massachusetts Institute of Technology

---

Other volumes:

1. Latin American Urban Research (1971)
   Francine F. Rabinovitz and Felicity M. Trueblood, Editors
2. Regional and Urban Development Policies: A Latin American Perspective (1972)
   Guillermo Geisse and Jorge E. Hardoy, Editors
3. National-Local Linkages: The Interrelationship of Urban and National Polities in Latin America (1973)
   Francine F. Rabinovitz and Felicity M. Trueblood, Editors
4. Anthropological Perspectives on Latin American Urbanization (1974)
   Wayne A. Cornelius and Felicity M. Trueblood, Editors

Latin American Urban Research

VOLUME 5

URBANIZATION AND INEQUALITY: THE POLITICAL ECONOMY OF URBAN AND RURAL DEVELOPMENT IN LATIN AMERICA

WAYNE A. CORNELIUS
and
FELICITY M. TRUEBLOOD
Editors

SAGE PUBLICATIONS
Beverly Hills / London

For information address:

SAGE PUBLICATIONS, INC.
275 South Beverly Drive
Beverly Hills, California 90212

SAGE PUBLICATIONS LTD
St George's House / 44 Hatton Garden
London EC1N 8ER

Printed in the United States of America

ISBN 0-8039-0437-1 (cloth)
ISBN 0-8039-0602-1 (paper)

Library of Congress catalog Card No. 74-83000

FIRST PRINTING

CONTENTS

VOLUME 5

LATIN

AMERICAN

URBAN

RESEARCH

ABOUT THE EDITORS

WAYNE A. CORNELIUS is Assistant Professor of Political Science at the Massachusetts Institute of Technology. He received his Ph.D. at Stanford University and has been a visiting scholar at El Colegio de México (Mexico City) and the Center for International Affairs at Harvard University. His fields of specialization are comparative urban politics and Latin American politics. He has done fieldwork in urban and rural Mexico, and is currently engaged in research on the impact of government policies and programs on out-migration from rural communities in that country. His recent publications include *Politics and the Migrant Poor in Mexico City* (Stanford University Press, 1975); "Urbanization and Political Demand Making: Political Participation Among the Migrant Poor in Latin American Cities" (*American Political Science Review,* September, 1974); and "The Impact of Cityward Migration on Urban Land and Housing Markets: Problems and Policy Alternatives in Mexico City," in John Walton (ed.) *The City in Comparative Perspective* (Sage Publications, forthcoming, 1976).

FELICITY M. TRUEBLOOD is Assistant Professor of Latin American Studies and History at the University of Florida, Gainesville. She also serves as executive secretary of the Latin American Studies Association (LASA), and edits the *LASA Newsletter.* She has published translations of Spanish language fiction and nonfiction.

Introduction

WAYNE A. CORNELIUS

Severe spatial inequalities in the distribution of wealth and socioeconomic development have been characteristic of most Latin American countries since the early colonial period (see Hardoy, 1972; Singer, 1974; Portes and Walton, 1975: ch. 2). In most of Latin America today there are huge rural-urban, interregional, and intra-urban disparities in personal income levels, occupational and educational opportunities, public services, and other public goods. And there is disturbing evidence that in recent decades these disparities have actually increased, even in countries which have achieved rapid rates of overall economic growth measured by GNP (Adelman and Morris, 1973; Chenery et al., 1974; ECLA, 1970; Figueroa and Weisskoff, 1974; Girling, 1973; Navarro, 1974). The rural poor have responded to growing rural-urban differentials in income and income-earning opportunities by abandoning the countryside in ever increasing numbers.

The fact that urban-industrial development in Latin America and other Third World regions since 1940 seems to have exacerbated rather than ameliorated spatial inequalities has prompted many scholars to reconsider their theories and assumptions about urbanization and the process of economic development. These scholars no longer accept the traditional view of urbanization as a process which invariably results in the most "rational" or "appropriate" national distribution of population and skills in relation to resources and demands for labor. They emphasize the need to evaluate both the benefits and the *costs* of contemporary patterns of urban growth, particularly the costs to those sectors of the population living outside the largest cities. Previously the diffusion of technology and material benefits from the largest cities to rural areas and smaller cities in the "periphery" was assumed to be inevitable; revisionist scholarship has

Editor's Note: I would like to thank Elisa M.D.C.P. Reis and Eusebio Mujal León for their assistance in preparing the papers in this volume for publication. I would also like to thank Felicity M. Trueblood, co-editor of Volumes 1 through 5 of the *Latin American Urban Research* series, for her editorial suggestions and bibliographic assistance.

argued that the diffusion or "spread effects" of the economic growth generated in capital cities and other large metropolitan areas to their hinterlands and other regions of the countries in which they are located are minimal, and that, in fact, decapitalization of the hinterlands may be the most likely outcome. The earlier emphasis on the creative, innovative, modernizing role of the large city in national development has given way to the notion that large cities—especially national capitals, or "primate" cities—maintain an essentially exploitative relationship with their hinterlands and are dysfunctional to achievement of national developmental goals (see, for example, Walter, 1973). Governments are increasingly criticized for using the surplus generated by the rural sector to finance industrialization and urban infrastructure and to maintain an abundant and cheap supply of food for urban consumers. The investment decisions of multinational corporations along with other aspects of Latin American dependence on foreign sources of capital and technology have been cited—especially by Latin American scholars—as key factors contributing to widening rural-urban and interregional disparities in development (Castells, 1973; Portes and Walton, 1975: ch. 2; Quijano, 1968; Rofman and Romero, 1973; Sunkel, 1970).

This volume of the *Latin American Urban Research* series was conceived as an interdisciplinary effort to explore more systematically some of the disturbing questions about the relationship between urbanization and socioeconomic inequality which have been raised in recent years. Most of these questions, of course, are as relevant to the experience of Afro-Asian countries as to that of Latin America (see, for example, Bates, 1974; Cohen, 1974). Thus it is hoped that the papers in this volume will encourage cross-cultural comparisons and contribute to our general understanding of the role of urbanization in development and underdevelopment in the Third World. The contributors—five economists, three sociologists, three anthropologists, one political scientist, one geographer, and one urban and regional planner—view urbanization as a social change process which has brought about major shifts not only in human settlement patterns but in national distributions of wealth and economic opportunity. They discuss the mechanisms or processes by which these shifts have occurred, and identify the groups or sectors of the population which have benefitted most from them, as well as those who have benefitted least. In the process, they suggest a number of ways in which the economic and political relationships between rural and urban sectors in Latin American countries might be reconceptualized so as to increase our understanding of center-periphery interactions and provide a more adequate basis for policy formulation.

The "political economy" subtitle of this volume underscores the theme common to all papers included in it: public policy and its relationship to social inequality. The contributors illustrate how government decisions, policies and programs have influenced the spatial distribution of wealth and population in Latin American countries, whether by design or as an unintended consequence of public policies not directly concerned with influencing the rate, pattern or consequences of urban growth. They identify the frequent tensions and contradictions between governmental efforts to reduce spatial inequalities and other policies with different objectives (especially relating to overall economic growth) being pursued by the same governments. Finally, they assess the experience of several Latin American countries in using a variety of policy instruments (regional development programs, housing policy, fiscal policy, etc.) to ameliorate the inequities which have accompanied urban-industrial development.

Urbanization and Uneven Development

A first step toward disentangling the complex relationships between urbanization and Latin America's increasingly uneven pattern of socioeconomic development is taken in John Walton's essay on "internal colonialism." Building on the work of theorists such as Pablo González Casanova (1965), Rodolfo Stavenhagen (1968), and Andre Gunder Frank (1969: 190-201), Walton carefully explicates and criticizes alternative conceptions of internal colonialism, and redefines it as "a process that produces certain intra-national forms of patterned socioeconomic inequality directly traceable to the exploitative practices through which national and international institutions are linked in the interests of surplus extraction and capital accumulation." In spatial terms, internal colonialism involves the concentration of resources among smaller numbers of major urban centers at the expense of smaller towns and rural areas. Although Walton's reformulation may not fully satisfy the objections of some scholars who have criticized the internal colonialism concept (Morse, 1971: 50-55; Chilcote, 1974: 11-12; González, 1974), he makes a strong case for its utility in describing and explaining the relationship between large cities and their hinterlands and provides a detailed list of empirical indicators which might be used to operationalize the concept for research (cf. Havens and Flinn, 1970; Hechter, 1974).

Walton also specifies a number of areas in which the practices of public and private institutions are especially likely to give rise to relationships of internal colonialism. He identifies the structure of trade and commerce as the most important determinant of internal colonialism in its geographic form, particularly unequal commodity exchanges and deteriorating terms of trade between the largest cities and rural areas and provincial urban centers. He also relates spatial imbalances to the activities of multinational corporations, which tend to concentrate their investments in national capitals and "move down the urban hierarchy only after successive encounters with saturated markets." Thus urbanization under conditions of externally dependent capitalism can be expected to intensify spatial inequalities in income and employment opportunities. In examining the implications of his analysis for theories of urbanization and urban social organization, Walton stresses the crucial role of cities as "nodes" in the process of surplus extraction and transmission from lower to higher levels of a society which is the essence of internal colonialism. He observes that in most developing countries, plans for decentralization of urban-industrial growth "remain only plans, not for want of some justification based on distributive economic justice, but because they run counter to the logic of internal colonialism."

The Rural-Urban Interface

The micro-level changes which occur in the economic and social life of rural communities as a result of urban-industrial development at the national level have been the object of considerable speculation but little systematic investigation. The two papers included in Part II of this volume help to remedy this deficiency in urbanization studies dealing with Latin America; both are based on first-hand observation and interviewing, and both deal directly with the costs and benefits of urbanization to specific provincial communities.

The study of the Mexican village of Tzintzuntzan by Robert V. Kemper and George M. Foster, based on data gathered over a thirty-year period, reveals that as Tzintzuntzan has come increasingly under the influence of urban-based government agencies and private businesses and individuals, it has profited in many ways, particularly as a result of local infrastructure development and the stimulation of local pottery and handicraft production linked to urban markets and tourism. The village has also benefitted substantially from the remittances of urban-dwelling emigrants from the village, in the form of money and merchandise, and from other services performed by the emigrants for village residents. (The emigrants themselves and their adaptation to life in Mexico City are described in Kemper, 1974.) Nevertheless, urbanization has increased income inequality within the community, thus increasing the potential for social conflict between the village's "haves" and "have nots." "Creeping urbanism" (cf. Guyot, 1969) has also encouraged buying on credit among the residents and increased their indebtedness to nonlocal businesses. It seems, however, that Tzintzuntzan's economy, based traditionally on pottery-making, has enabled it to benefit more than the average, predominantly agricultural village in Mexico from integration into the nation's expanding urban system.

Bryan R. Roberts' paper, based on fieldwork in the Mantaro Valley region of central Peru, stresses the resilience of provincial economic and social life in the face of a national development process dominated by the country's urban core. Building on his analysis of rural-urban linkages in Volume 4 of this series (Roberts, 1974), he provides a detailed case study of the development and functioning of the economy of a provincial city (Huancayo) and its hinterland, and their relationships with the capital and the national economy. Emphasizing the predominance of small-scale entrepreneurial activity in the provincial economy, Roberts shows that this kind of economic activity is not "marginal" to the national development process, nor "an outmoded form of economic activity in process of extinction"; rather, it is an integral part of the capitalist transformation of contemporary Peru, though until recently operating largely outside the sphere of government regulation.

In the second part of his chapter, Roberts presents a strong indictment of "centralist-biased" strategies of national development currently fashionable in Peru and many other Third World countries, as well as among North American development specialists (see Lowenthal, 1975; Kesselman and Rosenthal, 1974; Kimmerling and Lissak, 1974). He describes three kinds of national government intervention in the Mantaro region since 1968, and analyzes the consequences of these interventions for the local economy. He concludes that, lacking the proper basis in local social and economic organization and sufficient capital investments on the part of the government, State intervention has had the effect of restricting the expansion of small-scale enterprises while accentuating local inequalities in wealth distribution. The military regime's would-be structural reforms have thus failed to benefit the majority of the region's population. Roberts' case study illustrates the difficulty of promoting structural changes in the face of vital, ongoing local social and economic processes which are insufficiently understood—and respected—by central planners.

The Political Economy of Urban Poverty

The contributors to Part III of this volume are concerned primarily with intra-urban rather than rural-urban or interregional manifestations of poverty and social inequality. The two papers by Lisa Peattie and Susan Eckstein, however, provide a fascinating big-city counterpoint to Roberts' analysis of small-scale entrepreneurial activity in small-town and rural Peru. Both Peattie and Eckstein present detailed case studies of the microeconomy of low-income neighborhoods within a large city, and the relationships of local entrepreneurs with institutions and individuals operating in the larger urban economy.

Peattie focuses on low-income city dwellers engaged in "tertiary sector" activities—petty commerce and services. Drawing on recent fieldwork conducted in a peripheral *barrio* and a central-city area in Bogotá, she challenges much of the conventional wisdom concerning the nature and general economic and social functions of the tertiary or "informal" sector of the urban economy in developing countries. Although some students of Asian and African cities have urged a reassessment of the generally pejorative view of this sector held by most development economists (see, for example, Hart, 1973; McGee, 1974), Latin Americanists have continued to characterize the sector primarily in terms of "ease of entry," "marginality," low productivity, low earnings, and its role as an occupational "refuge" for unskilled migrants from the countryside. The rapid expansion of the tertiary sector in virtually all major Latin American cities in recent decades has been viewed primarily as a response to rapid population growth, rural-urban migration, and capital-intensive technology which reduces the rate of job creation within the secondary sector (cf. Friedmann and Sullivan, 1974). Peattie's research suggests that, in fact, many forms of petty commerce are not particularly suitable for entry by new migrants to the city, that earnings within the tertiary sector are not uniformly low, and that many of those engaged in tertiary activities would not necessarily opt for wage-labor employment in the secondary sector if jobs were available there. Indeed, Peattie's interviews reveal that being self-employed is positively valued by many people in the tertiary sector, who regard even petty commerce as a surer road to upward mobility than unskilled wage labor, especially in a nation lacking powerful unions and fringe benefits deriving from labor legislation. Peattie also stresses the role of government regulation–especially the official system of public markets and legal permits for selling–in restricting competition within the tertiary sector and raising barriers to entry.

Another perspective on entrepreneurial activity in low-income neighborhoods is offered by Susan Eckstein, who reports on a comparative study of the local economies of a central city slum zone, a low-cost public housing project, and a relatively old squatter settlement in Mexico City. She describes the problems confronting small businessmen in the three areas which contribute to extreme insecurity of income and high turnover of ownership. She finds that local businesses offer relatively few employment opportunities for neighborhood residents owing to discrimination in hiring practices (proprietors prefer to hire either relatives or recent migrants from rural communities). A major problem revealed by Eckstein's research is nonlocal control of economic opportunities in low-income neighborhoods. The largest factories in the central city slum zone included in her study had been acquired by U.S.-based multinational corporations, and the largest and most lucrative retail businesses in all three neighborhoods were also owned by non-residents. The main problem, she argues, is not the *absence* of local opportunities but the "inability to control access to those opportunities which do exist within the communities, particularly access to the most financially rewarding businesses." Eckstein also shows that in the areas under study, local business prospects have been strongly influenced by political-economic forces operating at the national level during the period in which each area was initially settled, and that even governmental inaction (e.g., selective non-enforcement of labor legislation) has powerfully shaped local opportunities.

This section of the volume concludes with two papers on the problem of housing for low-income city dwellers and governmental responses to this problem in Brazil and Chile. Clark W. Reynolds and Robert T. Carpenter analyze Brazil's Housing Finance System and its accomplishments both in terms of increasing the supply of low-cost housing and of redistributing wealth in favor of the poor. The authors employ a "flow-of-funds" analytical approach to identify the income groups which are the most important suppliers of resources to the Housing Finance System and the groups which have benefitted most from it.

Their analysis reveals that the system has been very successful in attracting savings that might otherwise have been directed to consumption, and that, at least in terms of its returns to low-income savers, "the Brazilian program is a definite step in the direction of social equity." However, confirming the early suspicions of some Brazilian housing and urban development experts regarding the probable outcomes of the military government's policies in this area (see Ríos, 1971), Reynolds and Carpenter note a disturbing trend in the utilization of funds attracted by the program: They find that a majority of funds have been used to finance "middle and upper income housing, other urban construction, and works of urban infrastructure rather than subsidized housing for the poor, and that this trend has been increasing." Despite the demonstrable bias favoring middle and upper income groups, Reynolds and Carpenter express optimism concerning the potentialities of the program for assisting low-income city dwellers and perhaps even the rural poor. They offer a number of policy recommendations for modifying the Housing Finance System in order to increase the flow of resources to the poor, especially the poorest 20 percent of the urban population which up to now has been virtually excluded from the system's benefits.

In the first of two papers included in this volume on urban and regional policy under Salvador Allende's Unidad Popular regime in Chile, Eduardo Lozano begins with a comparative analysis of approaches to the low-income housing problem pursued by Unidad Popular and its predecessor, the Christian Democratic administration of Eduardo Frei. Lozano's analysis of the Christian Democratic policies concludes that the housing targets established were inadequate, only partially achieved, and "with an outlook that subordinated the larger public interest to the smaller private one." Most importantly, the Christian Democrats opted to work mainly through the private construction industry and market allocation mechanisms. By contrast, the provision of low-cost housing became, under Allende, an integral part of the social revolutionary process, in which the government would attempt to "gain control of the housing production sector, to increase its efficiency, and to pass along to the people the cost-reduction benefits." A radical new conception of housing itself was developed under Unidad Popular: "Housing was withdrawn from the marketplace as an item to be purchased and sold and as a source of profit for investors. Housing took on the character of another right of the people, produced and allocated according to social criteria, not unlike education or health." Lozano's analysis suggests, however, that the housing targets established by the Allende regime were probably too ambitious to be realistic, given the extremely high levels of financial and human (technical) inputs they required, and the fact that in some respects the housing policy conflicted with other high-priority objectives of the revolutionary change process underway. Despite these limitations, Lozano estimates tentatively that housing construction goals for the first years of the program were largely attained, and observes that the government had been highly successful in enlisting mass participation in the program through political party, trade union and neighborhood committees. He suggests that high levels of popular participation combined with strong ideological commitment on the part of the government might have compensated temporarily for some of the technical limitations on the housing program's potentialities, had it been permitted to continue.

Public Policies as Determinants of Urban Growth and Rural-Urban Inequalities

There is abundant evidence indicating that the highly uneven patterns of human settlement and wealth distribution characteristic of most Latin American countries today are not simply the outcomes of "natural" processes of development, nor even of the normal operation of market forces within capitalist economies. These imbalances also stem from the decisions and policy preferences of national governments. The contributors to Part IV of this volume address themselves to public policies as *determinants* of inequalities in the national distribution of population, income, and developmental possibilities.

Joel Bergsman opens the discussion of this issue with a provocative essay emphasizing the importance of "accidental" policies for controlling the rate and pattern of urban growth. These policies usually lack an explicit spatial dimension or objective, and usually are formulated without consideration of their likely effects on the national distribution of population; yet their actual impact on settlement patterns and interregional inequalities in wealth and development is often greater than that of public policies implemented deliberately with spatial objectives in mind. As examples of such "accidental" urban growth policies Bergsman cites industrialization policies, import and export policies, pricing policies which favor industry over the agricultural sector, wage policies which create large interregional income differentials, and pro-natalist demographic policies which foster overpopulation of rural communities and, in turn, emigration from them to the cities. He offers one quantitative example concerning the impact of protectionist import policies on urban growth in Brazil, estimating that tariffs and other import controls are responsible for the residence there of perhaps one-fourth of the population of the former State of Guanabara (the city of Rio de Janeiro and some adjoining suburbs). Faced with forces as strong as these, Bergsman argues, deliberate policies for channeling or reducing urban growth may have only marginal or very long-run effects on the national distribution of population.

John J. Harrigan probes the tensions between urban growth planning and national economic development policy in Brazil in greater detail. Following a careful summary of the major features of Brazilian urban and regional development policies, he observes that implementation of most of these policies would divert scarce governmental resources into public services and unproductive infrastructure investments benefitting primarily the rural poor and promoting a redistribution of national income in their favor—outcomes incompatible with the strategy of national economic development which has been pursued by the Brazilian military regime since 1964. This strategy emphasizes maximum overall economic growth in the short run, deriving mainly from rapid industrialization. The industrialization effort requires the economies of scale and infrastructure advantages which large cities provide, as well as the maintenance of a favorable investment climate in such cities, where multinational corporations prefer to locate their operations. The development strategy is not premised upon a reduction of regional inequalities in wealth distribution. Thus in many ways, Harrigan argues, "the logic of the Brazilian model for economic development would seem to create pressures for minimizing the amount of resources devoted to urban and regional development programs." He notes that even those nominally "spatial" policies which have been implemented by the regime—such as colonization of Amazon basin lands—have actually had the effect of concentrating more wealth in the hands of a few private investors and multinational corporations whose initial capitalization enabled them to take greatest advantage of the new economic opportunities, while having little impact on national settlement patterns. Indeed, so long as the regime's top-priority objective remains rapid expansion of the country's GNP rather than a more rational and just distribution of population and wealth, these kinds of policy outcomes seem virtually inevitable. It comes as no surprise that recent data

> clearly demonstrate that all attempts have failed to weight the various systems of taxation, fiscal incentives and public investment in favor of the impoverished North and Northeast. . . . Far from correcting the excessive development of the Center-South at the expense of the North and Northeast, government policies are actually accentuating it. . . . [Government] investment is made because an industrial infrastructure exists; where it does not exist, there is no investment [Latin America, 1974].

Richard Webb's examination of the case of Peru since 1963 reveals many parallels with the Brazilian experience. Like Bergsman, Webb finds that the public policies which have had greatest impact on spatial inequalities are policies aimed primarily at other objectives, especially national economic growth. He notes that many policy instruments employed by Peruvian governments have a location-specific nature which biases them toward the urban sector. Even so, he argues, governmental passivity or inaction in the face of market forces tending to benefit urban areas disproportionately has been a more important source of regional inequality in Peru than actual government policies and programs. Webb's data indicate that the controversial structural reforms pursued by Peru's military government since 1968 have had little impact on regional inequalities. He notes that most income redistribution has occurred within the modern (predominantly urban) sector of the economy, and that income transfers within this sector "have not been a significant cause of, nor offset to, the regional inequalities produced by the market." Webb points to strong political, administrative, and psychological forces which have made horizontal income transfers between the urban and rural sectors very difficult to achieve. There has been no significant increase in the agricultural sector's share of the total credit supply, and rural areas have also suffered from the high priority attached by the regime to capital-intensive industry and mining. Webb concludes that most spatial inequalities in Peru today flow from the operation of market forces and not from public policies that decapitalize the countryside; but "public investment has, and continues to, *reinforce* urban-rural inequalities."

Regional Development Programs and Rural-Urban Inequalities

Most Latin American governments which have acted to reduce spatial imbalances in population and wealth have made use of a combination of policy instruments which can be subsumed under the rubric of "regional development programs." Such programs normally involve selective decentralization of industrial investments (both public and private), administrative activities and infrastructure away from the urban "core" region or regions and toward a number of "growth centers" or "growth poles" in the periphery. Thus far there have been very few detailed case studies of regional development policies or programs which would enable planners to assess the efficacy of this policy alternative for shifting national distributions of population and wealth in the context of Latin America (see Stöhr, 1972, and Geisse and Hardoy, 1972, for reviews of the literature bearing on Latin America). Thus the papers by Gilbert, Barkin and Lozano appearing in the final section of this volume represent important new "case materials" for those concerned with spatial planning in Latin American countries.

Colombia is one of the few countries in the world whose government has pursued an explicitly "pro-urbanization" policy, viewing accelerated urban growth as a stimulant to overall economic development and as a means of bringing about desirable changes in national patterns of production and consumption. As Alan Gilbert puts it, Colombia has been one of the first nations to seek "economic development *through* urban growth." Gilbert provides a comprehensive survey of Colombian policies for urban and regional development since 1951, with a view toward assessing the prospects for balanced regional development as an outcome of current policies in this area. Even though Colombia has a relatively balanced pattern of urban growth by comparison with most Latin American countries, which suffer from "primate" urbanization centered on a single city, Bogotá has outdistanced all other major Colombian cities in population growth in recent years, and industrial development patterns show an increasing concentration of investments and employment opportunities in the four largest cities. The concentration of government activities in Bogotá is identified by Gilbert as one of the principal factors explaining its disproportionate growth.

Gilbert is not very sanguine about the prospects for reversing trends toward concentration of urban and industrial growth through the regional development policies currently being implemented in Colombia. The efficacy of these measures—including decentralization of industrial investments and credit, administrative decentralization, infrastructure investments in intermediate cities, and investments to increase productivity and incomes in rural areas—depends on a high degree of interagency coordination as well as real decentralization in the governmental decision-making process. Gilbert finds that neither of these conditions is being met adequately in Colombia today. He argues that genuine improvements for Colombia's poorer regions are likely to result from the program, but questions whether the present incentives for decentralization are sufficiently strong to check the powerful social, economic and political forces leading to spatial concentration. He notes important conflicts between the regional dispersion program and the national economic development plan, which is actually biased toward urban concentration. Gilbert argues that the Colombian regional program suffers most fundamentally from a "lack of political will"—weak governmental commitment to the goal of balanced regional development. He concludes his chapter with a number of unresolved questions for future research, the answers to which would greatly assist spatial planners and government decision makers in all developing countries:

> Do we really know whether large cities are more "efficient" than medium-sized cities, and are we certain that our present methods offer good ways of measuring urban costs and benefits? Can we agree on the point beyond which regional income disparities are undesirable and actually begin to slow down economic growth? Can we suggest ways in which the poorest regions in a nation can develop without leading to the destruction of their cultures or the massive acceleration of out-migration?

Regional development programs have often led to rapid increases in agricultural production in the affected region, due to public investments in irrigation and other infrastructure, improved credit facilities, and better integration of the region into the national economy. By this criterion, many such programs might be considered eminently successful. But what are the effects of increases in production and regional development in general on the lives of poor people in the "benefitted" area? This is the basic question posed and answered by David Barkin in his chapter on the Tepalcatepec River Basin project in Mexico. One of the large number of regional development programs established in major river basins by the Mexican government since 1947 (see Cárdenas, 1972; Barkin, 1972; Carrillo Arronte, 1975), the Tepalcatepec program has been very successful if measured by traditional criteria of public investment analysis. Most of the government's investments were concentrated in the agricultural sector, where significant productivity increases have been achieved. Traditional subsistence crops have been replaced by commercial crops, and modern production techniques have been adopted. Barkin finds the results of the program to be far less impressive, however, when an equity criterion is applied. Within the "benefitted" region, landownership and income are now much more concentrated than before the project's initiation. Out-migration of the poor has exceeded in-migration to take advantage of new economic opportunities created by the program. Finally, the project failed to stimulate self-sustaining economic growth in the region, thus limiting the rate of job creation, especially in the industrial sector. Instead, government policy encouraged the transfer of profits to other, more industrialized parts of the country.

Barkin's analysis of "what went wrong" with the Tepalcatepec project, at least in terms of equity criteria, is rich in lessons for would-be regional developers. It is clear, however, that governments seeking to implement a regional development program may act out of a variety of concerns, only one of which may be improving the incomes and living conditions of people in the affected regions or reducing interregional imbalances in development. Barkin argues that what mattered most, from the Mexican government's perspective, was the contribution of Tepalcatepec and other regional development projects to the national industrialization effort; thus steps were not taken to increase their redistributive impact. In the absence of such measures, regional development programs may succeed in reducing income disparities *between* regions of a country while having a regressive impact on income and land distribution *within* the "benefitted" regions (see Alonso, 1968: 52). A similar outcome is predicted by Alan Gilbert with regard to Colombia, where the basic thrust of the government's regional development efforts toward large-scale agricultural enterprises may lead to "a deterioration in the living standards of the poorer groups in the regions."

Prior to the September 11, 1973, coup which ended the Unidad Popular regime in Chile, that country had developed one of the most coherent strategies of regional development in Latin America. The experience of Unidad Popular and its predecessor, the Christian Democratic regime, in formulating and implementing a regional development policy is recounted by Eduardo Lozano in the final chapter of this volume. Under the Christian Democratic administration, the strategy to counteract spatially imbalanced economic development was heavily influenced by conventional "growth pole" theory. In practice, according to Lozano, the Christian Democratic approach failed to generate new growth centers in the periphery, and interregional inequalities actually became more pronounced. Lozano attributes this outcome to the Christian Democrats' limited conception of the role of the State in economic development, i.e., that the State should act basically in support of the private sector, not directing it nor supplanting it. Thus "the short-range objectives of private capital—which are in conflict with a deconcentration approach—replaced the long-range public objectives of regional development." State intervention in the economy increased tremendously, of course, under Unidad Popular; regional development was to be furthered in part by taking investment decisions out of the hands of private entrepreneurs and entrusting them to the State and to the nationalized enterprises. The regime's extensive agrarian reform program was also an integral part of its regional development strategy. And one of its first steps was to increase the minimum wage level and to standardize it throughout the country. This measure immediately increased the attractiveness of the less developed regions, where living costs were considerably lower than in the "core" regions. As in the case of the Unidad Popular housing program, implementation of the regional development strategy was hampered by lack of technical capacity and the strong opposition faced by Unidad Popular in the Chilean Congress. Conflicts also arose between "academic" planners and the more pragmatically-oriented, "operations" staff charged with regional development; yet "political goals, defined in clear ideological terms, had explicit priority in the planning process." Lozano admits that the short lifespan of the Unidad Popular government does not permit a thorough evaluation of its regional policies, but argues that they represent creative solutions to the problem of spatial imbalances in development which might have proven applicable to other Latin American countries.

Conclusion

The weight of the evidence presented by the contributors to this volume, as well as other students of urbanization and the development process, is that in most Latin American countries it will be extremely difficult, at least in the short run, to bring about significant changes in the national distribution of population and wealth through governmental action. In view of the powerful forces promoting concentration and centralization in the development process, governments must intervene massively in this process in such a way as to alter the deeply-rooted propensity of individuals and business enterprises to locate within the largest urban centers. After a review of studies of spatial planning attempts in both Third World and advanced industrial countries, one investigator recently concluded that "policies to redirect investment away from areas to which investors might otherwise move requires sophisticated economic analysis and planning, the capacity for considerable administrative coordination, and *a degree of political support that most governments find difficult to achieve*" (Weiner, 1975: 40, emphasis added).

The task becomes even more formidable in the context of capitalist economic systems in which large numbers of investment decisions are occurring constantly outside the public sector, without regard to the objective of achieving a more equitable and rational dispersion of economic activity and population through the nation. As Hardoy (1973: M265-14) has observed,

> In a capitalist economy, subject to the pressures of interest groups, if one region gains comparative advantages it is very difficult–practically impossible, I might say–to achieve an adequate regional balance. Regional inequalities cannot be overcome in a laissez-faire economy. . . . Moreover, the inequalities continue growing in spite of government proclamations, plans, and attempts at regional decentralization.

Barkin, in his chapter in this volume, argues along similar lines that within a capitalist system, "policy can be designed only to mitigate some of the most oppressive side effects of concentration and centralization without threatening its basic premise. . . . Only when the negative effects of continuing geographic concentration become too great for the capitalists themselves–in terms of falling profit rates–will there be changes in the location of economic activity and therefore of population." Meanwhile, rural-urban income differentials and disparities in living standards continue to widen, the exodus of the rural unemployed and underemployed proceeds apace, population piles up in the nation's capital or "core" regions, and the social costs of these huge urban agglomerations rise precipitously.

Although such problems are not completely absent even in socialist countries (see, for example, Lang, 1975), the case of Cuba under Castro–and perhaps that of Chile under Allende, had the latter's experiments in urban and regional policy continued long enough–demonstrates that a Latin American government can achieve significant spatial shifts in wealth and population without decades of sustained intervention. In revolutionary Cuba, rural-urban gaps in income, employment, and living conditions have been narrowed substantially, rural out-migration has been drastically reduced and rechanneled toward intermediate urban centers where new sources of employment and public services have been concentrated, and the size of the capital city has been stabilized (Acosta and Hardoy, 1973; Hardoy, 1973). A number of factors appear to have contributed importantly to this outcome, including the small size of the country, socialization of the economy, strong political commitment on the part of Cuban leaders, and high levels of mass participation in government programs.

Whether the Cuban experience might be replicated elsewhere in Latin America is, of course, a question which goes far beyond the scope of this introduction. It is clear, however, that in countries with capitalist or mixed economic systems, a far more "activist" role must be assumed by the State in managing the development process, if current trends toward ever greater concentration of population and wealth are to be reversed. As Portes has observed, "the dominant role of contemporary public institutions [in Latin America] has not been to prevent capitalist distortions of urban development but rather to adapt the city, as well as possible, to the new and difficult conditions" resulting from the fact that market forces have determined the rate and pattern of urban growth. "It has been, by and large, an alleviating, 'patching up' function, not a regulatory or preventive one" (Portes and Walton, 1975: ch. 2). Moreover, the government actions which have been taken–particularly industrial investment decisions–have often encouraged further urban concentration. The locational criteria applied by government decisionmakers bent on accelerating national economic growth usually do not differ greatly from those applied by private entrepreneurs, leading to the concentration of both public and private investments in cities and regions already enjoying considerable comparative advantages.

The economic development strategies preferred by a majority of Latin American governments today clearly limit the capacity of these governments to deal effectively with problems of spatial inequality. And as most of the papers in this volume strongly suggest, until the goal of greater equity in the distribution of benefits flowing from the development process is given higher priority than other national policy objectives, even the few programs implemented in the name of redistribution are likely to discriminate against the poor, or at least fail to help them appreciably.

Addendum

This volume of *Latin American Urban Research* does not include a comprehensive bibliography of recent publications in the field. Due to the relatively small number of studies which have appeared since our last bibliography was compiled (see *Latin American Urban Research,* Volume 4 [1974], pp. 263-296) and delays in receiving some foreign serial publications, it has been decided to postpone publication of a new bibliography until early 1977, when Volume 6 of this series will appear. Thereafter the bibliography will be a regular biannual feature of the *Latin American Urban Research* series. Readers are invited to send citations of books, journal articles, dissertations, and papers presented at professional meetings for inclusion in the Volume 6 bibliography. Correspondence should be addressed to Professor Wayne A. Cornelius, Department of Political Science, E53-413, Massachusetts Institute of Technology, Cambridge, Mass. 02139, U.S.A.

REFERENCES

ACOSTA, M. and J. E. HARDOY (1973) Urban Reform in Revolutionary Cuba. New Haven, Conn.: Antilles Research Program, Yale University.

ADELMAN, I. and C. MORRIS (1973) Economic Growth and Social Equity in Developing Countries. Stanford, Calif.: Stanford University Press.

ALONSO, W. (1968) "Industrial location and regional policy in economic development." Institute of Urban and Regional Development, University of California, Berkeley, Working Paper No. 74.

BARKIN, D. [ed.] (1972) Los beneficiarios del desarrollo regional. México, D.F.: Sep/Setentas.

BATES, R. (1974) Patterns of Uneven Development: Causes and Consequences in Zambia. Denver, Col.: University of Denver, Monograph Series in World Affairs.

CARDENAS, C. (1972) "Regional rural development: the Mexican Río Balsas Commission," in G. Geisse and J. E. Hardoy (eds.) Regional and Urban Development Policies: Latin American Urban Research, Vol. 2. Beverly Hills, Calif.: Sage Publications.

CARRILLO ARRONTE, R. [ed.] (1975) "Desarrollo regional," entire issue of Ecopolítica: Revista de la Liga de Economistas Revolucionarios de la República Mexicana 1, 1 (January-March).

CASTELLS, M. [ed.] (1973) Imperialismo y urbanización en América Latina. Barcelona, Spain: Gustavo Gili.

CHENERY, H. et al. (1974) Redistribution with Growth: Policies to Improve Income Distribution in Developing Countries in the Context of Economic Growth. New York and London: Oxford University Press.

CHILCOTE, R. (1974) "Dependency: a critical synthesis of the literature." Latin American Perspectives 1, 1 (Spring).

COHEN, M. A. (1974) Urban Policy and Political Conflict in Africa. Chicago: University of Chicago Press.

ECLA [Economic Commission for Latin America] (1970) La distribución del ingreso en América Latina. New York: ECLA, United Nations.

FIGUEROA, A. and R. WEISSKOFF (1974) "Visión de las pirámides sociales: distribución del ingreso en América Latina." Ensayos ECIEL (Programa de Estudios Conjuntos Sobre Integración Económica Latinoamericana, Rio de Janeiro and Washington, D.C.) 1 (November): 83-154. (English version to be published in Robert Ferber, ed., Consumption, Prices and Economic Development: Proceedings of a Conference Sponsored by ECIEL and the Institute for Ibero-Amerika Kunde, Hamburg, West Germany, October 1-3, 1973.)

FRANK, A. G. (1969) Capitalism and Underdevelopment in Latin America: Historical Studies of Chile and Brazil. New York: Monthly Review Press.

FRIEDMANN, J. and F. SULLIVAN (1974) "Labor absorption in the urban economy: the case of the developing countries." Economic Development and Cultural Change 22: 385-413.

GEISSE, G. and J. E. HARDOY [eds.] (1972) Regional and Urban Development Policies: Latin American Urban Research, Vol. 2. Beverly Hills, Calif.: Sage Publications.

GIRLING, R. (1973) "Dependency and persistent income inequality," pp. 83-101 in F. Bonilla and R. Girling (eds.) Structures of Dependency. East Palo Alto, Calif.: Nairobi Bookstore.

GONZALEZ, G. (1974) "A critique of the internal colony model." Latin American Perspectives 1, 1 (Spring): 154-161.

GONZALEZ CASANOVA, P. (1965) "Internal colonialism and national development." Studies in Comparative International Development 1, 4: 27-37.

GUYOT, J. F. (1969) "Creeping urbanism and political development in Malaysia," pp. 124-161 in R. T. Daland (ed.) Comparative Urban Research. Beverly Hills, Calif.: Sage Publications.

HARDOY, J. E. (1973) "Spacial structure and society in revolutionary Cuba," pp. 1-16 in D. P. Barkin and N. R. Manitzas (eds.) Cuba: The Logic of the Revolution. Andover, Mass.: Warner Modular Publications. Module No. 265.

--- [ed.] (1972) Las ciudades en América Latina. Buenos Aires: Paidós.

HART, K. (1973) "Informal income opportunities and urban employment in Ghana." Journal of Modern African Studies 11, 1 (March): 61-89.

HAVENS, A. E. and W. L. FLINN (1970) Internal Colonialism and Structural Change in Colombia. New York: Praeger Special Studies.

HECHTER, M. (1974) Internal Colonialism: The Celtic Fringe in British National Development 1536-1966. Berkeley: University of California Press.

KEMPER, R. V. (1974) "Family and household organization among Tzintzuntzan migrants in Mexico City," pp. 23-45 in W. A. Cornelius and F. M. Trueblood (eds.) Anthropological Perspectives on Latin American Urbanization: Latin American Urban Research, Vol. 4. Beverly Hills, Calif.: Sage Publications.

KESSELMAN, M. and D. ROSENTHAL (1974) "Local power and comparative politics." Sage Professional Papers in Comparative Politics 5, 01-049. Beverly Hills: Sage Publications.

KIMMERLING, B. and M. LISSAK (1974) "Inner dualism: an outcome of the center-periphery relationship during modernization processes in Uganda." Sage Research Papers in the Social Sciences, 90-008. Beverly Hills: Sage Publications.

LANG, N. R. (1975) "The dialectics of decentralization: economic reform and regional inequality in Yugoslavia." World Politics 27, 3 (April): 309-335.

Latin America (1974) "Brazil: unto him that hath, much shall be given." Latin America Newsletter (Britain), 1 March: 71.

LOWENTHAL, A. F. [ed.] (1975) The Peruvian Experiment. Princeton, N.J.: Princeton University Press.

McGEE, T. G. (1974) "The persistence of the proto-proletariat: occupational structures and planning for the future of Third World cities." Paper presented to the Comparative Urban Studies and Planning Program, School of Architecture and Urban Planning, University of California, Los Angeles, April. (Comparative Urbanization Studies Series, School of Architecture and Urban Planning, UCLA)

MORSE, R. M. (1971) "Trends and issues in Latin American urban research, 1965-1970: part II." Latin American Research Review 6, 2 (Summer): 19-55.

NAVARRO, V. (1974) "The underdevelopment of health or the health of underdevelopment: an analysis of the distribution of human health resources in Latin America." Politics and Society 4, 2 (Winter): 267-293.

PORTES, A. and J. WALTON (1975) Power and Poverty in Latin America: Studies of Urban Politics from Above and Below. Austin, Texas: University of Texas Press.

QUIJANO, A. (1968) "Dependencia, cambio social y urbanización en Latinoamérica." Revista Mexicana de Sociología 30, 3.

RIOS, J. A. (1971) "The growth of cities and urban development," pp. 269-288 in J. Saunders (ed.) Modern Brazil: New Patterns of Development. Gainesville, Florida: University of Florida Press.

ROBERTS, B. R. (1974) "The interrelationships of city and provinces in Peru and Guatemala," pp. 207-235 in W. A. Cornelius and F. M. Trueblood (eds.) Anthropological Perspectives on Latin American Urbanization: Latin American Urban Research, Vol. 4. Beverly Hills, Calif.: Sage Publications.

ROFMAN, A. B. and L. A. ROMERO (1973) Sistema socioeconómico y estructura regional en la Argentina. Buenos Aires: Amorrotu.

SINGER, P. (1974) "Campo y ciudad en el contexto histórico latinoamericano. Revista Latinoamericana de Estudios Urbano Regionales 4, 10 (September): 9-21.

STAVENHAGEN, R. (1968) "Classes, colonialism, and acculturation," pp. 31-63 in J. A. Kahl (ed.) Comparative Perspectives on Stratification. Boston: Little, Brown.

STOHR, W. (1972) Regional Development: Experiences and Prospects in Latin America. The Hague and Paris: Mouton.

SUNKEL, O. (1970) "Desarrollo, subdesarrollo, dependencia, marginación y desigualdades espaciales: hacia un enfoque totalizante." Revista Latinoamericana de Estudios Urbano Regionales 1, 4.

WALTER, J. P. (1973) "The city as a source of regional economic disparity in Latin America." Review of Social Economy 31, 1 (April): 66-84.

WEINER, M. (1975) "Internal migration policies: purposes, interests, instruments, effects." Cambridge, Mass.: Monograph Series on Migration and Development, Center for International Studies, Massachusetts Institute of Technology.

PART I

URBANIZATION AND UNEVEN DEVELOPMENT

JOHN WALTON is Associate Professor of Sociology and Urban Affairs at Northwestern University. He received his Ph.D. from the University of California, Santa Barbara, and has specialized in political sociology, the sociology of economic development, and urban sociology. He has done fieldwork in Mexico and Colombia on the role of local elites in urban development, and is currently engaged in a critical reevaluation of theories of development in Third World countries. His major publications include *Cities in Change* (coedited with Donald Carns; Allyn and Bacon, 1973); *Power and Poverty in Latin America: Studies of Urban Politics from Above and Below* (coauthored with Alejandro Portes; University of Texas Press, 1975); and *Elites and Economic Development: The Social and Political Bases of Economic Change in Latin American Cities* (forthcoming).

Chapter 1

INTERNAL COLONIALISM: PROBLEMS OF DEFINITION AND MEASUREMENT

JOHN WALTON

The central feature of contemporary developmental studies is a fundamental shift in the theories and embedded concepts employed to explain the conditions of Third World societies. A decade of research and theorizing based on conventional notions such as "modernization" and "social differentiation" seems to have failed to answer the most compelling questions about the developmental process. If, for example, social and economic development were to have been the necessary consequences of urbanization, technological diffusion, communications, and the differentiation of social structures, then why do Third World societies that have been the objects of these influences find themselves underdeveloped (and underdeveloping) today? Why do standard indicators of economic development show that while the scope and activities of transnational corporations continue to grow (representing an ever increasing proportion of the GNPs of the advanced nations), Third World economies either stagnate or "develop" in the direction of great social and economic inequality (Sunkel, 1969; Magdoff, 1969; Müller, 1973)? Why are the political systems of these countries, which we were told would become more "integrative" and "democratized," still rent by the conflicts of class struggle and neocolonialism?

Author's Note: This article builds on portions of an earlier paper entitled "Urban Hierarchies and Patterns of Dependence in Latin America: Theoretical Bases for a New Research Agenda," presented at the Conference on New Directions of Urban Research in Latin America, Institute of Latin American Studies, the University of Texas at Austin, May, 1974. For their comments on that paper I am indebted to Richard N. Adams, Harley L. Browning, Michael Conroy, and James F. Petras. It should not be inferred that those commentators agree with the formulation developed here.

Such questions have prompted the suggestion that conventional theories and concepts have proven woefully inadequate to the task of explaining the fundamental causes of development and underdevelopment.

In the late 1960s a clear alternative to these approaches began to emerge under the familiar, if not definitive, rubric of "dependency" theory. Certainly this movement was not the first to challenge the basic premises of conventional modernization theories. Writers such as Paul Baran (1957), Raúl Prebish (1961), Gunnar Myrdal (1957), Reinhard Bendix (1967), Irving Horowitz (1966) and others had earlier leveled a compelling series of criticisms at the prevailing fashion. Yet, the "dependency" theorists gathered the momentum of earlier critics and began to produce both theory and data which suggested that underdevelopment in the Third World was, to some considerable extent, caused by the exploitative and accumulative tendencies of the metropolitan centers. Consequently, they argued, explanations of development and underdevelopment were not to be found in the internal conditions of Third World societies, but in the interface between these and the expansive thrusts of Western capitalism. Illustrative of this approach are the works of Cardoso (1966), Cotler (1970), dos Santos (1970), Frank (1967), and Furtado (1965), to mention only a few of the Latin American writers.

If this theoretical controversy ran hot for several years, the most current indications are that rival perspectives are themselves changing. Conventional approaches have given ground and attempted new syntheses, albeit without substantial change in their basic assumptions (Ilchman and Uphoff, 1969; Chodak, 1973). Alternatively, certain exponents of "dependency" have concluded that this historically specific concept has outlived its usefulness and that it is now time to turn to broader formulations based on the process of capital accumulation (Frank, 1974; Amin, 1974), contradictions within the advanced economies (Hymer, 1972) and world economic systems (Wallerstein, 1974). Other believe more attention should be devoted to the problematic and variable interface between given underdeveloped societies and the international system (dos Santos, 1969).

It is in the latter vein that the notion of internal colonialism may have some application. While the term clearly derives from dependency theory, it has so far paid no theoretical dividends. The reasons for this are easily identified. Few concepts have been the object of as much passionate debate and confusion as has the idea of internal colonialism. Around the concept have swirled polemics of a racial, ideological, and class, as well as an academic character. The term has gained currency in both the lexicon of social science and the rhetoric of politics; it has been used to describe settings as diverse as the black and brown ghettos of North American cities and the rural or indigenous communities of Africa and Latin America. Indeed, this range of application is symptomatic of the vagaries of the concept. Some have suggested that the conceptual morass is sufficiently hopeless to warrant eliminating the term from future analytic endeavors. The position I shall take in this paper is that the concept is useful, even essential, and that it does, or can, capture certain key features of the urbanization and developmental processes that are not incorporated in other ready substitutes. Yet, it is obvious that any convincing demonstration of this claim must first clear away the confusion surrounding contemporary usages and answer legitimate demands for conceptual precision and utility.

ALTERNATIVE CONCEPTIONS OF INTERNAL COLONIALISM

As it appears in the social science literature the term "internal colonialism" seems to be used in four distinct ways, all of which, I shall argue, are misleading or inadequate. Such inadequacies, of course, are at the root of the well known and justified criticism that the concept has so far defied operationalization.

1. Internal colonialism as a *domestic analogy* to the forms of social and economic domination characteristic of "classical colonialism." Conceptually this is the weakest usage of the term. By describing black ghettos in the United States in this vocabulary writers such as Clark (1965) and Carmichael and Hamilton (1967) were less concerned with definitional precision than with calling dramatic attention to a problem. The colonial analogy provided a tactical vehicle for pointing up value inconsistencies in the larger society. How could the United States, an (allegedly) anti-colonial country, tolerate a facsimile of that system within its own cities? In a more circumspect, though similar usage Blauner (1969) recognizes that the term is an imperfect analogy (e.g., U.S. blacks are not an indigenous majority ruled by an alien minority), but argues that it has important heuristic properties. While we would scarcely wish to deny the political or ideological value of this usage, it is unsatisfactory from a conceptual standpoint. Because the analogy is imperfect it is no more justified in principle than "internal racism" or some other surrogate. Conversely, it fails to give any distinctive content to the term.

2. Internal colonialism as the *perpetuation of social and economic inequalities after formal independence* from colonial rule. Although this usage moves beyond mere analogy, it, too, is rather weak. Typically authors addressing the topic provide no explicit definition, but simply note that formal independence has not been a panacea for the development of former colonies. Social and economic inequality characteristic of the colonial period continues to exist as a national bourgeoisie moves into positions of power in what is essentially the same structure of domination (Coleman, 1960; Fanon, 1961; Hoselitz, 1962; Mills, 1963). Colonialism is not "internal" in the sense of national elites bearing the legal and social responsibility for underdevelopment in the eyes of these analysts. As before, we note two drawbacks with the usage. First, it does not distinguish itself from alternatives such as "neocolonialism." Second, it fails to provide any unique content to the term or to characterize a distinct process.

3. Internal colonialism as the *intra-national exploitation of culturally distinct groups.* Here we encounter the most systematic and influential efforts at isolating the unique properties of internal colonialism. These efforts have been carried forth largely by Latin American scholars who challenge the basic premises of "dualist" theories of development, i.e., the notion of two relatively independent economies: one developing *because* it is urban, industrial, innovative, dynamic, and modernizing; the other underdeveloped *because* it is rural, agrarian, irrational, stagnant, and traditional. Against this view writers such as Bourricaud (1966), Cotler (1970), Frank (1967), González Casanova (1969) and Stavenhagen (1970) have argued that these are not two economies, but one intimately linked system of urban exploitation of the labor and products of rural communities, or "colonies."

> Indeed, the backward, underdeveloped regions of our countries have always played the role of *internal colonies* in relation to the developing urban centers or the productive agricultural areas. And in order to avoid the mistaken idea that there are two (or more) independent social and economic systems at work in the Latin American countries, we propose to describe the situation in terms of *internal colonialism* rather than in terms of "dual societies" [Stavenhagen, 1969: 106-107, emphasis in the original].

In the Latin American societies of reference rural and urban sectors have been historically more or less coterminous with Indian and Ladino populations respectively. Consequently, for these writers internal colonialism becomes a special form of exploitation existing in the relationship between distinct ethnic or cultural groups. Stavenhagen (1970: 235) advances "a conceptual scheme based on the role of internal colonialism in inter-ethnic relations" and González Casanova (1969: 130-131) goes on to provide a definition of this special relationship:

> Internal colonialism corresponds to a structure of social relations based on domination and exploitation among culturally heterogeneous, distinct groups. If it has a specific difference with respect to other relations based on superordination, it inheres in the cultural heterogeneity which the conquest of some peoples by others historically produces.

These formulations have merit. First, unlike previous usages, they provide an explicit definition of internal colonialism and include within its boundaries a special instance of intergroup relationships. Second, the definition does isolate an important empirical phenomenon found in Latin America and other societies that are pluralistic in terms of culture, race, or ethnicity. Nevertheless, the approach has several shortcomings. At the operational level it relies on the assumption that cultural heterogeneity can be reliably measured or that "culturally distinct groups" can be unambiguously defined. It is instructive to note that both González Casanova and Stavenhagen use Meso-American Indians as their illustration, perhaps because they stand out more. But how would they handle exploited *criollos, mestizos,* or racial and ethnic groups in other more integrated societies? What are the standards of cultural distinctiveness and, more to the point, are we willing to abandon the concept in cases where exploitation is blatant but cultural differences between exploiter and exploited are more subtle?

This suggests a second problem that moves beyond operational definitions to questions of the generality of the concept. Namely, is it advisable to restrict the concept to such a relatively narrow range even if standards of cultural distinctiveness could be established? Might there not be more fundamental forms of class exploitation that are partially masked by ethnic and cultural differences which, in some sense, we would want to address with the notion of internal colonialism? Forms of exploitation that conform isomorphically to culturally distinct groups may be so rare as to recommend efforts at a more general conceptualization (González, 1974).

Finally, this definition has nothing to say about what constitutes exploitation. Presumably, if we note social and economic inequalities between culturally distinct groups, we may infer that they result from exploitation rather than other historical, circumstantial or fortuitous factors. Of course, students of social inequality are advisedly skeptical of the later alternatives. But that does not excuse them from the burden of characterizing exploitation as a special kind of relationship.

4. Internal colonialism as *domination by a privileged minority of a dependent majority.* This is the most general usage current in the literature. It avoids most of the problems of the foregoing one, but in so doing it opens itself up to charges of vagueness and all-inclusiveness. Havens and Flinn (1970: 11) provide a good statement of the approach and its differences with earlier ones:

> For our purposes, internal colonialism refers to structural arrangements typified by a relatively small dominant group which controls the allocation of resources, and a large subjected mass composed of various groups with unarticulated interests largely divorced from participation in the development process and blocked from means of social mobility. We differ from the more common usage of the concept as found in the writings of González Casanova in that the subjected groups are not necessarily of different racial origin than the dominant group. Our major focus is not on racial differences but on the nature of the dependency relationship.

Subsequently Havens and Flinn add to this definition a discussion of the context in which the term is to be understood. Specifically, internal colonialism is seen as an intra-national relationship of dependency closely linked to the society's external dependence on the economic and political power of the metropolitan countries. But, this important consideration does not inform the definition per se. In a series of useful case studies that follow, Havens and Flinn (1970: 20) regard these international linkages as beyond the scope of their work and, therefore, simply "assume that external dependency and internal colonialism exist and that they interact to shape the pattern of resource allocation." In other words, they assume and set aside what may be the critical distinguishing feature of the concept. Consequently, the approach becomes vulnerable to the most basic charge leveled by critics; namely, that internal colonialism is a superfluous term connoting no more than conventional, neutral, and better established concepts such as stratification, power, privilege, domination-subordination, etc. In short, while the previous definition is too restrictive, this one is too diffuse.

INTERNAL COLONIALISM: A REFORMULATION

In view of the difficulties encountered by proponents of the several approaches reviewed, one might wonder if the concept internal colonialism is useful or justified. I shall argue strongly in the affirmative for two reasons. First, most Third World societies, and certainly the Latin American ones of special concern here, are former colonies. This historical fact is of central importance for contemporary social organization. National boundaries, patterns of urban structure, land use and tenure, social class structure, indeed, law and religion, all assume forms most decisively fashioned under the influence of colonialism. Note, for example, that of Latin America's twenty largest cities (in 1970), sixteen were founded between 1520-1580 and nineteen were in existence one hundred years before formal independence in 1810-1820. Both the physical layout and the economic function of these cities continue to reflect basic patterns established to suit the interests of the colonial era, though, of course, contemporary influences have engendered modifications and extensions of the colonial pattern (Portes, 1975). Second, as the dependency literature amply documents, these societies continue to be the objects of neocolonial trade and intervention policies of the more advanced economies. As a result, the term internal colonialism provides us, at the outset, with the conceptual imagery suited for incorporating both the contemporary structural conditions of Latin American societies and the ways in which their internal conditions may articulate with influences from abroad. It constrains us to think in terms of hierarchical relationships or transitive linkages rather than discrete, yet specious units such as the nation or the city. But, given these apparent advantages, we still have to address the definitional question.

In order to avoid the foregoing conceptual pitfalls, internal colonialism will be conceived of here as a *particular type* of exploitation giving rise to broadly distributed experiences of inequality. Rather than artifactually tying the definition to the characteristics of those (cultural, racial, ethnic, class, or geographical) groups which are parties to, or victims of the process of exploitation, we focus on the *nature of the process itself.*

Accordingly, *internal colonialism is defined as a process that produces certain intra-national forms of patterned socioeconomic inequality directly traceable to the exploitative practices through which national and international institutions are linked in the interests of surplus extraction and capital accumulation.* Stated differently, internal colonialism refers to those domestic structures of inequality whose origins lie in the interface between internal conditions and external influences stemming from metropolitan economies. Internal colonialism has reference to both a process whose central characteristic is exploitation, and to the patterned consequences of the process in the form of socioeconomic inequality. *Exploitation* is distinguished from potentially diverse sources of inequality by the use of *power* (as opposed to market or voluntaristic mechanisms) to obtain the necessary inputs to the capital accumulation process at the lowest possible costs and to enhance the profitability of that process through monopolistic restraints on its distributive impact (e.g., in areas of mobility, broader employment, income distribution, etc.).

It should be stressed that all forms of socioeconomic inequality found in Third World societies are not necessarily instances of internal colonialism, nor are particular manifestations of internal colonialism necessarily similar across underdeveloped societies. The definition is more exacting, requiring, first, that exploitation be demonstrated as the causal basis of the patterns of inequality, and, second, that specific causes be located in the external-internal dependency relationship. Moreover, internal colonial structures may vary widely as a result of special internal conditions such as the resource base, level of development, historical experience, or public policy. As dos Santos (1969: 57-63) emphasizes, it is in the special conditions of articulation between "internal" and "external" influences that the explanation of dependency patterns must be sought:

> Dependence is not an "external factor" as is often thought. . . . Dependence conditions a certain internal structure which redefines it as a function of the structural possibilities of diverse national economies. . . . Even if these national economies do not condition relations of dependence in general, they limit their possibilities of expansion, or rather, they redefine them at the level of their concrete functioning. . . . We must study the manner in which dependent national economies structure themselves internally (and how they do this within the context of the world system) and the role they play in the development of the world system.

What is assumed in this formulation, yet requires restatement, is that center-periphery ties do not systematically entail exploitation and unilateral benefits accruing upwards. In actual situations the relationship may be more complex. Periphery economies, under certain circumstances, prove to be more adaptive and resalient than crude versions of dependency theory have anticipated (Balán, 1974; Roberts, 1974). Exploitative schemes of the metropolitan centers sometimes boomerang as illustrated in recent political efforts to nationalize productive facilities or form cooperatives of raw material-producing countries. Without dismissing these considerations we can still maintain that center-periphery exploitation is more the rule than the exception and that the notion of internal colonialism provides a way of getting at this process.

In summary, internal colonialism is a process characterized by several distinguishing properties. It refers to *intra-national patterns* of inequality, that result from a *process* of *exploitation* through the use of *power*, with *origins* in the relationship of *structural dependency* between advanced metropolitan and underdeveloped periphery societies, and taking *variable concrete forms* depending on particular congeries of these factors. Illustratively, the concept of internal colonialism would include instances of Indian communities whose land was incorporated into large-scale commercial agriculture for export under internationally constrained, disadvantageous circumstances. It would also include cases in which middle-class consumer groups or working class urbanites were disadvantaged by foreign monopolies (or consortia of foreign and local capital) in areas such as loss of employment, higher prices, small business failures, etc. Moreover, while our focus is on the Third World, this definition allows for the occurrence of internal colonialism within the advanced countries which export neocolonialism. Certain forms of socioeconomic inequality within metropolitan countries may be traced to their neocolonial operations abroad.[1] Internal colonialism is essentially a relationship of socioeconomic exploitation with transnational origins, irrespective of whether that exploitation is visited upon culturally distinct communities, particular social and ethnic groups, certain classes, or residents of a given geographic area. Certainly, any empirical description of the workings of internal colonialism should disaggregate the variable impact of this exploitation by social strata. But the characteristics of the victims should not be confused with a conceptualization of the process of victimization.

MAJOR FORMS OF INTERNAL COLONIALISM

On the basis of the foregoing definitional considerations we may turn now to a discussion of the principal manifestations of internal colonialism in underdeveloped societies. Our intention here is not to provide a logically definitive typology of internal colonial relationships. While I recommend that task to subsequent commentators and critics, a more immediate priority would seem to attach to the delineation of the most salient concrete forms of inequality which properly fall within the concept's boundaries.

According to our definition, internal colonialism is, at bottom, a process of surplus extraction from lower to higher levels of a society. In the broadest sense the resources of a society can be conceived of as distributed by class and geographic levels or hierarchies. Surplus extraction moves resources up these hierarchies and, therefore, has fundamental implications for the class and geographic distribution of resources. If the movement of resources can be thought of in this dichotomous sense of spatial and social structures, then clearly the two hierarchies also interpenetrate. As a proportion of the population upper class owners are more numerous in the capital cities and provincial centers, while the working class and peasantry are proportionately more numerous in towns and rural areas. Nevertheless, the process of surplus extraction can be conceived of as analytically independent with respect to the two hierarchies. Surplus extraction in its *class form* involves the concentration of resources among smaller numbers of the upper classes apart from their geographical location (e.g., owners of industry and agricultural properties at the expense of rural and urban middle and lower classes). Surplus extraction in its *geographic form* involves the concentration of resources among smaller numbers of major urban centers apart from their class composition (e.g., in a few large cities at the expense of all classes in smaller towns and rural areas). Again, the two dimensions are interactive in concrete instances of internal colonialism, but the distinction is important if we wish to differentiate salient patterns and consequences.

Substantively, I shall suggest four key areas or sectors in which exploitative institutional practices contribute to a pattern of internal colonialism: (a) the state, (b) agriculture, (c) manufacturing, (d) trade and commerce. The discussion will focus on certain concrete illustrations of institutional practices in order to provide a denotative suggestion of the range of application allowed by the concept as it is used here. Obviously, it would be impossible to provide an exhaustive enumeration of the manifestations of internal colonialism that might fall under each category. Rather, the intent is simply to describe some of the more salient varieties.

Internal Colonialism and the State

Practices by the state that are linked to external dependence and tend to generate conditions of internal colonialism are numerous, the most obvious illustration being *foreign investment policy*. In contemporary Latin America such policy varies from open and concessionary (e.g., Brazil, Chile in 1974) to selectively restrictive and nationalistic (e.g., Velasco's Peru, Pérez' Venezuela, Allende's Chile). Open and concessionary policies contribute to internal colonialism in specifiable ways. Tax allowances, suspension of import duties, unrestricted local borrowing and profit repatriation are just a few of the concessions that enhance the oligopolistic position of foreign corporate investors (and their national affiliates) with respect to national enterprises. Such investments tend to be located in the largest urban centers, to affiliate with the wealthiest elements of the national bourgeoisie, to be capital-intensive and operate at the highest profit margins. Their consequences are, notably, monopolization, reduction of sources of employment (in wage labor and smaller entrepreneurship), and increased concentration of income. Of course, the victims are workers, small business, and consumers who suffer from less price competition.

Yet, these are only the more obvious illustrations. Government expenditure, particularly in the area of ***infrastructure,*** serves to create or entrench patterns of surplus extraction. As Hirschman (1958) argues, public investment in social overhead capital as opposed to direct product activities tends to favor foreign investors. Moreover, social overhead expenditures contribute to internal colonialism when they disproportionately benefit urban and upper class groups as is typically the case. Of course, particular works should be the subject of cost-benefit analyses, but common illustrations are: greater per capita investment in urban versus rural roads, schools, power, transportation, etc.; diverting rural resources (e.g., water) to the cities; urban infrastructure works that disproportionately benefit large commercial and industrial groups with external ties. Illustrative was a costly project in Mexico designed to bring natural gas for industrial use to a large urban center. This new source of energy was beyond the needs and the means of artisan industry and benefited overwhelmingly only the largest extant and prospective industries which also had heavy foreign participation. This is not to say that such a project represents internal colonialism per se, apart from a larger, more balanced developmental strategy of which it is only a part. Rather, it is to say that such works combine to form a pattern of internal colonialism when they outweigh more egalitarian or redistributive expenditure policies. In order to measure the extent to which public expenditures contribute to internal colonialism one would want to sum the cost-benefit ratios of all or a representative set of expenditures.

I am aware, at this juncture, that advocates of unbalanced growth or the "trickle-down effect" would argue that the policies I have labeled internal colonialism may ultimately benefit broad class and regional groups. While I believe the evidence is overwhelmingly against this view, the present discussion confines itself to the problem of clarifying the *concept* of internal colonialism.

A third area in which state action contributes to internal inequalities is the *fiscal system.* We have spoken of tax concessions to foreign investors and their local "partners." Internally, credit and tax structures may benefit interests associated with export dependency as opposed to indigenous industry. Also within the fiscal realm are regressive means of dealing with inflation such as Brazil's "indexing" method or a hard line on wage versus profit controls (Chile, Mexico). Parallel with these policies of austerity are the use of foreign exchange and foreign exchange rates influenced by the IMF and international banks (Hayter, 1971). In a sense, government fiscal policy, and the political considerations that motivate it, are the root causes of internal colonialism. Typically it is within, rather than outside, the norms of public policy that exploitation flourishes. There are few more reliable guides to the allocative values of a society than its tax system. Moreover, official and systemic rules for the allocation of resources pervade all of the illustrations considered here.

A fourth area of state involvement in practices of internal colonialism may be broadly characterized as *social policy.* Paramount here is the educational system, particularly the tendency to overemphasize credentialing in those elite, technical schools that prepare graduates for positions in transnational corporations or the more "advanced" national enterprises tied to structures of dependent capitalism. This policy results in the further specialized education of an already privileged elite and widens the gap between that stratum and the masses whose education in underfinanced primary and vocational schools, even if increasing on the average, paradoxically becomes a handicap as educational credentials are increasingly a requisite for decent jobs (Illich, 1970).

We should stress again that not all forms of social inequality and the policies that produce them qualify as forms of internal colonialism; the additional stipulation being that they are directly linked to external, neo-colonial structures. Nevertheless, a broad range of conventional ills of Latin American societies fits these stipulations. Illustrative are public policies that protect foreign owned and sometimes unused properties from land reform (e.g., Costa Rica) or permit the exploitation of indigenous communities in the interests of the export economy.

Internal Colonialism in Agriculture

In the agricultural sector internal colonialism is reflected principally in large scale commercial production for export. Note that agricultural production for export per se represents an important field for Latin American development and is not regarded as an instance of internal colonialism. Rather, that term is reserved for cases in which this external linkage is found in combination with patterns of exploitation in credit, land ownership or use, and marketing.

Perhaps the key to Latin America's stagnating agricultural sector is the problem of credit and land tenure. In the absence of effective mechanisms for insuring small farmers credit on reasonable terms, many are forced into either subsistence production or alienated commercial production in which the larger share of profit is extracted by local loan sharks. As a consequence, individual plots of land are often sold or rented to large commercial firms that can receive credit. The *campesino* may then turn to wage labor which represents a small share of the profit generated by his own (or formerly his own) property. The first consequence of this situation is a growing concentration of land ownership, or effective rights to the profitable use of land, and a growing concentration of profit in the hands of local proprietors.

At another level, and contributing to the process of surplus extraction, are large marketing operations that encourage mechanized monoculture by purchasing for export the entire crop of a region. Illustrative is the U.S. firm of Anderson Clayton which is the largest purchaser of cotton in Mexico's northwest. Having gained control over a regional market the firm is then able to set prices that squeeze both commercial farmer and peasant wage worker, adding again to the amount of surplus extracted. Such leverage is further enhanced in cases such as Central America's banana regions where foreign firms assume the roles of owner, creditor, and principal buyer allowing them total control over this sector of the national economy. Such total control means unbridled exploitation of campesinos and smaller commercial farmers, and the ability to stunt this national resource by maintaining low commodity prices. Indeed, it extends into authentically imperialistic political control of national policy as witnessed in the recent sabotage of efforts to organize a Union of Banana Exporting Countries (U.P.E.B.). The result is a three- or four-tiered system of surplus extraction based on credit, land ownership/control, marketing, and export dependency; moving up a hierarchy from campesinos, to local commercial farmers, to national and foreign controlled markets, to transnational corporations.

While we touch here only on the principal thread that ties this process together, it should be recognized that there are many other collateral forms of inequality associated with the process. Havens and Flinn (1970: 26-52), for example, indicate how access to agricultural innovations and their profit potential is similarly embedded in a process of internal colonialism.

Internal Colonialism in Manufacturing

In the industrial sector, of course, the archetypal agent of internal colonialism is the transnational corporation. By now an impressive literature has been produced on the sophisticated profit-maximizing strategies of corporations operating across national boundaries and often beyond the reach of regulation by the laws of any single nation (Müller, 1973; Sampson, 1973; Vernon, 1971; Barnet and Müller, 1974). But our concern is with the intra-national impact of these institutions. Most fundamental, perhaps, is the tendency for investment by transnational corporations to further concentrate the ownership of capital. This is due in part, though not primarily, to the relatively large sums of capital they bring to underdeveloped societies. More important is their magnetic attraction of local capital (Müller, 1973; Frank, 1967) which tends to abandon purely domestic investment in order to enhance itself as well as the absolute profit of foreign investors through repatriation of an increasing proportion of the gross domestic product. Moreover, such local borrowing by transnationals exacerbates capital shortages in the underdeveloped societies preventing the creation or expansion of national enterprise. At least three immediate consequences follow which illustrate the impact of internal colonialism on the national bourgeoisie. First, manufacturers who may not have preferred the arrangement are forced to affiliate with foreign capital to maintain a competitive financial position. Second, successful national enterprises simply sell out to transnational conglomerates. Third, the trend toward monopolization results in the failure of many long-established, smaller enterprises. Illustrative of the latter, a well known case in Mexico witnessed a large U.S. tile and bathroom fixtures company gradually take control of some ninety percent of this traditional market, formerly the source of income and jobs for thousands of small operators. While many dramatic examples could be provided, I cite intentionally this prosaic one in order to illustrate the pervasiveness of such practices, even in areas where none of the conventional justifications of foreign investment apply (e.g., "transfer" of technology, economies of scale, etc.). It should be noted, of course, that certain elements of the national bourgeoisie do profit from these arrangements while others suffer. The larger point, however, is that the principal beneficiaries are the transnational corporations and an increasingly reduced stratum of the dependent society.

Moving beyond the impact of these developments for the national bourgeoisie, foreign controlled or joint-venture manufacturing tends to be capital-intensive, resulting in a shrinkage of sources of employment and the creation of a "labor aristocracy" (Arrighi and Saul, 1973). Consequently, a growing number of less skilled workers displaced from traditional, labor-intensive enterprises join the rural-to-urban migrant, driven from the countryside by commercialization and technification of agriculture, to swell the ranks of the urban unemployed. These twin developments in the national bourgeoisie and urban unemployed contribute greatly to the maldistribution of income.

Finally, these changes in manufacturing affect low-income consumers most regressively. Dependent manufacturing prefers production of luxury goods where profits are highest and where a lively market has been artificially created among the consumption-oriented national bourgeoisie and labor aristocracy (themselves products of the same reciprocal causation model). Oligopolistic control reduces the availability of basic commodities, the competition among sellers and, thus, raises prices.

Here we have considered only some of the most obvious and "classical" consequences of external dependence for the manufacturing sector. Recent developments suggest a shift in the policy of transnational corporations away from outright ownership and/or control, toward sophisticated patent and licensing arrangements, particularly in advanced technologies (Science, 1973). Sometimes described as "technological imperialism" (Magdoff, 1969), these practices add a new level to the process of surplus extraction through the sale of patents and collection of royalties on manufacturing techniques adopted by industries in which the transnational corporation may already have a heavy stake. As in the area of agricultural production, we see again a process of surplus value added upon surplus value with proportionately larger increments of profit accruing to the higher reaches of the class and urban-metropolitan hierarchies.

Internal Colonialism in Trade and Commerce

For purposes of this discussion we need not dwell on conditions of dependency that characterize underdeveloped societies vis-à-vis international trade and commerce. Suffice it to say that unfavorable terms of trade, exchanging primary products for manufactured goods and new technologies, coupled with the debt service on international loans leaves most Third World countries in a position of chronic trade deficits (the major contemporary exception, of course, being the petroleum exporting countries). It is also commonplace to observe that, contrary to the standard defenses of foreign investment in manufacturing, the commercial sector of many underdeveloped nations is influenced by the imposing presence of transnational firms such as Sears Roebuck, Woolworth, Walgreen (owners of Sanborns in Mexico), numerous restaurant franchises, etc., which require no expertise not available locally.

From the standpoint of internal colonialism the principal consequence of trade dependency is to orient local and regional economies to the requirements of export, rather than self-sufficiency, diversity, and interdependence. Just as the colonial period in Latin America enforced monoculture and unilateral exchange between regions, cities, and the crown, so export dependency reinforces this traditional pattern and minimizes regional interdependence and generative reciprocities. Agricultural regions capable of producing a particular export crop engage in monoculture which, as we argued earlier, comes under the control of large commercial farmers. Profitable as such practices may be for large-scale proprietors and commercial-exporting elites (both national and foreign), they leave the region dependent upon imports of other basic agricultural commodities, not to mention manufactured goods. Consequently the agricultural wage worker, already suffering exploitation from the forced sale or rental of his land, must now pay higher prices for essential commodities.

Cities play a key role in this exchange network. On the one hand, they become nuclei of trade and distribution, the urban merchant class becoming the second beneficiary (after the commercial farmer) of surplus extraction. On the other hand, provincial cities are increasingly subject to structural rigidities in their economies. They, too, must import a diversity of commodities. But, more important, since their principal economic activity turns on the processing of agricultural products, linkage effects that might stimulate other industries are held to a minimum. The "inputs" to these processing industries are overwhelmingly in the form of raw materials rather than semi-elaborated goods from satellite industries. In like fashion the reciprocities between provincial cities are minimized, resulting in a national urban pattern not of multilateral interdependence and complementarity, but one of bilateral, unequal exchange along a "radial" pattern of spokes between the capital city (and perhaps a few others) and provincial urban centers. To borrow an intentionally cryptic phrase from James Petras, "The growth and expansion of capital cities is the story of internal colonialism." In our terms, it is the structure of trade and commerce that has contributed most to internal colonialism in its geographic form.

This discussion of trade and commerce has focused chiefly on the consequences of agricultural production for export (though much the same would apply to extractive industries). Yet, clearly there are other influences at work. Historically Latin American capitals were established by fiat and conquest to become the centers of a radial structure based upon trade as well as civil, military, and ecclesiastical jurisdictions. Subsequent industry located naturally in these trade and administrative centers, typically achieving manufacturing dominance prior to the industrialization of provincial cities and capitals (Monterrey, São Paulo, and Medellín being the notable exceptions—Córdoba and Valparaiso less so). Consequently, commerce in manufactured goods tended to follow the pattern of surplus extraction described in the case of primary products. Subsidiaries or suppliers of capital city-based industries dominated smaller cities, and these satellites also experienced the effects of surplus extraction. Of course, the most glaring instance of this process is native artisan industry, the products of which multiply in price many times before appearing in the large, tourist-oriented, commercial outlets in the cities. At the other end of the spectrum, transnational corporations, with their attendant ramifications on internal trade, typically locate in the national capital and move down the urban hierarchy only after successive encounters with saturated markets. Forlorn plans for industrial decentralization remain only plans, not for want of some justification based on distributive economic justice, but because they run counter to the logic of internal colonialism.

In concluding this section two observations are required. First, the institutional practices included under these four separate headings (indeed the headings themselves) are acknowledged to be closely interrelated. While we may separately characterize and even measure internal colonialism in, say, agriculture and industry, in any concrete situation they are inextricable elements of a single process and it is that process which commands our attention.

Second, in order that these very sketchy descriptions of the mechanisms of internal colonialism not be misunderstood, certain caveats should be recalled again. Here we are *not* intent upon faithfully describing *all* that goes on in the internal political economy of underdeveloped countries. Some might argue that the patterns of exploitation described here are the principal or dominant features of dependent societies. Others would argue the point, which I immediately grant, that these societies are much more complex than depicted here and reflect diverse forces endeavoring to counteract the accumulation of inequality. But those are empirical issues, while our purposes here are conceptual and methodological. Indeed, to the extent that we can arrive at a workable conceptualization of internal colonialism and typify some of its manifestations, we may then be in a position to measure and assess the *extent* of its occurrence. Accordingly, we turn to the final problem for this discussion, the measurement of internal colonialism.

MEASURES OF INTERNAL COLONIALISM

In what follows I shall attempt to specify a number of discrete measures of internal colonialism. As we have noted, the problem of operationalizing this concept has provided critics with a powerful argument and has frustrated many sympathetic with dependency theory. The problem of operationalization, of course, is twofold: conceptual and practical. If the foregoing discussion clarifies in one form the conceptual issues, we are still faced with practical problems. Specifically, many of the measures I shall suggest cannot be executed with the kind of data readily available to social scientists. On the contrary, some of them assume complex and painstaking investigation in areas where access may be most restricted. In that sense some of the following suggestions may appear quite "impractical." They are advanced, nevertheless, in the belief that it is better to indicate the kinds of data that would be necessary for a faithful operationalization of the concept than to sacrifice the concept to methodological convenience. The proposed measures are divided into three subdivisions, the first dealing with the economic bases of internal colonialism and the latter two addressing its social and political ramifications. The items included under the first subdivision move from the most general to more specific levels.

Economic Measures

Profit-Taking. The question of profit-taking is virtually synonymous with surplus extraction. Doubtless its measurement could be accomplished in a variety of ways. Here we would suggest a disaggregation of the ultimate market value of commodities and services linked with external influences (import, export, foreign investment, loans, etc.). Particular attention would focus on the distribution of successive fractions of profit by participants in the production process by class and geographical locations.

Income Distribution. Parallel with the first item would be the measurement of longitudinal shifts in income distribution, again by class and geographical strata where such shifts are the result of external economic linkages.

Public Expenditures. Cost-benefit analyses of government expenditures notably, though not exclusively, in the area of infrastructure (e.g., dams, roads, electrification, education, etc.). Obviously "cost-benefit analysis" is not an unambiguous or value-free technique. Yet one relatively objective operationalization would be to compute a ratio of the tax cost per capita to the use value of a particular public work or investment (i.e., the cost to the individual of duplicating the service rendered when and as often as it might be used).

Taxation. Again in areas linked to external dependency (e.g., import duties, debt service, etc.) to what extent is the tax structure regressive. As with income distribution the proportionate tax effort or tax burden could be represented in the form of a Lorenz curve or Gini coefficient.

Transnational Corporations. Simple in principle and most difficult in practice is the calculation of rates of profit repatriation both directly and through various forms of in-company transfers (Müller, 1973). Assuming such amounts could be reliably estimated, they could be expressed as a ratio of national corporate profits, sums borrowed locally or a variety of other critical denominators.

Credit. The distribution of credit, particularly in agriculture, in terms of both absolute amounts (expressed as a ratio of sales or profit) and interest rates. For example, compare the amount of public credit received by a large commercial farmer versus a small landholder as a percentage of the value of a year's crop.

Monopolization. Longitudinal analysis of the consequences of nonlocal firms in particular lines of activity for subsequent concentration of the number of enterprises, profit, market control, etc. Again, standard techniques for analyzing income distribution would apply here.

Monoculture. Similar to the above, a longitudinal analysis of concentration in regional primary sector production for export; measured in terms of crop diversification, centralization of marketing, etc.

Land Tenure. The longitudinal consequences of export production for the concentration of land ownership and use.

Trade Flows. Shifts in regional import-export balances in the direction of increasing volumes and prices of imports and a declining variety of exports. This could be accomplished by longitudinally spaced input-output analyses at regional levels. Similarly, a comparison of local demand structure with that of certain higher units to determine "imbalances" in the sense of local shortages and higher prices that result from the local economy's responsiveness to external markets.

Labor Absorbtion. Calculation of differentials in the absorbtive capacity of national versus foreign enterprises. Conversely, the amount of unemployment or job displacement produced by foreign-linked, capital-intensive enterprises.

Denationalization. The degree of penetration of foreign capital through joint ventures and, particularly, the outright purchase of national enterprises.

Political Measures

Elite Structure. Assuming the utility of available methods for identifying local elites and key organizations (Walton, 1971), it is possible to next determine the proportion of these that represent nonlocal influence as well as the bases of that influence (e.g., occupation affiliation of nonlocal influential persons and economic or political function of organizations).

Policy. While all of the foregoing suggested measures allow for some quantitative expression, we should not limit ourselves in this regard. Case studies of the decision-making process and differential consequences of development policies may provide a rich fund of material on the details, mechanisms, and impact of internal colonialism. Key policy areas would include land use and land "reform," public investment and infrastructure, credit and its distribution, conditions and reciprocities negotiated with nonlocal investors, etc. Each of these policy areas could be explored within a cost-benefit framework leading to some quantitative estimates of the impacts of alternatives.

Political Participation. In a formal structural sense this would include the centralization or decentralization of state power vis-à-vis urban hierarchies; representation in local, state, and national assemblies; and political party structure. With respect to the actual workings of political participation it would include the extent of local voting, electoral competition, interest group organization and influence, etc. Illustratively, research that appears, in part, to qualify the internal colonialism thesis indicates that for Mexico urbanization is regularly and increasingly associated with opposition to the official party (Walton and Sween, 1971). This is not to say that the same occurs in the economic realm, or that the official party's domination is ineffective. It simply demonstrates one way in which the issue can be addressed systematically.

Social Measures

Social Stratification. Here attention would focus on longitudinal changes in class structure, notably changes stemming from the economic forces discussed earlier and contributing to greater class inequality. Of course, the theory and measurement of social stratification is a complex and controversial subject. Some recent work illustrative of the approach suggested here includes a theoretical essay by Bendix (1974) and an empirical study by Gartrell (1974).

Communication Patterns. Once again quantitative procedures (ratios, Lorenz curve analyses, etc.) could be used to analyze communication flows such as postal, telephone, and passenger exchanges between the unit and others above it. Illustrative treatments of communication patterns are available under the rubric of the "integration (which might be interpreted as domination) of political communities" (Jacob and Toscano, 1964).

Racial and Ethnic Discrimination. Following the empirical analyses of Stavenhagen and González Casanova it would be possible to compare all of the foregoing measures "controlling for" racial and/or ethnic composition of communities to determine whether that factor contributes additively to disadvantage.

Language and Literacy. Similar to both of the above, attention could be devoted to the extent to which illiteracy and native dialects prevent a broad network of social relations and encourage unilateral reliance on certain power brokers.

IMPLICATIONS FOR URBANIZATION THEORY

Our discussion so far has characterized internal colonialism as a systemic and hierarchical process, and properly so I believe. Nevertheless, it is easy to lose sight of the crucial role of the cities in this process; an impression which I do not wish to leave. Earlier reference was made to the historical importance of cities as instruments of accumulation under colonialism. As Portes (1975) notes,

> Unlike "natural" forms of urban growth, where the city emerges as a service center for an already settled hinterland, the Spanish and Portuguese cities in the New World were established in unknown and often hostile territories as centers of conquest and political control. They were founded by *fiat*, projected on the land as branches of an imperial strategy, rather than crystalized as necessary centers for expanding commerce.

Because there is a high degree of continuity between the structure of the colonial city and the contemporary situation, many of the preceding measures of internal colonialism are simultaneously measures of the class and social organization of cities. But, the implications of this essay for theories of urbanization go beyond questions of measurement.

An important theme in various theories of urbanization holds that the location and growth of cities are to be explained by laissez faire market mechanisms or the individual rationality of migrants. Illustrative are the so-called "push-pull" theories of urban migration, "central place" theories of urban location, and "growth pole" strategies of urban development. Typically these theories assume a *deus ex machina* principle by which competitive forces resolve themselves into the particular form and structure which cities take. Such views, of course, are extensions of an older urban ecology tradition that stressed dominance and competition as the forces underlying the social and spatial structure of cities. Urban social structure is seen as the outcome of competitive forces in the market place; the distribution of groups and classes in urban space is a function of their unequal resources and choices.

What this position ignores is the importance of political and institutional interests that conspire to restrain market competition and to structure alternative choices. From the standpoint of internal colonialism, cities function, to an important extent, as nodes in a process of surplus extraction, expropriating resources from their hinterlands for purposes of packaging and subsequent transmission. As Marx suggested, urban migrants may be displaced from the countryside in order to provide an abundant and cheap urban labor force, a process better conceived as "push-shove." Urban social structures, at least in Latin America, tend to amplify the differences between social classes. Marginal service sectors and the working class expand while industrial and export elites draw away from a reduced middle class under the support of transnational enterprise. On the physical side, land prices skyrocket from upper class speculation resulting in further overcrowding against which calculated land invasions at certain vulnerable points become the only recourse for the homeless. And all of this has less to do with competition in the marketplace than with monopolization and power.

Once again, my intention is not to characterize urban social organization as undifferentiated or to suggest that class struggles have predetermined outcomes. What I would suggest is that current theories of urbanization and urban social organization rest on the *least* tenable sets of assumptions and that a superior, though not infallible, theory would *begin* with the understanding that cities in underdeveloped societies perform functions and support class structures better illuminated by the dynamics of internal colonialism.

NOTE

1. In this essay the notion of internal colonialism is discussed with general reference to Third World countries and specific application to Latin America. The context is more than one of convenience; essentially I believe that it confines the concept to those situations where it is best suited. Nevertheless, some scholars have attempted to apply the idea to internal features of the advanced countries, notably the United States. As we have seen, Blauner (1969) and others have done this in the analogical sense, while Moore (1970) has justifiably analyzed the structural conditions of Mexican-Americans in the Southwest using a post-colonial model.

According to the definition offered here, certain processes and patterns of inequality within the metropolitan countries could be characterized as internal colonialism by virtue of the fact that they are generated by transnational, exploitative activities. Illustrative are cases where national employment suffers from importing foreign labor or, as César Chávez and the United Farm Workers of America claim, illegal aliens are imported to undercut wages and union organizing strategies. Similarly, exporting material to cheap-labor assembly plants abroad is an instance when it results in loss of jobs and income. Certainly the massive historical importation of black slaves and Mexican factory workers are cases in point and some may wish to argue that the residual consequences of these policies (e.g., black and brown ghettos) also justify the concept.

However, in the general case of accounting for patterns of ethnic, racial, and class inequalities in the advanced countries, I would argue against this conceptualization. In widely varying degrees all classes and racial-ethnic groups in metropolitan countries benefit from neocolonialism abroad. Internal colonialism is less apt a characterization of the circumstances within countries most of whose colonialism is exported. Moreover, the class structures of the advanced societies are evolving and uniquely different from those of underdeveloped areas. Finally, the usefulness of any concept is a function of its specificity; what it includes as well as what it excludes. Since our major concern here has been to render conceptual clarity in the interests of theoretical and research progress, any overextension of the argument is to be avoided. Just as the nature of inequality in the Third World has its special characteristics, so with the more developed societies. If the conventional theories we spoke of made the mistake of applying ethnocentric Western notions to the developing world, it would be equally mistaken to reverse the error.

REFERENCES

AMIN, S. (1974) Accumulation on a World Scale. New York: Monthly Review Press.

ARRIGHI, G. and J. S. SAUL (1973) Essays on the Political Economy of Africa. New York: Monthly Review Press.

BALAN, J. (1974) "Regional urbanization under primary sector expansion in 'neo-colonial' societies." Paper presented at the Seminar on New Directions of Urban Research, Institute of Latin American Studies, University of Texas at Austin, May.

BARNET, R. and R. MULLER (1974) The Earth Managers . . . Their Global Corporations. New York: Simon & Schuster.

BARAN, P. (1957) The Political Economy of Growth. New York: Monthly Review Press.

BENDIX, R. (1974) "Inequality and social structure: a comparison of Marx and Weber." American Sociological Review 3 (April): 149-161.

--- (1967) "Tradition and modernity reconsidered." Comparative Studies in Society and History 9: 292-346.

BLAUNER, R. (1969) "Internal colonialism and ghetto revolt." Social Problems 16 (Spring): 393-408.

BOURRICAUD, F. (1966) "Structure and function of the Peruvian oligarchy." Studies in Comparative International Development 2, 2: 17-31.

CARDOSO, F. H. (1966) "Entrepreneurial elites in Latin America." Studies in Comparative International Development 2, 10: 147-159.

CARMICHAEL, S. and C. HAMILTON (1967) Black Power. New York: Random House.

CHODAK, S. (1973) Societal Development: Five Approaches With Conclusions From Comparative Analysis. New York: Oxford.

CLARK, K. (1965) Dark Ghetto. New York: Harper & Row.

COLEMAN, J. S. (1960) "Conclusion: the political systems of the developing areas," in G. A. Almond and J. S. Coleman (eds.) The Politics of the Developing Areas. Princeton, N.J.: Princeton University Press.

COTLER, J. (1970) "The mechanics of internal domination and social change in Peru," pp. 407-444 in I. L. Horowitz (ed.) Masses in Latin America. New York: Oxford.

DOS SANTOS, T. (1970) "The structure of dependence." American Economic Review 60: 231-236.

--- (1969) "La crise de la théorie du dévelopment et les relations de dependence en Amérique Latine." L'Homme et al Societé 12 (April-June).

FANON, F. (1961) Les Damnés de la Terre. Paris: Maspero.

FRANK, A. G. (1974) "Dependence is dead: long live dependence." Latin American Perspectives 1 (Spring).

--- (1967) Capitalism and Underdevelopment in Latin America: Historical Studies of Chile and Brazil. New York: Monthly Review Press.

FURTADO, C. (1965) "Development and stagnation in Latin America: a structuralist approach." Studies in Comparative International Development 1, 11: 159-175.

GARTRELL, J. W. (1974) "Development and social stratification in South Indian communities." Paper presented at the VIII World Congress of Sociology, Toronto, Canada, August.

GONZALEZ CASANOVA, P. (1969) "Internal colonialism and national development," in I. L. Horowitz, J. de Castro, and J. Gerassi (eds.) Latin American Radicalism. New York: Vintage Books.

GONZALEZ, G. G. (1974) "A critique of the internal colonial model." Latin American Perspectives 1 (Spring): 154-161.

HAVENS, A. E. and W. L. FLINN [eds.] (1970) Internal Colonialism and Structural Change in Colombia. New York: Praeger.

HAYTER, T. (1971) Aid as Imperialism. London: Penguin.

HIRSCHMAN, A. O. (1958) The Strategy of Economic Development. New Haven, Conn.: Yale University Press.

HOROWITZ, I. L. (1966) Three Worlds of Development: The Theory and Practice of International Stratification. New York: Oxford.

HOSELITZ, B. F. (1962) Sociological Aspects of Economic Growth. Glencoe, Ill.: Free Press.

HYMER, S. (1972) "The internationalization of capital." Journal of Economic Issues 6, 1: 91-111.

ILCHMAN, W. F. and N. T. UPHOFF (1969) The Political Economy of Change. Berkeley: University of California Press.

ILLICH, I. (1970) "The false ideology of schooling." Saturday Review (October 17): 56-58, 68.

JACOB, P. E. and J. V. TOSCANO [eds.] (1964) The Integration of Political Communities. New York: Lippincott.

MAGDOFF, H. (1969) The Age of Imperialism. New York: Monthly Review Press.

MILLS, C. W. (1963) "The problem of industrial development," pp. 150-156 in I. L. Horowitz (ed.) Power, Politics, and People. New York: Oxford.

MOORE, J. (1970) "Colonialism: the case of Mexican Americans." Social Problems 17: 463-472.

MULLER, R. (1973) "The multinational corporation and the underdevelopment of the Third World," pp. 124-151 in C. K. Wilber (ed.) The Political Economy of Development and Underdevelopment. New York: Random House.

MYRDAL, G. (1957) Rich Lands and Poor: The Road to World Prosperity. New York: Harper & Row.

PORTES, A. (1975) "The economy and ecology of urban poverty," in A. Portes and J. Walton, Urban Latin America: The Political Condition from Above and Below. Austin, Texas: University of Texas Press.

PREBISH, R. (1961) Nueva política comercial para el desarrollo. México, D.F.: Fondo de Cultura Económica.

ROBERTS, B. R. (1974) "The provincial urban system and the process of dependency." Paper presented at the Seminar on New Directions of Urban Research, Institute of Latin American Studies, University of Texas at Austin, May.

SAMPSON, A. (1973) The Sovereign State of I.T.T. New York: Stein & Day.

Science (1973) "Latin America: is imported technology too expensive?" Science 181 (July 6): 41-44.

STAVENHAGEN, R. (1970) "Classes, colonialism, and acculturation: a system of inter-ethnic relations in Mesoamerica," pp. 235-288 in I. L. Horowitz (ed.) Masses in Latin America. New York: Oxford.

--- (1969) "Seven erroneous theses about Latin America," in I. L. Horowitz, J. de Castro and J. Gerassi (eds.) Latin American Radicalism. New York: Vintage Books.

SUNKEL, O. (1969) "The structural background of development problems in Latin America," pp. 3-37 in C. T. Nisbet (ed.) Latin America: Problems in Economic Development. New York: Free Press.

VERNON, R. (1971) Sovereignty at Bay: The Multinational Spread of U.S. Enterprises. New York: Basic Books.

WALLERSTEIN, I. (1974) The Modern World System: Capitalist Agriculture and the Origins of the European World–Economy in the Sixteenth Century. New York: Academic Press.

WALTON, J. (1971) "A methodology for the comparative study of power: some conceptual and procedural applications." Social Science Quarterly 52 (June): 39-60.

--- and J. A. SWEEN (1971) "Urbanization, industrialization, and voting in Mexico: a longitudinal analysis of official and opposition party support." Social Science Quarterly 52 (December): 721-745.

PART II

THE RURAL–URBAN INTERFACE

ROBERT V. KEMPER is Assistant Professor of Anthropology at Southern Methodist University. He received his Ph.D. from the University of California (Berkeley) in 1971. He was founding Editor of *Urban Anthropology Newsletter* and is now Associate Editor of *Urban Anthropology*. Among his principal publications are: *Anthropologists in Cities* (with George M. Foster; Little, Brown, 1974); "Bibliografía comentada sobre la antropología urbana en América Latina" (*Boletín Bibliográfico de Antropología Americana*, Vol. 33/34, 1970/71); "Factores sociales en la migración: el caso de los tzintzuntzeños en la ciudad de México" (*América Indígena*, Vol. 33, 1973); and "Family and Household Organization among Tzintzuntzan Migrants in Mexico City" in W. A. Cornelius and F. M. Trueblood (eds.) *Latin American Urban Research*, Vol. 4 (Sage Publications, 1974).

GEORGE M. FOSTER is Professor of Anthropology at the University of California (Berkeley), where he received his Ph.D. in 1941. He has taught at Syracuse University, the University of California (Los Angeles), the National School of Anthropology in Mexico City, and for six years served as Director of the Institute of Social Anthropology (Smithsonian Institution). Among his principal publications are: *Empire's Children: The People of Tzintzuntzan* (with Gabriel Ospina; Institute of Social Anthropology Publ. No. 6, 1948); *Culture and Conquest: America's Spanish Heritage* (Viking Fund Publications in Anthropology No. 27, 1960); *Traditional Cultures: and the Impact of Technological Change* (Harper & Row, 1962; reissued in 1973 as *Traditional Societies and Technological Change*); *Tzintzuntzan: Mexican Peasants in a Changing World* (Little, Brown, 1967); and *Applied Anthropology* (Little, Brown, 1969).

Chapter 2

URBANIZATION IN MEXICO: THE VIEW FROM TZINTZUNTZAN

ROBERT V. KEMPER and GEORGE M. FOSTER

Much has been written about the dramatic growth of Mexican cities since the 1940s, the seemingly endless stream of migrants from countryside to metropolis, and the consequences of rapid urbanization for national economic development. Much less has been said about an equally important dimension of contemporary Mexican life: the entry of thousands of small rural communities into the urban orbit. This process of rural modernization provides a crucial counterpoint to the nation's urban and industrial growth. It reflects the formal and informal efforts of governmental agencies, private enterprise, and individual citizens to narrow the gap between village and city. These efforts, although uncoordinated and overlapping, have succeeded in transplanting many features of urban life to the rural setting. As a result, Mexican urbanization cannot be understood without examining its effects on rural populations,[1] which in 1970 represented about 65 percent of the total population and more than 99 percent of all localities (Corona Rentería, 1974: 298).

Authors' Note: We are grateful to many people and institutions for their support of the research on which this paper is based. The Institute of Social Anthropology (Smithsonian Institution) sponsored the original fieldwork in 1944-1946; the National Science Foundation (Grant G-7064), the National Institute of General Medical Sciences (Grant GM-1224), the Wenner-Gren Foundation for Anthropological Research (Grant 3027), and the Research Committee of the University of California (Berkeley) have provided assistance since 1959. In addition, it is a pleasure to acknowledge the courtesy of the Mexican government, and especially the Instituto Nacional de Antropología e Historia, which has permitted this long-term, continuing study to be conducted. Finally, we would be remiss if we did not thank the people of Tzintzuntzan, residents and emigrants alike, for their constant friendship and cooperation.

In this essay we shall examine the costs and benefits of urbanization for a single Mexican village: Tzintzuntzan, Michoacán. The data from this rural community, covering thirty years of first-hand ethnographic observation and supplemented by detailed household censuses for 1945, 1960, and 1970, provide a solid base for analyzing demographic and socio-economic changes in the face of urbanization. In addition, special studies of emigration and urbanization were carried out in 1969-1970 and 1974. Thus, it is possible to describe with some precision how the people of Tzintzuntzan once lived and how they live today.

The analysis is in two parts: the first sketches the major changes which have taken place in Tzintzuntzan during the past three decades; the second evaluates the roles of government, business, and individuals in changing the village and its inhabitants. Before proceeding with this analysis, however, it is important to stress the extent to which, in most of Mexico, the cultural gap between countryside and metropolis has been closed during the past generation. In spite of the remarkable urban and industrial development that has characterized Mexico, and in spite of the supposed conservatism of its rural population, the physical and psychological distance between town and country has narrowed appreciably during the post-World War II era. Today rural and urban Mexicans watch the same television programs, listen to the same soap operas, increasingly wear the same clothing made in the same factories, buy the same capital goods (e.g., television sets, stoves, blenders, refrigerators), eat the same packaged foods, follow the same educational curricula, and prefer medical doctors to *curanderos.*

What is especially striking about these changes is the role of the Mexican government in building a nationwide infrastructure. Some modest changes did occur without major infrastructure development. For example, gasoline-powered maize mills and Singer sewing machines were found in remote areas well before highways were built. And simple country schools long antedated rural electrification and hard-surfaced roads. Yet in analyzing the case of Tzintzuntzan, we find that most major changes awaited governmental decisions at state and national levels to develop the local infrastructure. Without these governmental efforts, particularly the establishment of a network of hard-surfaced roads and a system of rural electrification, Tzintzuntzan and many other Mexican villages would still look much like their nineteenth-century predecessors.

TZINTZUNTZAN: THREE DECADES OF CHANGE

Tzintzuntzan is a Spanish-speaking mestizo village located on the shores of Lake Pátzcuaro, 230 miles west of Mexico City. Although today Tzintzuntzan is, and appears always to have been, a typical Mexican village, appearances are deceiving. At the time of the Spanish Conquest, it was the capital of the Tarascan Empire, which included most of the modern state of Michoacán and adjoining areas—an empire which successfully held the Aztecs at bay. After the Conquest, however, Tzintzuntzan's eminence was short-lived. For the past four centuries, almost nothing has distinguished the village from thousands of other Mexican rural communities, except its fame for superior pottery and the richness of its ceremonial life.[2]

During the four centuries following the Conquest, the village's population appears to have been stable, fluctuating around 1,000 persons. A high birth rate was balanced by a high death rate, while limited in-migration from nearby hamlets seems to have just about matched out-migration. Resources, although limited, were apparently sufficient to meet the simple subsistence requirements of peasants who knew no other way of life (Foster, 1967: 264).

Then, beginning in the late 1930s, and gaining momentum in the 1940s and 1950s, Tzintzuntzan's population underwent a dramatic change. The 1,003 persons of 1930 became 1,077 in 1940; 1,336 in 1950; 1,840 in 1960; and 2,169 in 1970. This means that the population increased 0.7 percent per annum between 1930-1940, 2.2 percent per annum between 1940-1950, 3.2 percent per annum between 1950-1960, and just 1.7 percent per annum between 1960-1970. It appears, therefore, that Tzintzuntzan has passed through its period of most rapid population expansion.

A comparison of local and national crude birth and death rates shows the extent of recent population changes in Tzintzuntzan (Table 1). For the 1935-1945 period the net increase falls well below the national norm; in contrast, over the following two decades the rapid decline in mortality brought Tzintzuntzan into line with the national figures. Furthermore, the mortality decline was greatest in Tzintzuntzan during a period when out-migration was still relatively uncommon.

TABLE 1

BIRTH AND DEATH RATES: TZINTZUNTZAN AND MEXICO, 1935-1965

	Period		
	1935-1945	*1945-1955*	*1955-1965*
Tzintzuntzan[a]			
Birth rate per 1,000	46.8	50.7	44.1
Death rate per 1,000	29.8	16.8	8.7
Net increase	17.0	33.9	35.4
Mexico[b]			
Birth rate per 1,000	48.1	46.3	44.9
Death rate per 1,000	22.6	15.9	11.3
Net increase	25.5	30.4	33.6

SOURCES: a. Foster, 1967: 265. b. C.E.E.D., 1970: 8.

Emigration

Tzintzuntzan's recent population growth would have been even higher if out-migration had not drained off a considerable number of villagers (and their potential spouses and children) during the 1950s and 1960s. Household census data for 1945, 1960, and 1970, plus preliminary interview data for mid-1974, provide excellent documentation of emigration trends. Table 2 shows that while a plurality of Tzintzuntzan emigrants have remained in Michoacán, a significant minority have settled as far away as the United States. Furthermore, in recent years an increasing share of migrants have made long distance moves. Perhaps most significant is the apparent decline in the total number of emigrants since 1970. If this fall off is not just a result of under-reporting by the key informants who provided the bulk of our mid-1974 data, then it would seem that emigration from Tzintzuntzan has peaked and is stabilizing at a fairly high level.

Rural-urban migration has been much more important than village-village migration throughout the post-war era (Table 3). In fact, cityward emigration represents a steady 70 percent of all migration from Tzintzuntzan. Mexico City has been, and continues to be, the primary urban destination for Tzintzuntzeños, with about one-third of all emigrants having moved there either directly or by stages. The only other important urban destinations are Morelia (the state capital), Pátzcuaro (the major market town in the lake region), Uruapan (a rapidly growing industrial and agribusiness center in western Michoacán),

TABLE 2
MIGRATION FROM TZINTZUNTZAN: REGIONS OF DESTINATION

	Period of Migration					
Region[a]	*pre-1945*	*1945-1959*	*1960-1969*	*1970-1974*[b]	*Totals*	*%*
Michoacán	9	89	212	59	369	41.0
Mexico City	10	50	186	57	303	33.7
U.S.A.	1	6	36	31	74	8.2
Core region	0	29	11	12	52	5.8
North region	0	8	18	16	42	4.7
West region	0	0	17	6	23	2.5
South region	0	0	2	0	2	0.2
Unknown	0	1	10	24	35	3.9
Totals[c]	20	183	492	205	900	100.0
%	2.2	20.3	54.7	22.8	100.0	

a. Regions used here are modified from Cline (1963: 49).

b. Figures for 1970-1974 are estimates derived from interviews with selected key informants. All other figures are based on analysis of unpublished household census data for 1945, 1960, and 1970.

c. Return migrants are excluded from this table. Estimates of returnees are: none for the pre-1945 period; one for the 1945-1959 period; 42 for the 1960-1969 period; and 24 for the 1970-1974 period.

TABLE 3
RURAL-URBAN MIGRATION FROM TZINTZUNTZAN

	Period of Migration					
Destination	*pre-1945*	*1945-1959*	*1960-1969*	*1970-1974*[a]	*Totals*	*%*
Rural	1	53	94	41	189	21.0
Urban	18	126	354	140	638	70.9
Unknown	1	4	44	24	73	8.1
Totals[b]	20	183	492	205	900	100.0
%	2.2	20.3	54.7	22.8	100.0	

a. Figures for 1970-1974 are estimates derived from interviews with selected key informants. All other figures are based on analysis of unpublished household census data for 1945, 1960, and 1970.

b. Return migrants are excluded from this table.

Guadalajara (capital of Jalisco), Tijuana (a major city in Baja California), and Toluca (capital of the State of Mexico). Clearly, then, Tzintzuntzan emigrants prefer large urban destinations over small rural hamlets.

A final point regarding emigration: in earlier years return migrants were uncommon, but now they are much more frequent. Whereas only 43 returnees are known for the period from 1930 to 1970, at least another 24 emigrants have returned since 1970. Which of these returnees will depart the community again is unpredictable. Nonetheless, the recent increase in the number of return migrants is a result of declining selectivity within the expanding migrant group. This phenomenon corresponds to what Browning and Feindt (1969) have described as a "regression toward the mean" for the migrant group, as compared with the total population of their community of origin.

The Economic Situation

Demographic change in Tzintzuntzan has been accompanied by major changes in the way of life for the great majority of the villagers. Turning first to the local occupational structure, we see from the figures in Table 4 that pottery-making continues to be the primary occupation of most household heads. It has, however, declined in relative importance as potters' sons and daughters abandon the craft for commerce and day labor—or leave the village altogether to seek their fortune elsewhere. The percentage of farmers and fishermen has also declined during the past three decades. Land continues to be in short supply and the increased population has created added pressures on a limited supply of good agricultural properties. At the same time, severe over-fishing of the lake combined with an infestation of water lilies has so decreased fishing prospects that by 1974 only a single Tzintzuntzeño still derived his primary income from this activity.

While these occupations have declined in importance, the number of day

TABLE 4
OCCUPATIONAL STRUCTURE IN TZINTZUNTZAN: 1945, 1960, 1970

	1945			*1960*			*1970*		
Occupation	*No.*	*%*	*Rank*	*No.*	*%*	*Rank*	*No.*	*%*	*Rank*
Potter	118	48.0	1	167	52.2	1	167	46.4	1
Farmer	37	15.0	2	39	12.2	2	27	7.5	4
Pottery reseller[a]	26	10.6	3	14	4.4	5	17	4.7	5
Day laborer	20	8.1	4	37	11.6	3	53	14.7	2
Housekeeper	13	5.3	5	10	3.1	7	13	3.6	8
Fisherman	8	3.3	6	16	5.0	4	13	3.6	8
Miscellaneous	8	3.3	6	14	4.4	5	34	9.4	3
Construction	7	2.9	8	8	2.5	9	5	1.4	10
Storekeeper	5	2.0	9	5	1.6	10	14	3.9	7
Employee	4	1.6	10	10	3.1	7	17	4.7	5
Totals[b]	246	100.1		320	100.1		360	100.0	

a. For 1945, "pottery reseller" means muleteer *(arriero)*; for 1960 and 1970, "pottery reseller" means persons who own pottery stands or trucks.

b. The totals represent the primary occupation of household heads only; they do not include other workers nor do they include secondary jobs held by household heads.

SOURCES: All data are derived from analysis of unpublished household census materials.

laborers has greatly increased, as have the numbers of employees and "miscellaneous" workers. The "employee" category includes Tzintzuntzeños working in the local schools, in the village's small clinic, and in various posts with the local, municipal, and state government agencies based in the community. The "miscellaneous" category includes the growing group of specialists like bakers, butchers, and refreshment stand operators. And although their numbers had not grown dramatically by 1970, the impact of pottery resellers on village life also has been substantial. These middlemen traditionally took mules laden with local goods to the *tierra caliente* where they exchanged these goods for cheeses, dried meats, and other products of the lowlands. Today, local middlemen travel in the latest model pick-ups and half-ton trucks to the northern border cities where they sell substantial quantities of pottery and other craft products at considerable profits.

The past three decades have also meant rising standards of living for most households in Tzintzuntzan. In 1945, when the first ethnographic census was taken, many families still lived in houses little different from those their ancestors had inhabited several generations earlier. The contemporary contrast with the village of 1945 is obvious from the figures in Table 5 and Table 6. Aside from the raised hearth, a great convenience to a tortilla maker, most items listed have been introduced fairly recently. Progress has not been limited to house improvements; increasing numbers of villagers compete to be first, or among the first, to possess and display consumer goods once unknown on the local scene. As a result, many homes now have amenities usually associated with the urban

TABLE 5
HOUSEHOLD IMPROVEMENTS IN TZINTZUNTZAN: 1945, 1960, and 1970

Item	*1945* N	*1945* %	*1960* N	*1960* %	*1970* N	*1970* %
Raised hearth	148[a]	60.0	240	75.0	266	73.9
Patio water tap	54	21.8	152	47.5	230	63.9
Latrine	47	19.0	137	42.8	202	56.1
Electricity	35	14.2	156	48.7	232	64.4
Whitewashed exterior	n.d.[b]	–	148	46.2	159	44.2
Hard floor	n.d.	–	106	33.1	139	53.9
3 rooms or more	87	35.2	104	32.5	194	13.9
Glass window	n.d.	–	15	4.7	50	13.9
Shower bath	0	0.0	2	0.6	14	3.9
Flush toilet	0	0.0	0	0.0	4	1.1
	(N = 246)		(N = 320)		(N = 360)	

a. Estimated total and percentage.

b. n.d. = no data available.

SOURCES: Figures for 1945 are derived from Foster and Ospina (1948: 38); figures for 1960 and 1970 from analysis of unpublished census data.

middle class, including gas stoves, innerspring mattresses, television sets, stereo consoles, radios, electric blenders, flush toilets, and even automatic washing machines.

The improvement in standards of living has been so rapid and so recent that the figures in Table 5 and Table 6 do not fully reflect the situation in 1974. For example, in 1972 the Federal Commission of Electricity extended its lines to peripheral parts of Tzintzuntzan, for the first time making electricity available to all homes. In the extreme western barrio, El Rincón, 22 of the 27 home owners promptly signed up. Today the percentage of village subscribers to electrical service is probably between 85-90 percent. Similarly, the number of television sets has grown dramatically in the past four years. There were only 37 in 1970, and now there are well over 100. The number of gas stoves has also risen considerably since the 1970 census, with the current figure close to 100. Perhaps the most impressive measure of recent progress, however, is the increase in motor vehicles owned by Tzintzuntzeños. By 1974 there were five big vans, two light VW vans, 10 pickup trucks, 8 heavy-duty trucks, and 7 passenger cars–a total of 32 vehicles in all, and the number is still growing.

The intra-village disparities in living conditions resulting from this progress mean that the local saying "here we are all equal" ceases to describe accurately the reality of village life. One measure of increasing wealth differentiation in Tzintzuntzan is that most of the best homes are now located on or near the main plaza or along the highway through the town's center, whereas the poorest are found on the outskirts, either west in El Rincón or east in Yahuaro.

Nevertheless, changes in living standards in Tzintzuntzan are not irreversible:

TABLE 6
POSSESSION OF MAJOR CONSUMER GOODS IN TZINTZUNTZAN:
1945, 1960, and 1970

Item	1945 N	1945 %	1960 N	1960 %	1970 N	1970 %
Raised bed	143	57.9	221	68.7	268	74.4
Radio	20[a]	8.1[a]	124	38.7	242	67.2
Electric iron	0	0.0	100	31.2	156	43.3
Sewing machine	15[a]	6.1[a]	60	18.7	63	17.5
Store-bought mattress	8	3.2	53	16.6	73	20.3
Stove:						
propane gas	0	0.0	0	0.0	50	13.9
kerosene	0	0.0	0	0.0	16	4.4
Television set	0	0.0	0	0.0	37	10.3
Electric blender	0	0.0	0	0.0	17	4.7
Automobile/truck	0	0.0	1	0.3	11	3.1
Automatic washing machine	0	0.0	0	0.0	5	1.4
	(N = 246)		(N = 320)		(N = 360)	

a. Estimated totals and percentages.

SOURCES: Figures for 1945 are derived from Foster and Ospina (1948: 38); figures for 1960 and 1970 from analysis of unpublished census data.

few villagers are secure enough to weather a severe economic recession, particularly since the demand for local pottery and the prices which must be paid for consumer goods and services are determined externally by forces beyond local control.

Educational Progress

Unlike many rural Mexican villages, Tzintzuntzan has long had its own school, with a three-year primary program as early as 1869. However, attendance was sporadic because most parents believed education of little value to success as a potter, farmer, or fisherman. Even the construction of a fine, new school building in 1939, through the efforts of President Lázaro Cárdenas, instilled only temporary enthusiasm for education. The high drop-out rate for the fourth, fifth, and sixth grades during the 1940s and 1950s is clear from these figures: registration from 1940 to 1959 averaged between 175 and 200 students per year, but only 92 children graduated from sixth grade during this period. In fact, no class graduated for eleven of the twenty years, and the largest number of graduates was fifteen in 1947.

In the 1960s, however, most Tzintzuntzeños acquired a new interest in education. Local primary school registration is higher than ever and more children entering first grade now finish sixth grade. The school's physical plant was replaced by pre-fabricated modular units in 1970 because the old buildings had so deteriorated during thirty years of use and misuse. Moreover, the villagers have cooperated to an unprecendented extent to establish a secondary school program in Tzintzuntzan. Started on a trial basis in September, 1974, the secondary school should be attended by many children now pursuing or planning to pursue higher education elsewhere. Whereas before 1960 only 19 students had *ever* gone on to secondary school, at least 75 are currently enrolled in secondary schools, preparatories, normal schools, seminaries, and universities. In fact, of the 325 village children who completed sixth grade between 1960 and 1970, more than 100 have continued their studies. This dramatic increase in schooling is reflected in a rising literacy rate in Tzintzuntzan. In 1945 only 53 percent of household heads could read and write, and this figure improved only slightly—to 58 percent—by 1960. In contrast, the literacy rate climed to 70.3 percent in 1970 and today it probably has reached 75 percent.

Education also provides a popular career for many of Tzintzuntzan's young people. To become a school teacher is the most common, and most realistic, goal of many bright young students. From 1945 to 1970, some 30 villagers became state or federal school teachers. Since 1970, another 30 have been added to the rolls. Indeed, we believe that after pottery and other crafts, school teachers are one of Tzintzuntzan's principal contributions to Mexican development.

World View Transformation

Changes in population, shifts in occupational categories, improvements in living standards, and progress in education are all relatively easy to document in Tzintzuntzan's recent history. Changes in values, attitudes, and aspirations are much more difficult to assess. Some, such as a changed appreciation for schooling, are fairly obvious, and in this domain it is clear that the village has undergone a revolution during the past 15 years. Other changes can be inferred from close observation of the daily activities of Tzintzuntzeños. For instance, a "time-is-money" attitude is evidenced by a recent shift to buying tortillas rather than making them at home. Although the villagers recognize that machine-made tortillas are inferior to the hand-made variety, a majority of families now rely on *tortillerías* for their everyday supply. This allows women increased time for more productive work, which may include pottery-making, store-keeping, day labor, or commerce in arts and crafts.

Most striking of all the recent cultural changes in Tzintzuntzan is the breakdown of the traditional zero-sum game mentality that served to discourage innovation and modernization for many years. This cognitive orientation, labeled "the image of limited good" by Foster (1965), was calculated to maintain the status quo, and it was based on four major premises (Foster, 1972: 58-59):

(1) A normative individual behavior that minimizes the settings or situations in which ego may be exploited by others, i.e., rise at his

expense, is preferred. This behavior stresses the avoidance of close ties with others (unless validated by ritual safeguards), distrust, and concealment or denial of "good" possessed. The individual is confronted with a prisoner's dilemma payoff matrix in which cooperative urges are discouraged by the recognition that such action can be exploited by the other player, to ego's detriment.

(2) Violations of the preferred normative behavior are discouraged by invidious sanctions such as gossip, backbiting, witchcraft, and assault.

(3) Achieved or threatened power and wealth imbalances are neutralized through redistributive (or siphon) mechanisms such as fiestas and other forms of ritual hospitality.

(4) Acquisition of additional good is permitted (but not encouraged) by tapping sources outside the system: finding treasure, winning on the lottery, obtaining human and supernatural patrons (including pacts with the Devil), and working for wages beyond the boundaries of the system. Since such "good" clearly is not at the expense of others, it is "safe," and can be permitted without threatening the stability of the system.

Only in recent years have more than a handful of Tzintzuntzeños been willing to confront and reject the traditional world view. As early as 1965 Foster noted the appearance of people who competed openly for status and prestige through acquisition of material possessions and through visible house improvements (like constructing a second story). This tendency continues at an accelerated rate, and increasing numbers of villagers display their economic progress without fearing the envy of less successful neighbors. As a result, the "image of limited good" is being replaced by an "image of unlimited good." Tzintzuntzeños no longer treat the local system *as if* it existed in isolation from the national and international scene. And they perceive that progress within this larger system is possible without harming their fellow villagers' opportunities to get ahead.

This transformation of world view is not, however, a simple, one-way process. People oscillate between the old and the new rather than commit themselves wholly to the unknown. The opening up of Tzintzuntzan's world means that villagers must recognize and cope with risks formerly beyond their ken. The ways in which Tzintzuntzeños deal with this new situation represent a key element in their modernization. Those who refuse to change from traditional modes of behavior and those who see the old ways as silly and out-moded provide the poles of a continuum of responses in which the rest of the villagers can be placed. As just one example of the transition from tradition to modernity, we cite the case of a young woman who sometimes works in the capital as a domestic servant, but who normally lives in Tzintzuntzan with her husband and children. Several informants pointed out that this woman is highly adaptable: when she comes to the city she wears a mini-skirt, fashionable shoes, and has her hair styled high upon the head. When she is in the village she prefers to walk barefoot and wear traditional Indian dress. The informants have even given her a nickname, *"la polifacética,"* to convey the many facets of her personality. She is like a chameleon, changing her colors to suit the background, changing her attitudes and world views as the situation demands. And indeed, Tzintzuntzan is in a state of flux in which traditional behaviors are giving way, sometimes grudgingly, to new styles, values, and ideas.

THE URBANIZATION OF TZINTZUNTZAN

The major dimensions of Tzintzuntzan's transformation during the past three decades have now been described. At this point we can assess the extent to which urban forces have influenced the course of the community's recent development. The analysis is based on the belief that urbanization is a more complex process than just cityward migration and increasing proportions of the national population living in metropolitan areas. Urbanization also involves the diffusion of governmental programs, business actions, and individual decisions to communities that demographers define as "rural." When rural peoples, like those in Tzintzuntzan, come to see themselves as participants in this broader system of communication/interaction/decision-making, then the process of urbanization has taken hold.

The Impact of Governmental Programs

The first wave of governmental influences was felt in Tzintzuntzan in the 1930s. The *municipio* of Tzintzuntzan was formed by a decree on 2 October 1930, under the governorship of Lázaro Cárdenas, who "was anxious, even if only in a symbolic way, to restore some of the vanished grandeur of the former seat of the Tarascan Empire" (Foster and Ospina, 1948: 176). This municipio consists of Tzintzuntzan itself, as *cabecera,* plus another 30 or so smaller settlements. Thus, since the 1930s, the village has been a regional focus for governmental authority, just as its parish church for centuries has been an important religious center.

Infrastructure Development

Soon after the municipio was created, Cárdenas sent a Cultural Mission to Tzintzuntzan. This group consisted of "teachers specializing in plastic arts, social work, music, home economics, physical education, and 'small industries,' and a nurse-midwife and an agricultural engineer" (Foster, 1967: 26). While the Cultural Mission produced no immediate successes, it marked a turning point in village life. Tzintzuntzeños had their curiosity aroused, and they became less fearful of outsiders.

In the wake of the Cultural Mission, and as a consequence of Cárdenas' personal interest in Tzintzuntzan, the basic elements of a modern infrastructure began arriving. In 1938 the first electrical lines reached the community from nearby Pátzcuaro; running water was installed by laying iron pipes to a nearby spring; and an iron bandstand was even brought from the state capital to enliven the village plaza. In the following year, construction was completed on a paved highway linking Tzintzuntzan to Pátzcuaro and Quiroga, and thereby to the *tierra caliente* and to Morelia, Guadalajara, Mexico City, the rest of the nation, and the United States. Also in 1939, the village received its first six-year federal primary school, dedicated by Cárdenas himself.

Health Care Improvements

Because of World War II, and because of the government's post-war emphasis on urban-industrial development, little more occurred in Tzintzuntzan until the mid-1950s, when the Ministry of Health offered villagers assistance in latrine and shower bath construction, instructed them in the value of cement floors, offered immunization programs and, by 1960, built a small health center staffed by a nurse-midwife and *practicante* physician. These health services, in conjunction with good access to medical facilities in Pátzcuaro, Quiroga, Morelia, and even Mexico City, have had a significant role in lowering the villagers' mortality rate. As a further result, most Tzintzuntzeños now prefer physicians to *curanderos,* and except for childhood folk diseases like "evil eye" and *empacho,* people with money for fees and medicines seek the attentions of physicians. Commenting on the relative merits of the two types of treatment, one mother in her mid-thirties laughingly remarked that when her children were sick she always took them to a physician. Only in case he did not effect a quick cure would she turn to a curandero. This is an interesting reversal of the oft-noted pattern in which peasants turn to doctors only in desperation, after the local curers have failed. A more recent indication of the growing reliance on modern medical practitioners is that about 80 percent of recorded deaths now bear the name of an attending physician. Even in the mid-1960s, the figure was less than 10 percent. Government programs to improve the villagers' health have been very successful, but have had the effect, presumably unintended, of increasing the local population and creating further demands for medical services that the government does not provide in rural communities. Thus, health care improvements have brought Tzintzuntzeños into more intimate contract with cities where adequate health care is available.

The Bracero Program

The government program with the greatest impact on Tzintzuntzan was created early in World War II and continued through 1964. A series of

American-Mexican agreements allowed the temporary migration of farm laborers to the United States, where they were contracted primarily for agricultural stoop labor in the central, southwestern, and western states. During the quarter-century of the program, more than half of all Tzintzuntzan household heads worked as *braceros* at least once, and many men went north on a number of occasions.

The social and economic consequences of this massive, temporary migration have been significant and irreversible. Exposure to lifestyles wrought a permanent rise in aspirations, as men returned to Tzintzuntzan with new consumer goods and with the economic means to improve their living conditions. The program's stimulus to Tzintzuntzan's development also included many innovations. For instance, the braceros abandoned the traditional *calzones* for jeans and jackets, and women's costly home-made wool dresses were replaced by inexpensive cotton garments produced by Mexico's growing garment industry. In addition, braceros brought in most of the village's radios during the 1940s and brought in the first television sets in the 1960s. This exposure to American life also brought in new ideas and attitudes. As Foster (1967: 30) reports,

> It was a bracero, and not a stay-at-home, who once astonished me by asking, "Doctor, what can we do to bring industry to Tzintzuntzan? " He had noticed the same thing another bracero had observed: "In the United States, even in little towns, like this, I saw tall smokestacks, and at the bottom of the smokestacks, lots of people were working. Here our villages have no smokestacks."

The termination of the bracero program ended a vital economic transfusion for Tzintzuntzan, a community with too few employment opportunities and too many people. Moreover, while it lasted, the program had the effect of keeping most Tzintzuntzeños tied to their homes. When it ended, many quickly saw the excellent opportunities available in Mexico cities and emigrated. The long-term impact of the bracero program is still unclear, but without question many Tzintzuntzeños achieved economic progress impossible under traditional circumstances.

Mass Communications

The Mexican government has spent millions of pesos during recent decades to create a nation-wide communications system. The people of Tzintzuntzan have reaped many benefits from this policy. For a number of years villagers have been able to send and receive mail from Tzintzuntzan, but so far there is only one telephone to serve the community. It was installed in 1964 in a privately-owned store in the central plaza. Radio stations, both public and private, also help spread urban influences among the local population. In fact, the most recent "prestige" purchase is a stereo console, many of which have short wave receivers capable of receiving the Voice of America, Armed Forces Radio Network, and stations from Europe and other Latin American nations.

The most important element of the mass communications system is television, available to the villagers for 15 years. The government provided the infrastructure of microwave towers and ancillary equipment, while private consortia operate independent stations and provide their own programming. Tzintzuntzeños watch soap operas, movies, American westerns and detective programs (although the government recently banned many imported programs as being too "violent"). They also watch news programs, especially the popular 7 p.m. news and the late-night program called "24 Horas." Television, and news programs in particular, provide villagers with instant access to ideas and events that once took months or years to filter down to the Mexican countryside. For instance, in the summer of 1974 we found that many Tzintzuntzeños were familiar with the Watergate scandal. Indeed, a number of them watched Nixon's resignation speech on a live telecast dubbed into Spanish! Television is also the primary source of sports programs, ranging from soccer, boxing, basketball, and American football to the more exotic Olympic sports. Through television, therefore, villagers obtain a (sometimes distorted) image of urban life which broadens their horizons, increases their aspirations, and equips them to cope with urbanites—when they emigrate to the city or when they sell pottery to tourists passing through Tzintzuntzan.

Tourist Development

The natural beauty of the Lake Pátzcuaro area, and the attractions of its artisans and craftsmen, makes it one of Mexico's major tourist areas. The national and state governments have actively promoted tourism in the region and Tzintzuntzan has received a good share of attention for its famous pottery and its traditional religious festivals (e.g., The Day of the Dead, Holy Week, and the day of the local patron saint). The government also has done much to build the reputation of village craftsmen by purchasing their best works for resale in stores run by the Banco Nacional de Fomento Cooperativo and the Instituto Nacional Indigenista. These stores are located in Mexico City, Guadalajara, Morelia, and in several northern border cities. Furthermore, in 1974, the wife of President Luis Echeverría came to Tzintzuntzan to dedicate a new colonial-style arcade where pottery and crafts may be sold to tourists in a more "elegant" setting than that provided by the adobe and wood stands located across the street. Unfortunately, this arcade has fallen under the control of a single family and other villagers are upset that they are not able to obtain stalls.

Other government efforts to lure tourists to the Lake Pátzcuaro region are having mixed effects on Tzintzuntzan. The opening of the short-route highway from Morelia to Pátzcuaro bypassed Quiroga and Tzintzuntzan, with the result that many tourists headed for the famous Friday market in Pátzcuaro no longer go through Tzintzuntzan. At the same time, however, the state government and the National Fine Arts Institute have provided several hundred thousand pesos to restore Tzintzuntzan's convent and church to its sixteenth-century stature. They are using local labor–in itself a boon to the village economy–and are hopeful that the restoration will attract travelers to the community. And there is talk, as there has been for years, that the government will finally get the *yácatas* ("pyramids") fully excavated and restored to the condition in which they were when the Tarascan kings ruled Tzintzuntzan.

The Ejido Program

Tzintzuntzan is a land-poor community. In contrast to nearby hamlets where many families own twenty to fifty hectares, few Tzintzuntzeños own more than five hectares. Moreover, the government-sponsored *ejido* program has not been a local success because the lands assigned to Tzintzuntzan are located about five miles away. Only a dozen families possess ejido lands and most exercise their rights through sharecropping arrangements with farmers from other villages. In the long run, this program seems to have had little impact on the community.

Indirect Government Programs

We have discussed a number of government programs which have impinged directly on Tzintzuntzan during the past three decades. Tzintzuntzeños also have been affected by governmental actions carried out in other places for other purposes. For example, decisions to begin and terminate the bracero program were not made with Tzintzuntzan in mind. Planners examine the impact of such programs on all the "Tzintzuntzans" of rural Mexico, not just this one. Thus, when the government began massive construction projects for the subway in Mexico City, people from the whole nation responded–and Tzintzuntzeños were no exception. And as the flow of information into Tzintzuntzan improves, more villagers will likely respond to government-created job opportunities, whether in the local setting, in Mexico City, or in the United States.

International Development Programs

UNESCO's Fundamental Education Training Center for Latin America (CREFAL), established in the early 1950s at Pátzcuaro, carried out a major community development program in Tzintzuntzan for several years, stressing home egg production, pottery improvements, weaving, and furniture manufacturing. Foster has discussed the history of this project, and its sparse results (1967: 327-347). None of the projects survived, and in that sense the program must be considered a failure. In another sense, however, it was successful. International and Mexican Government interest in the village led people to see that they were capable of dealing with outsiders; many of today's leaders gained great self-confidence during the CREFAL period of activity. And students from Latin American countries living with village families aroused their curiosity about the outside world, and stimulated their desire to be more like this world.

The Role of Private Enterprise

While government programs improved Tzintzuntzan's infrastructure, private enterprise brough the villagers into the urban world of consumption. The products of a wide variety of businesses, including those of multinational corporations, are now available in Tzintzuntzan. Conversely, local entrepreneurs, especially pottery resellers, now sell locally-produced goods in Mexico City, Guadalajara, and the northern border cities. And although no direct industrial development has come to Tzintzuntzan, emigrants from the village have benefited from industrialization in other regions of the country.

Mass Communications and Advertising

Of the many outside enterprises influencing Tzintzuntzan, perhaps the most important are the urban-based mass media. The role of radio and television in bringing villagers news of the outside world has already been mentioned. In addition, Tzintzuntzan–and thousands of similar rural communities–has become a target for mass advertising campaigns, which change people's buying habits and consumption patterns, and in turn may improve their health and living conditions. The introduction of the detergent FAB some years ago illustrates one way in which Tzintzuntzeños have been influenced by advertising. First, the wonders of FAB were extolled on popular radio programs. Then, after they were familiar with the brand name, a panel truck with a roof loudspeaker came to town, stopping at each major intersection, where the announcer told villagers that FAB was available at a local store and that with each purchase came a valuable prize. FAB became an instant success and was quickly followed by competitors. Tzintzuntzan housewives presumably believed that their dishes, still washed in cold water, were cleaner than before.

Nowadays, packaged goods, cosmetics, clothing, and many other consumer products are constantly advertised on radio and television. The local reaction to these blandishments has meant that local stores have had to carry a much broader inventory than in earlier years. One small store, for example, stocks more than 400 items, representing everything from local agricultural produce to canned foods from the Mexican affiliates of American manufacturers like Del Monte, McCormick, and Nabisco. Nonetheless, Tzintzuntzan has no open-air marketplace nor any *supermercados* or chain-stores. Local residents and peasants living in neighboring hamlets must, therefore, travel to Quiroga, Pátzcuaro, Morelia, or beyond to acquire products and capital goods unavailable in the village. And it seems unlikely that outside investors will provide capital to build such facilities because of the small local population base and the presence of established competitors in nearby towns.

While radio and television are principal sources of news and advertising, newspapers and magazines are much less important in Tzintzuntzan. Beginning about 1965 the daily *Voz de Michoacán,* the main provincial newspaper in the state, was brought from Morelia to Tzintzuntzan. At the height of its popularity, the newspaper was distributed to about thirty subscribers. With the proliferation of television, however, the number of subscribers dropped to seven, and the local agent abandoned the service. Now, no newspapers or magazines come regularly to the village. In fact, because of their reliance on mass media originating in the capital, Tzintzuntzeños probably know more about life in Mexico City, key actors on the national scene, and major international news than they know about events on the other side of their own state.

Transportation and Tourism

Transportation enterprises also have had a significant impact on the community. The highway through town daily carries hundreds of trucks, busses, and cars. Many of these stop in Tzintzuntzan to load and discharge cargo and passengers. An average of twelve busses per hour stop during the day, and perhaps half as many at night. Thus, villagers easily can travel to Morelia, Mexico City, or other cities to buy goods or sell their products, to visit friends and relatives, to plead their case before state or federal officials, to seek temporary or permanent employment, or to receive specialized medical treatment beyond that offered in the local clinic. Furthermore, more and more Tzintzuntzeños now receive deliveries of liquid propane gas for their stoves from a Morelia distributor. And a few families even order purified bottled water from Morelia.

Outside business investment has been conspicuously absent in improving Tzintzuntzan's share of the growing tourist market. The village lacks a hotel, a tourist-class restaurant, a gas station, and a service garage. And it is unlikely that these necessary services will ever be available in Tzintzuntzan, since they exist in nearby Quiroga and Pátzcuaro. On the other hand, outside businesses have stimulated pottery and handicraft production. Large orders (e.g., a thousand ashtrays) from hotels and restaurants in Mexico City have provided considerable impetus to local pottery-makers. And recognition of the artistic merits of the pottery of the village's finer craftsmen has also meant improved sales. In order to meet the increased demands for their ware, Tzintzuntzan potters have "rationalized," at least partially, the production process. Whereas each family was traditionally an independent, vertically integrated production unit, in recent years a number of potters have tried to create a modified assembly line production system. They contract with other families for unfired "green" ware to be delivered in specific quantities on certain dates. Then they do the art work and firing of the pottery. Finally, the pottery is sold to a reseller, to one of the many pottery stands or stores (now numbering about fifty) which deal directly with tourists passing through town, or to the outside enterprise which contracted for the order.

Consumer Credit and Indebtedness

In recent years, a number of Tzintzuntzan families have gone into debt to outside creditors to purchase expensive consumer goods, to improve their homes, to buy a truck or car, or to expand their business. This installment buying is also encouraged by the government, whose agencies also sell many products to villagers on credit. Although no villagers currently have credit cards, some emigrants do and their ability to make large purchases on time is certain to impress the more affluent village families. In fact, one store specializing in reselling pottery and handicrafts to tourists became affiliated with the BANCOMER (and by extension, BANKAMERICARD) credit card system in late 1973. The net effect of increased credit buying and indebtedness to outside businesses is to draw Tzintzuntzeños even more irrevocably into the urban sphere. This suggests that a useful measure of urbanization for rural communities would be the amount of accumulated debt and the proportion of families with credit accounts in urban businesses.

The Impact of Individuals

Having examined the effect of government programs and private enterprise on Tzintzuntzan, we turn now to the impact of individuals on the community. The persons who influence Tzintzuntzan's development include persons born there who have emigrated as well as persons born elsewhere who pass through the village. Because documentation of the impact of individuals on the urbanization process is difficult, and because the role of individuals is rather informal and random in comparison with governmental and business activities, the following discussion is necessarily impressionistic.

Tzintzuntzeños: Returned Migrants and Permanent Emigrants

Urbanization does not always depend on strangers. Tzintzuntzeños also are active participants in Mexican development through their travels, their contacts with outsiders, and their permanent settlement in a number of cities. When they return to the village they bring new ideas, new aspirations, and new consumer goods. While returned braceros were responsible for many innovations, more recently local pottery resellers have become the most important native agents of change. Their contact with people traveling through Tzintzuntzan and their own travels to distant cities have convinced them that Tzintzuntzan is no longer an isolated village, but is instead part of modern Mexico.

The relative success of Tzintzuntzeño emigrants in Mexican (and American) cities has also been very important in the community's development. Emigrants provide those who stay behind with models of how to cope with urban life. When they return for brief visits, longer vacations, or even to live once again in Tzintzuntzan, the emigrants also provide images of the city to their fellow villagers.

Some migrants have returned to live in Tzintzuntzan because they lost their jobs in the city. More frequently, however, they go back home for non-economic reasons. One man said that his children were always ill in the city, where he and his family lived in a crowded *vecindad* (tenement slum), but now that they are once more in the village the children are healthy. Another family also returned because of their children, although in this case they wanted to provide their children more room to play than was available in their vecindad in Mexico City. And a few emigrants returned to care for elderly relatives who had been left alone as the children grew up and left the village to seek their fortunes in the city.

Most of the emigrants, therefore, do not return as "failures" from the urban scene; they choose to return, they do not seek refuge. Some emigrants even are buying lots and building vacation homes in Tzintzuntzan. And still others talk of retiring back to the village, where the cost of living seems to them to be less than in the metropolis. They hope that their pensions will buy more for them and their families, but this will only be true if they adjust their living standards to those of the village. In a sense, Tzintzuntzan emigrants moving back to the village from Mexico City face the same problems of adjustment that they once faced when going to the city. They must find housing, employment, education for their children, and meaningful social relationships. And at the same time, they must avoid tearing apart the fabric of village life by being haughty, by displaying disproportionate wealth, or by comparing Tzintzuntzan unfavorably with their former urban residence. So far, this has not been a problem, but as the number of returned emigrants grows, the potential for social conflict also increases.

Even those emigrants who seldom or never visit Tzintzuntzan contribute to its urbanization. First, they send remittances to their relatives back home. Although it is difficult to assess the quantity and frequency of money and merchandise sent back to the village, it is likely that most emigrants do send something with some regularity. One man now living in Mexico City, where he works for the government as a computer systems coordinator, sends about 1,000 pesos (U.S. $80) to his parents each month. Other migrants send from a few pesos to several hundred pesos regularly. If we suppose that the typical migrant sends an average of 100 pesos per month in money or merchandise, the aggregate remittance of the emigrant population would be over one million pesos a year. Even if the total remittances were half this amount, Tzintzuntzan is still receiving an excellent "return" on its emigrant "investment."

Second, emigrants provide their fellow villagers with assistance in looking for jobs and housing in the city. These ties to "senior" migrants have been crucial in the initial urban experience of more than 90 percent of Tzintzuntzeños now living in Mexico City. New migrants enter the urban scene as "clients" to those who preceded them. As a result, complex social networks bridge the gap between Tzintzuntzan and the capital, transforming what once were individual migration itineraries into a continuing, and expanding, social process. The set of actors is constantly changing, with each new emigrant profiting from the experiences–pleasant and unpleasant–of relatives and friends with whom he comes in contact (Kemper, 1974: 84-85).

Third, emigrants are sources of valuable information about city life. They take villagers sightseeing, escort them to religious shrines, show them national treasures, and in general convince them that the city is not a strange and dangerous place. Emigrants also serve as intermediaries when villagers need assistance in dealing with businesses, government agencies, or with admissions into the university system. In fact, with the current demand for higher education outstripping the government's ability to provide facilities, migrants are crucial middlemen in getting Tzintzuntzan's young people into normal schools, preparatories, and universities. The figures on current enrollment of Tzintzuntzeños in higher education indicate that they are very successful in this enterprise.

Finally, emigrants validate the importance of Tzintzuntzan in the eyes of those who stay behind when they return for ritual occasions. A number of emigrant women still return home to have their babies. Young children are often brought back to the local parish church for their baptism or confirmation. And many persons return for a few days during Holy Week, Christmas, or during the village fiesta in honor of *Nuestro Señor del Rescate,* held in the first part of February each year.

It should be noted that Tzintzuntzeños have no village-based voluntary association for emigrants. Nor is there any important voluntary association within the village. Emigrants and villagers interact, therefore, as individuals (or within family groups) and this ensures that the flow of ideas and material goods from emigrants to the people in the community is unpatterned and informal. Furthermore, the unevenness of emigrant contributions may have the effect of disrupting the traditional social structure or, at least, of heightening the cleavages caused by government programs and private enterprise.

Non-Tzintzuntzeños; Mexicans and Foreigners

In addition to the impact of Tzintzuntzeños on their own community, many non-villagers also influence its development. On the one hand, many Mexican citizens stop in Tzintzuntzan to climb the pyramids, to visit the church and convent, or to buy pottery and crafts at the roadside stands and stores. On the other hand, many non-villagers work in Tzintzuntzan or come to the village as representatives of various government agencies or private companies. These outsiders provide Tzintzuntzeños with clues to the latest urban lifestyles and they also help the local economy by their activities. There is, however, a small group of outsiders who come to the village whose influence upon it is primarily negative. In recent years, some 25 homes have been constructed on the lakeshore at the north end of Tzintzuntzan, which serve as weekend and vacation retreats for wealthy families from Morelia. These visitors have little contact with local residents, except for the few caretakers they have hired to guard their properties and except for the few occasions when they come into town to buy supplies they forgot to bring from Morelia. Their major impact has been to withdraw several hectares of good agricultural land from the limited local supply and to force up the price of other lakeshore properties in anticipation of further purchases.

While Mexicans represent the majority of tourists who stop in Tzintzuntzan, a number of foreigners also pass through the community. Because nearly all of these foreigners are Americans, the following discussion is limited to them. One consequence of their visits to the village is an increased interest in learning English. This, in turn, has had the unintended consequence of raising the status of adolescents and young adults, since they are more familiar with basic business English than are their parents. Another important effect of American tourists is in broadening villagers' horizons. Every day numerous Americans, ranging from children to hippies to retired persons, stop in Tzintzuntzan to see the sights and to haggle over the price of pottery and other handicrafts. In a sense, the Americans who pass through the village bear a responsibility of which they are probably unaware; they represent "Los Estados Unidos," the mythical land of opportunity, and this is particularly so for American tourists of Mexican ancestry. American tourists also provide Tzintzuntzeños with increased pride in their community. They ask questions about the Tarascan kings, about the church and convent, about who makes the best pottery, and about the future of the village. Many tourists already know much about Tzintzuntzan, either from reading travel books or one of Foster's monographs, and their knowledge about the village must be startling to the Tzintzuntzeños who come into contact with them.

Finally, the long-term involvement of Foster, his students, and a number of other social scientists with Tzintzuntzan must be mentioned as a foreign influence on the community. Analysis of the innovations introduced by these academics shows that few, if any, had not already been introduced by government, business, or villagers themselves. Indeed, the major impact of Foster et al. has been to demonstrate that Tzintzuntzan *is* an important place (for otherwise, why would the fieldwork be continued year after year?), that Tzintzuntzeños can hold their own with outsiders, and that they have progressed dramatically during the last thirty years.

SUMMARY AND CONCLUSIONS

Tzintzuntzan has undergone many changes during the past three decades. Its population has increased, the people are more healthy, and emigrants have settled in a number of other towns and cities, especially in the large metropolises like Mexico City. Its economy, still based on pottery production and sales, has expanded sufficiently to provide many villagers with living standards once unattainable. Its youth have educational opportunities that earlier generations never enjoyed. And, perhaps of greatest importance, its inhabitants now realize that the world they live in goes far beyond the local community.

This transformation is not primarily the result of local innovation and initiative. On the contrary, nearly all of the changes in Tzintzuntzan can be traced to urban-based institutions and people. The programs and policies of national and state governments, the investments of private enterprise, and the advice and assistance of outside individuals (emigrants and non-villagers alike) have provided the community with a present—and a future—that it never could have achieved on its own. Indeed, the people of Tzintzuntzan have received much more assistance from external sources than they have returned to the nation in skills, profits, or taxes (Foster, 1974: 54).

The urbanization of Tzintzuntzan began in the 1930s through government investment, which continues today at a much lower rate. Private enterprise soon followed, and found the community to be a good market for a variety of products and services. Individual initiative has become more important in recent years, particularly with the increase in cityward migration and rural tourism. This suggests that the people of Tzintzuntzan are now beginning to carry the burden of development once borne primarily by government and business. As a consequence, government should be able to turn its investments to other, less fortunate communities, and business should find Tzintzuntzan a continuing source of profits.

Tzintzuntzeños have benefited in many ways from the programs, policies, and actions that have characterized the Mexican urbanization process. Their gains have not been without some costs, however. In a single generation Tzintzuntzan has been transformed from a village where "here we are all equal" to a town inhabited by "haves" and "have nots." And the gap seems to be growing as some take advantage of outside opportunities and others remain trapped in the traditional way of life. In this sense, urbanization may have had the effect of increasing inequality within the community while decreasing the village's inequality with respect to other Mexican towns and cities.

An important aspect of Tzintzuntzan's urbanization has been the flow of villagers to Mexican cities, where they have participated in the nation's urban-industrial growth. These emigrants, who as a group represent some of Tzintzuntzan's most able people, represent one of the community's major contributions to national development. Conversely, their absence from the village has reduced the pressure on the local economy and has permitted those who remained behind to be relatively more successful. Moreover, if all the emigrants were to return to live in Tzintzuntzan, the community would burst its demographic seams. Thus, emigration has been a positive feature of urban development for Tzintzuntzan and for the nation at large.

In conclusion, the view from Tzintzuntzan suggests that Mexico's rural population is becoming an increasingly active participant in the expanding urban system. The transformation of Tzintzuntzan, through the efforts of government, private enterprise, and certain individuals, probably has been replicated in hundreds of similar communities. While urbanization has had both positive and negative effects on Tzintzuntzan, its overall consequences have been beneficial to the community's inhabitants and to the progress of the nation as a whole.

NOTES

1. Following the lead of Unikel (1968: 1-18), we have divided Mexican population centers into four categories: rural (less than 5,000 inhabitants); mixed rural (5,000 to 9,999); mixed urban (10,000 to 14,999); and urban (more than 15,000). Thus, in speaking of the urban population we have in mind those localities with population of 15,000 or more. This definition is more restrictive than that used in the Mexican government census, in which the cutting-point between rural and urban is 2,500 inhabitants.

2. For details on Tzintzuntzan's early history, see Foster and Ospina (1948: 6-21).

REFERENCES

BROWNING, H. L. and W. FEINDT (1969) "Selectivity of migrants to a metropolis in a developing country: a Mexican case." Demography 6: 347-357.

C.E.E.D. [Centro de Estudios Económicos y Demográficos] (1970) Dinámica de la población de México. México, D.F.: El Colegio de México.

CLINE, H. (1963) Mexico, Revolution to Evolution: 1940-1960. New York: Oxford University Press.

CORONA RENTERIA, A. (1974) La economía urbana. México, D.F.: Instituto Mexicano de Investigaciones Económicas.

FOSTER, G. M. (1974) "Limited good or limited goods: observations on Acheson." American Anthropologist 76: 53-57.

--- (1972) "A second look at limited good." Anthropological Quarterly 45: 57-64.

--- (1967) Tzintzuntzan: Mexican Peasants in a Changing World. Boston: Little, Brown.

--- (1965) "Peasant society and the image of limited good." American Anthropologist 67: 293-315.

--- and G. OSPINA (1948) Empire's Children: The People of Tzintzuntzan. México, D.F.: Smithsonian Institution, Institute of Social Anthropology, Publication No. 6.

KEMPER, R. V. (1974) "Tzintzuntzeños in Mexico City: the anthropologist among peasant migrants," pp. 63-92 in G. M. Foster and R. V. Kemper (eds.) Anthropologists in Cities. Boston: Little, Brown.

UNIKEL, L. (1968) "Ensayo sobre una nueva clasificación de población rural y urbana en México." Demografía y Economía 2: 1-18.

BRYAN R. ROBERTS (Ph.D., University of Chicago) is Senior Lecturer in Sociology at the University of Manchester, specializing in urban anthropology and sociology and in social and economic development. He has done fieldwork in Guatemala and Peru, and is currently engaged in research on urban and regional development in Spain and England (Manchester area). His major publications include *Organizing Strangers: Poor Families in Guatemala City* (University of Texas Press, 1973); "Interrelationships of City and Countryside in Peru and Guatemala," in W. A. Cornelius and F. M. Trueblood (eds.) *Latin American Urban Research, Vol. 4* (Sage Publications, 1974); and "Education, Urbanization, and Social Change," in Richard Brown (ed.) *Education, Knowledge, and Cultural Change* (Tavistock, 1973).

Chapter 3

CENTER AND PERIPHERY IN THE DEVELOPMENT PROCESS: THE CASE OF PERU

BRYAN R. ROBERTS

My aim in this paper is to explore those limitations on the effectiveness of central planning and national development policies that result from small-scale political and economic activity in provincial areas. Since I see this local level activity as being an integral part of contemporary development processes in Latin America, I also question government emphasis on centralized organization and planning in producing social and economic development. Such an emphasis contains a centralist bias which overlooks the extent to which national development continues to be influenced by the particular history of local populations and by their relative autonomy in social and economic organization.

I focus my arguments on Peru, which has experienced a recent attempt, on the part of government, to initiate a systematic reform of social and economic structures (Hobsbawm, 1971). This reform activity has taken place in the context of an explicit official ideology of choosing a path to development that is neither capitalist nor communist. According to this ideology, the primary obstacles to national development are rooted in the lack of social and economic integration of the rural and much of the urban population. This lack of

Author's Note: The data on which this paper is based were collected during a three-year study of the Central Sierra of Peru. This project was financed by the British Social Science Research Council and co-directed by myself and Norman Long of Durham University. During the course of the study the two directors and a number of other researchers worked in a large number of villages and small towns, and in the city of Huancayo. The range of data collected includes case studies of economic enterprises in rural and urban areas, survey material on different populations, archival data from town and village councils and from the provincial registry, and government data on flows of transport and agricultural goods.

integration is, in part, attributed to entrenched national or foreign economic interests, such as those of the large landowners or mine companies, which have benefited from the dependence of much of the population. In contrast to this official view, I argue that the problems facing Peru and its government are due to the disorganization of its urban and rural population by their integration, from early in this century, into modern forms of capitalism. This disorganization is expressed in a complex pattern of urban migration, in the proliferation of small-scale entrepreneurial activity, and in the absence of any well-defined class groupings in either towns or countryside. In such a context, government reform occurs without the active participation of the mass of the population and is likely to be overly sensitive to the pressures of centrally located groups in the bureaucracy or in the foreign and domestic business communities (Quijano, 1972). The Peruvian government's reform of structures from the center has not yet benefited much of the population; this outcome of a systematic and seriously undertaken reform program illustrates the centralist bias and the misconceptions of the development process that it produces.

Though views of underdevelopment and of the strategies required to counter this underdevelopment have differed widely in their theoretical approaches and their substantive content, most analyses have stressed central organization as the determinant of development. In the literature on regional planning, there is a stress on the need for a well-integrated urban hierarchy that effectively organizes the social and economic space of a region and articulates it with the national economy. From this perspective the underdevelopment of provincial regions is to be corrected by enabling space to be organized more efficiently through improved communications and other infrastructure and through the planned location of different types of industries. In this organization of space, centrally located groups such as urban entrepreneurs or administrators are described as the crucial agents of change (Friedmann, 1961). Related to the above perspective is that of development specialists who emphasize the importance of introducing rural populations to modern ways of life; rural energies are to be released by placing villages in better communication with the urban centers, through education and through the mass media (Lerner, 1958). In this approach, as in the first, government officials or technical advisors are given the main responsibility for "developing" the provinces by introducing new techniques of cultivation or industry and by advising on integration with the regional economy.

This emphasis on the central determination of local possibilities is one that is shared by commentators working from the very different theoretical perspective of "dependency theory." In the early accounts of the social and economic dependency of countries and regions in Latin America, underdevelopment is viewed as the product of vertically imposed structures of dependency; economic possibilities at the local level were determined by a chain of exploitation that ran through landowners and merchants, in lower-order centers, to the bourgeoisie of the metropolitan countries (Stavenhagen, 1964; Frank, 1969). In subsequent modifications of dependency theory, a greater stress has been placed on variations in the internal structures of class relationships that interpret the external domination; these structures are still, however, centrally determined and their analysis leaves little scope for considering the possibilities of internally generated change (Cardoso and Falleto, 1970).

One assumption implicit in these different approaches is that rural society in underdeveloped countries is relatively static and represents a social and economic configuration that reacts to external stimuli. I argue that these approaches underestimate the dynamic of provincial organization, and that this dynamic enables people not simply to respond to external stimuli, but to interpret them. People on the "periphery" initiate activity that involves them with the national polity and economy and play a part in transforming the pattern of national development. There is a considerable body of material that suggests that in Latin America, at least, even the poorest sectors of the population are active in coping with, and manipulating, their situation. Patterns of migration, "informal" economic and political activities, and the proliferation of "self-help" devices in town and countryside indicate that the less privileged sectors of the population organize their own environments as much as these are organized for them (Leeds, 1971; Peattie, 1968; Eames and Goode, 1973; Cornelius, 1974). These attempts to organize the environment affect, and even limit, the scope of action of the economically and socially superior classes by creating uncertainty and reducing their possibilities of controlling their environment (Roberts, 1973).

Apart from these suggestions as to the scope and importance of local level activity, there are fundamental reasons for questioning the capacity of central structures to determine development in Latin America. One of these reasons is the limited organizational capacity of the type of centralized capitalist economies that have developed in Latin America. Though primarily urban-based, industrial capitalism now predominates in most of the area, showing little capacity to expand so as to include an increasing proportion of the labor force and to effect a thoroughgoing transformation of local economic structures. This dominant capitalism controls the direction of economic activity; the expansion or contraction of other economic activities is, to a large extent, determined by the behavior of the capital-intensive and technologically sophisticated industrial sector. This sector is unable to impose the degree of discipline with respect to the behavior of entrepreneurs and of the labor force that characterized earlier capitalist industrialization. By discipline, I mean the routinization of tasks, the increasing standardization of working timetables and income levels, and the organized dependence of the work force, as consumers, on the market. This discipline was made possible in developed countries by the large-scale provision of specialized and relatively stable work in the factory environment; it enabled both government and capitalists to plan their investments in economically efficient ways. In Latin America, the development of productive capacity —mainly in capital-intensive industries and through sophisticated technology—has not occurred through a rapid expansion of the urban industrial labor force nor of the labor force in commerce and services associated with this modern sector. Webb (1974) reports that while employment in the modern sector of the economy (businesses with more than five employees) expanded from 18 to 21 percent of the labor force between 1950 and 1966, employment in the urban traditional sector rose from 24 to 32 percent in the same period. These gains in the proportion of each sector in the total labor force were at the expense of the agricultural sector. In practice, these trends mean that the growing urban populations of Peru have been absorbed mainly by small-scale enterprises, personal services and self-employed activities. Indeed, capitalist expansion in Latin America has not only provoked a degree of initial disorganization as customary rural activities were disrupted, but this disorganization has continued as the urban labor force expanded rapidly in the absence of a set of economic activities requiring their services.

There is another fundamental reason for emphasizing the significance of local-level activity; this activity is itself part of, and a dynamic part of, the contemporary capitalist transformation of Latin American countries. I do not view this transformation as mechanically dependent upon external capitalist stimuli; it is, basically, an internal process of transformation that, while often initiated by foreign capital, has its own logic and power of transformation. Part of this logic of transformation is expressed in the organization and expansion of small-scale economic activity. The prevalence and relative dynamism of such small-scale activity varies from country to country and from region to region; it depends upon the particular history of an area's penetration by capitalism. In this paper, I take the example of an area—the Central Sierra of Peru—that has been completely penetrated by the impact of the large-scale mining and agricultural enterprises. I do not claim that what is true for the Central Sierra of Peru is true of other areas of the continent; but the logic of the transformation that occurred there and which continues to affect national development is generalizable to other areas.

With regard to present government policy in Peru, my analysis has the concrete implication of questioning the possibility, let alone desirability, of planning from the center and for (instead of with) people. The capacity of any centrally located body to plan and effect a social transformation depends on the extent that the population can be, and is already, hierarchically organized in coherent and integrated economic and social systems. Integrated market systems and hierarchies of cities that embody such an organization are not the outcome of central control, but are the essential pre-conditions of it. The development of the national state and the extension of its bureaucratic apparatus has, until recently, accompanied the increasing social and economic integration of a society. It is well-known, however, that the situation in Latin America has been different in that the extension of the State and of mechanisms of central control have not been accompanied by such an increasing integration. In Peru, the State has, from the 1920s onwards, increasingly extended its apparatus to penetrate most geographical areas and most social and economic levels. As a consequence of the early predominance of foreign capital, there has been a notable absence of the other accompaniments of the centrally organized State: economic integration and a strongly entrenched bourgeoisie (Yepes, 1974).

Despite the limitations on its capacity to plan local development, the State in Peru is an active element in local social and economic organization and must be included as an element of study in any analysis of local organization. In this paper I seek to examine the implications, at the regional level, of this situation in which central control and planning proceed despite the low degree of social and economic integration. I view the situation as one in which two competing forms of organization are present: central and local. I do not assume that the central organization is the more powerful or the more likely to impose its pattern. I seek instead to analyze how the process of competition itself operates and affects the evolution of the society. The State in Peru affects the conditions of life of provincial populations (and of much of Lima's "marginal" population) mainly through price controls on food, indirect taxation, and the provision of public services; but this intervention is not systematically related to the economic activities that keep these populations alive (Webb, 1974). There is, for example, no relation between the nature and provision of educational services and the type of work available or likely to be available in the economy. Similarly, the indirect taxation and price control policies that affect these populations are, at best, very blunt instruments in terms of managing and directing economic activity among them. This is an essential limitation on the efficacy of state expansion; it does not form a necessary and integrated part of local-level economic development. At the same time, the expansion of the State has transformed, in indirect ways, the nature of local development by the regulation of large-scale activity and by the resources that state employment and the development of infrastructure have made available at the local level.

THE NATURE OF LOCAL LEVEL ACTIVITY

Though I focus, in this section, on the types of economic and social activity that occur in a provincial region, my argument is intended to apply also to the "marginal" populations of the capital cities of Latin America. Indeed, the interrelationships between these urban populations and those in the provinces are often an important factor in the vitality of small-scale activity in the city. The small-scale activities that I describe are not ephemeral or transitional in character. These activities display consistent patterns of development in different locations and in different economic sectors; they also contain the means to reproduce themselves and constitute relatively enduring features of the kind of economy that many Latin American countries now possess. In this sense, they are as much part of the structure of contemporary capitalism in Latin America as is the dominant form of urban-industrial capitalism.

Despite many decades of capitalist penetration into even the most remote provincial regions, there is often little evidence in the rural areas of Latin America of either the consolidation of landholdings or of the consolidation of industrial and commercial firms into larger enterprises. I shall take my examples from the Mantaro area in the Central Sierra of Peru, which is considered as the most economically and socially developed of the Peruvian Sierra regions and is well-connected to Lima and the coast by rail and a hard-surface road (Dobyns, 1970). In agriculture it is the *minifundia* that predominates, and the fragmentation of farmholdings has increased since the turn of the century. Whereas the average size of farmholding in the Mantaro valley was some three hectares at the beginning of this century, the contemporary average is approximately one hectare. Even before the current agrarian reform program began to expropriate the large hacienda holdings, there was no evidence, for this area, that either agricultural haciendas or large commercial farms (50 hectares or more) had extended their holdings. Even in the case of the highland pastoral haciendas, it is questionable whether they had actually extended their holdings at the expense of the small pastoral farmer. Much of the conflict between haciendas and local peasantry is most usefully understood as a competition between rival forms of capitalist expansion, small-scale and large-scale. As local farmers sought to increase their herds under the stimulus of market possibilities, toward the end of the last century and at the beginning of the present one, they came into conflict with haciendas and other jurisdictions over ill-defined grazing land or over rights to graze private animals when working as shepherds for the haciendas (Samaniego, 1974; Martínez Alier, 1972).

Commercial and industrial activity is also predominantly small-scale. The largest industry in the area (a textile mill) employs some 250 people; the next largest (a knitwear factory) employs about 50 people; the average number of employees for the factories of Huancayo, the largest city, is 7.1. Fifty-two percent of the manufacturing labor force in this city is employed in enterprises where there are five workers or less. The remaining large-scale industry is Cerro de Pasco Company's smelter and associated plants at La Oroya; this labor force, which numbered some 5,300 workers in 1970, has declined slightly in size from its height of 5,600 in 1956. Indeed, the trend in industrial activity has been clearly towards fragmentation and the dominance of the small-scale. Whereas in 1953 there were some 3,000 workers employed mainly in four textile factories in Huancayo, this work force has been replaced by some 1,600 workers in over 400 textile workshops. Commerce is also mainly small-scale and there has been only a very slow development of larger retail outlets; there are over 2,000 grocery stores in the city of Huancayo and three small "supermarkets." This situation is most marked in the transport sector, where the 658 trucks registered in the Mantaro area (Huancayo, Concepción and Jauja provinces) are individually owned and there is no single transport firm. The 81 bus companies servicing this area and linking it to the coast and to the northern and southern Sierras are also mainly individually owned, and a bus company is normally made up of ten or more owner-drivers.

These figures give a sense of the small-scale economic activity that characterizes this one provincial area. It is noteworthy that this small-scale activity pervades all economic sectors, despite the important differences in their modes of operation. The dominance and expansion of the small-scale also appears to be true of Lima's economy where, even in the industrial sector, a large percentage of the manufacturing work force is employed in enterprises of less than five people; and this proportion is likely to have increased from 1960-1972 (Webb, 1974).

The type of small-scale economic activity that predominates in the Mantaro area is similar to that activity which is included in the concept of the informal economy (Hart, 1973; McGee, 1971; Weeks, 1973). It operates largely outside the regulation of the State and is characterized by a heavy reliance on personal and often kinship relationships and by a tendency toward ad hoc decision-making and acts of exchange. I find the concept of the informal economy to be, however, a misleading one. The issue that is central to understanding the dynamic of small-scale activity is one of scale and not one of the existence of a relatively autonomous or relatively distinctive economic sector.

Small-scale economic activity is closely related to the large-scale sector of the economy. I include within this large-scale sector not only the larger enterprises in industry, commerce or the services, but also government employment.[1] In Lima and in the provincial cities, small enterprises and service workers "export" much of their goods and services to the large-scale sector and to those working within it (Webb, 1974). Likewise, those working in small enterprises or in personal services spend a good part of their income on factory goods, food and on "modern" services. The small-scale sector is not economically integrated and, often, the closest relationships of individuals or enterprises in this sector will be with firms or individuals belonging to the large-scale sector. The dependence of the small scale on the large scale is more indirect in the provinces; there is, for example, a considerable degree of interchange between a city like Huancayo and its hinterland and a relative absence of large-scale enterprises (with the important exception of mining). Even in Huancayo, our analysis of the purchases made by different groups of the population suggested the close relationship between the small- and large-scale sectors; lower income groups purchased factory goods and food originating in Lima and the bulk of the area's agricultural and industrial production was exported to the capital.

The significant factor in the economic activities of the majority of the population in city and countryside in Peru is that they are carried out within small-scale units. These units, whether in farming, manufacturing, commerce or services, do not make intensive use of capital; labor costs are likely to form the major part of the costs of the enterprise. At first glance, this small-scale enterprise has similarities to that which occurs in the earliest stages of capitalist development. There are no effective local monopolies and there is keen competition between individuals and enterprises over the price of the product or service they offer. Likewise, there is a relatively free labor market and enterprises are not restricted in their hiring or firing or in their wage bargaining by government regulation or worker organization.

This relative freedom of enterprise explains part of the persistence of small-scale activity; in itself, however, it would simply represent the last vestige of a system doomed to eventual destruction by the greater power of the large-scale modern sector which controls the most lucrative markets and the access to capital. Even the most successful of the small-scale enterprises that we studied did not expand much beyond ten or so employees. In the Mantaro area, at least, small-scale enterprise does not build up into large scale. Despite this finding, it was clear that small-scale activity continued to be dynamic and extended the scope of its operations; this occurred not through increase in the size or production of the unit, but through one unit giving rise to the establishment of new units designed to develop new resources.

Though incomes in the urban small-scale sector have not been rising nearly as fast as incomes in the large-scale sector, a small rise has occurred despite an increase in the numbers of those working within this sector (Webb, 1974). This capacity to increase per capita earnings indicates an internal dynamic that enables this sector to organize itself to take advantage of opportunities and to regulate competition. To understand the basis of this economic dynamism, it is necessary to consider carefully the logic of operation of the small enterprises.

An important feature of the mode of operation of small-scale enterprises is that they operate within a general context of market uncertainty. In part, this uncertainty is produced by the prevalence of small-scale activity; it also reflects the low level of economic development in Peru. In agriculture, the large number of small farmers, making individual decisions as to crops and the timing of the agricultural cycle, complicates both the coordination of production and marketing and the operations of large-scale agricultural traders. For example, in our study of the largest agricultural traders of the wholesale market of Huancayo, we found that their capacity to maintain a high turnover depended on a very complex network of contacts in the market and in the producing areas; these contacts enabled them to fulfill the supply contracts they had undertaken with the mining companies and Lima wholesalers. Even the largest of the traders had been unable to secure a constant supply by purchasing or renting land or by arrangements with large producers; the predominance of small landholdings in the area and the uncertainties of climate made such a process of vertical integration impossible.

The structure of trading was similarly affected; the necessity of working with a large number of producers, whether in agriculture or crafts, meant the development of personal relationships and local knowledge which required both time and considerable effort and which limited the expansion of any one enterprise. It was a common practice for a trader to prefer to delegate a new source of business to a relative or long-time associate, on the assumption that close personal attention was required for success. Small industry, which in this area produces mainly textiles, also operates in a situation of uncertain supply and demand; the extreme fragmentation of production is accompanied by a considerable degree of secrecy and lack of coordination among the producers. These small textile enterprises are closely tied to small traders who actively seek out markets in the villages of the Sierra, as well as travel to Lima and the coast. They purchase their wool or synthetic fiber in small lots from retail outlets in Huancayo or travel directly to Lima to obtain it.

Market uncertainties give a special character to the labor policies of these small enterprises: They tend to use labor in place of machines or other capital outlay. This avoidance of capital investments is not due to any reluctance to rationalize or innovate, but to the difficulties these small operators have in obtaining capital. Their credit is not good with the banks, and large-scale enterprises have become increasingly reluctant to grant extended credits to small operators. The capital of the small enterprises was obtained from savings (often pooled with those of a kinsman or friend) or from indemnity payments from previous employment. Several of the largest traders in the wholesale market of Huancayo began their businesses on the basis of savings from mine work; many of the small textile industrialists began on the basis of machinery and payments given to them when the large-scale industry closed in Huancayo. Capital emerged, in general, from a slow process of accumulation and, often, through informal means, as when agricultural credit was used to finance a trucking enterprise.

The intensive use of labor in the small enterprise is possible and profitable because the labor supply is differentiated in ways that enable it to be used flexibly and at low cost. One source of supply is family labor and, often, family labor which is given in the spare moments from other activities. In a survey of 400 small businesses in Huancayo (a random sample of the total of some 2,000 businesses in the city), I found that the majority of workers in these businesses were family workers; in bakeries and butcher shops where average employment was over four workers per business, 67 percent of all workers were family workers.

Even where these enterprises use non-family labor, it was common for this labor to be maintained and recruited in such ways as to reduce its cost to the firm. Board and lodging would be provided to a kinsman or fellow villager who had come to town to attend school, for health reasons, or to seek work; in return, the migrant would work part-time for the enterprise. Workers were also recruited from poorer regions and received wages lower than those normal in the city; though they might move on after a time, their place would be taken by other cheap labor.

The wages to some of these unskilled workers would, at times, be lower than those available in the rural areas; but the expectations of recent migrants about subsequent opportunities and their personal relationships with the owner often meant that they accepted such wages. Higher wages or percentages of the profits were paid to skilled workers, such as drivers or mechanics, but these payments were usually accompanied by the expectation that the worker take some responsibility for the cost of his work. For example, drivers and machine operators often had contracts whereby they were responsible for repairs. Such workers were taken on and laid off relatively easily, and small enterprises operated with a pool of contacts to obtain labor or services quickly.

Part of the mode of operation of the small enterprise is that its labor costs are subsidized by the uneven nature of development in Peru. In part, this subsidy derives directly from the different levels of development present even within a fairly small region. It is the small-scale enterprise that takes greatest advantage of the profits to be derived by the recruitment of a cheap labor force from remote and impoverished areas; in Huancayo, recent migrants from the remote villages are concentrated in the small enterprises. Also, labor costs are subsidized by the health and educational services provided by the government that attract people to the city and often lead migrants to accept low wages in order to be able to stay in the city and make use of its services.

The different levels of development present within regions have been important to the small enterprise in other ways. It was the small enterprise that articulated, through its labor force and economic activity, these different levels of development. The small enterprise permitted small surpluses to be marketed and goods and services to be sold at sufficiently low cost for them to be purchasable by even the poorest peasant. In this respect, the small enterprise could utilize resources that were too meager to be a source of profit to the larger enterprise, purchasing small quantities of wool, foodstuffs and craft products. This articulation of different locations and resources is an important element in the organizational capacity of small enterprises; they make use of the degree of differentiation that exists within regions and among even the poorest sectors of the population.

The operation of the small enterprise can be illustrated by the case of one of the principal agricultural traders of the central region of Peru—a Huancayo-based wholesaler and trucker. He was born in a small village of the neighboring Department of Huancavelica; his parents had little land and, from early on, he worked for others. He subsequently worked as a miner in one of the Huancavelica metal mines; he married there and his wife established a restaurant business for the miners. By the time the trader left the mine, on his wife's death, he had saved a small capital and, in addition, received an indemnity payment of some (U.S.) $720.

He and his brother-in-law, who had also been a miner, came to Huancayo to set themselves up as traders, pooling their capital. He met his second wife, a trader in cereals in the wholesale market, and together with the brother-in-law put his capital into this business. The two men travelled to small farms to buy produce. The brother-in-law had been born in a village near Huancayo and had family contacts in the agricultural villages nearby; these villages were one source of produce for the business. Another source was small farms in Huancavelica.

The business was expanded by contracting to supply the mines; the contracts were obtained through workmates and administrative staff that the two men had formerly known. The difficulty of persuading truckers to make the hazardous journey to the mines led the trader to invest in a truck. Throughout the growth of the business, which began in 1964, the trader was helped with loans and contacts by kin and former workmates. In 1972, he had a gross monthly income of some $2,100; of this, a percentage goes to the brother-in-law who supervises much of the work in the wholesale market and handles business with the small local traders and farmers. A driver is paid $70 a month, but with the condition of being responsible for the upkeep of the truck. The trader drives a second truck. He also has two full-time helpers to load and unload and accompany the trucks; they are paid an average of $25 a month, but receive board and lodging. These laborers are migrants from poor villages in Huancavelica. The trader has built a modern house in Huancayo and employs a full-time maid at $23 a month with board and lodging; the trader's wife helps with the business. The trader's son-in-law is paid $80 a month to keep the accounts. The trader also employs casual labor to help out at busy times. He estimates that his own net monthly income is $280 after paying wages, the small market overheads, and the (heavy) repayments on the trucks. Though he would finish paying for the trucks by the end of 1973, trucks in the Central Sierra do not have a long life on the type of roads on which they must travel.

Though the above observations may help us understand why the small enterprise continues to be a viable element in the contemporary economy of Peru, we need to relate small enterprises more systematically to the nature of capitalist development. Small enterprise represents the internal logic of capitalist transformation in Peru; it is the legatee of the impact of foreign capitalism and of the slow, locally-based processes of capitalist transformation that antedated the massive penetration of foreign capital. Although the effect of foreign investment has been to limit the development of a centralized, native industrial capitalism, foreign capital did stimulate local differentiation and diversity. This occurred primarily through the wages paid by mines and plantations, and through other local investments that the large enterprises made to improve transport facilities and to obtain foodstuffs.

These processes helped monetize local economies and weakened local jurisdictions and traditional obligations. These changes set in motion an irreversible internal development process. Mutual aid systems in agriculture are now in decline and, increasingly, work in agriculture is paid work. In the absence of dynamic, urban-based industrialization, the process of transformation was partial in the Central Sierra; it did not lead to a local specialization through families abandoning the land to work permanently in city factories, while others consolidated landholdings or worked as farm laborers. Instead, the transformation took the form of an increasing diversification of household and local economies; the possession of land was combined with other activities such as wage earning, trade or industrial production.

Within a household, the economic activity of each member became more specialized. The parents produced a small agricultural surplus; the children tended the animals, engaged in local trade or craft activity, or worked and traded in the urban centers. The exchanges between the various household members linked urban and rural economies and signified that local economies were no longer autarchic. There was no basis for a return to a subsistence agriculture and its associated crafts; survival depended upon combining and coordinating existing and new resources. This permitted enough specialization to raise productivity, but not enough to encourage centralization of economic activity.

In this context, the small enterprise becomes closely linked to the development of the modern sector of the economy. The small enterprise expands in response to the opportunities created by modern capitalist development. It is not an historical residue of traditional activities, but a qualitatively different form of activity that emerges out of earlier stages of transformation. The small-scale activities I am discussing are distinct from the customary ways by which villages or small towns obtained their manufactured goods and services. Rather, small-scale activities represent entrepreneurial attempts to take advantage of those needs created by capitalist transformation but not supplied by it: the feeding of urban or mining populations with new types of foodstuffs, whose production cycle is different from that of the more traditional foodstuffs; the provision of low-cost transport services based on a greater job mobility and movement of goods; the provision of specialized repair services and personal services; the production of clothing, made necessary by new patterns of life, which is quite distinct in form and mode of production from that of traditional dress.

The significant aspect about the "urban traditional activities" by which most of Peru's city dwellers earn their living is that hardly any of them are traditional (Webb, 1974). Indeed, they are as "modern" in the historical sense as the technologically-based activities which they complement. The danger of describing these activities as "traditional," "household" or "marginal" lies in giving the impression that they represent outmoded forms of economic activity in process of extinction. It is on this point of interpretation that I am most in disagreement both with Quijano's (1971, 1974) concept of "marginalization" and McGee's (1971: 170) concept of the "bazaar economy" in Southeast Asian cities.

The relation of the small enterprise to the large-scale, capital-intensive sector of the economy is that the small enterprise, for reasons that I have outlined above, possesses a flexibility which is a functional component of the current capitalist development process in Peru. This flexibility is most marked in the relative ease with which the small enterprise can change location, alter its labor force, and even change its lines of products or services. Even repair services show remarkable flexibility, as different combinations of tools and craftsmen allow a workshop to switch from auto body repair work, to engine work or to general metal repair work.

This flexibility ensures that resources are tapped and developed that are too uncertain for the profitable operation of large firms. The increasing intervention of the Peruvian government in the economy and the continuing strength of labor unions have restricted the operation of large firms. Size is crucial in this context, since it is only the smaller operations that can easily escape government regulation or labor organization. Large firms are responsible for standards of security, health precautions, and payments towards employees' social security. They are also obliged to give a certain security of tenure to workers and to pay indemnities on separation. Recently, the larger firms (with more than ten employees) have been required to organize *comunidades industriales,* through which part of the firm's profits are reinvested to purchase worker shares in the enterprise. These various costs do not seriously limit the profitability of large firms with sophisticated machinery; but they mean that centralization of economic enterprise is limited by the inability of the large firm to compete effectively with small enterprises on a variety of low-priced services and products, and in extracting small surpluses from widely dispersed producers.

The small enterprise is dynamic not simply because it is economically viable, but also because its operation draws more and more of the population into the orbit of the capitalist economy. The small enterprise, not the large, is the active agent of capitalist penetration in Peru. This dynamic means that the term "marginal" applied to much of the urban and most of the provincial population of Peru is misleading in at least one important respect: These "marginal" populations are not passively reacting to economic changes originating from above, but are engaged in their own internal processes of development and in using changes elsewhere in the system to further that development.

SMALL ENTERPRISE AND PATTERNS OF STRATIFICATION

Despite the degree of complementarity that exists between the small enterprise and the large, the relation is an unequal one. The large enterprise has greater capacity to raise productivity through technological improvement and controls the most accessible and profitable markets—the middle and upper income populations of Lima and of some of the provincial cities. The rate of increase in per capita incomes within the small-scale sector of the economy is low; the increases in sales and services to the rest of the economy have been achieved mainly by expanding the labor force.

In this context, small-scale economic activity has somewhat contradictory implications for social and economic differentiation. There is differentiation within the small-scale sector, since those individuals or enterprises most closely linked to the wealthiest sectors of the economy are likely to receive the most income. In Lima, for example, certain classes of domestic and craft service and certain small industrial activities that directly complement larger firms are likely to generate the most income. On the other hand, this differentiation is not based on any structural characteristics that enable particular sectors or individuals to consolidate their favorable position. The operation of the small enterprise is highly particularistic, depending on the skills and energy of the individual. These skills and energies enable certain people to secure a relatively favorable position; but there is no means of erecting monopolies to ensure continuing access to rewards.

One implication of this is apparent in the distribution of income among the different sectors of economic activity in Huancayo (see Table 1). The shares of income in this city, which is dominated by small-scale activity, are similar for all

TABLE 1
INCOME, WORK POSITION AND SECTOR OF ECONOMIC ACTIVITY OF MEN AGED 20-60: HUANCAYO, 1972 (in percentages)

	Up to 2000 Soles[c] *Monthly*		*2001-5000 Soles Monthly*		*5001 Soles and Above Monthly*	
Sector of Activity	*Self-Employed*[b]	*Em-ployed*	*Self-Employed*	*Em-ployed*	*Self-Employed*	*Em-ployed*
Mining	8	5	7	4	12	8
Manufacturing	25	13	17	11	14	9
Construction	5	17	10	5	10	5
Commerce	33	26	26	18	31	13
Transport	5	6	6	8	5	3
Non-government services[a]	24	26	28	33	25	20
Government	–	7	6	21	3	42
Total %	100	100	100	100	100	100
N	63	76	120	141	87	96

a. Non-government services are those personal,technical and professional services, repair activities and entertainment services in the private sector of the economy. Government employment is teaching, administration and other jobs in government institutions.

b. The self-employed category includes those retired people whose main source of income is their pension (usually from the mining companies or from the government).

c. The exchange rate of the sol was approximately 40 to the dollar.

SOURCE: Stratified sample survey of adult males in Huancayo, 1972.

economic sectors, with the exception of government. There is no evidence that any sector is a privileged domain of activity that ensures a higher income to its members. This is true not only for sector of activity, but also for two other significant indicators of economic structure—size of enterprise and work position. In the absence of any technologically advanced economic activity in Huancayo, bigger enterprises do not obtain higher incomes for their members; similarly, the difference between being an employee and being self-employed is not related to the amount someone is likely to earn (see Table 2).

These statistics indicate a process that is directly observable within Huancayo: Though the population is differentiated in terms of income levels and, to a certain extent, by habits of consumption, this differentiation does not occur in ways that are likely to lead to relatively enduring and visible class groupings. This is partly because the spatial mobility and economic flexibility entailed by small-scale activity discourages those commitments that allow differences in access to resources to be reproduced. These commitments relate to housing, educational facilities, local associations, and political activity.

Although income differences do exist in Huancayo, they are most pronounced between those employed by the government and those working in other sectors of the economy (see Table 1). Within the small-scale sector, income differences are diminished by the predominantly family character of these enterprises. Also, the logic of small enterprise encourages a sense of individual opportunity. This sense of opportunity encourages competition between peers, whether these are other owners or fellow workers, but may diminish tensions between owners and employees, who are often linked by particularistic ties. The

TABLE 2
INCOME, WORK POSITION AND SIZE OF WORK PLACE OF MEN AGED 20-60: HUANCAYO, 1972 (in percentages)

		Monthly Income				
Size of Workplace	*Work Position*	*Up to 2000 Soles*	*2001-5000 Soles*	*5001 Soles and Over*	*Total %*	*N*
Works alone	Self-Employed	27	43	30	100	60
	Employed	23	46	31	100	95
Less than 5 people	Self-Employed	24	40	36	100	78
	Employed	22	46	32	100	90
Between 6 and 12	Self-Employed	20	49	31	100	65
	Employed	25	42	33	100	75
Over 12 people	Self-Employed	23	46	31	100	69
	Employed	28	41	31	100	54

SOURCE: Stratified sample survey of adult males in Huancayo, 1972.

case of the wholesale merchant cited earlier provides a good illustration of this situation. There are clear income differences among the various participants in this enterprise; but even the owner works alongside his men. They depend upon him not only for wages, but for their board; however, they are able to make some extra money by doing work for others or by engaging in a little independent trade on the side.

The ambiguous nature of the pattern of stratification in Huancayo is further illustrated by the position of government employees and by that of the employees of the few large concerns (mainly banks). In terms of educational levels and income levels, these employees constitute the dominant social and economic group in present day Huancayo. The commercial and landed families that once had dominated city life have, almost entirely, moved permanently to Lima (Roberts, 1974a). This is not simply an accidental feature of Huancayo's history; it results from the general pattern of economic development in Peru, in which capital has become increasingly centralized in Lima, and provincial centers depend increasingly on government employment or on small-scale activity.[2]

These government and private firm employees are well represented in the activities of the provincial Council and in the prestigious social clubs of the city; but they are people who, in the main, have little long-term commitment to Huancayo. Many of them stay only two or three years; of all the occupational groups, these employees were the least likely, in our survey of Huancayo's population, to say that they would spend their life in the city (Roberts, 1973). Some of the most important officials have, in fact, not taken up permanent residence in Huancayo, but commute to Lima on weekends.

The degree of social fluidity encouraged by the contemporary economic structure is reflected in statistics on passenger transport flow and hotel and lodging house occupancy in Huancayo.[3] There is a considerable flow of professionals, white-collar workers and traders between Huancayo and Lima, numbering, for these categories alone, over 10,000 individual movements in one month. The traders are the largest category of people moving between the two cities; almost twice as many traders are recorded as professionals and white-collar workers. These traders are mainly based in Huancayo and its area; only a small proportion of those registering in hotels or boarding houses are traders, and our own observations of the pattern of trading activity confirms this relative absence of Lima-based traders. In contrast, the professionals and white-collar workers make up almost 60 percent of all registrations in the hotels and boarding houses. The picture is one of an outflow of local traders, moving down to the capital to sell local products and to return with manufactured goods. The reverse flow is that of government bureaucrats or of employees such as teachers and company officials who come to the Sierra to supervise, temporarily, the development of the local economy and polity.

In the villages of the Mantaro area, land has ceased to be the major determinant of social status; wage labor, salaried employment, trade and craft activity have become equally important factors in local stratification (Grondin, 1974; Samaniego, 1974). This pattern of stratification is complex and changing; though there are evident differences in the economic position of people in the villages, these are not based on resources (such as land) that reproduce the pattern of social differentiation. Mobility in this situation is also complex; it involves education, migration to different labor centers, and a possible return to the locality. The economic position of the parents affects all these factors; but there are no local monopolies over the crucial resources–education and job migration. Furthermore, local stratification is the more complex since the pattern of migration, including the return migration of certain sectors of the population, also disrupts the reproduction of economic and social differences. Wage labor migrants, originating from poorer families, return with the cash to build houses, set up businesses, and even to buy some land; migrants from richer families may have obtained stable jobs in the city and will stay there.

The complexity of the migration patterns in the Central Sierra is understandable in terms of, and partly underlies, the pattern of small-scale activity (Laite, 1974; Roberts, 1973). Migration is one means whereby individuals and households make use, over a lifetime, of the opportunities available to them locally, regionally and even nationally. In the relative absence of stable employment in cities, individual migration histories reflect the dynamic of small enterprise; individuals migrate to take jobs with kin, but still contribute to the family economy in their place of origin. Absent household members help parents or siblings to market products, send factory goods from the city, and provide information about job or educational opportunities.

Migration is not predominantly unidirectional; there are considerable return flows of migrants from Lima to the Central Sierra. Also, migration often takes the form of a series of movements between different urban and labor centers, only to settle "finally" in a village or town near the migrant's place of origin. These movements are closely correlated with the stage in the individual's life cycle and the type of job that he has; it is the interaction of these factors that influences the destination and sequence of migration. Lima is not, in any undifferentiated way, a dominant pole of attraction for migrants.

The Central Sierra is increasing its population at approximately the national rate of growth.[4] Population dynamics are affected by several different migration flows: migration out of the region to the coast or other parts of the Sierra; return migration of the locally born, often during the period when their families are growing; and the in-migration of people born elsewhere, usually in the poorer regions of the Sierra. These migration flows contribute to the dynamic of small enterprise and link the area to Lima and to other regions. They also increase the complexity of social stratification patterns by juxtaposing, within the same area, people whose social and economic characteristics are not simply different, but are only loosely integrated.

This situation is different, in several important respects, from that obtaining during the dominance of an agro-mining economy in this area. In the earlier part of the century, social and economic groups with clearly differentiated characteristics were detectable; the commercial and industrial elite was based in Huancayo and was of foreign or Lima origin (Roberts, 1974a). This elite organized the industry and commerce of the whole region. There was also a group of medium-sized farmers in the villages and small towns, whose land produced a large enough surplus to enable them to extend their fortunes through education, trade, and even small industry. The majority of the area's population of nearly 200,000 provided the labor for local businesses engaged in subsistence farming and, eventually, supplied the manpower for mines and plantations.

The interests of these different groups were relatively well defined. The pursuit of these interests provided the dynamic of political activity in the area, giving rise to labor organization in factories and mines, "peasant" movements, and the extension of political organization at the regional level through the APRA political party, Acción Popular and a number of locally based political organizations (Alderson-Smith, 1974). Even in this period, however, the articulation of the various organized interests did not result in clear conflicts of interest or of class position. For example, with the exception of the few resident landowners, the elite had no interest in controlling local resources and made their profits by selling imported goods (mainly to the mines) or through industrial speculation. They were often the allies of the medium-sized farmers, small traders, and small industrialists, to whom they extended credit and whom they helped in their attempts to destroy traditional obligations and jurisdictions (Roberts, 1974b).

The degree of political fragmentation now present in this area is much greater than in the earlier period. The dominance of small-scale economic activity and the complex patterns of stratification provide no consistent basis for the political organization of any sector of the local population. The lack of any basis for such organization does not imply that there are no conflicts of interest present at the local or national levels, or that people are political inactive. The economic dynamism of small-scale activity means that those involved in it have an inherent conflict of interest with large-scale capitalism and, even, with government. Though there is an important degree of complementarity in the economic system between small-scale and large-scale enterprise, the expansion of individual small enterprises is limited by the monopolies of large-scale enterprise and by government regulation.

The small-scale enterprise depends on securing even small gains by "cutting the corners" of existing regulations or economic practices; thus small-scale entrepreneurs are active in the struggle to control local political and administrative offices. We found that in the villages and towns of the area, there was a considerable degree of political activity, often directed against the implementation of government reforms, that was closely linked to the strategies of small entrepreneurs (Long and Winder, 1975). My argument is, however, a general one;

in the context of contemporary Peru, and possibly of other Latin American countries, the co-existence of two forms of capitalist development—large and small scale—entails a political dynamic based on the different interests of the two sectors. The intervention of the Peruvian government does not, consequently, occur in a political vacuum, but is part of this political process.

THE EXTENSION OF STATE INTERVENTION AND THE DILEMMAS OF PLANNED CHANGE

In this section I want to examine in greater detail the particular role that the Peruvian state has come to play in local and national development. In part, my object is to assess the ways in which government can effectively intervene to secure a more even distribution of national resources among the population, and in a way which best utilizes local capabilities. Such an assessment necessarily involves an examination of the degree of autonomy that central government agencies have in planning and initiating change.

The autonomy of the State is not only an issue in underdeveloped societies which have strongly entrenched propertied classes who permeate the State and orient its policies in their favor (Alavi, 1972); it is also an issue in nations like Peru which do not have such strongly entrenched groups. In such nations, the State has no class referents—whether a bourgeoisie, an industrial working class or a relatively homogeneous peasantry—by which to assess the effects and implications of its policies (Barratt Brown, 1974: 273-275). Moreover, without the degree of internal economic and social organization presupposed by the existence of such classes, it is difficult for the State to implement any policies without a considerable investment of its own resources. In this situation, public policies can become surreptiously affected by the centralist bias to which I referred earlier, so that centrally located groups, such as bureaucrats, managers or professionals, are disproportionately advantaged by state intervention.

The rapid expansion of government agencies in the provinces of Peru has coincided with the disruption of the forms of provincial social and economic organization that I described earlier. These agencies have been mainly "developmentalist" in character. In the 1960s their work took the form of community action programs, cooperative organizations, and agricultural extension work; the agencies had limited resources and operated by attempting to persuade local communities to cooperate in development projects. Much of the present military government's intervention in provincial life has been a consolidation of this previous work, especially by bringing together previously separate agencies in a greatly expanded "social mobilization" organization —SINAMOS. The important point, however, is that these government agencies replaced forms of local organization that had themselves been "developmentalist" in orientation and, in a particular way, had been effective in developing local resources.

The small-scale programs of local development that proliferated in the Mantaro area in the early part of the century were sponsored, and mainly paid for, by local communities (Dobyns, 1970; Adams, 1959). These programs included irrigation projects, road and bridge building, public buildings, water and electricity supply systems, schools and health clinics. They originated in the strategies and ambitions of the developing medium-sized farming group (owning 25 acres or more) of the area (Samaniego, 1974; Grondin, 1974). With the development of markets in the urban and labor centers, this group became more interested in commercializing their crops; its members held the main offices of the village, and they undertook development projects, using the free labor of the community. This group extended its political and economic contacts at the regional and national level, obtaining the help of their migrant relatives in the different centers. This was the period when Lima politics became penetrated by the lobbying and political strategies of provincial groups, and migrant associations proliferated in the capital and other work centers (Roberts, 1974b).

The local improvement projects were encouraged by provincial and national elites and by the large mining and agricultural enterprises, which often contributed to their financing. Such projects made the village or small town a more viable and attractive base from which a cheap, temporary labor force could be recruited. These projects also absorbed, at little cost for the government, the developmental pressures emerging at the local level. The provision of educational facilities by local communities, the construction of bridges and roads, all directly contributed to the development of the Peruvian economy and to its greater integration. It was also a form of development that more directly exposed provincial people to exploitation from the center.

This occurred because local communities undertook essential works of social and economic infrastructure that would otherwise have had to be financed by the State and, through taxation, by the large-scale enterprises. Also, the type of work undertaken contributed to destroying the basis for local economic autonomy. Community work was heavily concentrated in constructing schools and other social facilities; what was noticeably absent was investment in the development of local productive resources, whether in agriculture or in small-scale industry. This is not surprising since those mainly responsible for initiating the community works had diversified their economic activities and often based them on labor or other resources outside the village; they were less interested in providing local sources of work than they were in those facilities that would secure the comfort, prestige and mobility of their own families. The activities of these rural groups linked the provinces with the capital; but the type of development they sponsored was, ultimately, a disorganizing influence on local society. The community improvement projects did not provide the means to achieve self-sustaining local development; they contributed, however, to making people more aware of supra-local economic and political possibilities. With the shift from an agro-mining economy to one more concentrated in urban-industrial development in Lima, those groups—the Huancayo and village elites—who had maintained an element of control over local processes increasingly moved to the capital. It is in this context of increasing social and political dislocations produced by the decline of the previously dominant forms of provincial social and economic organization that government intervention in the provinces has increased (Alderson-Smith, 1974).

This situation presented the Peruvian government with a dilemma; it needed to incorporate the various and potentially troublesome local groups, but in such a way as not to encourage local autonomy and as not to impede the centralization of the economy. A constant preoccupation of the military government in the last six years has been that of securing an adequate and cheap supply of foodstuffs for the Lima market. The government has maintained strict price controls on agricultural foodstuffs and has made elaborate plans for rationalizing agricultural production through provincial branches of the Ministry of Agriculture. In the Mantaro area, these plans at one time included converting this mixed economy area into a dairy farming zone; the centralization of this dairy economy was begun in 1972 with the installation, with German government help, of a large and highly sophisticated milk processing plant in the center of the valley.

The first actions of the military government in the area were aimed at reducing potential sources of conflict. The agrarian reform program was applied most rapidly to the highland pastoral haciendas of the Central Sierra, which had been feuding constantly with the neighboring communities. This friction was widely believed to have been one of the bases for the guerrilla movement that had been strong in the area in the early 1960s. The object of the agrarian reform in the haciendas was to give the neighboring communities nominal ownership of the land, without rights to pasture on it, while retaining in government hands the effective control of production and profits (Roberts and Samaniego, 1973). This policy of maintaining the production structure of the old haciendas and not dividing the land among the communities was explicitly seen by officials as a means of removing a potential source of unrest, while retaining the efficient production of the haciendas.

The government's efforts at hacienda reform, reform of local peasant communities, and cooperative organization in the Central Sierra illustrate the difficulties of state planning where there is no social or economic organization on which to base it. In such a situation, the intervention of the State follows its own logic of centralization and control; but it does not have the capacity to improve the lives of the majority of the local population. Instead the intervention is often subverted to particularistic ends.

The agrarian reform program of the military government expropriated the large pastoral haciendas and reorganized them into cooperatives (Sociedades Agrarias de Interés Social—SAIS) in which the hacienda workers and the members of the pastoral communities bordering on the haciendas were eventually to be the owners.[5] Before the SAIS could become a full cooperative the debt to the hacienda owners had to be repaid; in the meantime the State retained important rights of supervision and control over the cooperative. A general assembly of representatives of the member communities of the cooperative was formed and two communities (Administration and Vigilance) were elected from the assembly; these constituted the government of the cooperative.

There was, however, a professional management—many of whom had served the haciendas—which executed the policy and administered the day-to-day running of the enterprise. The lands of the haciendas were kept as production units and were separated from the lands of the member communities; members of the cooperative were not permitted to graze their private animals on land of the production units (former haciendas). The members of the cooperative benefited in two main ways from the reform: They were entitled, as communities, to share in the profits after the debt payments and obligatory reinvestments had been made; and they received the services of a Development Division which worked with the communities to foster their social and economic development.

The member communities of the cooperative and the workers on the production units did not, however, participate in the day-to-day running of the enterprise. The position of the workers on the production units was especially difficult since, as co-owners, they were not entitled to form a labor union; moreover, they represented only a small percentage of the total members (the rest of whom belonged to the village communities) and thus had little chance to get their claims for better conditions or higher salaries properly evaluated by the general assembly.

These cooperatives contributed very little to improving the situation of their members. The people whom they included had only in small part been dependent on the hacienda system. The adjacent pastoral communities had come into conflict with the haciendas over grazing land; but these communities were themselves highly differentiated internally, with some families owning more animals than others. Over time, the economies of these villages had diversified to include craft and trading activities; many villagers had been migrants and many were still living in the various labor centers. Economic enterprise had become increasingly characterized by a household diversification in which one member tended the animals, another traded or farmed in the lowlands, and another worked in the city, exchanging urban products for agricultural ones. The dynamic of this activity, which increasingly came to include educating children to relatively high levels, had become directed away from the pastoral economy. To a certain extent, this was also true of the hacienda workers; many of these had tended privately owned animals alongside those of the hacienda and had worked in alliance with villagers and lowland traders.

The organization of the agrarian cooperative cut off some of these possibilities of enterprise and, at the same time, provided little useful help to the communities or workers. The amount of profits redistributed was so small as to only enable some minor community improvements to be undertaken. The Development Division of the Cooperative, staffed by government-appointed professionals and technicians, intervened in village affairs to encourage a greater redistribution of economic and social resources than had previously been the case; this hit at the heart of local economic enterprise, which was based upon local social and economic differentiation.

Under these conditions, the administration of the agrarian cooperative met with increasing hostility from their members which, at times, was expressed in attacks on the high salaries earned by the technicians and professional administrators. To the majority of its members, the cooperative was not a particularly significant reform; it did not, for example, affect their out-migration, which continued apace. Naturally, it created opportunities upon which the more enterprising seized. The office-holders of the cooperative were usually the better-off local farmers, and they benefited, privately, from the contacts the cooperative provided and from the use of cooperative facilities, such as trucks and road-building equipment, to transport their own produce to market.

This fundamental reform of existing rural structures made only a marginal difference to the economic and social situation of the populations most affected. This outcome was not due to any deficiency in the administration of the reform. For the reform to have had a deeper significance for this provincial population, it would have been necessary for them to have been previously organized in terms of the hacienda system. The agrarian cooperatives did not improve either the incomes or the sense of participation of most of their members, for these had never been vertically organized by previous social and economic systems.

The situation is similar in respect to the government's attempts to implement its Community Reform Statutes. The basic aim of these reform laws was to strengthen village agriculture by encouraging cooperative farming on the part of small-holders (see Plan del Perú, 1971). According to the Peasant Community Statute, membership in the new peasant community and access to its resources (the communal lands) were to be confined to people who were resident, full-time farmers, but who had only a small amount of land. The community land was intended to be farmed cooperatively, with profits redistributed or reinvested in local improvements.

One of the most radical features of the Statute was that of excluding from membership three, often overlapping, categories of people: non-residents, larger farmers (in the Mantaro valley, usually farmers owning four hectares or more), and those whose main occupation was not farming (Long and Winder, 1975). In this way, the Statute sought to homogenize the rural peasant population and to restructure agriculture in directions that would permit, with government aid, greater rationalization of production. The basic intent of the Statute was to secure a redistribution of local income in favor of the poorer village groups, by securing for them the communal resources.

A basic limitation on the impact of the Statute is that village communal lands are not extensive; there is hardly a village in the Central Sierra in which the vast majority of agricultural land is not held privately. The communal resources were, thus, small and made little difference to the economy of the larger local farmers and those with non-farm occupations. The basis for the vitality of village economic life remained the small-scale, commercial enterprises that combined farming with transporting, with trade or with some small-scale industrial enterprise.

These enterprises depended upon the maintenance of extended personal networks throughout the area and down to the coast. Migrant villagers were important to the development and maintenance of such networks. In one village, Matahuasi, events (such as the annual fiesta) which brought these dispersed people together were an important element in the success of the small enterprise (Long, 1973). The interpersonal networks were, to some extent, threatened by the Community Statute which deprived migrants of membership in the Community; equally threatening to migrants was the widespread suspicion that government policy would extend to limiting their rights to private land within the village.

There also was evidence in Matahuasi that the effect of the Community Statute was to polarize poorer residents against those villagers who controlled most economic resources and who also controlled most of the village's political institutions (Long and Winder, 1975). On the other hand, the reform did not provide sufficient resources to make the poorer residents self-sufficient. The *comuneros* (members of the community) still needed to work locally as laborers for the richer residents or to migrate temporarily to urban centers; by taking up these opportunities they risked the loss of their comunero status.

The richer, non-comunero residents found that some of their traditional sources of cheap labor were threatened, especially since the district authorities found it hard to obtain people for the *faenas* (communal workparties) any more, given the latent hostility between community residents and the authorities, who were mainly the richer villagers. One effect of this was to make the richer residents suspicious of government policy; it led them to a more determined attempt to organize politically to secure local offices and to prevent the full implementation of government reforms (Long and Winder, 1975).

Still another element of agrarian reform in the Central Sierra is government promotion of cooperatives. This policy is an extension of that initiated by previous Peruvian governments; it is aimed at promoting the development of cooperatives in the fields of production, marketing and services. The cooperatives receive tax concessions and are able to obtain government loans at low interest. They can also obtain the assistance of government and foreign technicians in their development efforts. In the Central Sierra, the government has promoted this policy in industry through the cooperative organization of a large textile mill, Manufacturas del Centro; through two agricultural marketing cooperatives that correspond to the left and right banks of the Mantaro valley; and through a series of smaller cooperatives, including one trucking enterprise.

The basic aim of the government policy has been to persuade people to pool resources and, by so doing, to effect economies, rationalize their enterprise, provide better services or products, and raise their own incomes. Our studies of the various cooperatives revealed, however, a different picture; the cooperatives tended to accentuate local economic inequalities.

In the case of the agricultural cooperatives this outcome resulted from the heterogeneity of interests and economic positions among cooperative members. Many members were large farmers, truckers and traders; for them, the cooperative offered an institutional means to obtain tax concessions on certain products and helped them monopolize a certain segment of local trade and production. Cooperative produce was transported in the private trucks of members; fertilizer was obtained, in quantity, at discount and often resold in more remote places at higher prices. Milk production in one of the cooperatives was in the hands of the more substantial farmers who obtained expert government aid and supervision and coordinated their production to secure the market.

The framework of the cooperative provided certain members with a set of institutionalized contacts which enabled them to extend their private businesses. In the case of one of the cooperatives, the office-holders were mainly traders and commercial farmers who were supporters of the APRA political party, and who used the cooperative to maintain their political contacts. Though there were constant attempts by the government and its agents to ensure that members kept to the spirit of cooperative organization, the interventions were largely ineffectual. The government had invested little material or technical resources in the cooperative and could not constantly monitor the activities of its members.

The textile cooperative has a different history; its industrial organization meant a greater homogeneity of interests and situations among members than was the case in the agricultural cooperatives. The textile workers, however, had interests which conflicted with the spirit of cooperative organization and which reflected the dominant pattern of small-scale enterprise in the area. Many retained land in the nearby villages and returned home daily or on weekends; others had set up their wives or kin in trade and used cooperative products in this activity. Also, the relatively high wages and high educational levels of these workers had enabled many to educate their children to levels at which they wished to take white-collar jobs.

The textile mill came to be seen by many members as a private resource to be exploited to the full in the present, rather than a community resource in which to make long-term investments that would provide work for themselves, their children and their relatives. To improve production and raise profits, the cooperative members, who were all aging after many years in the textile industry, took on surreptitiously contracted labor that was not protected by wage or social security legislation. Though the cooperative was highly successful economically, these practices led to government intervention and to a restructuring of the cooperative's organization and membership that strengthened the control of a professional manager.

These various cases illustrate the difficulty of promoting structural change in the face of an ongoing and vital set of local economic activities. Part of the problem in the Central Sierra was a lack of sufficient investments on the part of government to give members an equal and full-time commitment to the cooperative enterprise and to its social obligations. Apart from setting up the cooperatives, providing some technical aid and tax relief, the government maintained little consistent presence in these cooperatives; the dynamic that was present—that of the small-scale activity of the area—thus easily subverted these cooperatives to its own purposes.

A more fundamental problem was the lack of a suitable social and economic infrastructure for government planning and intervention. The cooperatives did not enclose homogeneous groupings which had previously been structurally dependent on other forms of organization. In the case of the textile workers, their relations with private management had been relatively harmonious in the last years of the factory; management had increasingly acceded to worker wage demands and control in the factory had become increasingly based on cooperation with the powerful textile union. The redistribution of income effected by the cooperativization of the mill was almost non-existent; most cooperative members had been highly paid loom operators, and these took a substantial cut in salary with cooperativization.

THE IMPLICATIONS

Despite the difficulties attending government intervention, the presence of the Peruvian state is increasing in provincial regions and has important implications for the course of local development. In the first place, the State has replaced the foreign and Lima-based commercial and industrial elites as the dominant external force in the provinces. The government is replacing the Cerro de Pasco Corporation as the largest single employer in the Central Sierra, employing some 19 percent of Huancayo's adult male population, as well as teachers and government agents in the smaller towns of the area. The government also pays the highest wages and has become one of the most important economic resources that the area now possesses. The position of the State adds a further dimension, as we have seen, to the complex patterns of stratification in the area.

In earlier periods the income-maximizing strategies of local people were oriented to making use of the opportunities of the agro-mining economy through migration and household diversification; now strategies have changed to tap the resources of the State. Education and white-collar employment have become, for many local families, the most important objectives to be pursued; much small-scale enterprise is geared to making profits for investment in education, or to locating itself so as to maximize educational opportunities. This orientation is another factor preventing the small-scale enterprise from expanding through further internal investments.

State intervention which is not accompanied by a thoroughgoing investment of personnel and capital produces an uneasy situation. Small-scale activity flourishes in the interstices of state regulation of large-scale enterprises; but this small-scale activity is restricted in its expansion and possibilities of rationalization by the governmental presence. This presence also diverts part of the area's entrepreneurial talent into "unproductive" careers in the growing bureaucracy.

There is little in the thrust of government policy that has positive implications for the economic development of the Central Sierra. As Richard Webb indicates, the effects of government policy on the national distribution of income are limited because this policy has been most effective in distributing income vertically within large-scale enterprises. Measures such as the *comunidad industrial* (worker participation in profits and ownership) or greater social security benefits redistribute income only in large-scale enterprises (Webb, 1974). Small enterprises largely escape such measures as minimum wages laws or union legislation.

Very little of the population of the Central Sierra is affected by the government's redistributive measures; indeed, the price controls on basic foodstuffs act to reduce the profit possibilities of the small-farming sector of the population, which is one of the bases of the area's economy. Little government attention has been given to these problems of horizontal distribution of income; yet, through indirect taxation, food price controls, and the scope of government regulation, the State already limits the dynamic of the small-scale sector. The primary beneficiary of the cheapening of food costs is the large-scale sector of the economy, which can most afford to pay them; much of the urban population even of cities like Lima is integrated into small-scale enterprises, which are either directly or indirectly linked to small-scale farming through economic and social exchanges. In the present situation, the state cannot organize economic activity and is an irritant to local development; the form of capitalism which is developing in the region and which articulates it with the national economy is not one that is susceptible to control or direction.

Unless the government in Peru can massively commit resources to a provincial area—and there are good arguments for making such investments—state intervention is simply a form of tampering with local structures that can become counterproductive. This is not meant as a total criticism of current reforms, but as a comment on the limited nature of the benefits that they entail for the mass of the Peruvian population. In this respect, it is important to remember the contribution made by small-scale enterprise to generating development, in what are uncertain and highly marginal economic circumstances. The limits on accumulation imposed by the small size of the enterprises, and the personal relationships on which their operation is often based, give the small-scale sector a continuing capacity to absorb labor. More than this, the nature of the accumulation dictates that, to a large extent, surpluses are invested locally. The profits of these enterprises are rarely more than sufficient to build a substantial house, furnish it, and maintain a comfortable, "urban" standard of living. Small-scale activity also impedes economic centralization and reduces the impact of economic monopolies by directly trading with factories and markets in Lima. Gone, for example, are the large merchants and industrialists who once controlled Huancayo's commerce and factories, and who remitted their substantial profits to Lima. The dominance of small-scale activity together with the wages paid locally by the government may have reversed, to a small extent, the outflow of capital from the Central Sierra to Lima that was characteristic of the period of the agro-mining economy.

An area whose economy is based on small-scale activity appears to have a relatively high capacity to retain population. In the last decade, the Central Sierra has increased its population and has not suffered a net loss of population through out-migration. This capacity to retain population in active and productive ways is, itself, a significant contribution to national development, given the rapid increase of Lima's population and the slow expansion of jobs in the large-scale sector of the capital's economy. The State retains an important role in provincial development, even where it is unprepared to invest substantially in that development; the infrastructure on which small-scale activity depends—roads, schools, electricity, water, health services—must be provided by the government. Likewise, facilities for small loans and for obtaining expert advice can usefully be made available by the State. What is unnecessary is the close supervision and direction of local activity by central authorities.

When state employees intervene in local processes to administer, regulate or to mobilize, they are usually outsiders with little understanding of local customs or of local social or economic processes. Though some of the employees may be local people, long absence to obtain education or to pursue a career has often made them unfamiliar with local events. The degree of information that these employees possess about local conditions is often not sufficient to enable them to define public policies to meet local circumstances. It is best left to local people to organize themselves; they are most capable of making the most efficient use of local resources.

NOTES

1. I prefer to use the term "large scale" in place of "modern sector" (cf. Webb, 1974). I do this to avoid the implication that small-scale activity is, necessarily, not modern. Within small-scale activity, I am including a range of rural and urban activities which, in general, are best analyzed separately; however, even the lumping together of urban and rural has the advantage of emphasizing that these two sectors are closely interrelated.

2. This tendency is not so marked in those provincial cities (such as Arequipa and Trujillo) in which there continues to be an expanding sector of large-scale activity.

3. These data are taken from one month's record of all the passengers on buses coming to and leaving from Huancayo, and from hotel and boarding house records. These records are centralized in the police department; it is a Peruvian government regulation that passengers and visitors must provide data on their place of origin and their occupation.

4. The census figures should, however, be treated with caution. From our own surveys, we detected a tendency to overreport local populations as a result of fears that only those listed as residents would have rights to property, under new government legislation. On the national census day, for example, many "permanent" migrants returned to their villages to claim residence.

5. Agrarian reform in Peru affects almost all productive land over a certain size. It has included expropriation of the large sugar plantations and their mills, foodstuff haciendas and pastoral haciendas; it is also being extended to reorganize local community management and to sponsor cooperative organization. The reform has been carried out quickly and almost all the large landholdings have now been affected. For a general account, see Zaldivar (1971).

REFERENCES

ADAMS, R. N. (1959) A Community in the Andes. Seattle: University of Washington Press.

ALAVI, H. (1972) "The state in post-colonial societies: Pakistan and Bangladesh." New Left Review 74 (July-August).

ALDERSON-SMITH, G. (1974) "Peasant land invasion in Peru: the example of Huasicancha, 1963 to 1968." Paper presented at the Ninth Annual Conference of the Society of Latin American Studies, University of Southampton.

BARRATT BROWN, M. (1974) The Economics of Imperialism. Harmondsworth, England: Penguin Books.

CARDOSO, F. and E. FALLETO (1970) Dependencia y desarrollo en América Latina. México, D.F.: Siglo XXI.

CORNELIUS, W. A. (1974) "Urbanization and political demand making: political participation among migrant poor in Latin American cities." American Political Science Review 68, 3 (September): 1125-1146.

DOBYNS, H. (1970) Comunidades campesinas del Perú. Lima: Editorial Estudios Andinos.

EAMES, E. and J. G. GOODE (1973) Urban Poverty in a Cross-Cultural Context. New York: Free Press.

FRANK, A. G. (1969) Capitalism and Underdevelopment in Latin America. New York: Monthly Review Press.

FRIEDMANN, J. (1961) "Cities in social transformation." Comparative Studies in Society and History 4 (July).

GRONDIN, M. (1974) "Land fragmentation and economic survival: the case of Muquiyauyo." Unpublished paper. Department of Anthropology, Universidad Iberoamericana, México, D.F.

HART, K. (1973) "Informal income opportunities and urban employment in Ghana." Journal of Modern African Studies 11, 1: 61-89.

HOBSBAWM, E. (1971) "Peru: the peculiar revolution." New York Review of Books (December).

LAITE, J. (1974) "Migration and social stratification in the Central Sierra of Peru." Unpublished paper. Department of Sociology, University of Manchester, England.

LEEDS, A. (1971) "The concept of the 'culture of poverty': conceptual, logical and empirical problems with perspectives from Brazil and Peru," in E. B. Leacock (ed.) The Culture of Poverty: A Critique. New York: Simon & Schuster.

LERNER, D. (1958) The Passing of Traditional Society. New York: Free Press.

LONG, N. (1973) "The role of regional associations in Peru," in M. Drake (ed.) The Process of Urbanization. Bletchley: The Open University.

--- and D. WINDER (1975) "From peasant community to production co-operative: an analysis of recent government policy." Journal of Development Studies (forthcoming).

McGEE, T. (1971) "Catalysts or cancers? The role of cities in Asian society," in Leo Jakobson and Ved Prakash (eds.) Urbanization and National Development. Beverly Hills: Sage Publications.

MARTINEZ ALIER, J. (1972) "Los Huacchilleros en las haciendas de la Sierra Central del Perú desde 1930: Algunas hipótesis preliminares." Paper presented at the Second Symposium on the Economic History of Latin America, Rome.

PEATTIE, L. (1968) The View from the Barrio. Ann Arbor: University of Michigan Press.

Plan del Perú (1971) Plan nacional de desarrollo para 1971-75: Volume I: Plan global. Lima: Instituto Nacional de Planificación.

QUIJANO, A. (1974) "Redefinición de la teoría de dependencia." Unpublished paper. Lima, Peru.

--- (1972) "Imperialismo y capitalismo de estado." Sociedad y Política (Lima) 1 (June).

--- (1971) "Pôle marginal de l'economie et main d'ouevre marginalisée," in Anouar Abdel-Malek (ed.) Sociologie de l'imperialisme. Paris: Editions Anthropos.

ROBERTS, B. R. (1974a) "The social history of a provincial town: Huancayo, 1890-1972," in R. Miller, C. Smith, and J. Fisher (eds.) Social and Economic Change in Modern Peru (Centre for Latin American Studies, University of Liverpool, Monograph No. 6, forthcoming, 1975).

--- (1974b) "The interrelationships of city and provinces in Peru and Guatemala," in W. A. Cornelius and F. M. Trueblood (eds.) Latin American Urban Research, Vol. 4. Beverly Hills: Sage Publications.

--- (1973) "Migración urbana y cambio en la organización provincial en la Sierra Central de Perú." Ethnica (Barcelona, Spain) 6.

--- and C. SAMANIEGO (1973) Unpublished paper presented at Institute of Development Studies, University of Sussex, July.

SAMANIEGO, C. (1974) "Location, social differentiation and peasant movements in the Central Sierra of Peru." Ph.D. dissertation. University of Manchester.

STAVENHAGEN, R. (1964) "Classes, colonialism and acculturation." Studies in Comparative International Development 1, 6.

WEBB, R. (1974) "Government policy and the distribution of income in Peru, 1963-1973." Ph.D. dissertation. Harvard University.

WEEKS, J. (1973) "Uneven sectoral development and the role of the state." Bulletin of the Institute of Development Studies, University of Sussex, 5, 233: 76-82.

YEPES, E. (1974) "Some aspects of Peruvian socio-economic history." Ph.D. dissertation. University of Manchester.

ZALDIVAR, R. (1971) "Elementos para un enfoque general de la reforma agraria peruana." Cuadernos Agrarios 1 (August).

PART III

THE POLITICAL ECONOMY OF URBAN POVERTY

LISA REDFIELD PEATTIE is Professor of Urban Anthropology in the Department of Urban Studies, Massachusetts Institute of Technology. She received her Ph.D. from the University of Chicago, and has done fieldwork in the United States, Venezuela, and Colombia. She is currently participating in a comparative study of economic dualism and sources of inequality in advanced industrial and developing nations. Her principal publications include *The View from the Barrio* (University of Michigan Press, 1968); "Structural Parameters of Emerging Life Styles in Venezuela," in E. Leacock (ed.) *The Culture of Poverty: A Critique* (Simon & Schuster, 1971); and "The Concept of 'Marginality' as Applied to Squatter Settlements," in W. A. Cornelius and F. M. Trueblood (eds.) *Anthropological Perspectives on Latin American Urbanization: Latin American Urban Research,* Vol. 4 (Sage Publications, 1974).

Chapter 4

"TERTIARIZATION" AND URBAN POVERTY IN LATIN AMERICA

LISA R. PEATTIE

There is a standard description of what has been happening in Latin American cities which links urban poverty to the "tertiarization" of the economy—the large expansion of employment in the commercial and service sectors, relative to employment in the commercial and service sectors, relative to employment in manufacturing. The story goes like this: In Latin America, as a consequence of rapid population growth and of industrialization along relatively capital-intensive lines of technology borrowed from the already industrialized nations, growth in industrial production has brought with it little expansion of opportunities for employment in industry. However, the low levels of earnings in rural areas and the possibility of having substantially higher incomes in the city generate a very rapid rate of rural-urban migration. This leads to the crowding of job-seeking migrants into an essentially unproductive service and commercial sector in which earnings are naturally low. According to Richard Morse (1965),

> It is often shown that rural-urban migration in Latin America outruns possibilities for employment in urban industry. The ratio of the tertiary "services" sector of employment to the secondary manufacturing sector is therefore much greater than the ratio prevailing in Western Europe. . . . [The Latin American] is heavily weighted toward petty commerce and street vending, domestic service, unskilled and transitory work, and disguised unemployment [cf. Frank, 1972; Cardoso and Reyna, 1968].

The occupations in the tertiary sector are viewed essentially as a sort of self-help, job-creation program. "Here the supply of labour creates its own employment opportunities by sharing out a given amount of work" (Bhalla, 1973). The persons in these occupations would prefer wage labor employment if the jobs were available; since they are not, they develop ways of scratching out a living in trade or petty services *faute de mieux*. According to Reynolds (1969) these occupations are seen as natural entry points for new migrants to the city:

> Entrance to the occupations in question is open. Most of them require little or no skill and also little or no capital. They thus provide a natural entry point for migrants from the country, who win a precarious foothold in the urban economy by crowding into petty trade, services and other small-scale activities. Overmanning of these activities contributes to low output and income per worker.

In summary, the growth of the tertiary sector in Latin American cities is seen as largely characterized by:

–easy entry and consequent "crowding"

–very low earnings

–a high proportion of recent migrants to the city

–having such low earnings and low security that it is seen by participants as substantially less desirable than a "regular job"

–a minimal contribution to the general process of economic growth, except insofar as it constitutes a source of support for the urban poor in the absence of sufficient industrial employment.

A recent bit of exploratory research on the tertiary sector in Bogotá casts very substantial doubt on all these propositions, at least in the simple form in which they are stated above.

I tried to look at tertiary sector activities in Bogotá in two general ways: first, by finding out something about all the enterprises, of whatever sort, located in one low-income barrio in the southern part of the city; and second, by exploring what would appear to be classic examples of "tertiarization"–e.g., street vending, lottery ticket sales–in the central city. This involved interviewing street sellers, talking with officials involved in regulation of markets and street selling, and interviewing leaders of organizations of lottery ticket sellers, masons, shoe shiners, newspaper venders, and porters.

"TERTIARIZATION" ON THE PERIPHERY

The barrio in which I did the first stage of my fieldwork was one of rather mixed but predominantly low incomes, in an area along the hills first opened up for brick-making and still containing a number of small non-mechanized brickyards. There is no such thing as a "typical" barrio, but this one seemed at least not atypical, and it had for me the very substantial advantage of base data; a rather extensive sample survey including a good deal of information on occupational and mobility histories and current family incomes had just been completed there.[1] I supplemented this material by walking the barrio, listing and mapping all the local enterprises I could find, and interviewing people in the various kinds of enterprises.

In this barrio of 955 households—5,400 persons in all—I found 181 local enterprises, including in this total some very minor sales ("ices" offered in a house not otherwise in commercial use) and services ("injections given"). The list also includes: 77 small groceries, including several which also sell meat; two meat markets; five street stands selling fruits and vegetables; 17 brick manufacturers; one sewer pipe factory; one ceramic flower pot factory, not currently in operation; one candy factory; two bakeries; one shop making metal doors and window frames; one general metal working shop; one mattress repair shop; one paper bag manufacturer; and one furniture manufacturer. There were also nine shoe and leather manufacturers and repair shops (mostly small shoe repair enterprises); two electrical repair shops; one plumber; one glass and parquet worker advertising his services; 14 women offering dressmaking or knitting services; and five dry cleaning agencies. There were even a few people keeping sheep and a family which supported four cows on the local grass and on garbage, and managed to collect 30 bottles of milk a day, most of it sold locally.

The upper end of the commercial spectrum in the barrio is represented by a drug and dry goods store which by its general spic-and-span air and large amount of stock suggests a higher level of capitalization than other local businesses; indeed, the proprietor, who had two years of medical school, started in partnership with a brother-in-law who has a number of such businesses and says that his contacts with bankers and manufacturers are excellent. I was not able to ascertain his volume of business or annual earnings. At the lower end of the scale, there are businesses of more fragile character, such as the street vegetable sellers, the man who collects scrap iron with a horse and wagon, and several ice cream vendors ranging from those with large, refrigerated carts to those having only small carts with newspaper insulation. A sunny weekend brings out still more evanescent enterprises: a woman selling beer and soft drinks from a stand down at the crossroads, an old lady on the main uphill street selling broiled entrails, and sellers of broiled corn and slices of pineapple.

While commerce in the barrio is clearly oriented to the local market, the goods sold are mostly acquired in the central city. The five dry cleaning establishments are collection and distribution points for central-city dry cleaners. The meat markets buy their meat wholesale at the central slaughterhouse. Fruits, vegetables, rice, brown sugar and other dietary staples sold in the barrio, whether in the little grocery stores called *tiendas* or by the vendors who spread their goods on the ground near the bus stop, come from the same place—the wholesale market at the western edge of the city. It may be that in Africa and/or in Southeast Asia petty commerce in the urban setting is tied to chains of distribution which reach directly out to the rural economy (see McGee,

1971); but in Bogotá it would appear that all this activity is funneled through a relatively small number of wholesalers.

Indicative of the controlling interests in this system is the fact that the wholesale fruit and vegetable markets—until recently a disorderly clutter around an old plaza in the central city—have just been moved to new, modern quarters located at the very edge of the city. The change makes matters more convenient for the wholesalers, and the market itself is a showplace; but small sellers now bear a heavy monetary and time cost of transportation, as they go to the market every few days on the bus to buy and pay truckers to haul the goods back. Presumably these costs are passed along to their customers.

Retailers in the barrio do not only the selling but a good deal of breaking of bulk themselves. Several families, for example, have as a source of income the selling of small sacks of coal for cooking; they buy the coal in large lumps by the truck load and then, in their spare time, hammer the coal into smaller pieces and fill small sacks. Similarly, a grocer will buy rice by the 125-pound sack and divide it on his scale into one-pound paper bags. The units of sale are often very small. It is not uncommon for a customer to buy one cigarette, one scallion, one beet; one does not typically buy "a cabbage" but rather a slice of cabbage.

Prices are negotiable at the wholesale end, but in the barrio they are fixed. I was not able to get a clear and complete picture of the way in which tienda owners do their pricing. Several shop owners told me that the retail price was arrived at by dividing the wholesale price by the number of retail units and then calculating what you "had to charge" for each retail unit. There must be some understood markup, but I do not know how stable it is over time or the degree to which it varies from one commodity to another. One shopowner told me that the turnover rate should not effect the markup.

There must be some granting of credit by small shopkeepers; but in all my hours of observing tiendas I saw only one purchase which was not for cash on the counter, that by a man who turned out to be 50 centavos short for a 2.50 purchase and was told he could bring it tomorrow.[2] Several tienda owners in the barrio heatedly insisted that the giving of credit is the sure road to ruin; debtors do not pay you back and will soon avoid you in the bargain. Both my observations in Venezuela (Peattie, 1968) and Robert Roberts' (1973: 81) account of the operations of a small shop in England would suggest that the operators of such small businesses, if they wish to survive, must be exceedingly selective in giving credit.

Shopkeeping is generally thought of as an "easy entry" occupation; and while with the intricacies of price policy, wholesale buying, social interaction with customers, and accounting through memory and mental arithmetic it seems like a rather complicated way to make a living, people in the barrio did agree it was easy to get started. One can, in fact, start a rudimentary business with neither capital, experience, nor credentials. A woman vegetable seller told me how she began, three years earlier. With seven children and a husband with a drinking problem, she had to earn something. The first day she went to the wholesale market with her oldest child, and he wrote down the things purchased and the prices so they could calculate what to charge. Now she does it herself. She gets up about 4:30 in the morning, takes the two bus rides to the wholesale market, buys a quarter sack of this, a dozen of that. She pays a truck to bring the vegetables back, and lays them out on two wooden boxes for sale. She has looked into getting a stall in the market below, but they want 900 pesos for the stall plus 15 pesos a day for cleaning and maintenance, and "the business won't support that." Similarly, to sell from a shop she would have to pay a much higher rent than that she now has. She may not have been aware that to establish a store she would need not only the start-up capital but–to do it legally–five different government documents, including a good-conduct certificate from the police and a health certificate. Another shopkeeper, a former construction worker who shifted to shopkeeper as a form of semi-retirement, saw no problem in mastering the art of shopkeeping, even though he spoke with great feeling about the problem of calculating the prices of each item, keeping track, keeping your wits about you, giving courteous service.

So it is not difficult to start a small business in the barrio. This part of the tertiary sector does appear to be classically "easy entry." It would appear that barrio business also fits the usual picture in terms of yielding rather low earnings. After many frustrating hours I concluded that it was practically impossible to get any reliable information on the incomes derived from these small enterprises for two reasons: first, because the operators are (no doubt with a number of good reasons) extraordinarily cagy, uninformative, and downright misleading as informants, no doubt feeling that any information may be used to raise their taxes or place them under some evaded regulation; and second, because they themselves do not have the information. Some shopkeepers keep a rough record of sales, but they do not appear to relate this to outflow for stock, capital investment, and shop rent; moreover, all eat off the shelves without recording the value of goods thus consumed. Indeed, it appears that the economy of the business is, in this category of enterprise, so intertwined with that of the household that it would be possible either to absorb profits in a higher level of personal consumption or to subsidize the business out of other family earnings without having an accounting of the process. Thus I drew a total blank in getting any precise data on earnings in this sort of enterprise. Nevertheless, there is every reason to believe that running a tienda or most other local barrio enterprises is no way to get rich.

With 77 small tiendas for 955 households, the grocery business in the barrio is obviously being divided up very finely indeed. Writers on retailing in developed economies seem to agree that overall profit margins are arrived at by combining very low margins (or even "loss leaders") on staples with higher margins on non-staples (Holton, 1973). This would suggest that the tiendas have very low overall profit margins, for only a miniscule part of their sales is represented by the sorts of goods on which supermarkets make their highest profits, and even the prices on staples would appear to be no higher—and in some cases lower—than in a middle-class Bogotá supermarket I checked for comparison. In the few instances in which I was able to determine the markup with any degree of confidence it seemed remarkably low considering the slow movement of the goods out of the store, onion by onion, as it were.

As to the many local services—dressmaking, giving injections and the like—it would appear that these in no instance constitute a primary source of income, but are rather a supplement like the "egg money" of U.S. farmers' wives. They are, after all, providing services with highly elastic demand in a market where discretionary incomes are minimal.

"TERTIARIZATION" IN THE CENTRAL CITY

It is when we move from the barrio to downtown Bogotá that some new aspects of commerce come into view. Here there is a dizzying variety of small enterprises, and many of them fit the classic picture of easy entry, low earnings, and stopgap functioning.

The "evanescent enterprises" mentioned above are equally present in the central city; what trade could be more evanescent than that of going around on election day with a rag and a basin of soapy water to wash off the excess ink on the forefinger which designates those who have already voted? Similarly, the week preceding Mother's Day brings the appearance on Avenida Décima of a row of (mainly female) sellers of ornate Mother's Day cards. From time to time, a new commodity makes its appearance in force—for example, rug hookers, demonstrated and sold mainly by young men. Certain commodities, such as books, incense, and herbal medicines, are found in only one or two locations. Others, such as newspapers, cigarettes, candies, and lottery tickets, are found at major traffic intersections all over the city. The same is true of services. Street typists with their stock of government forms congregate around the Ministries, especially at income tax time; shoe shiners are more widely distributed. Surely this variegated mass of entrepreneurial activity represents the classic phenomena of easy entry and unregulated, competitive markets. But as we shall see, the matter turns out to be more complex.

Permits for selling on the street are given out at the Alcaldía Menor (Little City Hall) of the sector in question. There is no charge, but the applicant must have an identity card, police certificate, and health certificate. Furthermore, he should demonstrate that he is not too well off. The official view of street selling is that it should be an easy-entry occupation for the poor; but to orient it in this direction it is necessary to erect entry barriers to the well-to-do, since higher-status applicants do find it worth trying to get in. Some no doubt succeed.

In the central (and obviously most desirable, commercially) part of the city no new permits are being given out except for "special cases of demonstrated need," to prevent the streets from becoming overcrowded. These permits are thus in great demand, and someone who decides to leave vending can sell his post to a successor. The Alcaldía recognizes a "right of inheritance"—and what goes on between the first permit-holder and his heir is their business. A man with a cigarette and candy stand at, admittedly, a splendid location on the main avenue near where the buses change, told me that he paid 10,000 pesos for his post.

The official in the Alcaldía responsible for the permit system told me that he did not believe that there is a single vendor in Bogotá who makes less than 30 pesos per day—the minimum wage. There are those who employ someone at 20 pesos a day to tend their stand.

There are, of course, non-licensed vendors: people who unfold a suitcase on the sidewalk or spread out a carpet, and who are liable to harassment by the police. My informant in the Alcaldía estimated that about half the actual street vendors might be unlicensed. Many of these unlicensed vendors may be in a less favorable position, but others here do not do so badly if, even without secure tenure, they have access to a desirable commodity with a high markup. The same informant in the Alcaldía claimed that some vendors might make 500 pesos a day, especially those who sell contraband radios. He also complained about the "Turcos" (Middle Easterners) who, he said, emigrate to Colombia claiming that they are going to work as technicians or in some enterprise and immediately open up a suitcase and start selling cloth so that they can make enough to open a regular store. The complaint, of course, implies higher earnings in street commerce than in other jobs.

Lottery ticket selling is one of the few occupations in Bogotá which requires absolutely no papers; it is possible to sell lottery tickets even with a police record. But, again, there is the problem of capital and of access to a supply which is, like central-city posts, limited. People buy tickets either by producing cash, by getting a co-signer, by having (in the case of some wholesalers) a line of credit, or by buying part of a ticket from a wholesaler. A social worker at the Loterías de Bogotá reported that there are 1,200 listed vendors, but she believes the actual number to be about 4,500, since included among the 1,200 are wholesalers who sell parts of tickets and charge a percentage. It follows that in addition to lottery ticket sellers with very low earnings, there are those who are making 3,000 or perhaps as much as 5,000 pesos a week. Some sellers even have automobiles and have put their children through secondary school.

It is clear that "street selling" does not constitute an altogether "unregulated and competitive market" or a situation of equally easy entry. Access to a high-markup commodity like contraband radios constitutes a form of semi-monopoly. A young man who spreads wallets out on the sidewalk constitutes a regular outlet for a producer of these goods in another city, and sees his position as quite a desirable one. Even lottery tickets are not in unlimited supply, so it is advantageous to occupy a position in the supply system where one will have no difficulty in getting these goods to sell.

Those who sell an identical and readily-available commodity like cigarettes or fruits and vegetables from the central market are differentiated by their capitalization, their security, and most of all by their location, critical to the access to a particular market. It is one thing to sell cigarettes and candies in a barrio on the outskirts of the city—"easy access," but a poor market—and quite another to sell cigarettes and candies on the main artery where many people change buses, as the man who paid 10,000 pesos for a post in the latter location understood. A fruit and vegetable seller has easy access to a post on two boxes at the entrance to the barrio. Getting a stall in a more central market would require a substantial capital outlay, a good deal of paper work, some manipulation of the bureaucracy, and a sufficient expansion of the business to cover a daily rental charge. Lacking such a stall, one can still sell on the next street over from the main artery—but then with the continual possibility of being arrested. "*Estamos todos aventurando aquí* (we're all risk-taking here)," a woman selling vegetables in this way told me.

The effect of public policy in regulating commerce is to increase the monopolistic character of competition in the field. Outside the Alcaldía Menor in the southeastern part of the city, the area where the barrio I studied is located, a new covered market is under construction. The official with whom I spoke said that the government planned to move into this market the persons now selling on the street in front of a church. The rent for a stall in the new market will be 100 pesos a month. On questioning, the official agreed that there might be some sellers who would have problems in expanding to cover this additional charge. Meanwhile, applications for stalls were coming in: While I was there a resident of "Ciudad Kennedy"—a rather prosperous neighborhood on the western edge of the city—who appeared to have some sort of inside track in the bureaucracy, came in to negotiate his application; I had no doubt that there would soon be, as in other Bogotá markets, an unofficial charge to "buy" a stall. The sellers who do not get into the new market and are left outside, "*aventurando*" with the police, will be in a relatively worse competitive position than before. When I raised this issue with my informant, he agreed that there was a problem, but said that after all, the city could not allow everyone to jam into the most desirable locations. "Nor would you like it in a nice residential district to come out of your door and find a vendor of potatoes or snacks in front of the house."

But of course it would be highly unrealistic to think of restricted competition as being "forced upon" the participants in the tertiary sector by the public authorities. The natural wish of every little group is to, in one way or another, fence out competition: to become a group of "ins" restricting entry by the "outs." In the case of Bogotá, it would appear that the groups most successful in this process have been those who were able to restrict entry by controlling access to a particular commodity. This had been achieved by the Syndicate of News Vendors, a combined distribution system and mutual-aid society with a number of rules on work discipline and a rather extensive system of benefits, and by the several organizations of lottery ticket sellers. The market porters *(zorreros)* also have a "syndicate" and its members wear an identifying badge; but they have evidently been unable to maintain any control over the flow of jobs which would differentiate their position effectively from unorganized porters. Indeed, I was told that the police impose only on organization members the requirement of having a complete set of papers–a substantial disadvantage. As for the shoe shiners, they tried during the mayoralty of the reformer Gaitán to secure regulation of the occupation and limit it to uniformed members of an organized syndicate; but, as the union secretary told me, "They said we couldn't monopolize it." Thus, while individual shoe shiners may protect their own corners, the occupation as a whole has unlimited entry, and consequently many very low earners.

TERTIARIZATION: A REASSESSMENT

Pondering my discovery of the well-to-do lottery ticket wholesalers and the tight organization of newspaper vending, I realized that it was foolish of me to have imagined that urban commerce could ever be characterized by universal "easy entry" or free competition. Commerce is particularly suited to the development of profitable monopoly, either of a desirable high-markup good (such as contraband radios) or of a desirable location (as on the main avenue where the buses change in Bogotá). The tertiary sector is thus not at all adequately conceptualized as characterized by free competition between a large number of individual entrepreneurs with roughly similar resources. It is institutionally structured so as to provide a number of different, and differentially profitable, semi-monopolistic shelters.

From the understanding that even petty commerce is characterized by the development of a variety of semi-monopolistic shelters, a number of other things can be deduced: that, as a whole, it is not particularly suitable for penetration by new migrants to the city; that earnings will show a substantial spread; and that average earnings would be low only if there were such a number of very low earners at the bottom to counter-balance the high earnings at the top. There is evidence to substantiate all three of these deductions.

First, as to migrants: It will be clear from the preceding description of the organization of commercial life in Bogotá that only certain kinds of commerce are particularly accessible to migrants. Anyone can sell vegetables on the corner in the barrio; but to get a street post in the center one must either be a person who held the place before the freeze on new permits or someone with the financial or political resources to negotiate a permit now. Similarly, wholesalers in the lottery ticket business must be people with a good grasp of, and contacts in, the system. Indeed, my informant, the social worker in Loterías de Bogotá, said that a substantial proportion of the sellers she interviewed came into the occupation "through inheritance," i.e., because their parents were lottery ticket sellers. Thus we should not be astonished by the finding that in Bogotá, in 1964, about the same proportion (15 percent) of the migrant labor force were in commerce as native-born persons (Berry, 1973).[3]

The fact that individual migrants come into the system with different sets of resources, and therefore enter the system at different points, and that on the other hand, some "easy entry" occupations have almost no upward mobility no doubt accounts for finding in several studies that there is a rather low correlation between number of years in the city and socioeconomic level—except with respect to level of formal education, characteristically much more readily available in the city (see Perlman, 1971; MacDonald, 1969; Rodríguez Espada, n.d.).

Nor do the available statistics confirm the picture of job-seekers "crowding" into the tertiary sector. As Berry (1973: 44) points out,

> The presence of labor surplus might be expected to lead not so much to decreasing wages as to a decrease in the average earnings of self-employed people in commerce [as opposed to hired laborers]. It would be expected at the same time to lead to an increase in the share of the sectoral labor force who are family helpers or self-employed. . . . There has over no extended period of time been any trend toward increasing use of unpaid family helpers nor increasing share of independent workers; rather the opposite has occurred.

In a recent paper, Alan Udall specifically tests the "tertiarization" hypothesis by looking at employment trends in Bogotá during the years when *"la violencia"* in the countryside was driving large numbers of rural persons to take refuge in the cities. Although the violence did increase the share of small-scale workers in the labor force, "contrary to the service employment hypothesis most of this increase is accounted for by changes in small-scale employment within sectors, with total employment expanding at about the same rate in each sector" (Udall, 1974: 16-17).

Berry's statistics show very clearly that the commercial sector in Colombia is not characterized by low earnings; on the contrary, average income in this sector appears to be somewhat above that for the labor force as a whole, and from 1954 to 1967 it has been increasing at least as fast as other non-agricultural wages (Berry, 1973: 39-40, 49). These findings are paralleled by evidence from Peru, where Richard Webb (1973) found "positive, if moderate, trends in income . . . within the urban traditional sector, i.e., the employees in small non-reporting establishments, domestic servants, and self-employed workers in a variety of occupations."

Figures are not at hand to corroborate the thesis of highly unequal earnings within the sector, but as Berry (1973: 50) puts it: "It is widely believed on the basis of impressionistic evidence that some of Colombia's largest incomes have been based on commerce, and it is also obviously true that many relatively low income urban dwellers are found in that sector."

The great range of earnings to be found in the tertiary sector should in turn prepare us for the discovery that, whatever economists may think about how these people should be earning their livings in a better-ordered world, they themselves are not necessarily anxious to move from the independence of self-employment to wage labor—or at least, to the kind of wage labor which they might reasonably expect to obtain.

Among my informants in Bogotá—admittedly, a skewed sample, for I was interviewing only people who did not have wage-labor jobs—I heard a kind of hostile commentary on wage employment which I cannot ever remember hearing in Venezuela, with its highly paid, fringe-benefited labor aristocracy. But after all, Colombia does not have the powerful unions or the wage and fringe benefit structure which the "ins" of Venezuelan labor enjoy; the minimum wage is by no means universal, and even the legal minimum is not princely: the daily equivalent of one pair of men's undershorts. And if Colombians see more chance for upward mobility from some little business enterprise than in an unskilled job, they are probably quite realistic.

Relevant here is comment of Douglas Uzzell (1974) on the *cholos* who are the "master artisans, skilled laborers, unskilled laborers, servants and independent entrepreneurs" of Lima:

> Development economists and others like to lament that industrial employment in the Third World countries is not keeping pace with the growth of the urban labor force. We should keep in mind, though, that in Peru large-scale industry is a creole institution, and like the rest, it is structured in such a way as to exploit cholos. In Lima, employment in even a highly skilled blue collar job is a dead end, both socially and economically. By contrast, the small clandestine manufacturer produces relatively cheap consumer goods for cholos, while avoiding taxes and other creole devices for reducing his income, and the cholo merchant may sometimes distribute those goods. In contrast to blue collar jobs, these activities are *not* necessarily dead ends, however great the odds may be against one's becoming wealthy. Cholos do, in fact, become wealthy, and those who do are not wage laborers.

Sometimes people choose petty commerce because they lack the physical stamina for a regular job, or the sort of regular job for which they would be eligible. Examples include the sick woman who nurses a perpetual headache behind her counter in the barrio, and the house painter who bought a street stand when he became unable to work. Sometimes the motives are more along the lines of what professors—who very much value keeping their own hours—call "lack of labor discipline." Illustrative are the following comments by my informants, beginning with a barber and dry-cleaning collector:

> When the business goes well, it is good to make yourself independent—you can work your own hours, get up when you want to. Working for a company you do have medical care . . .

An independent metal worker:

> Well, yes, this is better than a regular job; at least you don't have to rush over there in the morning.

But this "lack of labor discipline" easily passes over into other issues. For example, a furniture maker comments:

> I prefer an independent business. The salaries in industry are too low. Terrible to live on. [He describes at length a job in a plastics factory where he was required to work 18 hours a day at 35 percent overtime.] Not worth it. If you work a long day in your own place, you know you're getting the results of it. And [in a regular job] if you complain, they just tell you to leave—there are lots more to take your place.

A vendor of homemade ice cream substitutes:

> Of course it's better than a job. You're not under the domination of anyone.

A woman street vendor:

> Better than a job? Of course. At least you don't live humiliated.

A shoe repairman:

> At least with this you can escape from that tyranny—the humilation. They call you: Run, little donkey. Waiting hour after hour for them to pay you the little bit they owe you. I worked as a painter on a big building in the center—thirty pesos a day, working from seven to six, often overtime. The contractor was making lots of money, and had only to order people around. The oligarchy gets richer and richer—take from the poor to give to the rich.

This series of comments—I have tried to select quotes to represent a sort of gradient from the less to the more political—illustrates a number of different themes which shade into each other. There is the convenience and sense of ease in following one's own rhythm of the job—certainly a major theme in the troubled adjustment of the British to the Industrial Revolution (Thompson, 1967). There is wage employment experienced as status subordination, and earning inequality experienced as injustice. Finally, there is the placing of these experiential themes in the political context furnished by an ideology; so that "the rich" become "the oligarchy."

Here we are dealing with "cultural preferences," but preferences which must be shaped very strongly by the actual structure of economic opportunities available, and which must, therefore, vary a good deal from time to time and place to place. But given the preoccupation of the development economists with the employment (i.e., job) problem, and the limited labor-absorptive capacity of industry, it seems worth stressing that the independence and possibility of upward mobility in "informal sector" entrepreneurship may appear very attractive—especially if not counter-balanced by relatively high wages and mobility opportunities in the larger enterprises.

The fact that so many of the common generalizations about the tertiary sector in Latin American cities fail to stand up very well to close examination might make us look a little more closely at the common notion that all this activity contributes little or nothing to economic growth. Here certain theoretical difficulties stand in the way: A basic one is the rather faltering character of economic theory relating to commerce and services. Another is the fact that while we may speak of "productivity" as some kind of functional characteristic, in practice earnings are our only operational productivity measure; and where services are provided to a stratified market with highly unequal incomes this clearly gives a low weighting to services for the poor. A third problem is the difficulty of comparing economic functions which are carried out in economies of different levels and kinds of organization. It has been pointed out that activities like cobbling and millinery which are carried out in shops as in the barrios of Bogotá are likely to be censused as tertiary, whereas if carried out under factory conditions they would be treated as secondary (Bauer and Yamey, 1951). Still, the issue of economic function does not go away just because our conceptual apparatus is not capable of dealing with it adequately.

One point is amply clear so far as Bogotá is concerned: The commerce of the central city streets and of the peripheral low-income barrios, just as much as the commerce of the big shops, is part of the general economy of the city, not a separate sub-economy. The greater part of the goods sold everywhere are factory-produced. The prototypic "street vendor" is waving cartons of Marlboro cigarettes at the intersection. A Brazilian economist observes:

> The phenomenon which exists is not that of an "inflation" of the tertiary sector. The size of the latter, in an economy like the Brazilian and from the point of view of its share in total employment, is a question closely tied to urban-industrial accumulation. The acceleration of growth, whose epicenter came to industry, demanded of Brazilian cities—seats par excellence of the new cycle of expansion—infrastructure and service requirements for which they had not been previously prepared. The intensity of industrial growth, which in thirty years passed from 19 to 30 percent of gross production, *did not permit an intense and simultaneous capitalization in services*. . . . This contradiction was resolved through non-capitalist growth in the tertiary sector [Oliviera, 1973].

Here is a very large issue for future work, and the very fact that our conceptual apparatus has trouble dealing with it seems to suggest that we could get a good deal out of additional fieldwork to tighten up hypotheses and categories.

Finally, the very sketchy field observations reported here should be sufficient also to call into question the distinction often made between "institutionally-determined" and market-determined earnings. Social and political institutions affect earnings up and down the social structure, though they may do so in different ways. The official system of markets and legal permits for selling affects earnings for the people in the markets, and also changes the relative economic chances for persons outside the formal system; the same point applies to lottery ticket sales or newspaper selling. And if an occupation is very little structured institutionally, earnings in that occupation will be lowered by the existence of barriers to entry in other fields. One of the subjects for long-term research, then, is the way in which public policy and private organization affect the distribution of income among all those players in the making-a-living game for which these institutions set the rules.

NOTES

1. See Gauhan (1975). I am indebted to Mr. Gauhan for permitting me to examine his questionnaires.

2. In a survey in Cartagena, Colombia, 19 percent of those interviewed reported that they could respond to an economic emergency by buying on credit in local tiendas. See Triana y Antorveza (1974: 151).

3. Similarly, a study of the urban labor force in Tanzania (Sabot, 1974) found that only 6 percent of migrants had supported themselves in whole or in part through self-employment on arrival in the city, and that 69 percent of the self-employed had been living in the city for over five and a half years.

REFERENCES

BAUER, P. T. and B. S. YAMEY (1951) "Economic progress and occupational distribution." Economic Journal 61: 741-755.

BERRY, R. A. (1973) "Urban labor surplus and the commerce sector: Colombia." Unpublished paper. Economic Growth Center, Yale University, June.

BHALLA, A. S. (1973) "The role of services in employment expansion," in W. Galenson (ed.) Essays on Employment. Geneva: International Labor Organization.

CARDOSO, F. H. and J. L. REYNA (1968) "Industrialization, occupational structure and social stratification in Latin America," in C. Blasier (ed.) Constructive Change in Latin America. Pittsburgh, Penna.: University of Pittsburgh Press.

FRANK, A. G. (1972) Lumpenbourgeoisie and Lumpendevelopment: Dependence, Class, and Politics in Latin America. New York: Monthly Review Press.

GAUHAN, T. O. (1975) "Housing and the urban poor: the case of Bogotá, Colombia." Ph.D. dissertation. Rice University.

HOLTON, R. H. (1973) "Price discrimination in supermarkets," in K. A. Tucker and B. S. Yamey (eds.) Economics of Retailing. Baltimore, Md.: Penguin Books.

MacDONALD, J. S. (1969) "Migration and the population of Ciudad Guyana," in L. Rodwin (ed.) Planning Urban Growth and Regional Development. Cambridge, Mass.: MIT Press.

McGEE, T. G. (1971) The Urbanization Process in the Third World. London: G. Bell and Sons.

MORSE, R. (1965) "Recent research on Latin American urbanization." Latin American Research Review 1, 1: 35-74.

OLIVIERA, F. (1973) "La economía brasileña: crítica de la razón dualista." El Trimestre Económico 40, 2 (April-June): 411-484.

PEATTIE, L. R. (1968) The View from the Barrio. Ann Arbor, Mich.: University of Michigan Press.

PERLMAN, J. (1971) "The fate of migrants in Rio's favelas: portrait of the people." Ph.D. dissertation. Massachusetts Institute of Technology.

REYNOLDS, L. G. (1969) "Economic development with surplus labor: some complications." Oxford Economic Papers 21: 89-108.

ROBERTS, R. (1973) The Classic Slum: Salford Life in the First Quarter of the Century. London: Pelican Books.

RODRIGUEZ ESPADA, E. (n.d.) La incorporación de los migrantes a la estructura económica y social de la ciudad de Bogotá. Bogotá: Asociación Colombiana de Facultades de Medicina.

SABOT, R. H. (1974) "The meaning and measurement of urban surplus labor in an African context." Unpublished paper.

THOMPSON, E. P. (1967) "Time, work-discipline and industrial capitalism." Past and Present 38 (December): 56-97.

TRIANA Y ANTORVEZA, H. (1974) Cultura del tugurio en Cartagena. Bogotá: n.p.

UDALL, A. T. (1974) "The effects of rapid increases in labor supply on service employment in developing countries." Working Papers in Economics, University of Delaware, September.

UZZELL, D. (1974) "A strategic analysis of social structure in Lima, Peru, using the concept of 'plays'." Urban Anthropology 3, 1 (Spring): 34-46.

WEBB, R. (1973) "Government policy and the distribution of income in Peru, 1963-1973." Discussion Paper No. 39, Research Program in Economic Development, Woodrow Wilson School, Princeton University, June.

SUSAN ECKSTEIN is Assistant Professor of Sociology at Boston University. She received her Ph.D. from Columbia University, and has done fieldwork in Mexico and Chile. Her principal area of interest is the political economy of Third World countries, with special emphasis on the structural determinants of urban poverty. She is presently engaged in a comparative study of the social, economic and political consequences of Latin American social revolutions (Mexico, Bolivia, Cuba). Her chapter in this volume contains materials from her forthcoming book, *The Poverty of Revolution: Social Controls of Mexican Urban Poor* (Princeton University Press).

Chapter 5

THE POLITICAL ECONOMY OF LOWER CLASS AREAS IN MEXICO CITY: SOCIETAL CONSTRAINTS ON LOCAL BUSINESS PROSPECTS

SUSAN ECKSTEIN

The proliferation of squatter settlements on the periphery of Latin American cities has generated a belief that there are "slums of hope" and "slums of despair" (Stokes, 1962; cf. Portes, 1971; Mangin, 1967; Turner, 1968; Goldrich et al., 1967-1968; Cornelius, 1971; Rogler, 1967; Germani, 1967; Patch, 1968). Accordingly, scholars, city planners and politicians have tended to stress that not all lower-class residential areas are alike, that public housing projects are economically impractical as well as socially alienating, and that at least certain of the new self-built housing on the outskirts of cities is preferable to both inner-city tenements and housing projects. Emphasis on dwelling environments has overshadowed concern with the economic roots of urban poverty which the housing problem reflects, although some (e.g., Turner, 1968) have argued that the self-built housing may help mitigate poverty, in that residents of squatter settlements can augment their income both by opening stores or other small work enterprises in their homes and by renting out rooms.[1]

My study of three lower class areas in Mexico City suggests that recent optimism about the work opportunities generated by squatter settlements is ill-founded. Outlying areas do not necessarily provide better employment prospects than inner-city slums for the urban poor, largely because of the impact national political-economic forces have on the local communities. Economic possibilities within different sections of the city reflect societal conditions prevailing during the years the communities have existed. Because the structure of the economy has changed over the years, new areas do not offer the same opportunities that old ones once did.

Within the three areas under study, national and even international economic and political pressures have shaped the array of local productive and distributive enterprises, patterns of ownership, prospects of financial success, and relations within and among businesses.[2] As a consequence, residents have access to more distributive and service ventures than productive undertakings, particularly in the two new areas on the city's periphery; and the businesses they establish tend to be small and precarious, generating little profit. The most lucrative local enterprises are owned by people who do not reside in the areas; people who began their local businesses with a comparative economic advantage over the residents. These non-residents neither reinvest the income they generate locally to upgrade the local communities, nor primarily hire local residents so that money thereby is made available to members of the communities. Despite such "market forces," government policies have indirectly helped to create and maintain certain business opportunities for residents in the private sectors of the local economies. Also, residents have been able to assert a modicum of influence over local economic conditions.

The three areas investigated include a center city slum, part of which dates back to the Colonial period; a low-cost, publicly-financed housing development comprised of individual homes which opened in 1964; and a now-legalized squatter settlement first occupied in 1954. These areas were selected purposively to represent different types of lower class communities, in order to ascertain how the "life chances" of the poor vary in different types of urban dwelling environments.[3] The analysis of the economies of the three areas presented in this paper constitutes part of a larger, in-depth study I made of the areas. References to residents are based on formal interviews with a sample of three hundred inhabitants, selected randomly from a household census of blocks in different sections of the three areas. The information on shoe artisans derives from participant-observation, together with unstructured, informal interviews with shoe artisans and local priests who worked closely with the artisans. The material on factories stems primarily from interviews with factory owners and/or managers, and that on commercial and service enterprises derives from a questionnaire administed to persons in charge of seventy local shops. The sample of shopowners and managers was selected randomly from a census I made of all business enterprises visible from the streets in the areas.[4] All persons interviewed were asked about the organization of their businesses, how and why their operations had changed over the years, how the businesses were initially started, previous work experiences, other economic activities in which they presently engage, work histories of kin, and place of residence.

THE PRODUCTIVE SECTOR

While the Mexican economy as a whole has expanded rapidly in recent decades, local employment opportunities provide little evidence of this trend, particularly in the squatter settlement and housing development included in my study. The contrasting job profiles of the three communities reflect the structure of production in the society at large during the different historical periods in which the areas have been settled. Since the Colonial era the inner-city area has been a major center of craft production, and since the turn of the century it has also been a major center of small and medium-scale industries, reflecting the country's early industrial growth. Yet the old center city area does not exemplify a stage in the development process of local economies through which the two newer areas with time will pass, largely because technology and the organization of production have changed.[5]

Craft Production

While some residents in the squatter settlement and housing development sew clothing, make parts of shoes, or do other piece-work in their homes, and while some of them work out of their homes on a contract basis, in neither of the areas settled in the last two decades are there many local sweatshops. In contrast, the center city area continues in its long-established tradition to be a major hub of artisan activities, although the types of crafts located there have changed over the years, in response to overall changes in the national economy. Some of the new and most lucrative crafts in the center city area reflect recent technological developments which have been introduced into Mexico in the course of the century. Auto mechanic work is a case in point. However, other new local crafts, particularly shoe-making, have been transplanted from provincial communities. As the standard of living of city-dwellers has improved and the demand for non-luxury shoes has increased, shoe artisans have moved to the largest cities to produce and sell their goods. As illustrated below, shoe artisans in the center city area face severe competition and exploitation by employers, suppliers and distributors. They thus far have managed to survive as a class because the government protects the inefficient but labor-absorbing sector from competing shoe manufacturers.

Center City Cobblers

The shoe craft sector in Mexico City in general and the center city area in particular has expanded markedly in the twentieth century.[6] Its expansion demonstrates that urbanization is not necessarily associated with the rise of industry and the demise of artisan activities.[7] Interestingly, in fact, more shoe craft enterprises are situated in Mexico City than elsewhere in the country and most shoe factories are located outside Mexico City. Forced to compete with manufacturers, artisans seem to find it propitious to locate near the main market for their product.[8]

They established themselves largely in the inner-city "slum" because the area not only was residential but also a center of craft and commercial activity. Once the area became a center for shoe craft production, shoe artisans–mainly migrants and children of migrants from the provincial centers of shoe production–continued to locate there, because of easy access to requisite materials.

While the local shoe artisan sector has expanded greatly during the course of the century, the organization of production remains labor-intensive and guild-like. In the small *talleres* (sweatshops) only a few varieties of shoes are made. The *maestro* owns the shop, manages the production process, and is in charge of sales.[9] One or more workers cut the leather. The others sew, glue and adorn the shoes. If the maestro is poor he sends the leather out to be sewn and glued because he cannot afford to purchase the requisite machines. The skills are learned through an apprenticeship system. In contrast to most workers who learn only one skill, the maestro generally knows all the relevant skills so that he can substitute for any worker when absent, if he does not have other work to do. The workers are paid on a piece-work basis, not for the time they spend at work. Hence, when a cutter or sewing machine operator reports late to work, the others, unable to work, do not get paid.

The owners of talleres operate on a low margin of profit; competing with the more efficient manufacturers, they cannot readily pass on their costs to consumers. Their problem stems largely from the structure of the market. Competition among shoe artisans is stiff, since little capital and few skills are needed for most stages of the production process and since artisans have not organized to limit the number of people in the craft. Thus, the expansion of the craft reflects the way in which people with little education and few economic resources adapt to the general economic situation in Mexico, and the high turnover rate of shops is also a consequence of this general situation.

Profits, moreover, are limited because owners of talleres are exploited by retailers and distributors to whom they sell their merchandise, and by suppliers from whom they purchase their materials. Distributors pay less for the shoes than retailers, and retailers often either pay shoe craftsmen with postdated checks or pay only part of the cost of the shoes upon delivery. As a consequence, shoemakers, in effect, supply retailers with credit. In addition, if the shoes, which are made to order, are delivered more than approximately two weeks late, retailers and distributors pay less than the agreed upon price for the shoes. Because of such abuse, owners of shoe talleres often find themselves with insufficient cash to buy equipment and supplies and to pay workers. Production is thereby impeded; and since taller owners cannot fill orders when they are unable to maintain production, their businesses suffer.

Taller owners attempt to resolve their financial problems by buying equipment and materials on credit but, because interest rates are high, this drives up their production costs. Machinery, most of which is imported from the United States, sells on credit for double the cash price. In addition, tanners charge 5 to 20 percent interest on loans and insist that their debtors buy leather exclusively at their tannery. Tanners can thereby minimize competition which would drive down the going market price for their merchandise. Since most tanners are located within the center city area they can watch their clients fairly easily. Should they catch shoemakers breaking the informal agreement, they may refuse to loan the shoemakers additional money in the future.

The national association of shoe manufacturers and the government further reduce the potential profits of taller owners. All shoemakers are obliged to belong and pay dues to the national association, although some small producers have managed to stay out of the association. Theoretically, the organization represents the interests of all members, but because members' voting power depends on the amount of capital they invest in their business, in actual fact the association primarily looks after the interests of the large factories.

The government, in turn, taxes shoe producers. While local artisans evade business taxes, reputedly the large, non-local manufacturers also do. And even though the small shoe producers indirectly are protected by the government in that only large firms are required to pay workers the official minimum wage, provide them with Social Security, and abide by other stipulations of the Federal Labor Code, large producers benefit much more from tax loopholes for capital investments.

Moreover, there are plans to require taller owners to provide their employees with Social Security benefits. To date, differences between the social and economic benefits enjoyed by shoe artisans and blue collar employees in shoe factories stem from differences in government protection, not differences in productivity. If the Social Security regulation is enforced, the seemingly desirable and progressive plan may prove to work against the interests of taller owners, who will have to bear much of the cost of Social Security coverage, and, paradoxically, of employed artisans. Many of the taller owners who already operate on a small margin of profit may be forced out of business if they have to bear the additional labor cost, in which case artisans will lose their jobs.[10] Thus the plan would benefit indirectly the large-scale shoe manufacturers, since they will not be subject to higher labor costs: They already provide workers with Social Security coverage, and they can better afford the expense, as labor constitutes a much smaller percentage of total production costs in the mechanized firms than in the labor-intensive craft shops.

The craft sector has survived, despite these problems, since artisan labor is inexpensive. Labor is cheap because there is a vast "pool" of available workers and because shoe artisans are unorganized and unprotected by minimum wage legislation. In addition, taller owners keep labor costs low by employing the cheapest labor: migrants, women, and, in violation of the labor law, children. And because the Labor Code is not enforced in the artisan sector, taller owners can expand and contract employment as their seasonal business fluctuates. Consequently, they need not bear high labor costs when business is slow.

Despite the large supply of labor, taller owners have problems acquiring and maintaining a dependable work force. Labor commitment vacillates, due to the nature of work conditions. Because employers pay poorly, they do not offer sufficient inducement to attract the best and most reliable workers. While maestros are better able to maintain discipline and control production when their employees work under "one roof" than when they run their businesses on a "putting out" system, production often is impeded because one or more workers report late to work. Absenteeism and tardiness are particularly widespread after weekends. To minimize such problems some taller owners prefer hiring people who live near their shops; that way they can readily fetch those employees who fail to report to work.

Employers also are faced with the problem of finding workers they can trust. Workers tend to steal material from the shops because they are paid poorly. Some taller owners attempt to resolve this problem by hiring relatives, whom they feel they can trust more than non-kin. Or else they try to win workers' loyalty by providing "non-contractual" benefits. Taller owners, for example, periodically supply employees with shoes and cash loans, and provide workers with medical assistance when sick. The range of services offered partly depends on the maestro's contacts. For instance, one maestro paid part of his employees' medical bills, but required that his workers use a specific doctor, a friend of his. He had an agreement with the doctor: the doctor charged a reduced rate in exchange for the patients the maestro sent him. Workers realize that they are expected to cooperate with and occasionally do favors for their employers, in order to obtain such benefits. As a result, particularly during the busy Christmas season, artisans work very long hours, seven days a week.

Competition for customers and good workers exacerbates matters for taller owners. Formalized efforts to reduce competition have failed. A priest, for instance, tried to form a shoe artisans' cooperative through which artisans could purchase supplies collectively for less money than they pay when buying individually. However, while artisans liked the intent of the cooperative, they were reluctant to join, for fear that someone would run off with the group's money. Experience has taught them to be skeptical, for once before someone *did* steal money from a short-lived cooperative.

Kinship bonds are one of the few mechanisms which reduce competition among shoemakers. Relatives are expected to assist, not compete with one another. Thus, in one *vecindad* (center city tenement) where several related artisans make shoes, there is a tacit agreement among them to cooperate and help one another in times of crisis. However, rather than organize an efficient, profit-generating, collective enterprise, they engage in discreet, non-competing operations: The different households produce different types of shoes, find customers and occasionally buy materials for each other, and share the same car for delivering their products.

The various constraints described above limit the profits shoe artisans can make. However, the small number who either by chance or business skill succeed in generating a sizeable profit rarely use their liquid reserves for further mechanization of the productive process. If they invest their profits in the business, they generally use them to extend the existing labor-intensive system. They hire more cutters, sewers, and so on, on a piece-work basis.

Aside from lack of capital, disciplined labor, and markets for shoes, another major problem confronting many taller owners is an organizational one. The owners with bookkeeping operations are the most successful, since they can keep track of their costs and profits and economize so as to minimize their expenses. Unfortunately, many owners lack such skills.

In addition, scarcity of capital and extensive competition for buyers puts shoemakers in a weak bargaining position at both the supply and distributive ends of the production process. Their weak bargaining position, combined with poor organization, limit the profits they can generate. Craft production has expanded nonetheless, largely because the government has not enforced labor legislation. Thus, even when the government does not directly intervene in the local economy, local economic opportunities are importantly shaped by political as well as "market forces."

In sum, while shoe craft production in the center city area has persisted and indeed expanded in the present century it represents no mere continuation of the production process established locally under the Colonial guild system, and the changes which have occurred do not reflect autonomous economic developments. Today the division of labor in production and distribution is more specialized and the technology employed is more sophisticated than in the past. Because cobblers use imported machinery, local production is not replicating the independent pattern of development of shoe manufacturing as it evolved in the advanced capitalist countries.

Local Factories

Despite the expansion of craft production in such spheres of the urban and national economy as shoe-making, in general the country's major growth stems from the expansion of more mechanized industries. Yet, not only do the squatter settlement and housing development offer few artisan jobs, but due to zoning restrictions they offer no industrial opportunities. The structure of local manufacturing illustrates still another way in which the economies of the three areas under study are shaped by domestic and foreign market forces and by government policies.

Most of the factories in the center city area were started during Mexico's era of greatest industrial expansion, the immediate post-World War II period. Although most of the firms have changed hands over the years, they initially located there because land at the time was cheap and because the area was a major commercial district. However, because all but one local factory (discussed below) contrast markedly with the new, highly productive, capital-intensive subsidiaries of multi-national industrial corporations and large Mexican-owned firms, the factories are not representative of current industrial trends in the country.

Accordingly, most goods manufactured locally are characteristic of early industries, not recent consumer developments: There are firms manufacturing food products, textiles, paper bags, cardboard sheets, furniture, curtains, mattresses, candles, and electrical signs. Furthermore, although imported, the machinery utilized locally tends to be antiquated. This is true even in those firms which have "modernized" their production process over the years.

Since the machinery is not highly sophisticated, the employed labor force tends to be semi- and unskilled; and since the firms are small and medium in size, they are managed directly by owners. Only one factory has more than one hundred workers. However, while the size of the labor force employed in the factories in some instances reflects the degree to which the firms are mechanized and capitalized, it sometimes reflects the way in which production has been adapted to the legal code. Thus in several firms employment has dropped over the years as more capital-intensive machinery has been introduced; but in the case of the two local paper bag factories, management has deliberately limited the work force so as to maximize profits. The two firms are owned by the same person, a man who owns still another paper bag factory elsewhere in the city. He deliberately runs several different factories—each employing slightly less than one hundred workers—rather than a single large one, in order to circumvent the Constitutional stipulation that firms with more than one hundred employees must provide their workers with housing and other benefits.

Owned by non-residents, the profits generated in local factories leave the area. The monopolization of local industrial opportunities by non-residents partly reflects the fact that these capitalists are a select group.[11] Several of the owners are children of immigrants, particularly of Eastern European Jews. They have a post-primary school education and useful kinship contacts, and they received training relevant to their work before going into business for themselves. Since many parents and other relatives of the local industrialists had similar businesses, the local industrialists acquired business skills as children. From their kin they also acquired machinery and/or help in securing loans, and useful business connections. Such family backgrounds and personal experiences have given them a decided entrepreneurial advantage over local residents, even though few of them directly inherited their fathers' businesses. Partly because of these advantages they have not been faced with the same extensive competition limiting business prospects.

To illustrate, a local Jewish manufacturer of cotton textiles had help from relatives when he began his business. Although he did not get along well with his father, the owner of a similar factory in the State of Mexico, the father taught him useful business skills. Through his father he also acquired business contacts, including ones which enabled him to get financial backing and access to suppliers and buyers. Moreover, his brother gave him the plant and the machinery. The brother had owned the business before starting to manufacture luxury fabrics. Since the present owner invested less than $100 of his own money when he took over the firm, personal accumulation of capital was one of the least important factors enabling him to become economically successful. Moreover, since the family was of immigrant Jewish background, the "particularism" which facilitated his business does not reflect the persistence of a cultural trait generally attributed to Latin Americans.[12] Instead, the "particularism" in this case reflects an adaptive mechanism by which socioeconomic privileges are passed on from one generation to the next along family lines. The case of this Jewish family also suggests that kin at times are prone to establish separate but non-competing businesses, as also was true among blood-related shoe artisans. The relatives pool their efforts in ways which, on the one hand, give them greater control over the market situation and, on the other hand, maximize autonomy within their immediate work situation. However, they in part employ this strategy so as to circumvent certain tax and labor laws.

Because residents do not own the local firms, they cannot readily secure managerial and blue-collar jobs in the factories. The managerial posts tend to be reserved for relatives or personal acquaintances of the owners.[13] Although the owners do not hire kin as manual laborers, several local entrepreneurs and managers deliberately discriminated against local residents, claiming that they were drunkards and unreliable. Several owners also preferred hiring docile migrants from rural areas to natives of the city. Since most center city inhabitants were born in the capital, this management preference further limited residents' ability to secure work in local industries.

Thus, even more than in the artisan sector, residents tend not to be the main beneficiaries of the few industrial opportunities which exist locally. They are victims of informal social pressures which discriminate against them. Yet, as illustrated by the case of the one locally operating subsidiary of a foreign-owned corporation, international as well as domestic forces impinge on the local employment opportunities.

A Denationalized Chocolate Factory

Reflecting the post-World War II trend toward transnational ownership of large-scale Mexican industries, U.S. companies had acquired the two biggest firms—one manufacturing canned goods, the other chocolate—in the center city area by 1971. These businesses had been among the last major ones in the food industry to remain in Mexican hands. Upon purchasing the canning company, United Fruit moved the factory to Querétaro. The other firm, bought by Quaker Oats, still operates locally.

The chocolate factory was the largest of its kind in Mexico. It had been owned primarily by one man. He initially started the business in the state of

Michoacán, Mexico's cacao center, but moved it to Mexico City in 1930, when he fled to the capital to escape civil strife. By the 1960s the firm employed about 350 people, mostly women from his town of origin who had little or no schooling. He preferred hiring such workers because he believed them to be respectful, obedient, and willing to work for low wages. When he needed new workers he generally recruited through a few employees who were regarded by the other factory hands as "natural leaders." These "leaders" were migrants from the *patrón's* hometown who had worked many years for the firm.[14] By hiring migrant women the patrón successfully kept workers both from affiliating with a national union and from forming *cajas,* a type of informal credit association, against his will. He thereby minimized not only labor costs but also labor's independence from him.

Yet the old man was not a complete tyrant. He permitted workers to have *tandas*—rotating credit associations much less sophisticated than cajas—and lent money to workers upon request.[15] He also regularly donated money to the church in the provincial town from which he and most of his workers migrated, paid for the buses his workers took on their annual pilgrimage to the town, and provided flowers and fireworks for the town fiesta. He also contributed money for a special mass associated with an annual pilgrimage workers made in their native provincial costumes to the Basílica of Guadalupe in Mexico City, and occasionally invited the local parish priest to give mass in the factory chapel. In addition, he encouraged and institutionalized personalistic ties by serving as godparent to workers' children.

Nonetheless, the favors the patrón did for his employees never included extending opportunities for occupational advancement. The managerial posts were monopolized by the boss's sons, most of whom were college-educated, and by a few other relatives.

Yet kinship ties did not keep family members from fighting among themselves. Because the relatives differed in their commitment to the business, their entrepreneurial skills, and their honesty, the aging founder of the business decided to sell the firm to an American corporation when faced with the problem of succession.[16] As one of the foreign executives phrased it: "Who else was he to go to? "

The new owners still maintain certain aspects of the old business more or less intact. The few blue collar workers who have been hired since ownership changed hands come from the same provincial town as most of the other employees, and were hired through the same "natural leaders" as the other employees. The new management also continues to subsidize the provincial community, by regularly donating money to the town church. They also pay costs associated with the annual pilgrimages. One of the foreign managers even accompanied workers on the Michoacán pilgrimage, and attended both a special mass for the factory workers in the town and a lunch in the church for community leaders. According to the manager, the priest spoke in the mass of how fortunate the employees were to work for such a big company.

Interestingly, the foreigners have been more anxious to cultivate socio-religious ties with the migrants' town than with the local community in Mexico City; they have never invited the local priest to give mass in the factory chapel. Their selective continuation of policies established by their predecessor reflects their economic concerns. Since the new management continues to employ workers from the provincial town they do not wish to antagonize townsmen and employees in ways which would upset labor relations within the firm. Since they hire few local residents they feel little pressure to maintain the few community ties which the old patrón had established.

Certain changes, however, have been initiated since the takeover, and others are planned. First, only one son of the former owner, the one in charge of production, remains with the company. The rest of the managerial staff is foreign. Second, the new management has added several new departments, including sales and accounting departments, and a laboratory to help improve "quality control"–the "American way," to quote one of the foreign executives. Unlike the old patrón the new management is very concerned with introducing new products. They were disturbed by the fact that the old patrón had not marketed a new product during the last five years he owned the firm. In addition, the new owners have attempted to restructure labor-management relations within the firm. Thus, whereas formerly workers took their problems directly to the patrón or one of his sons, now authority is formally delegated. The Americans have introduced a hierarchical chain of command linking management to department heads, department heads to supervisors, and supervisors to workers, and they stress that decisions are to be made on the lowest level possible. However, these changes to date exist more in theory than in practice. Relations still tend to be personalized and centralized, as many workers continue to take their problems directly to "the top."[17]

The foreign staff also has attempted to make employer-employee relations more impersonal and efficient by introducing policies to treat workers categorically rather than individually. As a result, whereas workers formerly were not limited in the amount of money they could borrow from the firm, they now can borrow no more than the equivalent of one month's salary. Furthermore, while the old patrón had *compadrazgo* relations with many workers, the Americans do not. Only the patrón's son who continues to work for the firm follows the tradition established by his father. He finds that those workers with whom he has compadrazgo relations are exceptionally cooperative and subservient, willing to work overtime and sympathetic to management in labor disputes. While the personalistic ties maintained by the former owner's son appear to conflict with the organizational blueprint and objectives of the Americans, in actual fact the son helps link the workers, accustomed to a paternalistic firm, with the new-styled management. In the process, he helps to reduce tensions within the factory.

The new managers' limited success in "modernizing" relations within the factory reflects their being compelled to adapt to the environment in which they operate, in order not to antagonize labor. However, once the management introduces new imported machinery and a new system of production, as they intend to do, more of the now-established customs are likely to be curtailed, for the customs will conflict with management's new economic interests. Because the Americans will want a more skilled and experienced work force than they presently have and can recruit from the provincial town, undoubtedly many workers will be fired and ties with the provincial town severed. However, at that point management will feel less compelled to appease their present work force.

THE DISTRIBUTIVE AND SERVICE SECTORS: LOCAL PETITE BOURGEOISIE

While the more recently settled areas included in this study contain few productive enterprises and none of any scale, all three areas contain commercial enterprises. This commerce does not represent the persistence of a pre-industrial economy but a form of adaptation to an industrializing economy which absorbs only a small proportion of the labor force.[18] Both the abundance of these non-productive (or low-productive) enterprises locally and the organization and control of the shops reveal once again how national economic forces impinge on the local communities. Because of the contrasting epochs in which each area was settled, commercial as well as productive opportunities in the old center city slum are better than in the two newer areas.

All three areas are dotted with stores, particularly small "mom and pop"-type operations. The most typical ones are small merchandise operations, such as pharmacies, bakeries, grocery and furniture shops and, above all, "misceláneas" —small grocery shops that offer a limited supply of canned and bottled goods, and pastas. The number and diversity of stores mainly reflect the capital and contacts shopkeepers have, and their lack of better alternative economic opportunities—not local demand for the goods marketed.

In addition, there are numerous repair shops, including ones for shoes, watches, bicycles, metalwork, electrical appliances and cars. In the center city area there also are a few businesses servicing buses, automobile generators and motors. At times service shops are combined with artisan operations or with small merchandising outfits, if the owners have the capital. For example, some cobblers both repair and make shoes, and some owners of stores selling handmade furniture are also cabinet makers. However, most goods sold locally are not produced locally.

Although approximately two-thirds of the shops in the areas are owned by residents, non-resident businessmen increasingly are taking advantage of local economic opportunities. Consequently, the largest stores, particularly in the two newer areas, are owned by non-residents, including immigrants and children of immigrants. Unlike most of the Mexican shopowners, the shopowners of immigrant background generally are involved in a variety of business ventures. One Spaniard owns three bakeries in the center city area and another bakery elsewhere in the city; another Spaniard with local bakeries owns a total of seventy in the capital; and a third Spaniard owns a real estate business in Acapulco in addition to a large dry cleaning establishment in the center city area. The economic success of these immigrants stems largely from social and economic advantages they enjoyed before they became involved in local businesses. Of higher class background than the average native shopowner, they had better access to schooling and capital with which to begin their stores. And because many of their parents were involved in commerce, they had gained considerable experience with commerce before opening their own businesses. Commenting on economic advantages enjoyed by the shopowners of immigrant origin, the owner of a small furniture shop in the squatter settlement noted that

> About half the furniture stores here are owned by foreigners—by Jews and Spaniards. . . . There's a lot of competition among us. The only way I get any business is by selling for less than the big stores. They began with more capital. They therefore can offer better deals and can pay lawyers if they have problems collecting money. I have a lawyer who helps me out a little, but it's difficult.

In contrast to the shops owned by children of immigrants and other non-residents, those owned by local inhabitants generally are small. They tend to be run by spouses with the occasional assistance of children or other relatives. The shopowners rely on kin because they feel kin can be trusted more and paid less than non-kin. Not only do the businesses generate few employment opportunities, particularly for non-kin, but they also tend not to be a likely source of livelihood for the average resident. Shopowners tend to have at least a primary school education. They also tend to be offspring of men who either were independently employed, as *comerciantes,* or enjoyed considerable autonomy in their work. However, only a few shopowners directly inherited their businesses from their fathers, and some of those who did actually considered it a mixed blessing. An owner of an auto repair shop, for example, complained that in inheriting the store he also inherited large debts.

The shopowners rarely pulled themselves up by their own "bootstraps." Only about one-third of the storeowners I interviewed financed their businesses themselves, and few of those who did used money they had saved over the years. Instead, they used money from land they had sold, indemnization they received when fired from previous jobs, or other one-time financial gains. Much more frequently, relatives—brothers, cousins, and uncles, more than parents—or former employers loaned them money and/or helped them get bank loans and merchandise on credit. Thus, a carpenter began his business with money that his brother borrowed from his employer, and the owner of a local stationery store established his own business with a loan from his former boss. Similarly, the daughter of a resident of the squatter settlement who owned a furniture store in another section of the city helped her father get merchandise on credit from her suppliers. With this merchandise he opened his own furniture store in the squatter settlement.

Although the shopowners typically are of higher class background than the average resident, this is least true in the center city area. Nonetheless, resident shopowners in the center city area reported greater economic success than resident shopowners in either of the other areas. The success of center city area shopowners seems to stem mainly from the greater capital they initially invested in their businesses, their prior experience in related businesses, and the better sales opportunities in the area, which has been a major center of commerce in Mexico City ever since a national economy began to take shape in the nineteenth century.

In the two newer areas and, to a lesser extent, in the center city area, shopkeepers do not constitute a solidly established class. Although a class of "petty" merchants has persisted over the years, individuals have entered into and dropped out of it with great frequency. As a result, most shopowners have had their present businesses for only a brief portion of their working lives—for an average of five years in the center city area, less than four years in the squatter settlement, and about two years in the housing development—and few of them have a history of entrepreneurial employment. The brevity of ownership partly reflects the fact that the businesses are highly unstable, offering no economic security. However, the short "life-span" of stores in the two newer areas is also partly a result of the proliferation of stores in these areas in recent years; as the population of the areas has expanded, residents' buying power has improved, and jobs in the other sectors of the economy have become more scarce. However, the high turnover rate of store ownership seems to stem mainly from extensive competition within the small-scale commercial segment of the economy. It also probably reflects the fact that the people being attracted to such businesses lack sufficient skills. As the following comments reveal, the relevant training shopowners reported having was largely indirect and informal:

cabinet maker:	I learned the trade from my father and from practice.
owner of a plumbing shop:	A friend of mine offered me a job in his shop. From him I learned to be a plumber.
owner of an auto mechanic shop:	I lived around auto mechanics since I was young. My father and relatives taught me how to do the work.
owner of a stationery store:	I'm acquiring experience little by little.
owner of an upholstery shop:	I once was an apprentice in a shop. Then I worked many years in shops, accumulating experience.

The little prior experience shopowners had gained was mainly in trade rather than entrepreneurial skills. They generally opened their own stores either because they wanted to be their "own boss," in order to avoid the degradation and lack of freedom they suffered when working for others, or because they were too old or ill to find other jobs.

Yet business failure often has been influenced by shopowners' own perceptions of their economic prospects. Most of them view their situation as being determined by forces beyond their control. Seeing restricted opportunities, they respond in ways which make their prophecies come true. Many of them see the demand for their goods and services as fixed and limited, not expandable and manipulable.[19] Accordingly, they view their prospects in terms of the ratio of local buyers to sellers, and the buying power of customers. Comments which reflect this view include the following:

owner of a beauty salon:	Business is the same as two years ago because I have the same number of customers and equal profits.
owner of a miscelánea:	Sales are the same as they were a couple of years ago. Before, there were fewer people and fewer misceláneas in the area. Now there are more people but there are also more misceláneas.
owner of a photography studio:	Business has been pretty good. I'm one of the few photographers in the area with a studio.
owner of a small furniture store:	Business has been bad. The large stores in the area monopolize the clients.
owner of a miscelánea and a bicycle repair shop:	There's too much competition here.

Other shopowners felt they could not improve their businesses because they lacked sufficient capital with which to purchase equipment and merchandise or hire personnel, or because they were victims of national economic trends and government policies. Thus, an auto mechanic and a plumber felt their businesses suffered because they had no money with which to buy expensive materials and pay workers; a pharmacist complained that his business was bad because he could not afford to stock his store well; and an owner of a bakery felt his business failed because he could not afford quality bread. Those who saw their problem as being linked to larger societal forces spoke of general industrial developments, changing consumer preferences, and specific government programs which discriminated against them:

metalworkers:	People now prefer buying plastic rather than metal goods. Consequently I have less business than formerly.
owner of a shop selling handmade furniture:	People no longer order handmade furniture. It's out of fashion.
barber:	I have fewer customers than in the past because fashions have changed. Men don't go as frequently to barbers as they used to.

shoe repairman:	The new government controls capital. Therefore, there is no work now. Before, people had money and I consequently had more work.
tortilla maker:	My profits are low because the government regulates the price of maize.
pharmacist:	Now people rarely come to pharmacies. They all go to Social Security and ISSSTE [another type of government health facility].

Since they rarely evaluated their businesses in terms of entrepreneurial dexterity or organization, they tended not to consider restructuring their operations in ways which might enhance their profits. They therefore did not collaborate with other resident shopowners to restrict non-residents from capitalizing on the local consumer market, to form credit unions so that they could secure low-interest loans, or to buy large quantities of merchandise stock at lower prices than they pay when buying individually in small amounts. Generally, those who realized that their businesses were poorly organized did not know precisely what skills they lacked. Because their perceptions reinforced social, economic and political forces which in fact inhibit their business prospects, individually and collectively they rarely exploited the limited existing opportunities.

CONCLUSION

Since the areas included in this study were non-randomly selected, and since the economic analysis is based on limited interview and observational data, the findings reported here are necessarily exploratory. Also, since most residents do not work within the area where they live, the constraints operating within their neighborhoods are not necessarily the only ones shaping residents' job opportunities. Nonetheless, the situation within the three areas suggests that the structure of the local economies has been significantly influenced by political-economic forces prevailing in the society at large, currently and historically. Residents' business opportunities are limited locally, largely through no fault of their own. Since residents with local businesses began the operations at their own initiative, their problem is not one of lack of entrepreneurial or achievement motivation or lack of creativity, as proponents of cultural explanations of underdevelopment lead one to believe (cf. McClelland, 1961; Hagen, 1962).[20] Yet their limited organizational dexterity prevents them from taking advantage of those opportunities which exist.

While expansion of urban consumer demand has made possible the expansion of local productive and distributive enterprises, this demand in itself does not account for the proliferation of local enterprises. Most local businesses are distributive rather than productive operations, largely because distributive businesses require less capital investment. Similarly, differences in business opportunities among the three lower class communities, particularly in productive enterprises, do not stem from differences in local demand. Rather, they derive mainly from the contrasting political-economic eras during which the areas were settled.

Residents suffer not so much from lack of local economic opportunities as from an inability to control access to those opportunities which do exist within the communities, particularly access to the most financially rewarding businesses. Locally owned businesses have been proliferating over the years, but because they are hyper-individuated, poorly organized, and poorly capitalized, they are highly unstable. Such factors do not impede the business prospects of non-residents who establish businesses locally.

The most lucrative businesses are owned by non-residents, mainly because they have better skills, contacts, access to capital, and a better understanding of the market situation, which gives them a competitive advantage over local residents. Concerned as the non-resident entrepreneurs are with maximizing their personal profits, they have not taken a special interest in developing the local economies or in providing employment for local residents. To the extent that the employers want docile and inexpensive labor, they deliberately have hired migrants over city born workers. Such a labor strategy discriminates against center city dwellers, who are overwhelmingly native-born, yet the center city area is the only area with productive enterprises of any size.

Kinship ties are utilized by businessmen to gain control both over individual productive and distributive enterprises and over the market situation. Use of such ties is neither irrational nor a cultural residue from Mexico's pre-industrial past. Given the scarcity of socially and economically rewarding jobs, residents of the three areas have used non-economic means to serve their economic interests.

In contrast, economic relations among non-kin tend to link people of unequal status through a series of exchange relations. The owners and/or managers of the businesses assume non-contractual responsibilities for their workers, not merely because it is customary to do so but because it appears to make good business sense to them. They pay workers low wages, but supplement the income with other social and economic benefits, including job training. Workers consequently are indebted to and dependent on their employers, as long as they remain employed by them. Thus within most enterprises the interests of the people of lower rank are linked to those of higher rank; they are not entirely antagonistic. However, the very favors which employers extend to workers may, with time, work against employers' interests, for employees may use the on-the-job training they acquire, the entrepreneurial skills they observe, and the money they borrow to start their own businesses—businesses which may actually compete with those of their former bosses.

Because the small locally-owned businesses absorb labor and help circulate money to people with little or no alternative sources of income, they serve certain economic and, ultimately, political "functions," not merely for local residents but for the government and those with a vested interest in the status quo. Although highly unstable, these operations at least temporarily increase consumer demand while reducing unemployment and the potential for civil strife which long-term unemployment might precipitate.

NOTES

1. The literature on Latin American urban communities also suggests that settlement in squatter areas or shantytowns correlates with socioeconomic status (Flinn, 1968) and "consolidation" of socioeconomic status (Turner, 1968), independently of whether residents work where they live.

2. This article focuses only on legitimate enterprises not directly controlled and regulated by the government. It therefore excludes a discussion of economic conditions in the local government-administered markets, schools and public service institutions, and illicit activities.

3. The study excludes presently non-legalized squatter settlements, tenant-occupied housing projects, government-organized squatter settlements, and low-income subdivisions created by commercial land developers. On these types of settlements see Portes (1971) and Cornelius (1975).

4. Since small businesses which people operate in their homes are not always visible from the streets, the census necessarily only approximates the total number of locally operating enterprises. Due to this sampling problem, the survey findings should be viewed as exploratory.

5. Although I argue that the inner-city slum does not represent a "stage" that the two newer areas will replicate with time, the economies of the areas are not static. In particular, the number of shops in the two newer areas has increased over the years as the income level of residents has risen and jobs in other sectors of the economy have contracted. The improved level of well-being of residents mainly appears to reflect the fact that recent arrivals to the two areas are of higher class standing than their predecessors, although it also reflects the fact that long-term residents have improved their level of living somewhat.

6. For a detailed discussion of artisan and industrial shoe production in Mexico, see Galindo Muñez (1969). Approximately half the shoes produced in Mexico are made in small craft shops (Galindo Muñez, 1969: 76).

7. The literature on the economies of Latin American cities emphasizes the expansion of the service (tertiary) sector and, to a lesser extent, the industrial sector with urbanization—not craft production.

8. According to a local priest who works closely with local cobblers, shoe artisans are migrating to Mexico City partly because they find it increasingly difficult to compete with the shoe factories in the provinces.

9. The distinction between productive and distributive types of employment used here is an analytically, not empirically, derived distinction. Thus, the same individuals may be involved in both productive and distributive activities.

10. The case of these shoe artisans demonstrates that developments within the "primary" labor market are closely related to developments within the "secondary" labor market, and that specific government policies affect both the distribution of labor and the benefits which labor employed in each sector receives. It also demonstrates that the government to date has not been a mere tool of large manufacturers; if it were, it would enforce Social Security and minimum labor legislation in the artisan sector so as to drive the

small, inefficient producers out of the market. On the notion of "primary" and "secondary" labor markets, see Piore (1971: 90-94). According to Piore, the "primary" market offers jobs which provide high wages, good working conditions, employment stability and job security, equality and due process in the administration of work rules, and chances for advancement. In contrast, the "secondary" labor market involves jobs which offer low wages, poor working conditions, variability in employment, harsh and often arbitrary discipline, and little opportunity to advance.

11. Derossi (1972) in her study of 322 Mexican firms found that even three generations back, few managers were of worker or peasant background. Similarly, Vernon (1963: 157) found that Mexican business executives were not typically a rags-to-riches group.

12. On "particularism" as a distinctively Latin American cultural trait impeding economic development, see Gillin (1966) and Parsons (1951: 198-200).

13. Typically, Latin American enterprises represent an extension of the family system, not a break with it (Davis, 1972a: 60; Derossi, 1972). According to Derossi, family-owned or controlled businesses in Mexico are most prevalent among small firms and firms in traditional manufacturing activities.

14. Wilson's (1969) study of Mexican factories also shows that workers from particular provincial communities tend to concentrate in particular industries in the capital. If tensions are likely to develop among workers from different regions (and, often, from different ethnic groups indigenous to particular regions), it is expedient for management to hire workers of similar community origin—unless regional or ethnic conflicts help to prevent the work force from organizing in opposition to management. In the United States historically, manufacturers at times deliberately hired from different ethnic groups to keep the workers divided (Higham, 1969: 115); and during periods of labor unrest the capitalists hired spies and rumormongers to stir up antagonisms between ethnic groups, especially when such groups had little command of English (Brecker, 1972; Brody, 1960).

15. According to the plant manager, 99 percent of the personnel owed money to the company in 1965. The average amount borrowed was $80.00 (Davis, 1967).

16. While the changeover in ownership reflects a transition from family to corporate capitalism which also occurred in the United States historically, in the United States ownership remained in the hands of nationals whereas in Mexico and most other Latin American countries corporate industrial ownership increasingly has become "denationalized" since World War II.

17. Studies of Latin American firms typically stress the "particularistic" and hierarchical nature of employer-employee relations and the unique way each worker is treated by management. In contrast, studies of U.S. firms emphasize that workers are group-oriented and that all workers of a given rank are treated similarly by management. The different patterns are attributed to general cultural differences between the United States and Latin America. Examples of this interpretation include Williams et al. (1972) and Davis (1972a: 57).

18. The situation within the three areas suggests a development contrary to one predicted by Marx. According to him, the *petite bourgeoisie* would decline as industrialization advanced because they would be increasingly unable to compete with large-scale capitalists (Marx and Engels, 1959). Although the situation within the three areas suggests that few petite bourgeoisie are able to convert their businesses into progressively profit-generating enterprises, there is no evidence that the petite bourgeoisie are disappearing as a class. They are not disappearing because this class is absorbing many people who cannot get jobs in other sectors of the economy. It is probably more accurate to speak of cities such as Mexico City as being "petite bourgeoisified" rather than proletarianized, at the same time that industry and the interests of large-scale capitalists are expanding. The government is encouraging such "petite bourgeoisification" through maintenance and regulation of the market system and through such urban land distribution schemes as

legalization of squatter settlements and government subsidized housing developments. Land ownership is not identical to ownership of the means of production, although by renting out rooms and establishing shops in houses, land is used to generate income.

19. Foster (1967) has used the term "limited good" to characterize a similar attitude among peasants. According to him, peasants view their total environment as one in which all the desired things in life exist in finite quantity and in short supply. They feel that they connot increase the currently available amount of "good things." Actually, Foster seems to exaggerate the universality of the "limited good" orientation in peasant societies, for he associates fatalism with this orientation. However, "voluntary" peasant migration to cities suggests that not all peasants are fatalistic. Most peasants migrate because they feel their opportunities will be better in their place of destination than in their community of origin.

20. Hagen (1962) argues that one of the main impediments to economic growth in "underdeveloped" countries is the "uncreative" personality complex which predominates in such countries. According to him, people with such personality types have a low need for achievement and a low need for autonomy, and believe that the world consists of arbitrary forces. While I did not learn whether shopowners in the three areas lack a psychological "need to be independent," many of them clearly indicated a *desire* to be independent. Furthermore, since the shopowners did not attribute their business success or failure to "arbitrary forces," Hagen's explanation is unsatisfactory.

REFERENCES

BRECKER, J. (1972) Strike! San Francisco: Straight Arrow Books.

BRODY, D. (1960) Steelworkers in America: The Non-Union Era. Cambridge: Harvard University Press.

CORNELIUS, W. A. (1975) Politics and the Migrant Poor in Mexico City. Stanford, Calif.: Stanford University Press.

--- (1971) "The political sociology of cityward migration in Latin America: toward empirical theory," pp. 95-147 in F. F. Rabinovitz and F. M. Trueblood (eds.) Latin American Urban Research, Vol. 1. Beverly Hills, Calif.: Sage Publications.

DAVIS, S. (1972a) "United States vs. Latin America: business and culture," pp. 57-62 in S. Davis and L. Goodman (eds.) Workers and Managers in Latin America. Lexington, Mass.: Heath.

--- (1972b) "Authority and control in Mexican enterprise," pp. 300-305 in S. Davis and L. Goodman (eds.) Workers and Managers in Latin America. Lexington, Mass.: Heath.

--- (1967) "Social change in Mexican enterprise." Unpublished manuscript. Harvard Graduate School of Business Administration.

DEROSSI, F. (1972) "Familism in industry," pp. 75-84 in S. Davis and L. Goodman (eds.) Workers and Managers in Latin America. Lexington, Mass.: Heath.

FLINN, W. (1968) "The process of migration to a shantytown in Bogotá." Inter-American Economic Affairs 22, 2: 77-88.

FOSTER, G. (1967) "Peasant society and the image of the limited good," pp. 300-323 in J. Potter, M. Diaz and G. Foster (eds.) Peasant Society: A Reader. Boston: Little, Brown.

GALINDO MUNEZ, A. (1969) Desarrollo e integración de la industria del calzado en México. Thesis for Licenciado en Economía. Universidad Nacional Autónoma de México, México, D.F.

GERMANI, G. (1967) "The city as an integrating mechanism: the concept of social integration," pp. 175-189 in G. Beyer (ed.) The Urban Explosion in Latin America. Ithaca, N.Y.: Cornell University Press.

GILLIN, J. (1966) "The middle segments and their values," pp. 23-40 in R. Tomasek (ed.) Latin American Politics. Garden City, N.Y.: Doubleday.

GOLDRICH, D., R. B. PRATT, and C. R. SCHULLER (1967-1968) "The political integration of lower-class urban settlements in Chile and Peru." Studies in Comparative International Development 3, 1: 1-22.

HAGEN, E. (1962) On the Theory of Social Change: How Economic Growth Begins. Homewood, Ill.: Dorsey Press.

HIGHAM, J. (1969) Strangers in the Land: Patterns of American Nativism,1860-1925. New York: Atheneum.

MANGIN, W. (1967) "Latin American squatter settlements: a problem and a solution." Latin American Research Review 2, 3: 65-98.

MARX, K. and F. ENGELS (1959) "Manifesto of the Communist Party," pp. 1-41 in L. Feuer (ed.) Marx & Engels: Basic Writings on Politics and Philosophy. Garden City, N.Y.: Doubleday.

McCLELLAND, D. (1961) The Achieving Society. New York: Van Nostrand.

PARSONS, T. (1951) The Social System. New York: Free Press.

PATCH, R. (1968) "La Parada, Lima's market–part III: *serrano* to *criollo,* a study of assimilation," pp. 207-223 in American Universities Field Staff Associates, City and Nation in the Developing World (AUFS Readings, Vol. II). New York: American Universities Field Staff.

PIORE, M. (1971) "The dual labor market: theory and implications," pp. 90-94 in D. Gordon (ed.) Problems in Political Economy: An Urban Perspective. Lexington, Mass.: Heath.

PORTES, A. (1971) "The urban slum in Chile: types and correlates." Land Economics 47, 3 (August): 235-248.

ROGLER, L. (1967) "Slum neighborhoods in Latin America." Journal of Inter-American Studies 9, 4: 507-528.

STOKES, C. (1962) "A theory of slums." Land Economics 38, 3: 187-197.

TURNER, J. (1968) "Housing priorities, settlement patterns, and urban development in modernizing countries." Journal of the American Institute of Planners 34, 6 (November): 354-363.

VERNON, R. (1963) The Dilemma of Mexico's Development. Cambridge, Mass.: Harvard University Press.

WILLIAMS, L., W. WHYTE, and C. GREEN (1972) "Do cultural differences affect workers' attitudes? " pp. 17-24 in S. Davis and L. Goodman (eds.) Workers and Managers in Latin America. Lexington, Mass.: Heath.

WILSON, C. (1969) "Social organization of Mexican factories." Ph.D. dissertation. Columbia University.

CLARK W. REYNOLDS (Ph.D., University of California, Berkeley) is a Professor of Economics in the Food Research Institute at Stanford University. He has done field research in Chile, Mexico, Colombia, Brazil, Peru, Costa Rica, and Jamaica, and currently directs the Organization of American States' Capital Markets Program Flow of Funds Project. His current research deals with the impact of financial sector development on the pattern of production, accumulation and wealth distribution in developing countries. His publications include *The Mexican Economy: Twentieth Century Structure and Growth* (Yale University Press, 1970) and, with Marcos Mamalakis, *Essays on the Chilean Economy* (1965).

ROBERT T. CARPENTER is a doctoral candidate and research assistant in the Food Research Institute at Stanford University. He is currently affiliated with the Instituto Brasileiro de Mercados de Capitais (IBMEC), and is engaged in a study of flow of funds in the Brazilian Housing Finance System.

Chapter 6

HOUSING FINANCE IN BRAZIL: TOWARDS A NEW DISTRIBUTION OF WEALTH

CLARK W. REYNOLDS and ROBERT T. CARPENTER

This paper examines the performance of Brazil's Housing Finance System (SFH) since the mid-sixties as it has affected the distribution of wealth. Many of the phenomena commonly associated with urbanization in Latin America, such as rural-urban migration, explosive urban population growth, rapid expansion of urban infrastructure, and real estate speculation, help give rise to transfers of wealth in the form of both real and financial assets between different groups in the population. Quite often such transfers bring about an increased concentration of wealth. We will be examining the flow of funds through the Housing Finance System in order to determine what impact the resulting asset transfers have had on patterns of wealth distribution.[1]

A principal assumption of the study is that financial intermediation may be used to combine voluntary and contractual savings with partially-subsidized lending in order to effect shifts in the pattern of real asset ownership without major distortions in allocative efficiency. This approach is a recognition of the quasi-fiscal role of financial intermediation policy as it operates in many developing countries. For the purposes of the present volume we shall focus on the implications of our findings for strategies to alleviate the massive low-cost

Authors' Note: We wish to express our appreciation to the Capital Markets Program of the Organization of American States for financing a portion of the research; to the Instituto Brasileiro de Mercados de Capitais (IBMEC) for permitting research in residence during the period June-September, 1974; to students of the senior author's course on Analysis of the Flow of Funds and Financial Development in Latin America at IBMEC, August, 1974, for helpful criticisms and comments; and to the Food Research Institute of Stanford University for continuing support.

housing deficit that confronts urban Latin America. The Brazilian approach to public housing is basically a variation of earlier and, for the most part, less successful strategies employed elsewhere in Latin America. The scarcity of resources for public investment in developing economies means that wholly-subsidized housing is out of the question. Instead, several Latin American countries, particularly Peru, Chile, and Venezuela, have found it necessary to devise systems for capturing savings that can then be used to complement government subsidies (Elliot, 1966).

In the Brazilian case there is no outright subsidization. Most of the system's resources are captured in two ways: savings and loan passbook accounts, and an employee guarantee fund financed through payroll deductions. We consider both of these sources of funds to derive basically from the working class, an assumption not yet subject to statistical verification. In addition, some entities within the system capture funds by issuing bonds which, by being priced beyond the means of the working class, may be assumed to draw funds from upper income groups. With respect to the effect of the source of funds on the distribution of wealth, our aim will be to establish the relative degree to which different income groups are actually financing public housing in Brazil through the devices listed here. Of course, a proper assessment of the situation's welfare implications must take into account the return to the holders of these particular financial assets, in the form of interest and monetary correction for inflation.

Having identified those income groups which are the most important suppliers of funds to the Housing Finance System, we will move on to a more difficult aspect of the wealth transfer problem: namely, which groups are being afforded asset subsidies through the SFH's disbursements? Much of the imprecision in the identification of disbursement beneficiaries stems from top administrators' perception of housing not as a discrete problem but as one facet of an integrated set of urban problems. Consequently, funds are being allocated increasingly to community infrastructure projects in which housing units are included. This type of investment does not facilitate the pinpointing of those income groups which benefit most from its execution. As for the financial operations that can more easily be classified by income level, namely the financing of housing units themselves, there are two principal considerations which bear on patterns of wealth distribution. One is the scale of interest rates on Housing Finance System mortgages, which varies positively with income level. While the application of monetary correction is intended to avert the incidence of negative real interest rates which have been so prevalent in long-term financial operations in inflation-plagued Latin American economies in recent decades, the lowest-income SFH mortgagors nonetheless can be seen to enjoy an effective subsidy at the expense of those paying the higher interest rates.

The possibility of there being some element of subsidy even in the higher rates will require comparison with prevailing interest rates in the regular mortgage market. The use of the interest rate structure to create partial subsidies for low-income families complicates any assessment of the distribution of SFH-financed housing by income bracket. There is some validity in the argument of Brazilian public housing officials that the viability of the differential interest rates hinges on maintaining an adequate volume of high-interest mortgages to reasonably prosperous families. Data we have obtained to date indicate that the proportion of funds going into these mortgages has greatly increased in recent years.

The key question, taking into consideration our findings as to which groups are providing the funds for SFH operations, is to determine that proportion of high-interest to total mortgages required for effective and equitable functioning of the system. One may then determine whether that level has been exceeded.

This study is partial-analytical, in that housing finance, despite its increasing importance in total financial intermediation in Brazil especially as regards the mobilization of voluntary and contractual savings for investment, is treated independently of the general financial development process. Hence the fact that housing finance appears to have distorted the investment process toward urban residential (and other urban) construction is underplayed here. (A similar case is that of Colombia, where specialized financial instruments with monetary correction [UPACs] distorted financial flows toward an excessively large share of investment in urban housing, with major consequences for the distribution of wealth among income groups, rural and urban employment, and growth of the capital stock [Hanson, 1974].) Nor is it possible to go as far as desired in measuring the incidence of the program by income group, due to lack of data. However work is continuing by the authors on the welfare consequences of Brazilian housing finance and on the development impact of the structure and growth of financial intermediation in Brazil.

RECENT HISTORICAL BACKGROUND

Brazil's Housing Finance System came into being with the founding of the National Housing Bank, or BNH (Banco Nacional da Habitação) in August, 1964, shortly after the ouster of president João Goulart. This new program was conceived as part of a general overhaul of the financial system of which the architects included ministers of Finance and Planning, Octavio Bulhões and Roberto Campos respectively. Successive military regimes during the past decade have stressed the remodeling and expansion of the financial system as a core element in Brazilian economic development strategy, and a prominent role has been reserved for the Housing Bank throughout. This high priority is shown by the range and diversity of activities that the government has allowed to cluster under the BNH's financial and administrative umbrella. From its origins as an institution primarily responsible for tackling the ubiquitous low-cost housing problem, the BNH has evolved into a super-agency unparalleled in Latin America. Its concerns cover a full spectrum of urban affairs: sewage and water networks, mass transit, real estate markets, community facilities, the construction industry, building materials supply, and job-training. This broadening of the Housing Bank's purview has been based partially on a surplus of loanable funds for strictly housing purposes, and partially on a perception of the interrelationships among the many dimensions of the urban environment. The operational linkages established have, however, been of a predominantly financial nature. It would appear that the prime rationale of Brazilian urban policy, as embodied in the programs of the National Housing Bank, is to use it as a means of capturing funds to be used, if not to harness the dynamism of the urbanization process, at least to exploit its momentum to stimulate more planned economic growth. Also, the broad scope of the Bank's financial operations provides considerable leverage in influencing the way in which the fruits of that growth are distributed.

It is against this backdrop that we propose to examine the component of BNH operations encompassed by the Housing Finance System. The fact that this system claims to have financed more than a million dwelling units in the first 10 years of its existence—compared to a total of 120,000 units financed in Brazil in the previous 25 years (BNH, APC, 1974: 19)—points to a dramatic shift in the pattern of resource allocation. Our focus on the flow of funds through the Housing Finance System will show how that reallocation has been reflected in the pattern of financial assets and liabilities.

TAPPING POTENTIAL SAVINGS: SOURCES OF FUNDS

The key to understanding the effect of the Housing Finance System on asset holdings lies in the indexing mechanism imposed on many aspects of the financial system by the government in 1965 and staunchly defended against growing opposition since then. "Monetary correction," as it is called, entails periodic adjustments of the nominal values of financial assets and liabilities to correct for inflation. The corrective coefficient is based on changes in the wholesale price index. In the Housing Finance System, monetary correction is implemented through revaluation of a so-called *standard capital unit,* or UPC (Unidade Padrão de Capital), in terms of which all transactions within the system are expressed. The value of the UPC is adjusted quarterly in accordance with the monthly revaluations of indexed bonds issued by the Federal Treasury (see the discussion of monetary correction as applied in the Housing Finance System in Chacel et al., 1970: 123-132).

Of the numerous distortions wrought by the severe inflation that beset Brazil in the early 1960s, one that was of particular concern to Goulart's military successors was the drying up of investment in the housing market because of rent and interest rate ceilings, discouraging respectively both the demand for investment on rental housing and the supply of long-term funds for building construction. By applying monetary correction to the Housing Finance System, the government sought to stimulate housing-related investment. Since correction was also applied in other areas of the capital market, this was not expected to unduly divert funds. An essential element in this strategy was the introduction of new financial instruments to capture the resources necessary for the system's operations.

Seniority Security Fund

While still in its infancy, the National Housing Bank found that its operational needs were not being met from the funds provided in the original legislation: an initial budgetary allocation of 1 million cruzeiros, a 1 percent share of the salaries of all workers subject to the existing labor indemnification laws, and a 4 percent levy on all rent receipts (in return for which landlords received housing bonds redeemable after 20 years). In its approach to resolving the Housing Bank's difficulties, the government saw an opportunity to simultaneously correct perceived failings in the labor indemnification legislation then in effect and generate funds for the new program. The result was the creation, in September, 1966, of the Seniority Security Fund, or FGTS (Fundo de Garantía do Tempo de Serviço). For those workers eligible and opting for coverage by the Fund, employers were to deposit in a personalized FGTS bank account an amount equalling 8 percent of the previous month's wages. For eligible workers who did not chose FGTS coverage the 8 percent deposits were to be held in a common FGTS account, so that if desired the option could be exercised in the future.

With few exceptions these deposits earn 3 percent annual interest plus monetary correction as stipulated by law 5107 of September 13, 1966 (BNH, CGFGTS, 1974b: 6-7).[2] They may be withdrawn for a variety of reasons including retirement, dismissal, termination of a temporary contract, serious personal or family illness, initial investment in an enterprise, or acquisition of a residence through the Housing Finance System (spelled out in detail in BNH, CGFGTS, 1974a: 36-51).

What has been the significance of the Seniority Security Fund, which represents the government's recourse to a single contractual savings scheme for the pursuit of varied policy objectives? By far the majority of eligible urban workers have chosen FGTS coverage, offering as it does a better cushion against inflation than the alternative indemnification guarantee. Data available in the FGTS administrative center show that the accounts have been quite active, with withdrawals in the neighborhood of 35 to 45 percent of gross receipts on a quarterly basis since 1970. Withdrawals have predominantly been occasioned by retirement, unemployment, or illness. As yet, withdrawals associated with investment (i.e., acquiring housing or setting up independent business ventures) have been negligible.

Still, the primary importance of the FGTS for resource allocation lies in its capacity to place funds at the disposal of the National Housing Bank. Despite the appreciable withdrawal rate, the steady expansion of the urban work force has enabled the Fund to sustain a healthy rate of growth, as evidenced in Table 1. Independent research by the authors has revealed that in 1972, the most recent year for which national accounts data are available, the net increase in FGTS resources equalled fully 1 percent of GDP. Moreover, with a balance of 12.9 billion cruzeiros at the close of 1973, the Security Fund accounted for 9.3 percent of all non-monetary financial assets in the economy (5.5 percent when monetary assests are included).

Unfortunately, one key question regarding the FGTS remains unanswered for the time being, namely: what is the relative participation of different income groups in filling the Fund's coffers? Not only is this important in determining which groups are and will be receiving social security benefits from the Fund, but also in verifying the socioeconomic origins of resources that have long been the mainstay of the Housing Finance System (see the representational diagram in Figure 1). While employers and the self-employed are automatically excluded from FGTS coverage, along with civil service employees and those in miscellaneous other job classifications, the mass of the urban labor force that does have FGTS accounts encompasses a wage scale too broad to justify arbitrary weighting of the population's composition by income level.[3] Therefore, the income profile of FGTS contributors must remain unclear.

TABLE 1

EVOLUTION OF FINANCIAL SAVINGS IN THE HOUSING FINANCE SYSTEM (net annual increases in Cr$ millions)

Years	*A. Savings Deposits*	*B. Housing Bonds*	*C. FGTS*	*D. Total*	*(A + B)/C*
1966	18	6	–	24	–
1967	66	134	570	770	35.1
1968	244	320	993	1,557	56.8
1969	563	488	1,244	2,295	84.5
1970	1,188	774	1,529	3,491	128.3
1971	1,680	1,094	2,016	4,790	137.6
1972	3,952	1,908	2,843	8,703	206.1
1973	6,409	1,490	3,942	11,841	200.4
1974 (Jan./June)	4,199	487	2,621	7,307	381.5
Cumulative balance	18,319	6,701	15,758	40,778	158.8

SOURCES: Savings deposit and housing bond data from Boletim do Banco Central do Brasil, 10, 8 (August, 1974). FGTS figures acquired from Departamento da Receita, Banco Nacional da Habitação.

Voluntary Savings

As impressive as the growth of the Seniority Security Fund has been, it has been outstripped by the performance of the Housing Finance System's instruments for capturing voluntary savings, as reflected in the ratios shown in the right-hand column of Table 1. This is especially true in the case of the savings passbook accounts in the federal and state savings banks, savings and loan associations, and real estate credit companies, which together comprise the Brazilian Savings and Loan Association, or SBPE. Passbook balances have been growing faster than those of any other financial asset in the market. From 1.9 percent of total financial assets at the end of 1970, passbooks were able to increase their share to 6.1 percent by the end of 1973, comprising 10.2 percent of non-monetary financial assets. In conjunction with the FGTS and housing bonds issued by the real estate credit companies, this caused the liabilities of the Housing Finance System to represent a large and growing share of total sources of funds in Brazil as enumerated by the Central Bank. Thus by the end of 1973 the system's financial liabilities represented 14 percent of total financial assets in Brazil and 24 percent of total non-monetary financial assets (Boletim do Banco Central do Brasil, various issues; Contador, 1974: 105). This serves to demonstrate in part the formidable financial impact of the government's policy initiatives in the urban development sphere.

It should be realized that these voluntary savings instruments bear a significance for the Housing Finance System quite distinct from that of the Seniority Security Fund. One principal difference lies in the socioeconomic strata from which the savings are drawn. The most clear-cut case is that of the housing bonds. These bonds are sophisticated financial instruments, of which there are several types distinguished by maturity and the schedule used for determining monetary correction and interest, which is presently 6 percent for all.[4] Given the minimum denominations of 1,000 cruzeiros or 20 UPC's (equal to 1,489 cruzeiros at the average UPC value in 1973), housing bonds are beyond the financial means of the urban masses earning less than three minimum monthly salaries (see later discussion of urban income distribution).

There is more of an identity between the holders of savings passbooks and owners of FGTS accounts than is the case between housing bonds and the Security Fund. At the end of 1973 the number of passbook accounts had risen to nearly 4.8 million, while official estimates placed the total of active FGTS accounts between 7 and 8 million, with some incidence of multiple accounts in the name of the same depositors in both cases. There are strong indications that the gap between the two account totals is found principally among low-income wage earners, although this must remain a tentative conclusion in the absence of more evidence regarding the composition of the two depositor populations.

Certainly, thrift institutions have looked upon the field of potential savers in Brazil as almost virgin territory offering attractive opportunities for expansion.

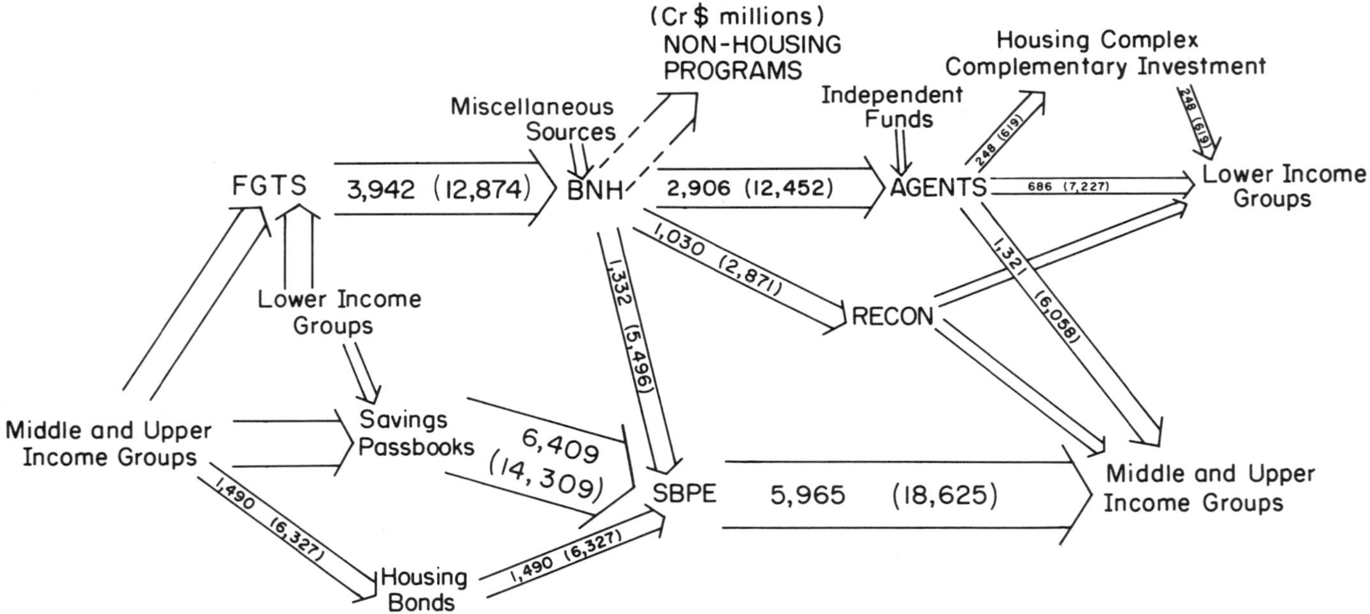

NOTE: Figures in parentheses give cumulative balances.

SOURCES: Tables I and III; BNH, Boletim Mensal, IV, no. 48 (1973): 6; Boletim do Banco Central do Brazil, X, no. 4 (April 1974): 22, 24.

Figure 1: FLOW OF FUNDS IN THE HOUSING FINANCE SYSTEM–1973

The 1970s have seen an aggressive publicity campaign carried out by savings and loan associations and real estate credit companies both individually and collectively in major Brazilian cities, in an effort to persuade people of modest incomes to open savings passbook accounts.[5] The campaign has received ample logistical support through the proliferation of branches of these two institutions, particularly in blue-collar urban neighborhoods, contrasting sharply with the non-expansionary policies of other financial institutions such as commercial banks and finance companies during the same period (BNH, SAF, 1974: 39).

While the advertising effort had a hand in the mounting influx of funds depicted in Table 1, not to mention the burgeoning ranks of depositors, which expanded at an average annual rate of 53 percent between 1970 and 1974, its success at bringing small savers into the system cannot be gauged by reference to the available data of fluctuations in average account balances over time. The average balance for the SBPE as a whole rose steadily from 1970 on, as did the average in the savings banks, which were not as active in seeking out new depositors as were the other two institutions. After seeing their average passbook balances decline in 1971 in the face of a stock market boom, both savings and loan institutions and real estate credit companies experienced rising average balances in the following two years. Even though the average savings bank passbook balance was still twice the size of the average real estate credit company balance at the end of 1973, the absolute increases in the two averages during that year were virtually equal (data in this paragraph derived from tables in BNH, SAF, 1974: 36, 70).

The determination of whether the rising account balances were basically attributable to higher incomes of new savers or merely to the accumulation of savings on the part of old ones, requires data more disaggregated than that presently available. The Brazilian government is doing its part to attract higher-income savers to passbook accounts. When the income tax deductions allowed for various types of investments were revised in mid-1974, SBPE accounts were accorded more favorable treatment than any other financial asset outside the stock market. While the legislation specified a limit on the average account balance for which the more advantageous deduction was applicable, the ceiling was set sufficiently high at 400 UPCs[6] (Jornal do Brasil, Rio de Janeiro, July 24, 1974: 21) that future deposits attracted by the tax advantage should boost average deposit balances even higher than they have already risen.[7]

Should savings passbooks follow the predicted pattern in response to the selective fiscal incentive, then we can expect a progressive divergence between the proportions represented by different income strata among FGTS contributors and among SBPE savers. This is noteworthy, not only because of its implications for future liquidity prospects for each institution in relation to changes in Brazilian income distribution, but also because the resources entering the Housing Finance System through different channels tend to end up being applied via separate conduits as well, as schematized in Figure 1. The distributional ramifications of the process will be dealt with in the treatment of the housing loans made by the system.

CHANNELING THE FLOWS: USE OF FUNDS

Having examined the origins of the funds being fed into the Housing Finance System, we now shift our attention to the destinations of those resources. Before beginning the discussion of the applications of funds in the form of housing loans, there is another conspicuous use of funds by the Housing Bank which deserves mention since it bears on our concern for changes in the patterns of asset holdings in the economy. An examination of the National Housing Bank's running balance sheet (which appears in the Central Bank's monthly bulletin) discloses a marked increase in the agency's holdings of indexed Treasury bonds during 1972. In relation to total BNH assets, the bonds' share rose from 13 percent at the end of 1971 to almost 20 percent a year later. During the same timespan, the increase in these holdings as a share of total financing extended by the BNH to its agents was even greater, going from 16 to 25 percent. Both proportions had declined slightly by the end of 1973, but the Housing Bank had already become the largest holder of Treasury bonds in the economy with its 23 percent share at the close of 1972 (Boletim do Banco Central do Brasil, April, 1974: 20-21).

The propriety of such a large proportion of Housing Bank resources being placed in government bonds rather than being used to finance residential mortgages would appear questionable at first glance. In effect the holders of FGTS accounts, the Bank's primary source of funds, are involuntarily financing the bond purchases. However, a satisfactory explanation for this type of investment was provided by an official of the Bank's Office of Planning and Coordination (responsible for preparing the BNH's budgets), in response to the authors' questioning. He claimed that the purchases of Treasury bonds were scheduled in accordance with future projections of Housing Bank revenues and expenditures, so that the return on government securities could be utilized to offset predicted deficits. This would, therefore, give the BNH more latitude in programming its credit operations in the urban domain.

Figure 1 helps illustrate the National Housing Bank's financial role within the Housing Finance System, which is basically that of a second-line bank, allocating funds to the various other intermediaries, which in turn make the actual housing loans. In this manner a large share of the Security Fund's resources, derived in part from the middle-and-upper-income groups, is channeled back to the same groups through the SBPE, while a smaller share also reaches them via other means. The bulk of the remainder passes through the intermediaries in the "Agents" category to the lower income classes.

The arbitrary boundary adopted for separating the "Lower-income Groups" from the "Middle-and-Upper-income Groups" is the maximum income in the target population of the Low-income Housing Finance System, or SIFHAP, which represents a family income of no more than three minimum monthly salaries.[8] Reference to Carlos Langoni's analysis of the 1970 census results reveals how preponderant the lower socioeconomic strata are in Brazilian cities. Minimum salaries at the time that the census was conducted ranged from 144 cruzeiros in the Northeast to 187 in the more prosperous Center-South (Conjuntura Econômica Supplement, December, 1973: 99), for a rough weighted average of 165-170 cruzeiros. Projecting this figure onto Langoni's profile of urban income distribution in 1970 presented in Table 2, we find that approximately 40 percent of the population was not even earning one minimum salary, and close to 80 percent was earning less than three. True, Table 2 is dealing with the distribution of individual rather than family income. But Langoni's comparison of personal and family income distributions for Brazil as a whole shows the relative shares of each decile to be essentially the same in both cases. There is no discrepancy larger than a single percentage point in the lower seven deciles, and for no decile does the variation exceed two points (Langoni, 1973: Tabela 1.1, 26). The Housing Bank's own estimates indicate that 20 percent of urban families earn less than one minimum salary and another 45 percent earning between one and three minimum salaries (BNH, APC, 1974: 99; Conjuntura Econômica, March, 1974: 75).

An item in Figure 1 that will not receive extensive treatment here is RECON, a subprogram for financing construction materials to individuals, used by families of modest income to build their own homes, as well as by families of more comfortable means for remodeling purposes. Available data provide no breakdown on the use of RECON loans. Yet is is worth noting in Table 3 that RECON has had the most impact of the three categories in inducing investment

TABLE 2
URBAN PERSONAL INCOME DISTRIBUTION IN BRAZIL, 1970

Percentile	*% of Total Income*	*Average Monthly Income (cruzeiros, 1970)*
10–	0.98	37
10	2.23	84
10	3.39	128
10	4.20	159
10	5.12	193
10	6.15	232
10	7.51	283
10	10.54	398
10	15.21	574
10+	44.67	1,688

SOURCE: Reproduced from Langoni (1973: Tabela 3.8, 70); based on 1970 Demographic Census, Instituto Brasileiro de Geografía e Estatística.

TABLE 3
HOUSING LOAN BREAKDOWN BY PROGRAM (Cr$ 000s)[a]

	BNH Funds	*Intermediary Supplement*[b]	*Other Sources*[c]	*Total Housing Investment*	*No. Units (000s)*
1971 Agents[d]	1,385	103	231	1,719	72
SBPE	553	454	425	1,432	26
RECON	362	–	881	1,242	18
Total	2,300	557	1,537	4,394	115
1972 Agents[d]	2,323	–27	280	2,576	66
SBPE	1,192	2,678	487	4,357	50
RECON	663	–	1,837	2,500	20
Total	4,178	2,651	2,604	9,433	136
1973 Agents[d]	2,906	–819	405	2,492	44
SBPE	1,392	4,573	2,197	8,162	157
RECON	1,030	–	2,565	3,595	21
Total	5,328	3,754	5,167	14,249	222
1974 (Jan./June)					
Agents[d]	1,269	61	334	1,664	8
SBPE	598	4,307	2,308	7,213	38
RECON	1,624	–	2,969	4,592	14
Total	3,490	4,368	5,611	13,469	60
Cumulative Totals[e]					
Agents[d]	13,721	894	3,568	18,183	576
SBPE	6,094	17,436	9,297	32,827	373
RECON	4,494	–	9,818	14,312	102
Total	24,309	18,330	22,683	65,322	1,051

a. All values include monetary correction.

b. Represents funds provided by the system's various intermediaries to supplement the loans received from the BNH, the total comprising the amount loaned to purchasers of housing.[10]

c. Represents funds derived from borrowers' saving or from other sources outside the Housing Finance System, to comprise the balance between loans received from the system and the total amount of investment represented by the acquired housing.

d. Refers to all BNH agents except those in the Savings and Loan System.

e. August, 1964, through June, 1974, in Cr$ millions.

SOURCES: Conjuntura Econômica (26, 3 [March, 1972]: 90); Conjuntura Econômica (27, 3 [March, 1973]: 106); various 1973 and 1974 issues of BNH, Boletim Mensal.

on the part of its borrowers, both in absolute terms and relative to the amount of Housing Finance System funding. This would suggest a comparatively high income level for RECON borrowers.

Emphasizing Larger Loans

The breakdown in Table 3 illustrates the extent to which the Savings and Loan System (SBPE) has come to exercise a predominant role in the Housing

Finance System's supply of credit to the mortgage market. The two left-hand columns when combined give the total amount of housing loans during the year in each category. The SBPE rapidly increased its share of total system financing from 35 percent in 1971 to over 60 percent in 1973 and into 1974. While part of this relative gain was due to the higher unit cost of residences financed through the Savings and Loan System, the far right-hand column in Table 3 shows the SBPE to be financing four times as many units as the BNH's other agents during the final year-and-a-half covered.

A comparison of figures in the two left-hand columns shows that the SBPE's expansion came about principally on the strength of its own capacity for capturing funds, as the relative BNH component in the SBPE loans dropped from 55 percent in 1971 to 23 percent in 1973. (The even smaller percentage in the first half of 1974 should be viewed in the context of the inevitable administrative discontinuity accompanying the installation of a new president and directorate at the Housing Bank in March, which means that it does not necessarily indicate a trend toward continuing reduction of the BNH component in SBPE financing.)

Keeping in mind the government's objectives for housing finance as a stimulus for investment in Brazil's urban centers, we find that the volume of investment in the form of residence acquisition induced by the SBPE has been close to that generated by RECON, although a much larger flow of credit has been required. The sizable gap between the respective amounts of investment induced by those intermediaries within and those outside the Savings and Loan System is to be expected, owing to the disparate income levels of the clienteles served by the two systems.

While there is no limit on the value of dwellings that can be financed through the Savings and Loan System, there is a loan ceiling of 2,250 UPC's (174,200 cruzeiros at the average 1973 UPC value). In an effort to obtain broader distribution of SBPE credit by income level, the housing loans are divided into 5 size classes in increments of 450 UPC's. Effective interest rates (including fees and service charges) on monetarily corrected assets range progressively from 10 to 12 percent in the first four classes, to no limit on rates in the uppermost class, while the maximum ratio of financing to value of the dwelling varies inversely by class, from 90 to 76 percent. To keep SBPE institutions from concentrating their loans in the highest class, where interest rates are determined by the market, the Housing Bank limits these high-interest loans to 30 percent of each member institution's total financing. Conversely, a minimum of 10 percent of total financing must go to the two lowest credit brackets (IBMEC, 1974: 137-139), where the maximum loan amount, 900 UPC's, is the same as the ceiling on credit operations by non-SBPE agents.

The consequences of this latter provision for the redistribution of credit in favor of low-income families are not as great as they might appear at first glance. It is a reasonable assumption that the 10 percent quota is concentrated in the next-to-lowest SBPE credit bracket rather than the lowest, thereby serving

TABLE 4
CREDIT TERMS IN THE HOUSING FINANCE SYSTEM[a]

Program	Maximum Loan Value	Nominal Interest Rate (%)	Maximum Commitment of Monthly Family Income (%)	Terms Under System of Constant Amortization		
				Initial Installment	Average Installment	Maximum Family Income
Low income	120	1	18	.50	.45	2.70
	160	2	20	.80	.67	4.00
	200	3	20	1.17	.92	6.00
Economic	240	4	20	1.60	1.20	8.00
	280	5	21	2.10	1.52	10.00
	320	6	22	2.67	1.87	12.00
	360	7	24	3.30	2.25	14.00
	400	8	25	4.00	2.67	16.00
Intermediate	480	9	25	5.20	3.41	20.80
	600	9	25	7.00	4.76	28.00
	720	10	25	10.00	7.02	40.00
	900	10	25	12.50	8.77	50.00

a. Values expressed in UPC's (units of constant purchasing power) unless otherwise indicated. For definition of UPC see text.

SOURCE: BNH, Assessoria de Planejamento e Coordenação (1974: Quadro 2, p. 62).

families earning at least 4.5 minimum salaries.[9] For such families, the 10 percent real interest rate available from the Savings and Loan System is competitive with the 9-10 percent interest rates charged elsewhere in the Housing Finance System for loans of equivalent size (see Table 4). On the other hand, families earning less than 4.5 minimum salaries are entitled to interest rates ranging from 1 to 8 percent on monetarily corrected loans from non-SBPE agents. Therefore, provided they are adequately informed regarding the alternative credit terms available to them, only tight conditions in the mortgage market would lead families below 4.5 minimum salaries to seek higher-interest financing in the lowest loan bracket of the Savings and Loan System. Thus, even though SBPE agents themselves should be largely indifferent as to how their 10 percent loans are distributed between the two lowest brackets, demand factors can be expected to keep the majority of those loans in the higher of the two.

The differential described here between the interest rates on loans up to 400 UPC's offered by the two basic types of intermediaries is justifiable on financial grounds: the cost of funds is higher in the Savings and Loan System because of the 6 percent interest (plus monetary correction) paid on housing bonds and passbook accounts, compared to the 3 percent (plus monetary correction) paid on most FGTS accounts. The point to be stressed is that if one is seeking to identify features of the Housing Finance System that effectively increase the flow of mortgage credit to low-income families, the 10 percent minimum quota on SBPE loans up to 900 UPC's cannot be considered very significant.

One approach that might facilitate greater participation by the Savings and Loan System in extending credit to families for whom its interest rates are normally too high would be a modification of an already existing Housing Bank financing operation. Since September, 1973, the Bank has made available to its associated thrift institutions especially designated additional financing, for the express purpose of encouraging the concession of loans of less than 900 UPC's. However, the terms offered to the intermediaries for such financing are the following: 8 years to repay at 8 percent annual interest, plus initial administrative fees and technical service charges of 1 percent (BNH Directorate Resolution 72/73 of September 28, 1973, reproduced in BNH, Boletim do Serviço, October 30, 1973: 11-12). That is to say, the interest rate is the same as that which applies to ordinary BNH credits for SBPE members who have not yet complied with a timetable established in October, 1971, for instituting newly-lowered interest rates for their borrowers. Thus for members who have complied with the timetable and therefore have qualified for a reduction from 8 to 6 percent on regular BNH refinancing (BNH Directorate Resolution 53/71 of October 5, 1971, reproduced in CENPHA, 1971: n.p.) there appears to be scant incentive at present for them to seek the credits earmarked for smaller loans.

In order to strengthen this incentive, our suggested modification would call for the Housing Bank to lower the rate on this line of credit to 5 percent, which is the estimated cost of capturing resources through the Seniority Security Fund when administrative costs are taken into account. To justify such a substantial reduction, the Bank would require institutions accepting the special loans to supplement them with their own resources, complying with a minimum ratio to be established by the BNH directorate. By charging 5 percent itself, the National Housing Bank could then set quotas for the resulting loans granted according to a specific subsidized interest rate schedule, ranging perhaps as low as 7 percent. In this way, a modest volume of SBPE resources would become available to families of income levels close to those served by the National Low-income Housing Plan, or PLANHAP (see the following discussion of PLANHAP), where the maximum nominal interest rate is now 6 percent. This extension of SBPE loans to lower income levels than are presently being served could be viewed as compensating for the expansion upward that has been taking place in the top SBPE loan bracket, where interest rates are not regulated. The last few years have seen a growing participation of Saving and Loan System entities in the financing of luxury units.

A similar compensatory principle is one of the basic characteristics of the present Housing Finance System, embodied in the 1 to 12 percent range for interest rates that spans all income levels of mortgagors (see Table 4), save for the case of loans larger than 1,800 UPC's made through the Savings and Loan System. In an indirect fashion, borrowers paying the SBPE interest rates of 10 to 12 percent or higher are helping to subsidize borrowers who are paying the 1 to 6 percent rates on loans made through the Low-income Housing Finance System. Our characterization of the subsidization as indirect is grounded in the fact that the lending institutions involved are not the same for all sizes of loans and rates of interest.

The subsidy mechanism operates through the differential between the interest rates charged to borrowers of different categories and those paid by the various institutions on refinancing received from the Housing Bank. In the Savings and Loan System, the refinancing rates are either 8 or 6 percent, as mentioned above. All other financial agents for the Housing Bank pay rates set at 1 percent below the nominal rates charged to their borrowers (as set forth in Table 4, BNH Directorate Resolution 68/71 of November 25, 1971, reproduced in CENPHA, 1971, n.p.). Only because of this differential is it possible to maintain the spread of more than 12 percentage points between the smallest loans granted through SIFHAP and the largest ones granted through the Savings and Loan System.

PROVISION OF HOUSING CREDIT OUTSIDE OF THE SAVINGS AND LOAN SYSTEM

We shall now examine the housing credit operations carried out by BNH agents apart from the Savings and Loan System. The great majority of these operations cannot be considered to be directed towards families of modest income. That is because an examination of the credit terms offered by these agents, as set forth in Table 4, indicates that the middle category or "Economic" program enjoys the maximum degree of subsidization to which these operations have access, and that this does not equal the terms offered to families which fall into our definition of the "low income group" (i.e., no more than 3 minimum salaries). The middle category also represents the upper limit of the range of financing of credit under the National Low-income Housing Plan which is designed for families with 1 to 3 minimum salaries and with maximum loan values of 320 UPC's.

A variety of agents are active in promoting and financing housing in the loan range of 320 to 900 UPC's, including housing cooperatives, the National Social Welfare Institute, mortgage companies, state and municipal pension funds, businesses (for their own employees), military clubs, and even the state housing companies, which are the key agents in the execution of PLANHAP. The data on completed housing loan contracts that are published by the Housing Bank are classified solely by program, which prevents an exact determination of the breakdown of loans between those less than and these greater than 320 UPC's. Of course, all loans in the "Intermediate" program are larger than 320 UPC's. Available data show that, whereas the cruzeiro volume of financing handled by this program has been expanding steadily since 1970, the volume in the other two programs has been diminishing sharply since 1971. In the cumulative totals for financing granted by the three programs through the end of 1973, the "Intermediate" share was only 14.6 percent (based on data in BNH, 1974: 11, Table 1.2).

During 1972, however, the agent's operations through these three programs had begun to experience difficulties in disbursing loan funds (Conjuntura Econômica, January, 1973: 36). This turn of events is reflected in Table 3, where the agent's supplementary contributions for 1972 and 1973 show negative results. Whatever the nature of the difficulties that cropped up, they primarily affected the smaller loans. In a compensatory effort, the volume of loans in the "Intermediate" program was stepped up, with the result that its share vis-à-vis the other two programs jumped from 10 percent in 1971 to 30 percent in 1972, and reached 43 percent in 1973 (based on data in BNH, 1974: 11, Table 1.2). It is reasonable to assume that a similar shift was taking place among the sub-classifications in the "Economic" program category. Judging from the rapid growth of the "Intermediate" program relative to the other two serving lower-income families, it would appear relatively conservative to assume that at least 50 percent of all financing in the "Economic" category was for loans between 320 and 400 UPC's. This, therefore, was the ratio used in arriving at our estimate for the flow of credit from SBPE intermediaries to the "Middle-and-Upper-income Groups" appearing on the far right-hand side of Figure 1.

Focusing on Low-Income Housing

The picture that has been emerging in the course of our examination of the distribution of loans within the Housing Finance System is one in which the early 1970s saw a steady growth in the proportion of loans going to the most comfortable 20-30 percent of the urban population. Nor was this trend strictly a function of the dynamism of the Saving and Loan System's sources of funds. Notwithstanding the fact that a sizable number of families living on moderate incomes was given opportunities for home ownership that never had existed prior to the establishment of the National Housing Bank, it was clear that the financial apparatus as it stood was not geared to ensure an adequate assault on the massive housing deficit that still faces Brazil.

Out of a recognition of the inadequacy of existing structures and mechanisms came the first firm step in utilizing the Housing Finance System's proven capacity for capturing resources to help expand the supply of low-cost housing on financial terms suitable to those with modest incomes. In January, 1973, President Emilio G. Médici unveiled the National Low-income Housing Plan, calling for an investment of 30 billion cruzeiros during the next decade in the construction of 2 million units for families earning between 1 and 3 minimum salaries. The proposed activities were to be limited to the following: metropolitan areas, regional "growth poles," cities of over 50,000 inhabitants, and selected smaller cities showing abnormally high demographic growth rates (BNH, COS, 1973: 38-39). Once again, as with the creation of the Seniority Security Fund in 1966, the Brazilian government had used a modification in the structure of the Housing Finance System to attend to other concerns besides housing. In the case of PLANHAP the related issue was not worker indemnification but wealth distribution. Government officials had been stung by widespread criticism from abroad of distributive inequities in Brazil's ongoing economic boom. The built-in redistributive mechanism of the new initiative represented an effort to allay such adverse commentary.

In order to implement the National Low-income Housing Plan, a new Low-income Housing Finance System (SIFHAP) was formed within the framework of the regular Housing Finance System. Unlike the creation of the Savings and Loan System, the implantation of SIFHAP did not involve the formation of any new financial institutions. Instead, new relationships were specified between existing BNH agents and cooperating state and local governments. The state housing companies were to constitute the keystone of the system, which would encompass all of their housing loans up to 320 UPC's plus various complementary financing operations.

The incorporation of state and local government in the new system has produced one new instrument: the State Low-income Housing Funds, or FUNDHAP's (Fundos Estaduais de Habitação Popular). This type of fund constitutes the Housing Finance System's first significant recourse to government subsidization since the 1964 federal allocation of initial capital for the National Housing Bank. FUNDHAP's are to receive 2 percent of the annual tax revenues of their respective state governments, plus additional contributions that the states may require from localities benefiting from PLANHAP activity (BNH Administrative Council Resolution 1/73 of January 23, 1973, reproduced in BNH, COS, 1973: 42). The function of these Housing Funds is to supplement BNH loans for specific PLANHAP projects. The determination of the respective proportions for the sources of funds is one of several mechanisms intended to encourage housing projects serving small borrowers; the percentage of BNH financing conceded for a particular project is to be inversely proportional to the average unit value of the project, with the balance to be made up by the respective FUNDHAP (BNH Administrative Council Resolution 1/73 of January 23, 1973, reproduced in BNH, COS, 1973: 45-46).

Beyond merely seeking to foster the construction of low-income housing so as to benefit disadvantaged urban groups, the PLANHAP regulations permit these borrowers certain advantages in the financing terms to which they are subject. From Table 4 it can be seen that those receiving loans of less than 320 UPC's pay the lowest interest rates charged in the system, which should result in the lowest installments relative to family income. By way of a reference, the ceiling on relative commitment of family income on SBPE loans varies from 25 to 40 percent depending on family size and income level (IBMEC, 1974: 140). The gap between the percentage commitments allowed by SIFHAP and SBPE seems appropriate in view of the much higher proportion of their income that SIFHAP borrowers may be expected to spend on necessities.

At the time of this writing (September 1974), some twenty months after news of PLANHAP's impending implementation was first released, the process of cooperation between the Housing Bank, the COHAB's, and the state and municipal governments has been operational for only a short time. The same is true for the numerous complementary programs spawned by PLANHAP, some of which will be touched upon here. Our personal inquiries at the Housing Bank Office of Planning and Coordination turned up some specific explanations for the delay in getting PLANHAP into operation, in addition to the inevitable bureaucratic obstacles: It was pointed out that many state governments were reluctant to sign accords with the Bank setting up FUNDHAP's because of budgetary constraints, and that several COHAB's experienced difficulty in acquiring real estate at prices low enough to make the construction of low-cost housing viable. In addition, the Housing Bank claims that only one percent of Brazil's nearly 4,000 municipalities possesses the capacity for indebtedness essential to participation in most local PLANHAP projects (BNH, APC, 1974: 100). Nevertheless, at this juncture PLANHAP and its auxiliary sub-programs offer promising long-term prospects to increase the relative share of credit going to families earning less than three minimum salaries within the Housing Finance System.

Complementary Programs

Our examination of the distribution of credit provided by the system, as between low-income groups on the one hand and the rest of the urban population on the other, has hitherto remained focused on loans for the purchase of housing. But there are several sub-programs within the scope of PLANHAP which provide loans that can definitely be identified as benefiting the residents of the housing complexes built and financed by the COHAB's, even though they do not go directly to buyers of low-cost dwellings. The consolidated total of such programs is presented in Figure 1 as "Housing Complex Complementary Investment" and is shown to benefit the low-income groups exclusively.

In these programs the Housing Bank initially makes credit available to COHAB's at 6 percent to purchase land for the construction of housing complexes (BNH Directorate Resolution 90/73 of October 19, 1973: 63, 65). While this practice cannot obviate the scarcity and concomitant over-valuation of real estate that have plagued PLANHAP from the start, the credit does bolster the capacity of the COHAB's to compete under otherwise unfavorable market conditions. It should be noted, however, that this credit may also serve to inflate land values still further, thus exacerbating the costs of the program. In cases such as this, the right of eminent domain, which justifies the state acquisition of land at "fair value" for purposes serving the public interest, might be more vigorously applied by the government housing institutions in order to save scarce financial savings by alleviating the cost of land purchases.

As part of its broadening outlook on the necessary integration of housing with other features of the urban habitat, the Housing Bank has set up a battery of sub-programs for financing diverse public and private enterprises directly linked to housing complexes financed by members of SIFHAP, including complexes built prior to SIFHAP's existence. The types of installations they support include public works and utilities, landscaping, various community service facilities, and even small-scale commercial establishments. An interesting feature of this set of credit operations is its deliberate impetus for a regional redistribution of resources. Interest rates charged to the borrowers, whether they be state or local governmental agencies or individual entrepreneurs, are scaled from 4 to 8 percent, varying according to the per capita tax revenues of the state in which the complex is located (BNH Directorate Resolutions 31/73 of April 26, 1973, and 56/73, of June 28, 1973, reproduced in BNH, COS, 1973: 52-56, 84-87). In this way, the more prosperous states who make use of these sub-programs contribute a proportionately larger share to SIFHAP support than do the poorer states.

Yet another line of credit of this nature is destined for families living in units within the scope of PLANHAP who have not fallen behind in their payments and who seek additional financing to make improvements in their homes. For such families, the BNH authorizes the COHAB's and other agents to extend loans at one percent interest (BNH Directorate Resolution 84/73 of September 27, 1973, reproduced in BNH, COS, 1973: 136-137).

The low-income Housing Finance System also administers credit to families wishing to build their own dwellings on previously acquired lots, as long as they earn at least one minimum salary. This scheme is similar to others tried elsewhere in Latin America with mixed success (e.g., see Laun, 1973: 19-20). By way of minimum standards for the units thus financed, the Housing Bank requires that the lot size comply with local ordinances, and that there be connections with public utility systems. Interest rates are the same as in Table 4 and, in another provision aimed at directing credit to lower income groups, each agent is required to apply at least 45 percent of such loans towards dwellings valued at under 200 UPC's (BNH Directorate Resolution 92/73 of October 8, 1973, reproduced in BNH, COS, 1973: 154-155). While this approach is potentially conducive to cooperation among borrowers in the purchase of materials and in the building process, in practice actual construction often proves quite burdensome on the time and physical resources of individual families (Perlman, 1974: 32).

Through the elaboration of PLANHAP's principal lines of action, we have seen the BNH somewhat slacken the financial moorings of a portion of the Housing Finance System, as its directors have become more aware of the necessity for flexibility to serve the needs of families at low levels of income. Still, it is apparent that even the less rigorous standards of PLANHAP are overly demanding for the poorest families (i.e., those with an unstable income averaging less than one minimum salary a month), which are estimated by the Housing Bank to comprise 20 percent of the urban population. Consequently, BNH policymakers have recently decided to let out still more slack in the program by announcing in September, 1974, the adoption throughout the Housing Finance System of a type of core-housing project that has been operating for a few years on an experimental basis in the northeastern city of Recife. This approach entails the provision of a basic housing unit of two or three rooms, equipped with utilities, which can be easily enlarged. The proposed monthly installments are the same as in the Recife project—15 to 20 cruzeiros—over a period of 20 years (Jornal do Brasil, September 4, 1974: 16). While the model project in Recife has not been free of problems, the report of one observer (Perlman, 1974: 24-25) indicates that its difficulties seem to be peculiar to its particular setting. In a more positive vein, the housing in that project is described as sturdy, which is somewhat surprising considering that the installments are less than 10 percent of the effective minimum wage in Recife. This offers hope that the same quality might be achieved in other locales with the same-sized installment. However, it has not been explicitly stated whether these minimal installments have been subject to monetary correction, or that they will be when the project is adopted on the larger scale.

MONETARY CORRECTION REVISITED: PROBLEMS FOR THE USE OF FUNDS

Earlier we pointed out the fundamental role played by the indexing mechanism in the capture of voluntary savings by the Housing Finance System. Just as significant and far more controversial is the application of monetary correction to the amortization of loans received from the system's agents. On the one hand, monetary correction is deemed essential under inflationary conditions in order to prevent the recurrence of the situation prevailing in the real estate market in the early 1960s when the real value of both rents and housing payments declined precipitously due to rent controls and nominal interest rate ceilings. As a result, investment in real estate dried up, leaving an acute housing shortage at all income levels. Another reason given for applying monetary correction to loan balances is that monetary correction is being paid on the system's three chief sources of funds, so that failure to index the use of funds would lead to losses and illiquidity of the financial intermediaries involved in the housing program.

Nonetheless, from the mortgagor's standpoint, monetary correction has inspired a greater outcry than any other single feature of the Housing Finance System. Under the System of Constant Amortization that was adopted for loan contracts throughout the program in 1971, the real value of the installments decreases relative to the minimum salary over the course of the amortization period. The rising nominal value of the installments resulting from monetary correction has taken a large segment of the mortgagors by surprise, and their reaction has been rapid and vociferous. Indeed, no amount of reform in the methods of calculating the amount of correction has yet been able to still the clamor directed at the Housing Bank.

At present mortgagors in the system can choose between two methods of readjustment of debt balances and installments. One method has been in effect since the early days of the Bank and functions in approximately the same manner as the indexing of financial liabilities of the Housing Finance System institutions, with quarterly readjustment made equal to changes in the value of the UPC. The more popular method, probably because it involves fewer adjustments and therefore makes a family's financial planning easier, involves annual readjustments based on increases in the minimum salary (IBMEC, 1974: 142-143). The opportunity for choice between the two systems has tended to result in the equalization of their respective adjustments. As one may note in Table 5, since the second scheme was adopted in 1969, the amount of monetary correction based on the UPC has never exceeded the relative increase in the minimum salary.

Taking monetary correction into account, along with other difficulties, how secure has been the ownership of housing for those relying on mortgages of the Housing Finance System? Rough estimates of amortization delinquency rates

TABLE 5
ALTERNATIVE MONETARY CORRECTION DETERMINANTS
(increases in percent)

Year	*UPC*[a]	*Minimum Salary*[b]
1966	35.9	27.33
1967	26.7	24.79
1968	23.7	22.92
1969	17.8	20.11
1970	19.3	20.00
1971	18.9	23.96
1972	17.6	20.10
1973	12.9	15.93

a. Increase in value of UPC from final quarter of preceding year to final quarter of years indicated.

b. Minimum wage set on a regional basis, which is higher in the South than in the North. Figures given here represent average increases among 7 cities: Rio de Janeiro, São Paulo, Belo Horizonte, Curitiba, Pôrto Alegre, Salvador, Recife.

SOURCES: UPC data from Boletim do Banco Central do Brasil (10, 4 [April, 1974]: Quadro IV, 73, p. 92); minimum salary data from Conjuntura Econômica (27, 12 [December, 1973], supplement: 99).

vary widely, depending on the characteristics of a given project, but regardless of these rates, ownership is claimed to be relatively secure. While the Housing Bank does not release data on delinquency rates, its current president Mauricio Schulman claims that only 3 percent of the 270,000 units currently administered by COHAB's have been vacated because of the residents' inability to keep up their payments (Jornal do Brasil, September 4, 1974: 16). A 1973 survey of COHAB projects in various sections of Brazil found several locales where the share of residents who were keeping up with their payments reached 80 or 90 percent, while in others it was less than 20 percent (Perlman, 1974: 11-12).

CONCLUSION

This study illustrates the way in which one program, the Brazilian Housing Finance System, serves as a vehicle to attract voluntary and contractual savings for the benefit of low income lenders and borrowers for housing purposes. On the source-of-funds side, the system has provided to voluntary savers both passbook accounts and housing bonds which are subject to monetary correction. These programs have been amazingly successful. The indexing of the financial assets has protected their real value (at least until recently when the degree of monetary correction appears to have understated increases in the price level), making them appealing to savers of all income groups when faced with inflation rates of from 15 to 30 percent per annum in recent years. Without the program, some of these funds would have otherwise gone into consumption (especially for those with small passbook accounts) rather than savings, and other funds would have been used to purchase alternative real or financial assets (as in the case of the larger passbook accounts and the housing bonds).

Since most other financial assets in Brazil, except for corporate stocks, are also indexed, the program cannot be said to divert financial resources from other uses on the basis of yield alone (such as occurred in the recent, ill-fated UPAC program in Colombia where indexing was almost exclusively applied to savings accounts of the housing program). For Brazil these policies have resulted in a massive increase in the resources available to institutions involved in the Housing Finance System. These funds, together with those from contractual savings, have permitted the Savings and Loan System and other agents not only to keep pace with the rapidly expanding demand for upper income housing (those in the upper 20 percent of the income distribution) in Brazil's major cities, but also to make important inroads into the low income housing deficit as well as into the need for general urban infrastructure programs.

A major benefit of the program for all savers has been the provision of indexed financial assets capable of insuring the real value of their savings. Progress has also been made in the use of such funds plus contractual savings to subsidize loans for borrowers of modest means. The method used has been to charge differential loan rates to borrowers ranked in terms of capacity to pay, while offering monetarily corrected deposit rates to all. Hence on the source-of-funds side the program has offered proportional rather than progressive or regressive yields on its financial liabilities, benefiting all income groups to the same degree. On the use-of-funds side, an attempt has been made to provide lower lending rates to poorer borrowers, favoring the objective of progressive wealth redistribution in the form of owner-occupied dwelling units.

In the face of policies in most developing countries which tend to be regressive in terms of yields on financial assets, such that low-income groups usually receive lower and even negative real interest rates on their financial savings, the Brazilian program is a definite step in the direction of social equity (or away from social inequity). However, in terms of the *use* of funds, our study indicates that the majority of funds in the program to date is used to finance middle and upper income housing, other urban construction, and works of urban infrastructure rather than subsidized housing for the poor, and that this trend has been increasing. One reason for this is that the policy of monetary correction which accounts for the success of the program in attracting funds implies continual adjustment in the nominal value of interest and amortization payments to permit the program to retain its liquidity. Although these payments do not increase in real value, there is a politically unpopular aspect to the readjustment process, especially for those in the lower-income groups who have experienced erosion of their real incomes owing to wage adjustments which have tended to lag behind price increases. It remains to be seen whether a true housing loan subsidy program on a mass basis could be mobilized which would be at once capable of eliminating a large share of the low-income housing deficit and at the time retaining the liquidity of the program. It is likely that such a program would have to depend upon additional interest rate subsidies from the government, if voluntary and contractual sources of funds were to retain their positive real rates of return. And if this were not true, then the sources of voluntary savings might well dry up, and contractual savers among the lower-income groups would be "taxed" on the one hand, through negative yields on their payroll deductions, while on the other hand they were being subsidized.

At the present time, the net flow of funds between the private and public sector through the housing program appears to be toward rather than away from the government, as the program is used to finance works of government infrastructure and the acquisition of government debt. Thus until recently the Housing Finance System has represented a channel of financial savings of the private sector into expenditures of the public sector—some of which are more progressive in their incidence than others—as well as a channel of funds from all income groups in the direction of lower, middle, and upper-income housing, with an increasing emphasis on the latter two groups. However, there is nothing in the nature of the program or its institutions which requires this situation to continue. Indeed, its original concept was quite different from recent practice. Now with the new impetus provided by the implementation of PLANHAP's assorted credit programs since mid-1973, the Housing Finance System may have begun to realize its potential for providing the mass of the urban labor force with secure, subsidized access to home ownership. Still, much remains to be done to improve the accessibility of indexed savings accounts and low-cost housing credit for the rural poor. It is hoped that the program might eventually be extended in this direction as well.

NOTES

1. The methodological innovation of the present study is the application of source and use of funds analysis (flow of funds) to the study of a major financial intermediation subsector in the development process. The study attempts to determine through the association of financial flows with major activities and income groups the impact of housing finance policy on the pattern of resource allocation and the distribution of wealth. As such it forms part of a more general program of research by the authors on the interactions between the real and financial sectors in the development process, their relationships to financial policy, and the implications for growth and welfare. For an introductory description of this program, see Reynolds (1973).

2. The exceptions are accounts that have been receiving deposits from the same employer since before the 1971 standardization of the rate of interest accruing to the accounts. In this limited case, accounts are entitled to periodic increments in the rate of interest earned, up to a maximum of 6 percent after the tenth year, provided the employer remains the same (BNH, CGFGTS, 1974b: 25-27).

3. Long hampered by difficulties stemming from the complex transfer system developed for collecting the FGTS deposits, only now are the administrators of the Seniority Security Fund implementing procedures for gathering the type of data needed for such an analysis.

4. Prior to the standardization of housing bond interest rates in May, 1974, they ranged from 6 to 8 percent.

5. Apparently the publicity campaign pitched to the small saver was successful enough that the financial institutions eventually grew concerned that they were limiting their potential market. Witness the opening lines of a real estate credit company advertisement appearing in the September 19, 1973 issue of the weekly newsmagazine *Veja:* "Caderneta de poupança (the savings passbook) sò é interesante para o pequeno aplicador, certo? Errado uma verdade que sómente agora começa a ser descoberta pelos aplicadores . . ."

6. The value to be used for converting UPC's to cruzeiros was to be that in effect during the final quarter of the tax year. Thus, for 1973 the UPC value would have been Cr$77.87, thus setting a deposit ceiling for benefiting from the advantageous 6 percent deduction of Cr$31,400, approximately 10 times the average passbook balance in the Savings and Loan System in December of 1973.

7. The very concept of fiscal incentive, which the Brazilian government has made liberal use of to influence the distribution of investment throughout the financial system, favors the wealthy. Not only does the amount of the deduction increase with the taxpayer's income under a progressive tax system, but also the deduction can only benefit those who pay income tax. For the 1973 tax year, annual incomes of up to 10,700 cruzeiros were exempt, including the thirteenth salary to which Brazilian workers are entitled by law. The annual figure represented a monthly income of 2.9 average minimum salaries, or 2.6 times the minimum salary effective in São Paulo, Rio de Janeiro, and Belo Horizonte during 1973. Furthermore, when the standard deductions were taken into account, taxpayers had to earn at least 13,000 cruzeiros before they owed as much as Cr$100 in taxes (tax schedule in Ministério de Fazenda, SRF, 1974: 12).

8. The 12-UPC maximum family income in this category has approximated 3 minimum salaries in the years since 1970. Average UPC value: 1970–Cr$45.21; 1971–Cr$54.21; 1972–Cr$65.30; 1973–Cr$74.43. Rough weighted average of urban minimum salary, for the seven cities listed beneath Table 5: 1970–Cr$165-170; 1971–Cr$205-210; 1972–Cr$240-245; 1973–Cr$280-285.

9. We arrived at the figure 4.5 minimum salaries in the following manner: The upper bound of the lowest SBPE bracket is 450 UPC's, reasonably close to the upper bound of the "Economic" program shown in Table 4. The "Economic" program serves families earning up to 16 UPC's monthly, a value which equalled between 4.2 and 4.5 minimum salaries during the years 1970-1973, using the average minimum salary for the cities listed beneath Table 5.

10. Because of irreconcilable discrepancies between the loan totals for non-SBPE agents in the two sources consulted, the proportional shares of the three programs (as calculated from Quadro 1.2 in BNH, 1974a: 11) were applied to the sum of the "BNH" and "Intermediary" components for Agents in 1973, obtained from Table 4. In other words, the entire "Intermediate" program's 43.3 percent share and half the "Economic" program's 45.0 percent of the 2.0 billion cruzeiros in total Agent loans–or 1.3 billion cruzeiros–was estimated as having gone to families earning more than 3 minimum salaries. The same procedure was followed for the cumulative balances (from BNH, Boletim Mensal, January, 1974: 3).

REFERENCES

Banco Nacional da Habitação (1974a) "BNH–uma avaliação de 1973." Rio de Janeiro (mimeo).

——— (1974b) BNH–1974. São Paulo: AGGS Indústrias Gráficas.

———, Assessoria de Planejamento e Coordenação (1974) BNH: avaliação e perspectivas. Rio: Secretaria de Divulgação do BNH.

——— , Carteira de Operações de Natureza Social (1973) PLANHAP: objetivos e normas de execução.

——— , Coordenação Geral do FGTS (1974a) Instruções sobre o FGTS, 4a. Rio: Secretaria de Divulgação do BNH.

——— , Coordenação Geral do FGTS (1974b) Legislação do FGTS, 4a. Rio: Secretaria de Divulgação do BNH.

——— , Superintendencia de Agentes Financieros (1974) O sistema Brasileiro de poupança e empréstimo. Rio: Secretaria de Divulgação do BNH.

CHACEL, J., M. H. SIMONSEN, and A. WALD (1970) A correção monetária. Rio: APEC Editôra.

CHALHUB, M. N., D. P. ALVES, E. P. VIEIRA (n.d.) Financiamento da casa própria: noções básicas. Rio: Imprinta.

CONTADOR, C. R. (1974) Mercado de ativos financieros no Brasil: perspetiva histórica e comportamento recente. Rio: IBMEC.

ELLIOT, S. M. (1966) Financing Latin American Housing: Domestic Savings Mobilization and U.S. Assistance Policy. New York: Praeger.

HANSON, J. (1974) "Estimación de ahorro familiar en Colombia." Unpublished paper.

Instituto Brasileiro de Mercados de Capitais (1974) Sistema financiero da habitação. Rio: IBMEC.

LANGONI, C. G. (1973) Distribuição de renda e desenvolvimento econômico do Brasil. Rio: Editôra Expressão e Cultural.

LAUN, J. (1973) "Low-cost urban housing in Colombia, 1942-1972: the rhetoric and reality of reform." Unpublished paper. University of California, Berkeley.

Ministério da Fazenda (1974) 1974 Imposto de renda pessoa física: manual de orientação. Rio: Secretaria de Receita Federal.

PERLMAN, J. (1974) "Report on squatter settlements and low income housing systems." Unpublished paper. Dept. of City and Regional Planning, University of California, Berkeley.

REYNOLDS, C. W. (1973) "The use of flow of funds analysis in the study of Latin American capital market development." Documents and Summary of Discussions, III Annual Meeting, Organization of American States, Capital Markets Development Program, July 31-August 2, 1973, Mexico, D.F. (Spanish translation: "Uso del análisis de flujo de fondos para el estudio del desarrollo del mercado de capitales en la América Latina," Revista de Economía Latinoamericana [Caracas] 38.)

PERIODICALS CITED

Banco Nacional da Habitação, Boletim do Serviço. Rio.

——— Boletim Mensal. Rio.

Boletim do Banco Central do Brasil. Brasília.

Centro Nacional de Pesquisas Habitacionais (CENPHA), "Legislação 15" (loose-leaf binder). Rio: Departamento de Documentação e Intercambio Científico.
Conjuntura Econômica. Rio: Fundação Getúlio Vargas.
Jornal do Brasil. Rio.

GLOSSARY OF ACRONYMS

BNH–National Housing Bank
COHAB–State Housing Company
FGTS–Seniority Security Fund
FUNDHAP–State Low-income Housing Fund
PLANHAP–National Low-income Housing Plan
RECON–BNH Sub-program for Financing Construction Materials
SBPE–Brazilian Savings and Loan System
SIFHAP–Low-income Housing Finance System
UPC–Standard Capital Unit

EDUARDO E. LOZANO is Associate Professor of City and Regional Planning, and Assistant Chairman of the Department of City and Regional Planning, at Harvard University. Originally an Argentinian architect, he obtained a Ph.D. in City and Regional Planning at Harvard, and taught later at Princeton University. His two contributions to this volume are based on field research in Chile during the Allende period.

Chapter 7

HOUSING THE URBAN POOR IN CHILE: CONTRASTING EXPERIENCES UNDER "CHRISTIAN DEMOCRACY" AND "UNIDAD POPULAR"

EDUARDO E. LOZANO

An historical event of the first magnitude took place in Chile in November, 1970, when the broad leftist coalition called Unidad Popular (People's Unity), led by Salvador Allende, was elected to power. It replaced the Christian Democratic Party, of centrist-reformist orientation. The program of Unidad Popular called for radical changes in most areas of Chilean life.

This event suggested the possibility of studying, from their inception, the new urban policies that a revolutionary government might implement. Such studies could be focused, first, on the reorientation of policies and planning activities, and second, on their comparative performance vis-à-vis previous policies—once sufficient time had elapsed to permit such an analysis. This paper concentrates mainly on the reorientation of housing policies in Chile under Unidad Popular. Considerable caution should be exercised in any study of this type. The commonly found gap between proposals and accomplishments and the difficulty of comparing the performance of previous regimes with the incomplete record of Unidad Popular have to be kept constantly in mind. I have attempted to deal with these problems by comparing not only the plans of the Unidad Popular

Author's Note: This paper is based on information and analysis developed during the summer of 1971 and supplemental data collected subsequently. The Chilean Ministerio de la Vivienda y Urbanismo (Ministry of Housing and Urbanism, MINVU), the Oficina de Planificación Nacional (National Planning Office, ODEPLAN), and other agencies collaborated fully, generously contributing time, space, documents, and personnel; to all my warm appreciation. The Program for Latin American Studies at Princeton provided the necessary financial support.

government with those of its predecessor, but also the actual achievements of the Christian Democratic administration with a realistic assessment of the probable results of Unidad Popular programs in the area of housing.

THE HOUSING CRISIS BY 1970

At the time of the electoral victory of Unidad Popular, the magnitude of the housing crisis was cause for deep concern in Chile. The wide gap between the people's income and the current market price for housing had led the Christian Democratic government to admit that no housing alternative was open to 12 percent of the population, and that 47 percent could obtain only very precarious solutions to their needs (MINVU, 1970). Thus, almost 60 percent of Chile's ten million inhabitants were deprived of housing that met minimum standards. It should be noted that the standards used were those developed by Chilean planners, reflecting the official consensus on what decent housing meant within the national context and resource limitations.

The disparity between the housing needs and economic capacity of the poor was reflected in the mushrooming of squatter settlements around the major cities. This was an urbanization of despair, caused more by chronic unemployment in many rural areas than by the emergence of new industrial employment opportunities in the cities. During the 1952-1960 period, the population of Chile grew by 2.4 percent and the population of Santiago, the capital city, increased by 3.9 percent; but the population concentrated in the central-city slums and peripheral shantytowns grew by 12.3 percent (MINVU, n.d.). In the capital city, migrants from the countryside and small towns constituted half of the economically active population.

According to the 1960 Census, more than 200,000 dwelling units in urban areas alone were classified as substandard. In 1970 the estimated average of housing space in Chile was 75 square feet per person, or an average dwelling unit of 375 square feet for a typical five-person family. To give an idea of the magnitude of the effort required to improve, even modestly, those standards, an example may be useful. The Christian Democratic administration set as its goal an average of 130 square feet of housing space per person; this would have required an investment equal to half of the country's Gross Geographic Product, or equal to the total Gross Geographic Investment for three years (ODEPLAN, 1970). And it must be remembered that this expenditure would have covered only the existing (accumulated) housing deficit; no allowance was made for the annual needs of a population that will increase at an estimated rate of 2.3 percent per year during the 1970-1980 decade.

The financial inability of the country to provide housing meeting minimum standards for all of its population was rooted in the underdeveloped nature of Chile's economy. By 1970, per capita income in Chile was $500 per year, a figure that had been growing at an annual rate of only 1.5 percent for a considerable time (ODEPLAN, 1970). Even more important, the unequal distribution of income further curtailed the economic capacity of large sectors of the population. In 1970 an estimated 30 percent of Chilean families were earning less than one "salario vital" (minimum wage), and 56 percent were in the one-to-four "salarios vitales" income bracket, still a very modest sum (MINVU, 1970). The "salario vital" equalled the minimum income necessary for an average size family to live at the lowest acceptable level. In 1971, the government increased the "salario vital" from 220 to 840 *escudos* per month.

Within the marginal population of shantytowns and slum dwellers, the statistics were even more dismal: 43 percent of those families were earning less than one "salario vital," and 49 percent were earning between one and two "salarios vitales" (MINVU, n.d.). The growing need for housing, and the economic impossibility of closing the gap, forced the adoption of "illegal" solutions—the invasion of land by low-income groups and the formation of shantytowns, whose residents were to become strong supporters of Unidad Popular.

Before 1950, the invasion process involved an aggregation of families who acted in response to individual decisions. The 1950s witnessed the slow emergence of a mass movement organized by and dependent on the decisions of large groups of invaders, backed by some political organizations. The invaded land was still marginal, being unsuitable for most other uses, but this also was to change. In the early 1960s the invasion groups, now with a more developed political structure and even technical assistance, began to occupy land that was appropriate for other uses. This trend has continued, along with the strengthening of neighborhood committees and other local organizations in the *"callampas"* (squatter settlements).

As discussed below, every administration made attempts at solving the housing crisis, but the hard-core problem of the "callampas" remained largely untouched. One squatter and cooperative president summarized the problem in this way:

> When the wife of some squatter comrade needs the ambulance, it is necessary to go far away to look for a telephone to request it. When it arrives at the shantytown, does the ambulance enter? It does not, because the streets are pure mud. Besides, we still have not obtained potable water. We build the houses by self-help. They are humble, . . . but we are happy with our efforts.

The Christian Democratic Planning Experience

The Christian Democratic years in power, 1964 to 1970, can be defined as an experience in typical reformist policies. The government's stated aim was "to give priority, in its direct action, to a sufficient supply of permanent housing oriented to the lower income sectors, [and to] temporary housing solutions for those families lacking the means to acquire permanent housing" (MINVU, 1969a).

The Christian Democrats' reliance on the market mechanism to supply low-cost housing was consistent with their emphasis on financial instruments to implement housing policies, since these instruments "permit on the one hand the regulation of long-term mortgages for the purchase and construction of houses and, on the other hand, stimulation of the supply of social-oriented housing" (MINVU, 1969b). The government's role was seen mainly as one of control and stimulation of the market mechanism. One of the most important features of the financial system was the readjustment of the mortgage loan repayments to keep up with inflation. This was welcomed by the lending bankers—who operated in a country with 30 percent inflation—but caused hardships for small homeowners, shifting to their shoulders the burden of inflationary pressures.

During those years a number of programs were started, the most important of which were "Operación Sitio" (Operation Site), consisting of provision of urbanized home sites; cooperatives and self-help projects with government assistance; and urban renewal projects. These programs have been assessed critically by planners in the Christian Democratic administration, who stressed the following problems (MINVU, 1969a): (1) The exclusive focus on a physical solution—houses and buildings—resulted in an impossible race with a deteriorating economic situation and a widening gap between needs and capabilities; (2) the affected people did not participate in the elaboration or implementation of plans; and (3) the social policies were sectarian, traditionalist, and paternalistic, leading to no structural changes.

Other criticisms must be appended to this list. The temporary solutions proposed for low-income groups became permanent by default, resulting in a process that institutionalized substandard conditions. "Operación Sitio" was, theoretically, a sound program, providing urban infrastructure in areas where the people could build houses according to their own needs and at their own pace. Unfortunately, political expediency and lack of administrative coordination led to the multiplication of pseudo-urbanized sites which were only lots with a legal property line—hence the popular nickname "Operación Tiza" (Operation Chalk). The result was widespread frustration and irritation. It aroused suspicion of "site-and-services" approaches and this, subsequently, led Unidad Popular to reject it. The Christian Democratic self-help projects suffered heavily from the exclusive stress on physical solutions, since this approach, to be done well, would require extensive organizational efforts, training programs, suitable designs, and follow-up programs including job placement, transportation, and community facilities for education and health. The urban renewal projects comprised a few medium-rise structures for low-income families. Their failure is apparent in these grim buildings, where large families of rural origin cannot maintain their way of life cramped in tiny (570 square feet) apartments. Though these units are larger than the national housing space average per family, their layout in mid-rise structures prevents the effective use of open space, which is essential to many family activities.

Analysis of data on the performance of the Christian Democratic housing policies leads to further insights (see Table 1). It appears that there was wide fluctuation in housing production in both the private and public sectors, but this was especially strong in the latter sector. In the worst interval, 1964-1965, the fluctuation in the public sector was of the order of more than five-to-one. Full use was not made of the public sector's capacity to build almost 40,000 dwelling units per year. The causes of this fluctuation are complex, but it must be noted that the lowest year in the public sector (1964) was an election year, and the highest (1965), the first full year of the Christian Democratic administration. Thus political factors seem to be important in explaining the fluctuations in the public sector, at least. The public sector was responsible for producing 59 percent of the units built in the period 1960-1967, but this represented only 50 percent of the total housing investment. The reason for this difference lies in the lower dwelling unit cost in public projects, due to their smaller size and lower quality. However, public financing of housing—in contrast to direct construction—represented up to 80 percent of the total investment in some years. On the average, 86.4 percent of the planned construction was achieved over the eight-year period, which is not a bad record.

But even if the Christian Democratic plans had been fully achieved, they would not have been adequate to end the housing deficit, as defined by Chilean planners. These plans were based on two limited goals: (a) providing units for new households being formed in the 1960-1970 decade, and (b) replacing demolished or lost units. It must be noted that the plans did not include provisions to start reducing the accumulated housing deficit.

During the 1960s, Chile was building housing at a rate of 4.5 units per 1,000 population, investing between 2.1 percent and 3.4 percent of its Gross National

TABLE 1
URBAN HOUSING TARGETS AND CONSTRUCTION IN CHILE, 1960-1967
(in dwelling units)

Year	*Plan Target*	*Total Built*	*Private Sector*	*Public Sector*	*% Plan Achieved*
1960	32,900	30,480	8,400	22,080	92.6
1961	34,800	36,189	11,129	25,060	104.0
1962	36,500	37,924	20,309	17,615	103.9
1963	38,500	27,428	15,440	11,988	71.2
1964	40,600	19,843	12,905	6,938	48.9
1965	42,600	51,538	15,051	36,487	121.0
1966	45,000	27,761	14,328	13,433	61.7
1967	47,500	44,000	15,715	28,285	92.6
Total	318,400	275,163	113,277	161,886	86.4

SOURCE: MINVU, Dirección de Finanzas.

Product, or between 12.6 percent and 19.6 percent of Gross Capital Investment. If Chile were to eliminate its housing deficit in the 1970-1980 decade, including accommodations for new families, replacement of demolished units, and elimination of the accumulated deficit, it would be required to build at a rate of 97,000 dwelling units per year. This represents a construction rate of 9 units per 1,000 population, or double the 1960-1967 rate. Since inflationary pressure is particularly strong in the housing sector, some government officials estimated this hypothetical increase would represent a tripling of the past investment level in housing. This implication was not lost on the new leaders of Unidad Popular, as revealed by comparison of the 1969 Christian Democratic and the 1971 Unidad Popular budgets. The former budget allocated 1,143 million escudos (E°) to public investments in housing, which, accounting for inflation, represents, in 1971 values, E° 2,000 million. The 1971 budget of Unidad Popular more than doubled this commitment, allocating E° 4,200 million.[1]

In summary, the housing policies of Christian Democracy set inadequate targets, only partially met, with an outlook that subordinated the larger public sector to the smaller private one. Housing statistics for this period reveal production levels that suggest unused capacity, uncertainty, and cyclical unemployment. Though some programs could have been developed successfully, if there had been sufficient political commitment and citizen participation, as a whole the Christian Democratic program was inadequate.

THE HOUSING PROGRAM OF UNIDAD POPULAR

According to their expressed political goals, housing was a key issue to the parties which formed Unidad Popular, long before 1970 (see Programa Básico de Gobierno de Unidad Popular, n.d.). Before the election, Unidad Popular published what it called *Las Primeras 40 Medidas del Gobierno Popular (The First 40 Actions of the People's Government),* a sort of party platform, six elements of which relate to urban and housing problems:

"A house, electricity, water for everyone."

"No more readjustable mortgage payments."

"Rents at fixed levels . . . 10 percent of the family income as maximum rent."

"Empty sites, no! Residential communities, yes!"

"Taxes only on luxury houses . . . free from taxes all residential units up to a maximum of 860 square feet."

"Work for everyone . . . new jobs with public works and housing plans."

After Unidad Popular took power in November, 1970, the Ministry of Housing and Urbanism (MINVU) rapidly became engaged in a revision of housing policies. From the beginning, there was popular pressure for immediate implementation of new policies in this area. This occurred at a time when the new political leadership was faced with the challenge of bridging the gap between campaign promises and planning operations. The apparent lack of planning preparation at the moment Unidad Popular took power can be traced in part to the political erosion of the concept of planning since 1964. In the electoral campaign of 1964, most parties offered "planning" as the solution to the country's problems. After the frustrating Christian Democratic experience the concept of planning was discredited, and by 1970 both contenders were extremely cautious in advocating "planning" again. This attitude may have pervaded the leadership structures of the political organizations, resulting in the low priority accorded to advance planning.

To further complicate the scenario, during the final weeks of the Christian Democratic regime some MINVU officials began the indiscriminate allocation of unurbanized housing sites to party followers, in a culmination of the "Operation Chalk" (Operación Sitio) program. This resulted in an even larger number of families demanding provision of basic urban services and housing units.

Transitional Policies

The period immediately after Unidad Popular took power demanded a set of transitional policies that could be implemented at once, even before studies could be undertaken. A few concise and radical policies with considerable multiplier effects were selected, among which the most important were:

(1) The threat of legal action against speculators and developers building residential subdivisions without services and community facilities.

(2) The establishment of rent control.

(3) The abolition of readjustments of mortgage loan repayments.

The impact of these transitional policies was considerable. The elimination of the readjustments of mortgage loan repayments unburdened the small home-owner of inflationary pressure, and encouraged low and lower-middle-income families to solve their housing problem through existing credit channels. The stringent rent control law—more radical than the Christian Democratic version—resulted in a drastic reduction of rent levels. The new maximum rent level was to be computed as 11 percent of the assessed value of the property for real estate tax purposes. Since the assessed values generally had been considerably lower than the market value, the new rent levels were, in most cases, much lower than before. One result was that many rental houses and apartments were sold to tenants at attractive prices, and cooperatives and condominiums were organized to manage the acquired housing. Also as a consequence of the rent control law, the speculative construction of housing for middle and upper-income groups—a typical outlet for the Latin American investor—came to a virtual standstill. Many unfinished high-rise apartment buildings could be seen in Santiago, stopped during construction.

The Unidad Popular government expected that part, if not all, of the capital that would have been invested in luxury housing would now be channeled into either economic development or social-oriented projects, including low-cost housing. Since the government also controlled the banking system, the usual remittance of domestic capital to foreign countries was made more difficult. Also, it was anticipated that private construction firms would be more willing to participate in public projects due to the curtailment of speculative housing.

As a result of Unidad Popular's transitional policies, housing financing in Chile underwent an important transformation. As mentioned above, many working-class families were finding that the savings and loan system was a valid option due to the elimination of readjustments of mortgage loan repayments. This was obviously a benefit for the middle-income groups purchasing houses as well. Private funds, either as voluntary savings or as new corporate taxes, constituted an important source for the financing of housing. The expressed goal was to allocate housing according to family needs with payment scaled to the family's economic capacity—a fundamental departure from the criterion of market allocation.

Although not explicitly announced as a housing policy, the work of Unidad Popular affecting the squatter populations residing in the shantytowns must be considered one of the most important undertakings of the transitional period. The government was working along two lines: politically, to radicalize these groups; economically, to create jobs for them at the highest possible rate. The importance of such policies cannot be overemphasized, since about 500,000 families lived in slums and shantytowns, at the bottom levels of income and employment, but beginning to develop political self-consciousness.

The 1971 Emergency Housing Program

The Emergency Housing Program made public by the Housing Ministry on July 29, 1971, was the core of Unidad Popular housing policy. Political and technical issues have equal importance in the Program (see MINVU, 1971), which was based on three key premises:

(1) It must be coordinated with the national strategy of economic and social development.

(2) It must help to broaden the political base of Unidad Popular by fulfilling its campaign promises.

(3) It must reflect the characteristics of the country—not only the physical, topographical conditions, but the fact that Chile is an underdeveloped country with severe social needs and economic constraints.

The most important goals of the Program, apart from the specific housing priorities to be discussed below, were:

(1) To generate direct and indirect employment through housing construction.
(2) To reduce the cost of services and urbanization.
(3) To make full use of the productive capacity of the housing industry.
(4) To stimulate the active participation of the people in the decision-making process.

In order to understand the approach of Unidad Popular, the overall housing problem must be viewed within the national economic and social context. Chile's housing deficit and its apparent incapacity to deal with housing needs are rooted, according to the Program, in five main causes:

(1) Underdevelopment, with its high unemployment and low-income consequences.
(2) The profit-seeking practices of the private sector of the housing industry.
(3) Rural-to-urban migration caused by regional disequilibria in development.
(4) Legal and institutional obstacles.
(5) A lack of political will to confront the issues (a criticism directed at previous administrations).

Wisely, Unidad Popular did not attempt to find a narrow technical "cause" for the housing deficit; rather, it took a much broader view and, accurately, indicated the range of constraints that makes a housing "solution" impossible as long as the social system of the country is not changed. Conversely, once those constraints are lifted, specific technical solutions might be successfully applied.

The huge housing deficit in Chile was interpreted as the logical result of misguided policies in the past. Special criticism was made of the housing industry, plagued by 24 percent unemployment, using a low-skilled and unstable labor force whose wages were subject to wide fluctuations, and lacking modern technology and standardization practices. Yet, during the Christian Democratic administration private construction firms often developed official connections which gave them a free hand to determine price levels. Faced with this supply structure and an allocation of dwelling units based on capacity to pay, the population in the lower-income brackets was forced to live in overcrowded and substandard housing.

This criticism of the Christian Democratic regime is warranted. To make things worse, its information and data control system was not adequate for monitoring the development of its programs; often there were long delays in completing projects, with an average of twenty months between initial decision and allocation of completed dwelling units. There was no success in industrializing the construction industry; and relationships with local MINVU offices were plagued by widespread administrative irregularities. The Christian Democrats did not develop a rural housing policy, and their urban low-cost projects resulted in increased physical segregation of the working-class population within the city.

In terms of specific goals, the Emergency Housing Program of Unidad Popular assigned top priority to assisting the 82,000 families who lived in squatter settlements. Decisions on whether the existing settlements would be improved or relocated were to be based on the physical characteristics of the sites—eliminating those with obvious handicaps—and on a set of urban development criteria, which were not clearly specified. Government officials estimated that about half of the squatter settlements could be improved in their present location, and that the other half would have to be moved to better sites.

The second priority of the program was to complete the "Operación Sitio" projects started before 1970, but not to initiate similar projects. "Operación Sitio" had been handicapped politically by the careless way in which it was implemented by the Christian Democrats; its mismanagement by the previous administration led the Unidad Popular government to terminate it—which, as argued below, was not a sound technical decision.

Finally, the Emergency Housing Program was to provide assistance to subscribers of the Popular Savings Plan, oriented toward moderate-income groups; to CORVI (Housing Corporation), an official agency that constructed housing using the surplus pension and retirement funds; and to cooperatives and trade unions engaged in providing housing for their members. In general, the housing program of Unidad Popular was structured so as to benefit, in the first place, the lowest income groups living in the large squatter settlements around every city, and, in the second place, the regularly employed working class.

The strategies selected by Unidad Popular to implement its housing goals were a combination of transitional and radical approaches. Private construction firms cooperating with the government's housing program were to be assured of a regular and substantial volume of business, which would enable them to maintain a certain level of profit. Prices were to be controlled by freezing the cost of inputs in the housing industry and by purchasing large stocks of materials from those building material firms needing revitalization. Employment stability in the housing industry was to be promoted by creation of a public agency to organize workers' brigades—a program which would have led eventually to the formation of a national construction consortium. Finally, monopolistic enterprises producing basic construction materials were to be nationalized. These strategies were aimed at increasing government control of the housing industry, increasing its efficiency, and passing the cost-reduction benefits along to the general public.

On the consumer side of housing, the object of the Emergency Housing Program was to distribute dwelling units in accordance with family size and economic activity of the household head, as well as with the ecological nature of the housing site. Specific allocation criteria were not detailed, since they were to be developed in cooperation with the affected community. The overall aim was to replace the criterion of "ability to pay" with one of "need and suitability."

In terms of housing targets, the Emergency Housing Program was quantitatively ambitious. During 1971, it proposed to provide 80,688 dwelling units, 72,045 of which were new units and 8,643 were units to be finished (started in 1970). In addition, more than 45,000 homesites were to be provided with urban infrastructure and services. As discussed in the following section, the proposed targets were unrealistically high.

The planning criteria implicit in the Emergency Housing Program can be clarified by analyzing the regional and sectoral allocation of housing. In regional terms, the plan, rather pragmatically, did not follow the long-range guide lines promoting regional decentralization postulated by the government, but was oriented to immediate needs. Almost 60 percent, or 47,747 dwelling units, were to be located in the capital city of Santiago, which accounts for a large share of the country's population in slums and shantytowns. The danger was that a dramatic improvement in housing conditions in Santiago would attract even more migrants, frustrating the regional goal of decentralization. Nevertheless, in terms of expenditures, Santiago was apportioned only 40 percent of the total housing investment, due to the concentration of housing efforts there on dwellings for the squatter population having a lower average unit cost, and to the existence of infrastructure.

The allocation of housing by population groups was arrived at by following the priorities established in the program and designating time periods in which the deficits in different sectors would be eliminated, limited only by economic and industry capacity constraints. The sectoral allocation of housing is highly indicative of the character of the Unidad Popular policies. More than 37,000 dwelling units in the Emergency Program were planned for politically organized shantytowns *("campamentos")* and 20,000 additional units were designated to complete the old Operación Sitio and similar projects. As a result, more than 80 percent of the new units planned for 1971 were allocated to the lowest income groups. Due to unit size and cost differentials, investment analysis shows that 50 percent of the financial inputs were assigned to units for shantytowns and other marginal groups and 40 percent to units for moderate and middle-income groups.

In terms of building types, only 6,000 units were planned to be walk-ups for low-income groups, most of which were to be located in Santiago; the rest were low-rise housing units. Planners noted that the multi-story buildings would cost almost twice as much to construct as the low-rise units for the same low-income groups (E^{o} 50/square feet against E^{o} 90/square feet), and it was feared that they might generate social and cultural conflicts among resident families.

The goal of obtaining people's participation, one made explicit in the Emergency Housing Program, was to be achieved through the rich network of political channels within the Unidad Popular coalition—party, trade union and neighborhood committees—in which broad popular involvement was the rule.

The Emergency Housing Program was to be financed through domestic sources, but with the expectation of some deficits. Funds were derived from a 1 percent tax on all wages and salaries, a new 5 percent tax on all corporative profits, normal mortgage loan repayments, the surplus of pensions and retirement funds, and, mainly, the government's contributions, which represented about 48 percent of the total financial inputs. As mentioned above, the 1971 housing budget totalling E° 4,200 million was more than twice the 1969 budget, at constant-escudos value.

Among the specific benefits to be provided by the Emergency Housing Program, the most important were:

(1) For squatters and the homeless: settlements with urban services and a choice of three dwelling types (a 390-square feet expandable unit built with masonry or with industrialized components, or a 610-square feet unit in four-story walk ups).

(2) For Operación Sitio settlers: full provision of urban services and the same housing choice as for squatters and the homeless.

(3) For Popular Savings Plan subscribers: choice of a 460-square feet masonry unit or a 570-square feet walk-up unit.

(4) For Pension and Retirement Fund members: normal mortgages.

Emphasis was also placed on the provision of community facilities such as nurseries, meeting halls, health and education centers, and cultural centers. Furniture and household equipment were to be provided by government agencies over the next few years.

EVALUATION OF THE HOUSING PROGRAM OF UNIDAD POPULAR

The Emergency Housing Program of 1971 was the most ambitious housing program ever attempted in Chile. This is apparent in a comparison with the performance of previous housing programs: In 1965, the most productive year of the past decade, slightly more than 51,000 units were constructed; and on the average, only 34,000 units were built each year during the 1960s. This means that the 1971 plan sought to achieve a level of production equivalent to 150 percent of the level of the best year and 230 percent of the average level for the decade. In terms of housing ratios, the goal of the 1971 plan was to practically double per capita production, jumping from the previous 4.5 dwelling units per 1,000 population to not less than 9 dwelling units per 1,000 population. As noted above, this meant that the housing deficit in Chile—both accumulated and yearly increases—could be eliminated in the decade of the 1970s.

Keeping in mind the problem of comparing past achievements with proposals for future ones, the high targets of the Unidad Popular program can be interpreted, at least, as an expression of political priorities. As will be discussed below, their technical feasibility could be seriously questioned. The few countries in the world that have reached such housing production levels were backed, in every case, by organizational, technological, and social resources mostly absent in Chile.

The level of inputs demanded by the plan was very high. In terms of financial inputs, to repeat, the 1971 Program more than doubled previous public investment in housing. This higher investment level could have been a serious distorting factor in the Chilean economy. A government study found that to reach such high levels of housing production, it might be necessary to have a 6.4 percent rate of growth in the GNP and a 4.0 percent increase in the per capita income (ODEPLAN, 1970). Unfortunately, Chile's income per capita has been growing, historically, at only 1.5 percent per year. Furthermore, the first years of the transition towards socialism could be expected to have been riddled with experiments, conflicts and even contradictions, precluding any immediate climb in per capita income. As a result, it appears that the housing program, if interpreted in an orthodox way, may have lacked economic preconditions, and that the new, higher levels of investment in housing may have unduly reduced investment levels in other key sectors.

In terms of human inputs, the plan was equally demanding. Assuming construction productivity coefficients of 540 square feet per man per year for traditional construction, and 2,700 square feet per man per year for industrialized systems, with a completion schedule of 8 months and 4 months, respectively, the Emergency Housing Program would have required the employment of more than 60,000 workers during some period of the year. In contrast, during the last decade, the employment level in housing varied between 22,000 and 26,000 workers. Thus, the 1971 plan implied more than a doubling of the work force previously engaged in housing construction.

Expansion of the labor force in housing could not have occurred at the expense of the nonhousing construction sector—which accounts for more than half of total construction employment—because the country's development plans, as well as the housing program itself, would have generated a large need for roads, bridges, industrial plants, drainage systems, community buildings, and other types of construction. The usual assumption that construction jobs could be filled by unskilled workers from the large masses of unemployed is only partially true, especially in cases where the housing program involved rather orthodox construction demanding semi- and fully-skilled labor in many tasks. Housing ministry officials believed that this bottleneck could have been avoided only by a top-priority, crash training program to provide an adequate labor force for the housing construction industry.

Further constraints on the implementation of the Unidad Popular housing program could have been expected to originate in the private sector of the housing industry. The transition to socialism, with its severe regulation of the private sector, could easily result in a reduction of production levels, due either to voluntary contraction of some firms hostile to the new government, or simply to unprofitable operating conditions. Therefore, it could be assumed that the private housing sector, which had accounted for 40 percent of the total production of dwelling units, would be drastically reduced and become marginal within a few years, and that the public sector would become increasingly responsible for national housing production. Shortages of skilled labor, equipment, and materials probably would have added more pressures for a total takeover of the construction industry by the government.

The impact of the housing program on the national economy cannot be disregarded. Strict price-cost controls were necessary to reduce the inflationary pressures of such an ambitious plan. Yet, the uncertainty prevalent in the private sector of the economy could have demanded that the Emergency Program be used as a countercyclical device to introduce more dynamism into the economic system. (The multiplier effect of housing is approximately 1 to 2.8 in Chile.)

Privately, some government planners and administrators realized that the housing targets would not be reached, but those at the highest levels within MINVU refused to change strategies. In order to forecast the possible level of achievement, before data became fully available, three hypotheses were selected and used by the author to estimate ranges of performance:

(1) Under optimistic assumptions, the private production of housing in 1971 would be equal to its best year of performance (1962)–20,000 dwelling units. Public sector production was set at a level 20 percent above its highest previous year, 1965, with a new peak of 43,000 dwelling units. This hypothesis resulted in a total production of 63,000 dwelling units, or only 80 percent of the planned target.

(2) Under more realistic assumptions, the private sector would build at the same level as its average in the 1960-1970 decade, i.e., 14,000 dwelling units. The public sector would repeat its past peak level of 36,000 dwelling units. This middle-range hypothesis resulted in a forecast of 50,000 dwelling units, or only 60 percent of the planned target.

(3) Under pessimistic assumptions, the private sector would contribute only 9,000 dwelling units, equal to its lowest year (1960). The public sector would build at the same level as its average in the past decade, 20,000 dwelling units. This results in a total of 29,000 dwelling units, or only 35 percent of the planned target.

At the time of these estimates (1972-1973), it was clear that if Chile reached the construction level of the middle-range forecast, fulfilling 60 percent of the Emergency Program, it would be a technical and organizational triumph. This would have equalled the highest housing production level of the past decade, and would have been attained while the country was undergoing the radical changes of the transition to socialism. Nevertheless, such a level of performance could have been used as the basis for political attacks by opposition groups, and it might have caused disappointment among supporters of Unidad Popular.

In summary, it was concluded that the Emergency Housing Program's target would not be reached, and that the most probable implementation level was 60 percent of the planned target, although it might have ranged from 35 to 80 percent of the target. Reaching the middle-range estimate, technically a formidable achievement, could have been interpreted, politically, as a liability.

Data on the actual performance of the program, due to appear at the end of 1973, may never be published. However, in early 1974 it became known that ODEPLAN and MINVU had estimated the housing production levels of 1971 and 1972 and were using this data for planning purposes. The actual achievements confirm the middle-range forecast presented above. During 1971 approximately 60,000 dwelling units were built or completed from the previous year, but in 1972 the production dropped to about 35,000 dwelling units–to the best recollection of government officials involved in planning activities. This means that, considering 1971 only, the Program was fulfilled at a 75 percent level, but if both 1971 and 1972 are considered–and retaining 80,000 dwelling units per year as the planned target–performance drops to 60 percent of the Program.

Returning to the scenario in 1971, it was apparent that high priority should have been assigned to the nationalization of several key industries (construction materials and machinery, household equipment), training programs for workers, the organization of a number of construction firms into a national construction consortium, and the development of interregional transportation systems for building materials. Also, it may have been necessary to encourage some transitional policies, such as the reorganization of uncooperative construction firms under the management of workers and technicians, as was done in manufacturing industry.

The gap between goals and means apparent above, and the urgency of using financial resources wisely, should be considered in evaluating the Unidad Popular housing program. Allocating large investments to housing means smaller shares for other sectors, such as industrial and rural development, education and health. However, housing is one of the few sectors that allows sizable trade-offs between cash and noncash inputs.

Consideration of noncash inputs in the Unidad Popular housing program could have had widespread effects. At the lowest income levels, construction of a small, 390-square feet dwelling for a squatter in 1971 cost E° 18,000, to which E° 7,400 must be added for urbanization costs, resulting in a total of E° 25,400 for the dwelling unit on a lot with services. If the occupant family were headed by an unskilled or marginal worker, its average income in early 1971 would have been about E° 350 per month, which means that the family's housing investment would be six times its annual income. This ratio—typical of low-income groups in many Latin American countries—is unacceptable because it forces either below-minimum levels of expenditures for other items, or substandard housing. Increasing the "salario vital" to E° 840 per month could have reduced the housing cost-to-annual-income ratio to 2.5:1; however, few families in the squatter settlements could have benefited to this extent, due to the high levels of unemployment and underemployment characteristic of these groups.

The alternative to this dilemma is to provide only the urban infrastructure—too technical in nature and too closely related to the city and neighborhood pattern to be left to individual initiative—and to train and organize the squatters to enable them to build their own homes, in accordance with their needs, available time, and changing economic possibilities, making maximum use of their tradition of building for themselves. Basically, this implies a strategy that is more egalitarian and less paternalistic, fully involving the people's initiative, efforts, and imagination. From the financial standpoint, this strategy would enable the government's cash investment to be reduced by almost two-thirds; conversely, the benefits of land with urban services could be made available to three times as many people.

Suggestions for revising the Unidad Popular housing program in accordance with the ideas outlined above were not acceptable to high officials of the Housing Ministry. The reason was what they felt to be the political liabilities of a housing program that might recall, even vaguely, the Christian Democrats' "Operación Sitio." Though some officials agreed that such a housing approach could be very successful now, all felt that the irresponsible management of "Operación Sitio" by the previous administration was too fresh in the minds of the people. Also, it must be noted that most Latin American politicians prefer projects that can be officially inaugurated within a relatively short period, rather than projects evolving over a number of years—a preference based on short-range personal considerations.

Finally, the locational effects of the housing program must be considered, especially in relation to the regional policies of Unidad Popular (see Chapter 13 of this volume). One of the most important strategies proposed by the new government was the rejuvenation of small and medium-sized towns, in an effort to divert rural migrants away from the big cities. Another important strategy was to "urbanize the countryside"—an objective closely linked to the agrarian reform—to provide urban-type services to rural communities, in an effort to keep people in the rural areas. There was obviously some inconsistency between these policies and the allocation of large numbers of dwelling units to the large cities, since the latter would increase the attraction of large cities for potential migrants. It is understandable, on the other hand, that housing was allocated where the need was most concentrated—a need that was most acute among the squatters who were among the most important supporters of Unidad Popular.

However, the large share of housing planned for large cities should have been reduced as soon as the existing need had been satisfied, increasing the share allocated to provincial towns.

CONCLUSION

The development of the housing program, like most planning activities in Chile under Allende, was pervaded by a strong awareness of its political implications. The planning approach of Unidad Popular tended to compensate for technical shortcomings with strong political commitment, ideological clarification, and enthusiasm. This phenomenon was manifested in the recurrence of unimaginative proposals in the area of housing policy. The housing program should have incorporated more experimental ideas, because planning and design alternatives must also reflect the radical character of the political system if success is to be achieved. Such ideas would have been in keeping with the radical new conception of housing itself being developed under Unidad Popular: Housing was withdrawn from the marketplace as an item to be purchased and sold and a source of profit for investors. Housing took on the character of another right of the population, produced and allocated according to social criteria, not unlike education or health.

The contrasts between the Unidad Popular and the Christian Democratic housing programs are of particular significance. The 1971 Emergency Housing Program indicated that Unidad Popular was prepared to allocate considerably more resources to housing, and, most important, to allocate more of them to the benefit of lower income and working class groups than ever before. The transitional policies implemented soon after the electoral victory of 1970 demonstrated that Unidad Popular was committed to fulfilling its promise of radical change to solve the country's critical housing problems. The Christian Democrats, on the other hand, began some technically innovative programs, but were not able to develop and implement them to their full potential.

The stress on political issues shown by Unidad Popular, together with its relative technical weaknesses, were probably the result of the drastic transformation which Chile was undergoing in 1971-1973. It could have been expected that once the political preconditions of Unidad Popular's programs were fairly well established, the technical level could have been raised.

It must also be remembered that, during this period, the highest priorities were rightly assigned to policies changing the economic structure of the country, such as nationalization of basic activities in foreign hands, redistribution of land and personal income, and control of inflation—in addition to the continuous political struggle for survival. It may be speculated that these areas of economic transformation, such as agrarian reform or nationalization of mines, are the ones in which considerable revolutionary experience was accumulated. Housing received less attention, suggesting that there was less experience with innovative change in this area.

Perhaps the two most distinctive characteristics of the Unidad Popular Program were that it showed a better understanding of the roots and causes of the housing problem, and that it aimed at a radical revision of the institutional framework in which housing is produced and allocated.

Chile was one of the few countries in Latin America in which housing was being recognized as a critical problem by the incumbent government, within a process of transition from a reformist to a revolutionary regime. It would have been very valuable to follow the experiment in years to come.

NOTE

1. It is very difficult to translate Chilean escudos into U.S. dollars because there was no floating exchange market. Instead, there was a set of fixed exchange values, such as \$1 = E^{O} 14 for industrial imports (in 1971), or \$1 = E^{O} 30 for foreign tourists (1971).

REFERENCES

MINVU [Ministerio de la Vivienda y Urbanismo] (1971) Programa habitacional de emergencia 1971. Santiago, Chile: MINVU.

--- (1970) Política de desarrollo urbano y vivienda. Santiago, Chile: MINVU.

--- (1969a) Análisis y programas de atención a urbanización marginal (callampas). Santiago, Chile: MINVU.

--- (1969b) Informe sobre misión de asistencia técnica al Ministerio de la Vivienda y Urbanismo de Chile. Santiago, Chile: MINVU.

--- (n.d.) Migraciones internas, marginalidad y desarrollo urbano. Santiago, Chile: MINVU.

ODEPLAN [Oficina de Planificación Nacional] (1970) El desarrollo económico y social de Chile en la década 1970-1980. Santiago, Chile: ODEPLAN.

Las primeras 40 medidas del gobierno popular (n.d.) Santiago, Chile.

Programa básico de gobierno de Unidad Popular (n.d.) Santiago, Chile.

PART IV

PUBLIC POLICIES AS DETERMINANTS OF URBAN GROWTH AND RURAL-URBAN INEQUALITIES

JOEL BERGSMAN, an economist, is Chief of the Community Development and Housing Section, Congressional Budget Office, Washington, D.C. His previous positions include teaching economics at the University of California, Berkeley; research in Brazil with IPEA, the Institute of Applied Economic and Social Research of the Ministry of Planning; and research at the Urban Institute, Washington, D.C. Among his principal publications are *Brazil: Industrialization and Trade Policies* (Oxford University Press, 1970); "The Agglomeration Process in Urban Growth," *Urban Studies,* October 1972; and "An Econometric Model of Employment Growth in U.S. Metropolitan Areas," *Environment and Planning,* to appear in 1975.

Chapter 8

URBAN GROWTH POLICY IN BRAZIL: INTENDED AND ACCIDENTAL

JOEL BERGSMAN

The message of this paper is simple and rather obvious: all kinds of public policies affect urban growth and urban problems; many policies that have important urban effects are designed with other objectives in mind and without consideration of the urban effects; and there is not much that can (or perhaps even should) be done about this. The importance of "accidental" urban growth policies, while obvious, is often neglected in discussions of urban policy. Such discussions often smack more of fantasy than of reality. The raison d'être of this paper is the need to recognize the importance of unintended effects, and thus make urban policy analysis more practical.

The paper is organized as follows: In the first section I will describe the objectives of urban growth policies and identify the most important policies that might influence them (intentionally or accidentally). In the second section I make a rough estimate of the quantitative importance of one "accidental" urban growth policy, as an example.

OBJECTIVES AND INSTRUMENTS OF URBAN GROWTH POLICY

Urban priorities of course differ, from country to country and from time to time. One is struck, nevertheless, by the similarity of concerns in many

Author's Note: A shorter version of this paper was presented at the Symposium on Urban Development sponsored by the Banco Nacional de Habitação, Rio de Janeiro, August 21-25, 1973, and was published as "Política de crescimento urbano–intencional e accidental" (*Estudos Econômicos,* Universidade de São Paulo, Brazil, Vol. 2, 1974).

countries, especially those of the less developed world. Which country does not have its low-income region, its rapidly growing large city, its urban slums? Which has fully adequate urban transport, water supply, or public health facilities? In which is pollution of air and water not a source of growing concern? These problems shape the objectives of urban policy.

Urban policy is first concerned with the distribution of people, jobs and income throughout the nation: the populations and rates of change of population of major regions and cities, the average income of different regions, and concentrations of poverty wherever they may be. One set of policy objectives stemming from these concerns relates to "regional balance," including such goals as increasing incomes in poor regions, reducing out-migration from these regions, improving the "human capital" in the regions, and so on. Brazil's Northeast is a classic example of such a region, as is Appalachia in the United States. Another set of objectives has to do with the sizes of cities and often includes reducing the growth of the largest cities, promoting the growth of other cities, increasing the diffusion of modern methods down through the urban hierarchy, and the like. Rapid growth of primate cities is often a cause of alarm (rightly or not). In Brazil, there is no single primate city, but the rapid and sustained growth of São Paulo has created some interest, at all levels of government, in diverting some of that city's future growth to other places.

In Brazil, still another policy objective relative to population distribution exists: the settlement of the undeveloped interior. This objective is partly based on geo-political motives—the government wants to secure its sovereignty over the territory by occupying it, and also wants to provide fuel for nationalistic pride—thus, "conquering the Amazon." Just as an earlier populist government had its Brasília, the present military government, even though wishing to appear more austere, similarly has its trans-Amazon highway. But the thrust towards the interior is not completely explained by such motives, any more than going to the moon can be completely explained by the needs and power of the military-industrial-aerospace complex in the United States. Evidently the spirit of the *bandeirantes* is still strong in the human race.

In addition to aspects of the distribution of people, jobs and income, urban policy commonly has another set of objectives to deal with the rapid growth of large metropolitan areas. These objectives include better administration of urban programs, increasing resources for providing public services in cities, reducing congestion and pollution, and some means of abating or dealing with rapid increases in land values.

Still another set of urban policy objectives relates to poverty. Poverty seems to be something that virtually every country has, because it is always defined in relative terms (see Jencks et al., 1972). Only extreme redistribution, such as in China or perhaps Cuba, can eliminate poverty. But most countries have not done so. Poverty, obviously, is the basic reason for inadequate housing, public services, and so on, and it is the basic reason why governments (sometimes) worry about subsidizing not only housing but other necessary services to the poor. The *urban* poor, being more visible, at least potentially more active politically, and easier to reach, usually get almost all of such subsidies.

Partial palliatives such as housing subsidies are seen by some as sops thrown to the poor, to reduce discontent caused by the highly unequal distribution of income typical of capitalistic development. The same policies are characterized by others as doing what is possible about income inequality, given tremendous political resistance to explicit redistribution policies. In the United States, we are slowly learning that the relative effectiveness of these policy alternatives depends crucially on market performance. In housing, we are starting to realize that housing supply responds quite well to demand, and that by far the best way to help poor people get better housing is to give them the means to buy it.[1] In health care, on the other hand, we have found that increasing people's effective demand has resulted in rapidly rising costs, partly because the supply of medical personnel has not responded so well to increased demand. Thus, direct income redistribution would probably solve most "urban problems" for some services (e.g., housing), but for others (e.g, health care) government action to assure adequate supply may also be necessary.

A final set of objectives of urban growth policy centers around unemployment and underemployment. Rapid population growth, rising agricultural productivity and more pervasive communication are causing rapid increases in urban labor supply, while the small size of the urban industrial sector, often combined with slow growth of output and use of capital-intensive technology, severely restricts the demand for this labor in most less developed countries (Baer and Herve, 1966). This is not much of a problem in southern Brazil today, but it is common around the world. The policy objectives here include both providing more jobs (usually through industrialization) and stemming the flow of migrants and perhaps also of babies.

Policies and Their Effects

The policies that affect urban growth can be grouped into four types, which I call physical, economic, and demographic policies, and "grand schemes."

"Physical" policies include many of those most commonly thought of as urban policies–in the terminology of this paper, "intended" urban policies. They include the provision of housing, transportation, communication, water, sanitation, and other elements of urban infrastructure. The differential provision of these facilities in different places may affect where people live. This idea follows the well-accepted model which posits that the potential supply of migrants to large cities is very large, and that actual in-migration continues until economic and other opportunities in the city are completely used by current residents (Todaro, 1969). Thus, provision of additional infrastructure may attract some additional migrants. I know of no empirical test of this particular hypothesis; such a test would be very difficult to perform, due to the (probably) high correlation between infrastructure services and other attractions of the city. However, it seems not unreasonable that superior education, health, and other services can and do attract migrants to cities.

In any case, the provision of these services certainly does have a major impact on the welfare of the people served. This is obvious and I will not pursue it further—although, of course, the accurate estimation of the benefits flowing from some of these services is a difficult and important problem in planning just how to provide the services.

Most of the policies that I classify as "economic" affect urban growth or geographic settlement patterns only accidentally. There is, however, one major exception: differential tax rates and other tax subsidies, depending on location. A classic example is the British scheme of taxing firms that locate in the most prosperous areas, and subsidizing those that locate in poor areas. Brazil's well known Article 34-18 is a less common policy of this type. Here the incentive consists of forgiveness of corporate income taxes that would be owed on operations elsewhere, if the funds are invested in a poor region (see Hirschman, 1968).

Of greater interest in this paper are the economic policies that affect urban growth in unintended ways. The most important way in which such policies work is the link between movements of people and movements of jobs (see Greenwood, 1973; Muth, 1971; Olvey, 1972). Obviously, any policy that affects the location of economic activity will affect patterns of urban growth. These policies may include various incentives to industrialization, such as tariffs or other restrictions on imports, export subsidies, favorable treatment of foreign private investment, and the like. Wage differentials are also important, not only among different places but also among different productive sectors (e.g., industry and agriculture).

Favoring industry over agriculture has obvious effects on urban growth: Most industries locate in cities, and in countries at Brazil's level of development, most industries locate in the largest cities, because of their superior infrastructure and communication, and other positive economies of scale. (Manufacturing has recently been decentralizing in the United States, but I suspect this to be a unique or near-unique experience.) Industrialization policies probably have the biggest effect on national settlement patterns in Brazil, and many other developing countries, of any single set of policies—and the effects are completely unintended.

Differential protection *among* industrial sectors also has important effects —sometimes quite deliberately. High protection for textiles in Brazil is a good example. At least until recently, there was wide variance in productivity among textile mills in Brazil (United Nations, 1963). The least efficient mills tended to be in the Northeast, and the most efficient ones in the Center-South. For many mills in the Northeast, high protection was probably necessary for survival. Thus, lower protection would have decreased employment in the textile industry in the Northeast and increased it in the South. Similarly, protection of inefficient production of salt, caustic soda, and coal in Brazil was enacted largely out of political concern for regions that were strongly dependent on these activities.

In general, more even-handed treatment of different economic activities would almost certainly tend to widen gaps between prosperous, growing places and poorer, lagging places. This is principally because the most efficient plants in any one industry tend to be in the prosperous, growing places; therefore the plants that would be shut down in case of a reduction in favored treatment tend to be in the poorer, lagging places.

Policies affecting regional income differentials are also important. For example, wage differentials have been shown to be important determinants of migration in country after country, including Brazil (Sahota, 1968). Government policies that promote or permit such differentials are certainly going to affect urban and regional growth patterns. The effect of place-specific differentials is direct and obvious; wage differentials among economic activities have the same effects, because different activities have different location patterns.

For the same reasons, all policies affecting income distribution will have urban growth effects, whether the policies have an explicit spatial dimension or not. Because high incomes are always relatively concentrated in large, rapidly growing metropolitan areas, increases in income inequality will tend to increase migration to these areas. This is true even though the migration itself probably tends to reduce income inequality (Yap, forthcoming).

Demographic policies obviously have important influences on settlement patterns. High birth rates mean high urban growth, both because of the natural increase of the urban population and higher out-migration from overpopulated rural areas. Recent Brazilian governments have not favored schemes to reduce birth rates. Their acceptance of (or even desire for) high rates of population growth seems to be motivated at least partly by their concern for settling large unoccupied territories in the interior of the country. This seems a bit ingenuous, to say the least, when it is perfectly obvious that most of the additional people are going to end up in existing cities, regardless of colonization schemes even on the Brazilian scale.

The fourth category of policies, earlier called "grand schemes," includes such projects as the creation of a new capital city (Brasília) in the interior and the highway network including the Belém-Brasília, Acre-Brasília, and Trans-Amazon highways. My statements elsewhere in this paper that these projects will have only small effects on urban growth in other parts of Brazil (e.g., they will not appreciably slow down the growth of Rio or São Paulo, at least for a long, long time) do not in themselves imply that the projects are not good ideas, nor that the projects do not have important effects in their own areas. The integration of the national territory is probably not something to be planned solely on the basis of formally rigorous cost-benefit analysis, as policy-makers in the eighteenth and nineteenth century United States well understood.[2]

As one final example of sometimes-intended, sometimes-accidental urban growth policy, let me cite state ownership of industry. Social and political forces are far more likely to affect the location of state-owned facilities than of privately owned ones. The location of Brazil's first integrated steel mill, the C.S.N. mill at Volta Redonda, is between Rio and São Paulo for a variety of political reasons. It is hard to imagine a private firm locating a steel mill at that site. More recent development of the steel industry seems to be based on the principle that each major port city should have one mill, rather than on any efficiency criteria. Private industry, on the other hand, shows a tremendous preference for São Paulo and other very large cities. Private profits tend to be greater in large, prosperous, rapidly growing places, and some observers believe that, in addition, private decision makers overestimate whatever profit differentials exist.[3]

This brief survey has covered only policies of *national governments.* Many other actors affect urban growth, including sub-national governments, supra-national bodies such as common markets, and private organizations both national and multi-national. When the effects of all actions taken by all these institutions are taken into account, intended urban growth policy appears even weaker in relation to accidental urban policies.

AN EXAMPLE OF ACCIDENTAL POLICY: THE EFFECTS OF TARIFF PROTECTION FOR INDUSTRY ON THE DISTRIBUTION OF POPULATION

To illustrate the impact of accidental urban growth policy, I present below a rough calculation of the effects of industrial protection—tariffs and other import restrictions—on the population of the former State of Guanabara (i.e., the city of Rio de Janeiro and some suburbs). The model used to make this estimate is crude and so the numerical result should be taken only as a first-order approximation.

The logic of the calculation is as follows: Protection increased the growth of manufacturing in Brazil. Part of this additional manufacturing located in Guanabara, and employed workers who—with their families—would otherwise have lived elsewhere. These residents in turn created jobs for other workers providing local services.

The calculations are simple. In a previous study, I estimated the amount of manufacturing in Brazil that would be eliminated in a move to free trade (Bergsman, 1974). In the year 1967 this amounted to NCr $10,567,000,000 (in terms of value added). I applied the percentage of all Brazil's value added that was produced in Guanabara (11.6 percent) and the national ratio of value added per worker in manufacturing (about NCr $10,000) to obtain an estimate of the number of jobs in Guanabara that would be affected. This number is about

121,000.[4] If the typical worker has a family of four people, then the direct population effect was roughly 500,000, or about 12 percent of the population of the State. However, protection existed for many years, and thus the jobs it created directly were augmented by "multiplier" effects–our 121,000 workers and their families also attract school teachers, policemen, grocers, maids, and others. Since the multiplier is probably two or more, a first guess at the total impact amounts to about one-fourth of the population of the state. This is an extremely rough estimate, but it suggests the practical importance of what has been said earlier.

Who would have recommended against import controls in order to reduce the population of Rio de Janeiro? How much merit would such a recommendation have? Those concerned with urban problems are right when they urge consideration of urban effects when other policies are designed. But they must themselves consider non-urban effects when worrying about urban growth policies. Moreover, it must be admitted that very little is known about the welfare effects, or even the income effects, of different patterns of urban growth (see Alonso, 1971). Until we know that one given pattern is so much worse than another, those concerned with urban problems will have to accept that they are not going to have all that much influence on national settlement patterns, and that dealing with the problems of people where they *do* live is more important than worrying about where they *should* live.

Brazil with its vast undeveloped territory comes closer to being an exception to this dictum than almost any other country. Brasília, and the various roads built through the interior, now capped by the Trans-Amazon highway, have already started to influence settlement patterns, and will no doubt have significant effects at some point in the future. But we have merely to look around in Rio or São Paulo to see that even these important projects have not seriously dampened the growth of the major cities, with all the benefits, and the problems, that such growth brings.

NOTES

1. I neglect problems of racial discrimination here. This whole discussion of market performance is, needless to say, highly simplified.

2. I base this conclusion not on approval of nationalism or grand schemes for their own sake, but rather on skepticism about the degree to which an analyst can predict with any accuracy the values of the variables that enter into a cost-benefit analysis of such large-scale projects. Indeed, many such variables are not even determined by the projects, but on the contrary are subject to further influences of government policy.

3. Hirschman (1958: 185), for example, has noted that "the external economies due to the [growth] poles, though real, are consistently overestimated by the economic operators."

4. This is probably an underestimate, since the greatest error probably lies in the use of the *average* percentage of manufacturing located in Guanabara ((11.6 percent) rather than the *marginal* percentage, which would be higher.

REFERENCES

ALONSO, W. (1971) "The economics of urban size." Regional Science Association Papers (European Congress, London, 1970) 26.

BAER, W. and M. HERVE (1966) "Employment and industrialization in developing countries." Quarterly Journal of Economics 80, 1 (February).

BERGSMAN, J. (1974) "Commercial policy, allocative efficiency and 'X-efficiency'." Quarterly Journal of Economics 88, 3 (August).

GREENWOOD, M. J. (1973) "Urban growth and migration: their interaction." Environment and Planning 5.

HIRSCHMAN, A. O. (1968) "Industrial development in the Brazilian Northeast and the tax credit scheme of Article 34/18." Journal of Development Studies (October).

--- (1958) The Strategy of Economic Development. New Haven, Conn.: Yale University Press.

JENCKS, C. et al. (1972) Inequality: A Reassessment of the Effect of Family and Schooling in America. Cambridge, Mass.: Harvard University Press.

MUTH, R. F. (1971) "Migration: chicken or egg?" Southern Economic Journal (January).

OLVEY, L. D. (1972) "Regional growth and inter-regional migration: their pattern of interaction." Review of Regional Studies (Winter).

SAHOTA, G. S. (1968) "An economic analysis of internal migration in Brazil." Journal of Political Economy (March-April).

TODARO, M. P. (1969) "A model of labor migration and urban employment in less developed countries." American Economic Review (March).

United Nations (1963) The Textile Industry in Latin America, Vol. II: Brazil. New York: United Nations. (E/CN.12/623, October)

YAP, L. (forthcoming) "Internal migration and economic development in Brazil." Quarterly Journal of Economics 89.

JOHN J. HARRIGAN is an Assistant Professor of Political Science at Hamline University, St. Paul, Minnesota. He received his Ph.D. from Georgetown University. His major fields of research and teaching are urban politics and comparative urban policy-making. Among his publications are *Political Change in Metropolis* (Little, Brown, forthcoming) and "Geography and Planning in Brazilian Urban and Regional Development" (*Luso-Brazilian Review,* Summer, 1975).

Chapter 9

POLITICAL ECONOMY AND THE MANAGEMENT OF URBAN DEVELOPMENT IN BRAZIL

JOHN J. HARRIGAN

The purpose of this chapter is to examine the hypothesis that the nature of the political economy in Brazil inevitably leads to incompatibilities between urban development planning and national economic development planning. This hypothesis is suggested by articles in popular as well as scholarly publications which have implied and often asserted that urban housing plans are subordinated to the interests of private investors (Rios, 1971), that rapid industrialization has failed to absorb the growing urban work force (Salmen, 1972), that the real income of the urban poor has declined rather than increased since the advent of the military government in 1964 (Poppino, 1973), that plans to colonize the Amazon primarily benefit large cattle ranchers and international corporations (Tamer, 1970), and that, despite the concentrated regional development plans in the Northeast, there has been very little redistribution of the wealth, the land or the income in that region (Tamer, 1970; SUDENE, 1969; Salmen, 1972).

There are no systematically collected data available for testing the hypothesis stated above. Consequently, the procedure to be followed here will be to analyze the rationale for this hypothesis through an examination of appropriate popular and scholarly literature. Four questions are central to this endeavor. First, what are the major features of Brazilian urban and regional development policies? Second, in what possible ways might there be incompatibilities between urban development planning and national economic development planning? Third, how have the theoretical concepts of "growth pole" and *"amenagement du territoire"* provided a rationale for resolving these potential incompatibilities? Fourth, what are some of the practical and theoretical consequences of these developments for the Brazilian political economy?

BRAZILIAN URBAN AND REGIONAL DEVELOPMENT PROGRAMS

Brazilian urban and regional development programs in recent years have had four principal objectives. First, programs have been instituted for the purpose of deterring migration into the developed metropolitan regions of the Center-South. Second, other programs have promoted population resettlement schemes in the interior (especially the Amazon basin) and within the larger cities (involving relocation of slum dwellers). Third, there has been established a national system of incentives to local, metropolitan, and regional organizations to engage in comprehensive development planning. Fourth, there have been increasing attempts to gain public control over land use practices in the larger cities.

That the government hopes to deter future migration into the metropolitan regions of the Center-South is well documented in statements by public officials (see, for example, Velloso, 1970). It is also apparent in the policy of constructing a national network of highways to provide access from the seacoast cities to the interior. This policy has been followed consistently for the past two decades. The problems of the Center-South are accentuated by the fact that a megalopolis is emerging between and around the two giant metropolises of Rio de Janeiro, with 7.1 million people, and São Paulo, with eight million people.[1] Within a contiguous region of about 50,000 square miles covering parts of four states[2] there exist three cities of over a million people and 29 other cities of over 100,000.[3] The entire region is highly urbanized and possesses a population of over 20 million people and an average density of over 300 persons per square mile. In the entire Western Hemisphere, the only region of comparable size with more big cities is the Northeastern seacoast of the United States.

A high population growth rate ensures continued growth of the Rio-São Paulo megalopolis through natural increase; and the huge population of over 42 million (Revista Brasileira de Estatística, 1971) in its hinterland ensures a steady supply of rural-urban migrants for many years to come. Outside of the State of São Paulo, the population is 60 percent rural (Rattner, 1972: 14). If growth continues unchecked, metropolitan São Paulo is expected to have 12 million people by 1980 and metropolitan Rio de Janeiro, 10 million (Visão, 1973c: 26). Because the government has consistently rejected a population birth control policy, the only prospects for limiting the growth of the megalopolis lie in a policy of population dispersion. And consistent government programs over the past 20 years suggest that such a policy has been pursued.

The policy of population dispersion has had two broad objectives: (1) channeling population growth away from the metropolises and into the interior, and (2) within the metropolises, instituting broad programs of slum removal and relocating the slum populations to satellite cities on the metropolitan fringe. The programs to channel internal migration into the interior are essential if the growth of the Rio-São Paulo megalopolis is to be limited. The largest source of migrants has been the impoverished Northeast. One study found that almost two-thirds of those migrating from this region end up in the Center-South megalopolis (Visão, 1973a). Programs to channel this migration into the interior have included the construction of the new capital, Brasília, the construction of a national highway network, and sporadic attempts at colonization. Of course, these programs have not stopped the growth of Rio and São Paulo; but they have siphoned into the interior much of the potential migration that otherwise would have ended up in the megalopolis. Just in Brasília and along the Belém-Brasília highway, there are now nearly three million people living in towns and settlements that did not even exist fifteen years ago. During the 1960s, the number of settlements along the Belem-Brasília highway increased from 10 to 120 (Sanders, 1973b). Had it not been for the construction of the new capital and the highway, many if not most of those three million people would now be living in the Rio-São Paulo megalopolis.

The most dramatic highway construction project has been the completion of the Trans-Amazon Highway. There are no reliable estimates for population settlements along it. During the 1970s, however, the government can realistically hope to attract several hundred thousand people out of the Northeast into the settlements that are emerging along the eastern portions of the Trans-Amazon and related highways.[4] In the western part of Amazônia an estimated 200,000 people migrated into the territory of Rondônia between 1970 and 1972 (Jornal do Brasil, 18 Feb. 1973). The government is now studying the possibility of creating two new states out of the southern flanks of the present states of Para and Mato Grosso (Veja, 1974: 21-22). It is thought by the sponsors of this plan that the creation of new states in those parts of Amazônia would make it easier to populate them and develop their agricultural potential.

The second objective of population dispersion has been to remove the *favela* (slum) dwellers from their inner-city sites and relocate them in satellite towns on the periphery of the cities. This program has been financed through a quasi-social security trust fund administered by the Banco Nacional de Habitação (BNH). Because employer and employee social security contributions have been earmarked for this fund, the BNH has been blessed with enormous capital to carry out its relocation projects. The most extensive slum removal project has been in Rio de Janeiro, where some 175,000 *favelados* were relocated by the BNH's urban renewal agency (CHISAM) between 1968 and 1971; another 600,000 were slated for removal between 1971 and 1976 (Rios, 1971; Salmen, 1972: 429). The program has been severely criticized for its exclusive reliance on relocation in dealing with urban problems (Rios, 1971; Salmen, 1972: 426-429; Leeds, 1973, 1974), but it has been stoutly defended by the government and the pro-government media (see Visão, 1973e: 43-49). Because it has strong elite support, it seems likely to continue as government urban policy for some time to come.

The government has also established an elaborate system of national incentives for local, metropolitan, and regional planning (Harrigan, 1974). At the regional level, planning has aimed primarily at promoting economic growth within the planning regions. The most notable examples are the regional superintendencies in the Northeast (SUDENE) and the Amazon (SUDAM), which have both had considerable success in attracting industries to their regions (Diégues Júnior, 1973). But they have been much less successful in promoting redistribution of land and distributing the new industrial wealth broadly (SUDENE, 1969: 270; Tamer, 1970). At the metropolitan and local levels, planners have also sought to attract new industry, but there has been a greater tendency at this level to focus on urban infrastructure problems and some of the consequences of economic growth. A national agency (SERFHAU) was created within the BNH to ensure that all municipalities create their own development plans (SERFHAU, 1971b). To accomplish this, SERFHAU uses a carrot and stick approach. Most of the planning is financed by SERFHAU and carried out by SERFHAU-trained or SERFHAU-sponsored planning technicians; but local governments that refuse to cooperate with SERFHAU in its planning objectives are faced with the threat of having their municipal budgets cut (Britto, 1970: 59).

Finally, urban development planning has progressed increasingly in the direction of gaining public control over land use practices. Typically, Brazilian cities have grown with very little regard for coordination or planning.[5] In Rio de Janeiro, for example, a recent wave of new office building construction in the central business district has been permitted by the city government without receiving any input from appropriate agencies on the construction's impact on automobile traffic, water supply, sewerage, or the availability of electrical energy (Visão, 1974b: 25). The lack of planning has had negative consequences for other aspects of urban life as well. In recent decades there has been a chronic shortage of housing; in metropolitan Rio de Janeiro alone, at least 1.8 million people live in substandard housing. A Ford Foundation study found that living conditions and real income among the poorest urbanites declined throughout the 1960s (Salmen, 1972: 426). In São Paulo, the death of 200 people in a single skyscraper fire was attributed to lax building and fire safety codes in the city (Visão, 1974c: 22-23).

The response to these problems has been to create metropolitan institutions capable of guiding future land use development and coping with some of the related urban problems. Legislation in 1973 established metropolitan councils in eight metropolitan areas. Although these councils are not without their critics (Visão, 1973d: 21), it is hoped that their development plans will begin to cope with urban sprawl and other urban problems. Metropolitan development plans are already far advanced in São Paulo and Belo Horizonte. In Rio de Janeiro, the two states of Rio de Janeiro and Guanabara, which share the metropolitan area, have been fused into a single state, partly in order to facilitate the creation of a metropolitan council and a development plan for greater Rio (Visão, 1974a: 20).

INCOMPATIBILITIES BETWEEN URBAN AND ECONOMIC DEVELOPMENT PLANNING

Most Brazilian officials would, no doubt, deny that the objectives of the country's urban and economic development plans are in any sense incompatible. Nevertheless, certain patterns have emerged in national planning that give reasonable support to the hypothesis that some aspects of the two types of plans are in conflict. Potential incompatibilities can be seen in four respects: internal migration policies, the role of urban planning in diverting scarce resources away from industrial development, the role of urban planning in redistribution of the national income, and environmental protection.

Incompatibilities in Migration Policies

There is a certain ambivalence in Brazil regarding migration to the Rio-São Paulo megalopolis. On one hand, urban planners articulate the point of view that continued in-migration is dysfunctional in Rio de Janeiro and São Paulo and must be curbed. On the other, the BNH's housing programs and favela eradication schemes do not resettle the favelados outside of the megalopolis: They simply resettle them out of the central city, where the favelas had become eyesores occupying very valuable land that could be more lucratively exploited by real estate speculators (Rios, 1971). The most rapid growth in the megalopolis has occurred not in the central cities of Rio de Janeiro and São Paulo but in the industrial satellite cities near them. The most striking example is Nova Iguaçu, a satellite city within the boundaries of Greater Rio, which grew from 135,000 people in 1960 to 732,000 in 1970, and to an estimated 1,000,000 by 1973 (Fundação IBGE, 1971a; Visão, 1973b). Similarly, in São Paulo, plans for dispersing urban growth apparently aim not so much at dispersing it out of the metropolitan area as at channeling as much of it as possible along the highways toward Rio de Janeiro (Visão, 1970: 150-158). This may be more realistic than trying to stop the growth altogether, but it does suggest an ambivalence toward stopping it.

Closely related to the question of limiting growth as opposed to channeling it is the need of expanding industries in the megalopolis for increasing numbers of workers. Despite some findings that Brazil's industrial growth has not kept pace with the growth of the labor force (see, for example, Salmen, 1972: 423), the present Finance Minister insists that there is a shortage of industrial laborers in the megalopolis, not a surplus (Simonsen, 1972: 42). It is also true that wage and salary costs to employers may be kept down more easily if the supply of industrial laborers and service workers greatly exceeds the demand. The Finance Minister's statement may, therefore, suggest that continued growth of the urban work force is economically functional, even though it may be dysfunctional from the perspective of urban planning.

Urban Planning as Diverting Scarce Resources

A second incompatibility between urban planning and economic development policies concerns the role of urban planning in diverting scarce resources away from the government's drive toward rapid industrialization. To the extent that urban growth planning diverts public and private investments into urban services and infrastructure, it limits the amount of investment capital available for developing key sectors of the economy. Conversely, to the extent that public investments have been channeled into productive sectors to stimulate industrial expansion, this has reduced the resources available for limiting the growth of the Center-South megalopolis and for improving the quality of life in urban areas.

Implementation of urban development plans is likely to be very costly. It was estimated in 1970 that only 55 percent of the nation's urban population had public water service and only 30 percent had public sewers. In São Paulo, the figures were one-third without water and two-thirds without sewers (Salmen, 1972: 422). Plans have been announced to raise the figures for the national urban population to 80 percent with public water supply and 50 percent with sewers (Velloso, 1972: 12-13). This construction of sewer and water facilities, if it can be achieved, will be enormously expensive. The BNH's plans for favela eradication are also very expensive; in Rio de Janeiro alone, over $100 million has been spent in destroying favelas, and the new dwellings constructed for relocated favelados have cost about $1,000 each (Salmen, 1972: 429-430). In addition to housing, water, and sewers, the growing urban population will also require health care facilities, schools, electricity, and other public services.

Urban Planning as Redistribution of Income

It seems fairly clear that the Brazilian model of development is based upon a forced austerity among the poorer classes in order to concentrate national income in the hands of the so-called producing classes who will reinvest it in basic industries (Poppino, 1973: 109-111). This policy is partially contradicted by urban development programs. To the extent that such programs provide housing, water, sewers, electricity, schools, health care facilities, and other public services to poor people who could not afford to purchase them from their own earnings, these programs promote a redistribution of the national income. Thus, in a country such as Brazil, which is seeking to industrialize as rapidly as possible, urban planning represents a waste of needed resources, because it redistributes income in what is thought to be an unproductive fashion. The logic of the Brazilian model for economic development would thus seem to create pressures for minimizing the amount of resources devoted to urban development programs.

If one accepts Jorge Hardoy's definition of urban development as encompassing urban land reform, there is clearly an incompatibility between urban and economic development planning in Brazil. In Hardoy's terms, such urban reform would include public control over (if not ownership of) all metropolitan land, limiting the influence of urban pressure groups, making basic modifications in the urban occupational structure, and reorganizing governmental institutions for the purpose of gaining greater centralized control over the metropolises (Hardoy, 1972: 31-37). Attempts to institute several of these reforms in Brazil would probably be unsympathetically received by the government, and would surely provoke strong reactions among certain interest groups in the private sector.

Environmental Protection

A final indication that urban development planning may be antithetic to the government's plans for economic development is provided by its stand on ecological and population control questions. Brazil opposed attempts at the Stockholm Conference to promote international agreements on ecological concerns. The government's position seems to be that as much as possible will be done to protect the environment, but such concerns will not be allowed to stand in the way of the country's rapid industrialization (Sanders, 1973a). A similar posture has been adopted in relation to limiting population growth. Given huge expanses of virgin territory to be exploited, given the conventional military viewpoint that a large population is a necessity for strategic strength, and given a strong official belief in the need for a rapidly growing labor force for industrial growth, the government sees no reason to limit population growth. Even if the plans to rechannel migration into the interior are successful, a substantial proportion of the future population increase—probably more than 50 percent—will occur in the metropolitan areas. Thus from an urban planning point of view, both the policy of unlimited population growth and the tendency to minimize the ecological consequences of industrialization compound the problems of promoting orderly development in the megalopolis.

RESOLVING THE INCOMPATIBILITIES

It is clear that any urban or regional plan which stands a chance of being implemented by the incumbent regime in Brazil must come to terms with the conflicting economic priorities described above. Urban planners must indicate how their objectives can be achieved and at the same time contribute to the realization of the higher priority national goals of industrialization and increased economic productivity.

Their task has been facilitated in recent years by the rapid popularization in Brazil of two French concepts of regional development. Just as Brazil's economic development is disproportionately concentrated in the Center-South megalopolis, French development has been concentrated in the Paris region.

When French officials decided to decentralize their country's economic growth, planners promoted the concept of *amenagement du territoire.* Eight equilibrium metropolises were designated to counterbalance the growth of Paris and to receive public investments that would encourage industries and people to relocate there rather than in Paris (Rodwin, 1970; Hall, 1971). At the same time, French economist François Perroux and French geographer Bernard Kayser were promoting the concept of "growth poles." In Perroux's view, space is one of the independent variables affecting economic development. Development is never diffused equally throughout a nation; rather, it centers on specific geographic areas which he calls growth poles.

Brazilian geographers and planners viewed these concepts as relevant to the Brazilian experience for several reasons (see Harrigan, 1975). The concept of *amenagement du territoire* was, of course, entirely consistent with the establishment of regional development agencies such as SUDENE and with the ideas of economists such as Celso Furtado (1961; 1962), who had argued for several years that special regional development programs must be devised to eliminate the regional disparities in economic development. The growth pole strategy of development, as envisioned by Brazilian planners, would enable public investments to be concentrated in a few rationally determined growth poles rather than dispersed throughout the country according to patterns of political influence. This would serve to discourage the over-concentration of development in the Rio-São Paulo megalopolis. The new growth poles, rather than becoming cities that drain the human resources and economic vitality out of the surrounding countryside, would instead stimulate development in the surrounding region. Once this rationale gained wide acceptance, the major task for planners was to identify the localities that were to serve as the development poles.

Once articulated, the idea of growth poles enjoyed a rapid rise to popularity. For the residents of economically depressed regions, it provided a rationale for seeking the alleviation of regional deficiencies. For those persons concerned primarily with industrialization and economic productivity, it meant that decentralizing industry around predetermined growth poles would produce more economic development more rapidly than allowing further concentration in the megalopolis (Faissol, 1972). From the urban planning perspective it justified attention to the spatial dimensions of development and supported efforts to reverse the excessive congestion of Rio de Janeiro and São Paulo. For those interested in populating the interior, it provided a rationale for attempts to channel migration into newly identified and in some cases (e.g., Brasília) newly created development poles.

SUDENE sponsored a seminar on the application of growth pole concepts in the Northeast (Andrade, 1967). A methodology was developed for ranking cities at different levels of growth pole development (Faissol, 1972). São Paulo was designated a national growth pole; nine other major cities were designated regional growth poles; and 113 smaller cities were designated subregional or local growth poles (Babarovic, 1972: 117). The concepts of *amenagement du territoire* and growth poles were also used to justify the government's policy of constructing the Trans-Amazon Highway in 1970, connecting it with a national network of highways, and promoting the establishment of new towns along these new highways. These policies were referred to collectively as the Programa de Integração Nacional. In the broadest sense, this program could be rationalized by urban and regional planners as channeling migration away from the Center-South and toward secondary development poles in the Amazon. This would also avoid an economically unproductive dispersion of population along the Amazon roads, as had occurred along the Belém-Brasília highway where deliberate colonization policies were lacking (Geiger, 1969; Sanders, 1973b). The Ministry of Planning spoke of establishing *pólos de irradiação* at the larger Amazonian cities such as São Luis, Teresina, and Pôrto Nacional, and *pólos de atração* at the more remote Amazon cities such as Santarem and Macapá (Godolphim, 1972). The Ministry called for an integrated program of economic investments in these poles, the construction of a road and communications network connecting them, and the relocation of the armed forces in order to "protect" them.

It is likely that the Brazilian government would have proceeded with its plans to occupy the Amazon regardless of the rationale provided by the new concepts of *amenagement du territoire* and growth poles. Their importance was to provide an intellectual framework within which the Amazon policies could be rationalized. They also, as indicated above, provided some operational guidance as to the form which the Amazonian occupation should take.

IMPLICATIONS OF GROWTH POLE THEORY FOR BRAZILIAN URBAN AND ECONOMIC DEVELOPMENT

To recapitulate the argument to this point, one of the most significant aspects of Brazil's political economy since the mid-1960s has been a growing concern for the spatial distribution of economic development. This concern has permitted an attenuation, but not an elimination, of several basic incompatibilities that appeared to exist between economic and urban development planning objectives. If it is true that continued economic progress for the nation is dependent upon a more selective stimulation of development in several regional growth poles rather than in one megalopolis, it can then be argued that economic development demands the implementation of urban development programs in the newly designated growth poles.

Because the government wants to promote migration to the new growth pole centers in the interior, it has a strong incentive to provide the urban services that will help to attract people to them. When the government announced its original plans for colonizing the Amazon through a proliferation of *agrovilas* (agricultural settlements) along the Trans-Amazon Highway, it promised that a wide range of urban amenities would be made available to each settlement—military security, a post office, medical and dental facilities, schools, a meteorology station, and telecommunications facilities, among others. There is little evidence that the government has been able to keep its promises. But the major point is that in order to induce people to migrate to the agrovilas, it was necessary to make such promises. If the government seriously wishes to develop new growth poles in the interior, it would seem that the diversion of capital into urban infrastructure is an absolute necessity.

Support for such an investment policy may even be forthcoming from the private sector. As noted above, São Paulo and Rio de Janeiro employers might have reason to object to plans to diminish the growth of the labor supply in their cities. But other employers who are relocating in the new growth poles (under the stimulus of government tax incentives) have an equally important reason for wanting to see potential laborers migrate away from the megalopolis rather than toward it. The industrial relocation policies have thus helped to create a new set of interests which may support policies that promote migration into the interior.

It should be noted that the population of the interior and the creation of new growth poles there may reduce demands for redistribution of the nation's wealth. One of the government's motives for constructing the Trans-Amazon Highway and in settling the interior was very clearly to dissipate the concentration of hundreds of thousands of underemployed and impoverished males in the Northeast (Velloso, 1970). The rural population there continued to grow throughout the 1960s and still constitutes a major source of cityward migrants. Although the government has redistributed a substantial amount of land within the region, provision of arable land to all landless Northeasterners would require a massive redistribution effort which would seriously affect agricultural productivity, at least in the short run. If landless workers could be induced to resettle in agrovilas or in other population centers in the interior, pressure for redistribution of land and income in the already overpopulated parts of the country would be lessened.[6]

A final implication of the population-of-the-interior and growth-pole schemes should be noted. If the government commits itself to financing urban development projects in the interior, the net result cannot help but increase the competition for already scarce funds for providing urban services in the established metropolises. São Paulo, for example, with a population of five million in 1970, has a city government budget of only about $170,000,000 (Salmen, 1972: 421-422). Not only must it face competition for public investment funds from the industrial sector; it must also compete with the new urban centers of the interior which also seek national government assistance in providing urban amenities. One must ask whether the Brazilian government is not creating conditions analogous to those in the United States, where the oldest metropolises are by and large the most neglected and underfinanced in the public sector.

In the final analysis, given the nature of the political economy in Brazil, urban planning objectives will continue to be subordinated to the top-priority goals of rapid industrialization and higher GNP. Where urban objectives coincide with national economic and political objectives, then promotion of the urban objectives will be feasible. Perhaps the most notable example of such congruence was the creation of elaborate and extremely profitable fiscal and tax incentives for industries to locate in the Northeast and in such interior cities as Manaus and Goiánia (Simonsen, 1972). Not only did such measures help to attain the geopolitical objective of populating the interior and the economic objective of regional development, but they also helped to divert a portion of the migratory flow away from the Rio-São Paulo megalopolis. However, where urban planners' objectives have conflicted with powerful interests in the established metropolises, planning has been much less successful. The most important example of such conflict has been in the urban housing program. A program of favela improvement might have dealt more successfully and economically with the housing shortage in Rio de Janeiro than has the BNH's favela eradication program; but the confluence of powerful interests among real estate speculators, the construction industry, and BNH planners made the more lucrative favela eradication scheme a much more salable program (Rios, 1971).

The concepts of growth pole and *amenagement du territoire* have helped to legitimize urban and regional planning in a planning environment that has been heavily oriented toward the objectives of rapid industrialization and increased productivity. They have not, however, enabled urban planners to prevail over those within the military government whose principal preoccupation is the achievement of these economic objectives.

NOTES

1. Unless otherwise noted, all population data are for 1970 and are taken from Fundação IBGE (1971b).

2. These states were São Paulo, Rio de Janeiro, Guanabara and Minas Gerais. In 1974 the two states of Rio de Janeiro and Guanabara were fused into a single state.

3. The third city of over a million people is Nova Iguaçu, a satellite city of Rio de Janeiro; its population reached the million mark in 1974. If the megalopolis continues expanding to include Belo Horizonte, it will contain four cities of over a million people, and another three million people (in 1970 data) must be added to the total megalopolis population (Harrigan, 1974). Many of the 29 cities of 100,000 are included in the metropolitan areas of Rio de Janeiro and São Paulo.

4. These comments are not intended as an endorsement of either the economic or the ecological feasibility of the Trans-Amazon Highway. The highway has been bitterly criticized by some observers and resoundingly praised by others. There are some indications that the government is abandoning its Trans-Amazon colonization scheme of a network of *agrovilas* in favor of a more modest attempt at creating a few experimental cities (Visão,

1974d: 21). However, there are other indications that maintaining the present highways, constructing new ones, and promoting the settlement of people along them remains a policy of high government priority (Sanders, 1973b). None of the questions surrounding the Trans-Amazon Highway can be resolved in the short confines of this chapter. What can be stated with certainty, however, is that the Trans-Amazon Highway was completed and that many thousands of people have come to live along it (Sanders, 1973b).

5. The two major exceptions to this are Brasília and Belo Horizonte, both of which were created according to elaborate plans. In both cases, however, after the initial implementation of these plans, urban growth occurred with little regard for the careful guidelines established by the original planners (see Epstein, 1973).

6. It should be pointed out that the new wealth to be generated in the interior is not likely to be distributed very widely. The mineral wealth and other natural resources are being exploited primarily by large corporations, which are not likely to reinvest much of their profits in the interior. This is also true of the new industries established by large corporations in places such as Manaus and Goias. And while the agrovilas along the Trans-Amazon Highway are organized into relatively small farming plots, much of the land along the Belém-Brasília highway and other highways leading into the Amazon basin is being occupied primarily by large ranchers, who want the land not for cultivation but for cattle grazing (Tamer, 1970). This is a pattern that does not seem likely to produce much redistribution of whatever new wealth is created.

REFERENCES

ANDRADE, M. C. de (1967) Espaço, polarização, e desenvolvimento: a teoría dos pólos de desenvolvimento e a realidade Nordestina. Recife: Centro de Administração Municipal.

BABAROVIC, I. (1972) "Development poles and rural marginality in Brazil: toward a definition of regional policy," in G. Geisse and J. E. Hardoy (eds.) Latin American Urban Research, Volume II: Regional and Urban Development Policies: A Latin American Perspective. Beverly Hills, Calif.: Sage Publications.

BRITTO, L. N. de (1970) "O federalismo na constituição de 1967." Revista Brasileira de Estudos Políticos 28 (January).

DIEGUES JUNIOR, M. (1973) "Os orgãos de desenvolvimento regional e o processo de integração." Revista de Ciencia Política 7 (October-December): 117-132.

EPSTEIN, D. (1973) Brasília, Plan and Reality: A Study of Planned and Spontaneous Urban Development. Berkeley and Los Angeles: University of California Press.

FAISSOL, S. (1972) "Pólos de desenvolvimento no Brasil: uma metodología quantitativa e uma exemplificação empírica." Revista Brasileira de Geografía 34 (April-June).

Fundação IBGE (1971a) Censo demográfico de 1970: resultados preliminares. Rio de Janeiro: Fundação IBGE.

--- (1971b) Sinopse preliminar do censo demográfico do Brasil, 1970. Rio de Janeiro: Fundação IBGE.

FURTADO, C. (1962) A pré-revolução Brasileira. Rio de Janeiro: Editôra Fundo de Cultura.

--- (1961) Desenvolvimento e subdesenvolvimento. Rio de Janeiro. Editôra Fundo de Cultura.

GEIGER, P. P. (1969) "Regionalização." Revista Brasileira de Geografía 31: 5-25.

GODOLPHIM, W. da C. (1972) "Amazônia e seus problemas," pp. 133-149 in Brasil: realidade e desenvolvimento: 1972. São Paulo: Suggestões Literarias.

HALL, P. (1971) The World Cities. New York: McGraw-Hill.

HARDOY, J. E. (1972) "Urbanization policies and urban reform in Latin America," pp.

19-44 in G. Geisse and J. E. Hardoy (eds.) Latin American Urban Research, Vol. 2: Regional and Urban Development Policies: A Latin American Perspective. Beverly Hills, Calif.: Sage Publications.

HARRIGAN, J. J. (1975) "Geography and planning in Brazilian urban and regional development." Luzo-Brazilian Review 12 (Summer).

--- (1974) "The emergence of the Brazilian megalopolis and the national system of metropolitan planning." Paper presented at the Annual Meeting of the Rocky Mountain Council of Latin American Studies, Lubbock, Texas, March.

--- (1973) "Some racial implications of urban and regional planning in Brazil." Paper presented at the Annual Meeting of the Midwest Association of Latin American Studies, Terre Haute, Indiana, October.

LEEDS, A. (1974) "Housing-settlement types, arrangements for living, proletarianization, and the social structure of the city," pp. 67-99 in W. A. Cornelius and F. M. Trueblood (eds.) Anthropological Perspectives on Latin American Urbanization: Latin American Urban Research, Vol. 4. Beverly Hills, Calif.: Sage Publications.

--- (1973) "Political, economic, and social effects of producer and consumer orientations toward housing in Brazil and Peru: a systems analysis," pp. 181-211 in F. F. Rabinovitz and F. M. Trueblood (eds.) Latin American Urban Research, Vol. 3. Beverly Hills, Calif.: Sage Publications.

POPPINO, R. E. (1973) "Brasil: novo modelo para o desenvolvimento nacional." Revista Brasileira de Estudos Políticos 36 (July): 105-114.

RATTNER, H. (1972) Industrialização e concentração econômica em São Paulo. Rio de Janeiro: Fundação Getúlio Vargas.

Revista Brasileira de Estatística (1971) "Evolução da população Brasileira." Revista Brasileira de Estatística 32 (July-September).

RIOS, J. A. (1971) "Social transformation and urbanization: the case of Rio de Janeiro." Discussion Paper No. 24, University of Wisconsin-Milwaukee, Center for Latin America, Milwaukee, Wisconsin.

RODWIN, L. (1970) Nations and Cities: A Comparison of Strategies for Urban Growth. Boston: Houghton Mifflin.

SALMEN, L. F. (1972) "Urbanization and development," in H. J. Rosenbaum and W. G. Tyler (eds.) Contemporary Brazil: Issues in Economic and Political Development. New York: Praeger.

SANDERS, T. G. (1973a) "Development and environment: Brazil and the Stockholm Conference." American Universities Field Staff Reports 17, 7 (June).

--- (1973b) "Colonization on the Transamazon Highway." American Universities Field Staff Reports 17, 3 (March).

SIMONSEN, M. H. (1972) Brasil: 2002. Rio de Janeiro: APEC Editôra.

SERFHAU (1971a) SERFHAU: Programações executadas 67/70. Rio de Janeiro: Ministério do Interior, Serviço Federal de Habitação e Urbanismo.

--- (1971b) Orientações quanto e elaboração e a presentação dos planos micro-regionais. Rio de Janeiro: Ministério do Interior, Serviço Federal de Habitação e Urbanismo.

SUDENE (1969) SUDENE dez anos. Recife: SUDENE.

TAMER, A. (1970) Transamazônica: solução para 2001. Rio de Janeiro: APEC Editôra.

Veja (1974) 24 April.

VELLOSO, J. P. dos R. (1972) Brasil: Emergência da nova sociedade. Rio de Janeiro: Ministério do Planejamento e Coordenação Geral.

--- (1970) "A estratégia de desenvolvimento e o programa de integração nacional." Revista do Serviço Público 105 (May-August): 15-30.

Visão (1974a) 15 May.

--- (1974b) 29 April.

--- (1974c) 25 February.

——— (1974d) 11 February.
——— (1973a) 10 September.
——— (1973b) 27 August.
——— (1973c) 23 July.
——— (1973d) 14 May.
——— (1973e) 29 January.
——— (1970) 21 November.

RICHARD WEBB, a Peruvian economist, received his Ph.D. from Harvard University. He is currently a research associate of the Woodrow Wilson School of Public and International Affairs at Princeton University, and is director of a cross-national study of public policy and income distribution in Third World countries. He also teaches development economics in the Center for Latin American Development Studies at Boston University. His publications include *The Distribution of Income in Peru* and *Government Policy and the Distribution of Income in Peru, 1963-1973* (Discussion Papers No. 26 and No. 39, Research Program in Economic Development, Princeton University, 1972 and 1974, respectively).

Chapter 10

PUBLIC POLICY AND REGIONAL INCOMES IN PERU

RICHARD WEBB

In this paper I consider the way in which public policy has affected regional income differences in Peru since 1963. Most of the discussion refers to urban-rural differences, but some comments are also made on other regional income differences. The stress is on policy. In the context of an underdeveloped market economy there are strong market forces affecting regional income trends, usually in the direction of greater inequality. My question is whether government policies have tended to reinforce or to offset such forces. In the first section of the paper I will describe the starting point: the principal regional income levels and trends in 1961. The second section analyzes the ways in which policy instruments can discriminate between regions. The final section reviews the main discriminatory effects of policies since 1963.

REGIONAL INCOME IN 1961

The 1961 statistics on income levels shown in Table 1 reveal a great deal of regional diversity. The urban-rural income ratio was almost 3:1 (after excluding corporate profits). The geographical poles of the income distribution are perhaps best represented by the city of Lima and by the "Mancha India," five contiguous departments[1] in the southern Sierra which concentrate much of the Indian population. Their incomes differed sharply: 7,400 *soles* per annum in the Mancha India, 23,300 soles in Lima (33,800 if profits are included). Leaving Lima aside, the ratio between incomes in other Coastal provinces and in the Sierra was still 2:1.

TABLE 1
INDICATORS OF REGIONAL PERSONAL INCOME DIFFERENCES IN 1961

Region	*Average Annual Income*[a] *(in thousand soles)*	*Index*	*Labor Force (thousands)*
All Peru	11.6	100	3034
Rural	7.3	63	1735
Urban	19.5	168	1299
Modern[b]	(30.2)	(260)	(587)
Traditional	(10.9)	(94)	(792)
Coast (excluding Lima)	12.4	107	707
Sierra	6.6	57	1492
Jungle	7.8	67	246
Lima	23.3	201	619
Mancha India	7.4	64	750

a. Excludes corporate profits.

b. Mostly urban, but includes about 80,000 rural sugar estate workers, miners, and rural-based government employees.

SOURCE: Webb (1972).

The spread of provincial incomes is summarized in Table 2. The figures indicate the wide range that existed between the poorer and richer provinces outside Lima; thus, the unweighted average incomes of the ten richest and ten poorest provinces were 15,300 and 3,100 soles respectively. The data also point up the income cleavage between Coast and Sierra, with Jungle incomes falling toward the middle of the range.

At the same time, there was much diversity of income within the major regions. In both Lima and the Mancha India, for instance, incomes spanned the four quartiles of the total income distribution. The spread was greater in the Mancha India, where half were in the lowest quartile, 14 percent in the top

TABLE 2
SIZE DISTRIBUTION OF INCOME BY PROVINCES, 1961

Mean Annual Income (thousand soles)	*Number of Provinces*			
	Total	*Coast*	*Sierra*	*Jungle*
up to 3.9	12	–	12	–
4.0 to 5.9	37	–	33	4
6.0 to 7.9	40	2	29	9
8.0 to 9.9	15	4	9	2
10.0 to 11.9	20	7	7	6
12.0 to 13.9	8	7	1	–
14.0 +	11	8	2	1
Total	143	28	93	22

SOURCE: Webb (1972: 17).

quartile, and 6 percent in the top decile. Similarly, 31 percent of the total rural population belonged in the upper half of the income distribution, and 12 percent in the top quartile. Conversely, 25 percent of the urban population fell into the bottom half of the distribution; these were chiefly members of the urban traditional labor force and the inhabitants of smaller towns.

The evidence also suggests that urban and Coastal incomes were growing faster than incomes in other regions during the fifties and early sixties. The main trends are summarized in Table 3: Urban incomes were growing at more than twice the rate of rural incomes, while, within the rural sector, the rate of increase was rapid on the Coast (3.0 percent per annum) and slow in the Sierra and Jungle (0.7 percent p.a.).

The growing urban-rural differential was not a reflection of rising incomes in Lima alone, nor in the modern sector only. Some of the fastest rates of income growth occurred outside Lima, such as on the sugar plantations (some of which are classed as urban), in mining centers and among the widespread bureaucracy. At the same time, more than half of the Lima labor force consisted of self-employed or small-firm employees whose incomes were rising more slowly, for instance, than those of Coastal farm workers.

Furthermore, though the Sierra as a whole was lagging, the region cannot be described as stagnant. In fact, all parts of the Sierra seem to have been involved in an awakening to modern life that is perhaps best described by the phrase "commercial revolution": a rapid increase in the movement of money, goods, and people. This was accompanied by changes that precede or accompany income growth, such as the creation of physical infrastructure (particularly roads and urban facilities), and the spread of schooling. The impact of such changes, however, was uneven; the evidence suggests that most income growth accrued to two groups: (a) regions with easiest access to Lima and the central coast, and (b) the inhabitants of small towns, chiefly the merchants, artisans, bureaucrats, medium-sized landowners, and other members of the rural bourgeoisie.

Thus, the growth in Sierra small-town population (2.3 percent per annum versus 0.8 percent for the rural population), the impressive increase in savings

TABLE 3
TRENDS IN PER CAPITA REAL INCOME, 1950-1966

	Annual Rate of p/c Income Growth
Urban[a]	2.8%
Modern sector	4.1
Traditional sector	2.0
Rural	1.3
Coast	3.0
Sierra and Jungle	0.7

a. The "urban" modern sector estimate includes a small number of rural labor force in sugar estates, mines and government service.

SOURCE: Webb (1974b).

deposits (5.0 percent p.a. in real terms), the expansion of the road system and of vehicle traffic, and the relative increase in the non-farm labor force (2.9 percent p.a. versus 0.8 percent for farm workers) all indicate growing *urban* incomes within the Sierra. The towns, rather than the farm labor force, seem to have been the direct beneficiaries of the expansion in commerce and transport. The urban population was also the principal beneficiary of the growth in the government sector, most notably in the early sixties. The influx of educational, health, police and rural development personnel raised government payrolls chiefly in provincial and district capitals. Average town incomes were raised by the compositional effect of government wages–which were high by provincial standards–and by the local multiplier effects of the government payroll.

Growing regional inequality was clearly the result of both market and policy forces. In fact, the two are hard to separate. "Market" forces, for instance, include the bargaining strength of unions in the modern sector, most of whom are in cities. Yet, union strength is partly the consequence of past government policies towards unionization and union activity. The following section will discuss the ways in which public policy can affect regional inequalities either directly, as by the regional distribution of schools, or less directly, by affecting market behavior.

REGIONAL INCOME POLICY: SOME GENERAL POINTS

Before looking at some of the data which reflect on the regional bias of public policy in Peru it is useful to discuss how and why policies do discriminate between regions.

A first point is that most regional discrimination is a by-product of policies primarily aimed at other goals. Peru, as probably most LDCs, has had a "regional policy," certainly under the Belaúnde (1963-1968) and the current administrations. To a large extent, that policy was motivated by a desire for a better income distribution. But "regional policy" in itself has been a minor component of the total impact of government on regional income differences. "Regional policy" in Peru has been implemented largely through minor changes in the regional allocation of public investment and through modest efforts to influence the allocation of private investment. A much greater impact on regional incomes has resulted from the general design of tax, industrial, government expenditure, and other policies which were aimed principally at economic growth or at income redistribution towards powerful middle-income groups.

In any case, regional policy in Peru has been directed chiefly at fostering the growth of smaller cities as an alternative to the growth of Lima. Though "excess urbanization" is often decried, no measures of importance have been directed at stemming the overall growth of the urban population nor at deliberately redistributing income from urban to rural sectors. Peru's regional policy has therefore had some effect on the regional allocation of industry, most notably to Arequipa, but that policy has not attempted to reverse the predominantly pro-urban bias of both market forces and of various government measures.

Second, much of the regional discrimination by government is a consequence of the location-specific nature of many policy instruments. Roads, medical facilities, and water supply systems, for instance, are highly location-specific, and are therefore biased in favor of urban dwellers. To some extent, this urban bias is admittedly less of an inflexible technical datum than it appears to be: it partly results from the cultural biases of urban and middle-class government officials. Roads, school curriculums, and health delivery systems, for example, could all be designed in ways that would make them more appropriate for rural families, and more easily delivered to a dispersed, rural population. Nevertheless, there remains a large element of locational inflexibility in many items of public investment and public services which tends to favor the urban population.

Neither of the points made above—the by-product nature of most regional discrimination, and the urban bias of many policy instruments—imply that regional discrimination is not perceived or intended by dominant groups. They do imply, however, that regional discrimination is not easily reversed. To achieve a pro-rural bias it becomes necessary to modify many "non-regional" policies, as well as the underlying attitudes and perceptions responsible for the pro-urban orientation built into the design of many instruments.

The final point is that regional inequality in Peru is less the product of discriminatory government policy than of its absence. The government is best pictured as passive before the pro-urban bias of market forces. Passivity does not mean neutrality, because government is pulled into providing complementary infrastructure and services that reinforce pro-urban and polarizing market forces. A pro-rural stance would instead require an active *anti-urban* program aimed at offsetting the considerable natural advantages of urban centers, and at extracting income from the urban population and transferring it, for either current consumption or investment, to the rural population.

The last point can be explained more fully by noting the strongly dualistic nature of the Peruvian economy. In 1961, 86 percent of total income was generated in the urban sector plus the sugar and mining enclaves in the countryside. And between 1961 and 1970 per capita value added in the urban and modern sectors grew at 3.2 percent annually versus only 1.4 percent in the rural economy. Government policies are reinforcing these broad differences, but so large a gap must be explained largely in terms of market forces. In this setting, only a very active pro-rural government program would achieve a significant degree of regional equalization.

The dualist model is a useful starting point for examining the actual regional impact of different policies since it suggests a convenient distinction between policies that equalize by transferring current market income from urban to rural sectors, and those that equalize by transferring productive resources, and thereby, by reducing future disparities in market incomes. Both are forms of horizontal redistribution in the sense that they extract from one sector and give to another. The principal instruments for horizontal transfers are fiscal and price policies, and to a lesser extent, credit allocation and other influences on the regional distribution of private investment. Most redistribution that has occurred in Peru, it should be noted, has been of a third kind, consisting of "vertical" transfers *within* the urban or the rural sectors. Such redistribution, which takes the form chiefly of wage increases and property transfers, including the agrarian reform, has no direct impact on regional incomes; it merely redistributes existing income within regions. It can, of course, have indirect effects on regional incomes, by altering the direction and nature of future investments. In the following section I will review the record in Peru with those policy instruments that do redistribute income horizontally, between urban and rural sectors, and I will also discuss the possible indirect effect on relative regional incomes of vertical transfers.

THE REGIONAL IMPACT OF POLICIES, 1963-1973

Urban-Rural Transfers of Current Income

The principal transfers of current income between the urban and rural sectors are summarized in Table 4. Both fiscal and price transfers between these sectors appear to have been small, both in 1961 and 1970. Furthermore, they have tended to offset each other so that the net horizontal transfer through these instruments has been small relative to total value added in each sector. The fiscal data in Table 4 cover only those public expenditures whose benefits could be assigned to another sector. If general or non-assignable expenditures (chiefly police, defense and some major infrastructure) were allocated in proportion to income or to population, the figures would show a more favorable net horizontal transfer to the rural sector: it would be neutral or slightly positive in both years. Even excluding those "general expenditures," the transfer—as shown in Table 4—is only slightly negative, though the trend has been towards a worsening for the rural sector, from −2 percent of rural value added in 1961 to −7 percent in 1970. These figures, of course, do not reveal the redistribution that has occurred *within* the urban and rural sectors, through traditional instruments such as fiscal wage policies, or through radical changes such as the agrarian reform. The net horizontal transfer, however, does summarize a major form of possible regional redistribution. The following paragraphs attempt to explain these aggregate estimates by examining the impact of specific measures on the subsistence and commercial components of the rural sector, and on the modern and traditional components of the urban sector.

The *rural subsistence sector* amounted to about 40 percent of the total rural

TABLE 4

MARKET INCOMES AND INCOME TRANSFERS, 1961 and 1970
(all values in 1970 U.S. $ per worker)

	1961		*1970*	
	Urban	*Rural*	*Urban*	*Rural*
1. % of labor force	49.7	50.3	54.7	45.3
2. Value added[a]	1505	530	1908	600
3. *Net budget transfer*[b]	*–95*	*20*	*–210*	*30*
4. Taxes	–265	–30	–415	–50
5. Education	55	20	100	50
6. Health	70	10	70	10
7. Public investment	45	20	35	20
8. Price effect[c]	30	–30	70	–70

a. Equals national income originating in the sector.

b. Equals sum lines 4-7; the sum of urban and rural net budget transfers is negative because about half of public expenditures were not allocated.

c. Calculated by comparing the current situation with a uniform external tariff and no food price controls or rationing.

SOURCE: Webb (1974a: 31).

population, if all haciendas and their *colonos* are classified as commercial. By and large, subsistence farmers are more easily helped than hurt by fiscal or price policies. However, since most sell at least a small proportion of output, and purchase some taxed items, they are affected to a minor extent–in both cases negatively–by price policies and taxes. The tax burden is very low, but price policy is discriminatory: Food imports continue to be exempt of tariffs while the average duty on all other goods has risen from about 30 percent in 1961 to over 70 percent in 1970. Cheap beef imports compete with what is often the principal source of cash income for small farmers: In 1961, over 70 percent of beef cattle were owned on farms under five hectares. Meat imports grew so fast during the last ten years that rationing has now been imposed to reduce demand. Yet most meat is consumed by middle-class families. Tariff-exempt wheat imports favor the consumption of bread; a nondiscriminatory general tariff, or a reverse discrimination in favor of domestic foods, would raise Sierra income from potatoes and other substitutes for bread. Potatoes in particular are thought to be in relatively elastic supply, so that a potential exists for import-substitution with large benefits to small farmers.

On the other hand, government expenditures do benefit the subsistence economy. The largest direct transfer is education. The Belaúnde administration extended primary schooling to most of the rural sector, where enrollment rates now reach 70-80 percent. Much more, however, could be spent on education in backward rural areas, where school materials are scarce, teachers are poorly prepared, secondary schooling is unavailable, and illiteracy remains high.[2] The

1971-1975 Development Plan recognized all these needs, but its projections did not add up to a large financial effort. There was no indication, for instance, of funding for a massive literacy program. Additional financial effort, however, may be less important than improvements in the quality of rural education, which remains strongly urban-oriented and which therefore adds little to the welfare or the future income of the *campesino* who does not emigrate.

Less money is spent on two more fruitful types of fiscal transfers to the small farmer: rural infrastructure, and agricultural extension plus credit. Small roads and small irrigation projects in the Sierra were minor components of Belaúnde's investment program, and there has been no major change in the priority given to those programs. On the other hand, there is a larger allocation for trunk roads and other major routes through or into the Sierra, and these also favor small farmers; about one-third of 1971-1975 projected road expenditures were allocated to the Sierra. Most of the national road program is a continuation of projects that were initiated or planned under Belaúnde. Though less is spent on roads in the Sierra in per capita terms, road construction may well be the single most productive transfer to the poorer rural population.[3] By contrast, potential small irrigation projects in the Sierra have been, and continue to be, almost entirely ignored.

The record of agricultural extension and credit to small farmers in the Sierra is one of extreme neglect. The extension service claimed a total of 117,000 assisted families in 1969, but about two-thirds were on the Coast or in the Jungle; thus only 40,000 families, or about 4 percent of Sierra small farmers, received direct assistance. The distribution of farm credit was similar. It is difficult to judge how much more the present regime is doing. The Plan's preoccupation with land tenure changes and with large irrigation and colonization schemes has directed most effort and money to the 10-20 percent of the small farmer population who are receiving land, including many on the Coast. The 1971-1975 Agricultural Development Plan, for instance, said little about a major constraint on the reach of extension activity: the limited number of field workers who know more about Sierra farm techniques than the campesinos themselves, and who are also able to communicate with and persuade the campesinos to change. The official programs do not plan for a substantial increase in the size and quality of technical assistance to small farmers.

The *commercial* part of the rural traditional sector is defined to include most Coastal and Jungle farms (excluding sugar, here classified as "urban"), Sierra haciendas, and most small farmers in the Central Sierra. Market participation is a mixed blessing for these farmers, since it opens them to large negative transfers via price and tax policies. Political weakness plus vulnerability to tax and price policies have combined to make this the most victimized sector in Peru, as it is in many LDCs.

Since 1963 there has been a great deal of income redistribution both *within* commercialized agriculture and *from* this sector to the urban economy. Large landowners were clear losers. In the case of small farmers and wage-earners, it is harder to determine the net incidence of better wages and public services on the one hand, and higher taxes and worsening terms of trade on the other. The sector as a whole was penalized by overvaluation, which reduced cotton and coffee earnings and cheapened competing food imports, and by the combination of food price controls and low tariffs on foods. Furthermore, some of the growing burden of indirect taxation spilled over to this group, while public investments complementary to *existing* commercial agriculture (e.g., improvements of existing irrigation systems and silos) received low priority.

There has been a remarkable continuity in the pattern of redistributive policy toward the rural sector, characterized on balance by negative horizontal transfers and a vertical redistribution of income and property from landowners to wage-earners and some small farmers. Under the agrarian reform law, the vertical transfer has become radical. On the other hand, the negative incidence of both price and tax policies appears to have been heightened with the growth in excise and sales taxation, and a more rigid and extensive application of food price controls.[4] Also, positive fiscal transfers to the sector of both the productive and welfare type continue to be of relatively minor order of priority.

Over the period under study, most income redistribution in Peru has taken place within the *urban modern sector.* The net result has been some gain for labor, at the expense of capital, though some measures transfer in the reverse direction. The sector as a whole appears to benefit at the expense of commercial agriculture, and to lose to both the urban traditional and the rural subsistence sectors. As may be seen in Table 4, however, any such horizontal transfers are small in proportion to the size of the urban modern sector.

This sector transfers income to other sectors through the budget: It had a net budgetary loss equal to 15 percent of value added in 1970, versus small gains in the other sectors. The modern sector has the highest tax burden: In 1970, 23 percent of its value added was paid in taxes, versus 20 percent in the urban traditional, and 9 percent in the rural sectors, respectively. The modern sector paid three-quarters of all taxes. However, the tax ratio has been rising faster in other sectors, particularly in the urban traditional sector, thereby lessening the degree of progressivity that existed in 1961.

Government expenditures are also far higher in the modern sector, though not sufficiently to offset the greater tax burden. Of the three components of government expenditure whose benefits could be allocated by sector (accounting for about half the total budget), the 1970 per capita benefits were all significantly higher in this sector: (U.S.) $260 per worker versus $170 in the urban traditional, and $80 in the rural sectors. In contrast to tax policy, the incidence of expenditures improved over the period: Their absolute growth between 1961-1970 was about equal in each sector, implying a faster rate of growth in the poorer sectors.

On the other hand, it could be argued that most of the nonallocated expenditures (chiefly defense, police, and some basic infrastructure) provide services that are more relevant to urban than to the rural inhabitants, or, to some extent, consist of subsidized wages that accrue to modern sector employees. More clearly, price policy works in favor of this sector. Though it is both conceptually and statistically difficult to measure the amount involved, the estimates shown in Table 4 indicate the direction and changing size of that transfer, both favorable to the modern sector. The overall impact of government measures may therefore be judged neutral or mildly negative.[5]

Since about two-thirds of the *urban traditional sector* in Peru are self-employed, and the rest are employees in small businesses where profits per worker are low, vertical redistribution in this sector is largely irrelevant. Furthermore, minimum wages or similar legislation would be hard to enforce in small firms and households, and high price elasticities of demand for labor in this sector would cause large employment effects. What can be done for the poor in this group must therefore be done at the expense of other sectors. The major horizontal transfers received are public services and low food prices; both become available to all urban residents, though with varying degrees of discrimination.

Neither of the last two governments has a good record of transfers deliberately aimed at the urban poor. Both have given greatest publicity and money to housing, though it is the least effective way of reaching the very poor: Costs per beneficiary are high, and in the best of cases few benefit. In practice, subsidized housing has gone almost entirely to middle-income employees. Recent government-subsidized housing is on the average reaching poorer groups than under Belaúnde, though prices still exclude the poorest, while credit-worthiness standards still imply a bias against the self-employed.[6] Public expenditures on streets, water, sewage, and the like in squatter settlements have been minimal over the whole period.[7] Between 1964-1970, the Paseo de la República (an expressway linking downtown Lima to the richest residential areas) absorbed half of the total investment by the municipal government of Lima; from 1970-1972 the extension of this expressway to the beaches continued to be the largest municipal project.

Urban health services are far better than rural: In 1961, per capita health expenditures in 15 cities were (U.S.) $15 versus $1 for the rest of the country. Urban health expenditures have risen since 1961, but neither the Belaúnde nor the current government has seriously attacked the discrimination built into the three-tiered health system: The military, police, and white-collar workers have better services than modern sector blue-collar workers, who in turn get more attention—from the social security system—than do the self-employed or unregistered *obreros* of small-scale business, who must resort to Ministry or charity hospitals. More than any other urban public service, the health system neatly discriminates between the modern and urban traditional sectors. The military government has made some moves in the right direction: it incorporated domestic servants into the social security system and has begun some sharing of facilities between the white- and blue-collar social security systems, but most of the traditional sector is still excluded from the social security system.

The nature of the urban traditional economy makes it difficult to raise incomes in that sector by raising productivity. The single greatest public expenditure in the sector is education, which is clearly of value as a current transfer; whether it raises money incomes is less clear. Would consumers spend less on traditional sector services and goods if workers in that sector were less educated? My feeling is that total expenditure would be similar, but more persons would be employed, thus increasing the wage differentials between the modern and traditional urban subsectors, but reducing them between the urban traditional and rural sectors. In any case, governments since 1961 have been heavily committed to the provision of education to the urban population, with no significant discrimination against the poor. The only apparent change in emphasis under the military government since 1968 has been the reduction of the university budget, though planned improvements in the quality of education are potentially much more significant.

On the debit side, the urban traditional sector has not fared well as a taxpayer. Its 1970 tax burden of 19.7 percent was almost as high as that of the modern sector (23.0 percent). Belaúnde's tax policy was particularly regressive with regard to this sector: its tax burden rose from 10.2 percent in 1961 to 20.5 percent in 1969. Though the tax burden is unlikely to rise as fast under the current regime, recent tax changes also appear to discriminate against this sector. Recent tax reductions largely benefit modern producers, while excise tax increases and the conversion of the sales into a value added tax hit low-income consumers most. The net fiscal burden worsened for the traditional sector under Belaúnde, despite a doubling of educational expenditure per capita; since 1969 it has probably changed little.

In summary, the nature of the urban traditional economy makes it hard to help this sector; vertical redistribution is ruled out, and productivity-raising horizontal transfers in the form of education and productive infrastructure probably change the distribution of incomes and employment within the sector more than its total income. It does receive substantially more welfare transfers than the rural population, though less than the modern sector. Also, income is transferred from the rural population through food price policies. Most of the fiscal transfer is paid for through taxes, but the urban traditional sector is clearly a net recipient of income from other sectors, once the effect of price policies and of unallocated public expenditures are counted. Finally, on all major aspects of distributive policy toward this sector, there has been considerable continuity between the Belaúnde and military governments.

The first major conclusion to which we are led by this analysis of urban-rural income transfers is that such transfers have not been a significant cause of, nor offset to, the regional inequalities produced by the market. Second, the relative insignificance of horizontal transfers in the Peruvian economy—despite the strong redistributive intent of both the Belaúnde and Velasco regimes and despite the vigor of other (vertical) forms of redistribution—supports the proposition that horizontal redistribution is more difficult to achieve than vertical transfers. There are also good a priori reasons to expect this: Political, administrative and psychological factors are mostly biased against horizontal transfers. However, if regional inequalities cannot easily be reduced ex post, more dependence must be placed on changing the market structure of production to generate a more equal set of regional income levels. The following section, therefore, discusses the impact of policy on regional growth rates.

Policy and Urban-Rural Growth Rates

The principal market determinants of the urban-rural income differential are the rates of investment and of productivity increase, and the rate of labor absorption in each sector. Between 1950 and 1970, per capita value added grew almost three times faster in the urban sector (2.9 percent annually) than in the rural sector (1.1 percent). This differential reflects the predominantly urban and modern sector orientation of most private and public investment over that period. The income growth differential would have been greater but for the high rate of rural-urban migration, which drained off about two-thirds of the natural population increase in the countryside.

Peruvian governments have affected the urban-rural allocation of investment through their own decisions regarding the location and composition of public investment, and also by influencing in numerous ways the allocation of private investment. In absolute terms, public investment has been larger in the urban sector (Table 4), though in proportion to regional income it has favored the rural sector. This judgment, however, is based on necessarily arbitrary assumptions regarding the incidence of benefits of many forms of public investment, and it omits large outlays on major infrastructure. If those major forms of public infrastructure (e.g., ports, airports, power plants) are assumed to give a more than proportional benefit to the modern and urban sectors, the overall picture would be much more favorable to urban families. Such in fact is the conclusion of two other studies of public investment. Wicht (1973), for instance, estimated that about 95 percent of public investment under the 1971-1975 Plan would be allocated to the modern sector (including sugar and cotton farms). And after a detailed regional and sectoral breakdown of 1971-1974 investment projects, Wilson (1974: 11) concludes that "real public investment has largely reinforced the trend towards spatial and sectoral concentration of foreign technology and of high productivity." Though the methods of allocation are crude, and a more careful analysis is warranted, the tentative conclusion must be that public investment has reinforced urban-rural inequalities, and continues to do so.

The impact of government on the regional flow of private investment is more complex. One form of influence is through the financial system. Until 1969 the principal allocational devices were the system of state development banks and interest rate controls. After 1969, the use of development banks was supplemented by a system of sectoral credit allocation ratios for commercial banks. Despite these allocation controls, and the continuing priority attached to agricultural credit throughout the period, there has been no significant increase in the share of agriculture in the total credit supply; in fact, the proportion appears to have fallen somewhat, from 27.2 percent in 1960 to 21.0 percent for the period 1965-1968, and 18.6 percent in 1971-1972.[8]

A second instrument for influencing the regional distribution of private investment consisted of various tax, duty-exemption and interest rate incentives offered under both the Ley de Promoción Industrial during the sixties, and since 1970, under the new Ley de Industrias. During the sixties these laws were supplemented by the promotional activities of regional development offices, such as ORDESUR (Oficina Regional de Desarrollo del Sur), which created an industrial park in Arequipa. Under the military regime, the legal incentives are supplemented instead by direct controls on siting, particularly in the case of larger industrial projects. For our purposes, however, the important aspect of these various decentralizing measures is that they do *not* attempt to steer capital to the countryside in the form of dispersed rural factories, small cottage industries, or other rural enterprises.

The principal influences on regional capital flows have been unintended by-products of two directions taken by policy since the early sixties, both amounting to an attack on rich farmers. One was land reform, and the other a price-cost squeeze on agriculture effected chiefly through wage, exchange rate, and tariff policies. The combined effects of the long gestation of agrarian reform, especially since the land reform bill of the 1962-1963 military junta, and of the squeeze on farm profitability during the sixties, drastically reduced interest in agricultural investment. Investment in agriculture may be rising at present due to the control over the agricultural surplus that is exercised by the cooperatives and other agrarian reform organizations. At best, however, current policy may prevent the outflow of rural savings; there is no policy for drawing in large amounts of private capital. In fact, policy towards the use of agrarian reform bonds, which can be cashed in if invested in industry, amounts to an institutionalization of a savings transfer out of agriculture.

In sum, government has sought some transfer of savings to the rural economy, chiefly via credit policy, but this effort has been swamped by the unintended negative effects on rural investment of other distributive policies.

The preceding paragraphs have discussed the impact of government on the regional allocation of capital. By and large, public policy has tended to increase the resource disparities between urban and rural sectors. Regional income differentials have also been worsened by various policies favoring capital-intensive forms of technology in the modern sector. The bias towards capital-intensive technology has resulted in a slower rate of employment expansion in the urban sector. At the same time, urban wages have risen because the modern sector demands more highly skilled workers, or because large capital investments create the opportunity for wage increases through union or political pressure. The traditional policies responsible for this capital-intensive bias are familiar. They have consisted chiefly of various capital-cheapening and wage-raising measures.

At present, the dualism of the productive structure is being further reinforced in several ways, of which the most important is the change in the projected composition of sectoral output, with much higher priority being given to the highly capital-intensive heavy industries and to mining. The race to establish a foothold in several branches of metal-working, petrochemical, and chemical industries, in advance of the complementarity agreements that are to be worked out under the Andean Pact, is giving an extra edge to the high degree of priority already enjoyed by those industries. The Andean Pact will also discourage efforts to sacrifice industrial efficiency in the interests of labor-intensity. In other activities, the government plan is strongly oriented towards large-scale investments that will be part of, or complementary to, the modern sector.

Dualism is also being increased by factor-price policies, which are not only maintaining, but are probably increasing the previous distortions favoring capital-intensive techniques. Wages have been allowed to rise substantially in high productivity establishments, while numerous incentives built into the Ley de Industrias and other sector laws tend to cheapen the cost of capital. Finally, the newly created workers' communities in most of the private modern business sector tend to resist employment expansion; they seek to maximize dividends per worker by maximizing capital per worker. Greater dualism will increase the concentration of value added in the urban sector, and the consequent need for horizontal transfers.

CONCLUSION

Government policies have on the whole reinforced urban-rural inequality in Peru. The principal negative effects have resulted from measures that have unintentionally reduced the rate of investment in agriculture and increased the degree of dualism, or of productivity disparities, of the economy. Public policy, however, has not been the major source of those inequalities, most of which can be attributed to market forces.

The case of Peru, therefore, provides only weak support for the theory of internal colonialism between sectors. The budget transfer, for instance, has favored the traditional sector on balance, and though it was offset by a negative price effect, the net loss to the rural economy from the two types of transfer was negligible in 1970. Most inequality now flows from the present unequal distribution of resources, and not from policies that "extract" or transfer income between sectors. On the other hand, government discriminates not only by its passivity in the face of major regional inequality, but also by policies that on the whole reinforce that inequality.

NOTES

1. I define these as the Department of Apurimac, Ayacucho, Cuzco, Huancavelica, and Puno. See Cotler (1967) who originated the concept and who also includes Ancash.

2. For an account of rural education in one part of the Sierra during the fifties, see Vásquez (1965).

3. Implicit in this evaluation is an optimistic view of the effects on the Sierra of integration into the country's market economy, based to some extent on the relative prosperity of Sierra regions already integrated. Integration, however, could also be accompanied by greater penetration of Sierra markets by factory (and tax-bearing) products, and other negative "polarization" effects of the kind described by Hirschman (1958: 187-190).

4. Estimates of the redistribution caused by price policy are very tentative, but the estimates in Table 4 (line 8) indicate the order of magnitude of non-neutral tariffs and price controls on foods. To estimate the potential for raising rural incomes through price policy with a deliberate rural bias, one could assume, for instance, prohibitive tariffs on most imported foods, no food price controls, and possibly a higher exchange rate favoring agricultural exports. Rough calculations of the value of import-competing and export farm products and of the domestic price elasticity of demand for foods suggest that such policies could raise incomes of individual farmers in the order of 10-50 percent, depending on the fraction of output that is marketed, and by over 20 percent for the sector as a whole.

5. Though I prefer to treat general expenditures such as defense, police, and general administration as social costs, rather than benefits, it is useful to test the effect of this treatment by calculating the implications of other treatments. Thus, a minimum share of unallocated expenditures could be estimated by allocating on a per capita basis; this yields a figure of $120. An allocation proportional to income raises budget receipts per worker, instead, to $280, while a higher figure would result from assuming, as suggested above, that most non-allocated expenditures are primarily of benefit to the modern sector.

6. See Tapia (1971) for statistics on housing prices and urban income levels.

7. A 1967 survey of squatter settlement residents by CISM (1967) revealed that 58 percent of the homes had no piped water, 61 percent had no sewers, and 87 percent were located on unpaved streets. On the other hand, only 2 percent of the families had children who were not attending primary school, and what is more surprising, only 11 percent had children aged 13-21 who were not attending secondary school.

8. Calculated from data in Superintendencia de Banca y Seguros, *Memoria 1972* and Banco Central de Reserva del Perú, *Cuentas Nacionales del Perú 1960-1969,* Anexo Estadístico, Tomo II, 1970.

REFERENCES

CISM (1967) Barriadas de Lima. Lima: Ministerio de Trabajo y Comunidades.

COTLER, J. (1967) "La mecánica de la dominación interna y del cambio social en el Perú," in Perú Problema No. 1. Lima: Instituto de Estudios Peruanos.

HIRSCHMAN, A. O. (1958) The Strategy of Economic Development. New Haven, Conn.: Yale University Press.

TAPIA, A. (1971) Acción de las instituciones de crédito especializadas en el financiamiento de vivienda en el Perú. Lima: Imprenta del Hogar de la Clínica San Juan de Dios.

VASQUEZ, M. (1965) La educación rural en el Callejón de Huaylas: Vicos. Lima: Editorial Estudios Andinos.

WEBB, R. (1974a) Government Policy and the Distribution of Income in Peru, 1963-1973. Princeton, N.J.: Research Program in Economic Development, Princeton University. Discussion Paper No. 39.

--- (1974b) Trends in Real Income in Peru, 1950-1966. Princeton, N.J.: Research Program in Economic Development, Princeton University. Discussion Paper No. 41.

--- (1972) The Distribution of Income in Peru. Princeton, N.J.: Research Program in Economic Development, Princeton University. Discussion Paper No. 26.

WICHT, J. (1973) Seminar presentation at Catholic University of Peru, based on Harvard University Ph.D. dissertation in progress.

WILSON, P. (1974) Influencias institucionales en el Perú: la regionalización de las inversiones públicas. Lima: CISEPA, Universidad Católica. Documento de Trabajo No. 21.

PART V

REGIONAL DEVELOPMENT PROGRAMS AND RURAL-URBAN INEQUALITIES

ALAN GILBERT is a Lecturer in the Economic Geography of Latin America at University College and the Institute of Latin American Studies, London. He received his Ph.D. from the London School of Economics (University of London), and has engaged in planning and field research in Colombia and Peru. His current research interests include education and health care provision in Latin America and national urban and regional development programs in Latin America. Among his principal publications are *Latin American Development: A Geographical Perspective* (Penguin Books, 1974) and "Industrial Location Theory: Its Relevance to an Industrializing Nation," in B. S. Hoyle (ed.) *Spatial Aspects of Development* (Wiley, 1974).

Chapter 11

URBAN AND REGIONAL DEVELOPMENT PROGRAMS IN COLOMBIA SINCE 1951

ALAN GILBERT

Regional development is currently in vogue in Latin America (Utria, 1972; ECLA, 1971). It is manifest in a variety of national programs concerned with modifying the present distributions of population, income and economic activity. At their most grandiose, these regional programs embrace projects as ambitious as the construction of the trans-Brazilian roads and the development of the massive industrial complex at Ciudad Guayana. At their most limited, they have aimed to improve the provision of health, education, sanitation and road facilities in the poorest regions. Between these extremes, a wide variety of programs have been introduced, including the establishment of industrial parks, the offer of tax incentives to encourage industrial dispersal, the construction of new roads and infrastructure, colonization programs, and new schemes for exploitation of natural resources (Gilbert, 1974a; Stöhr, 1972). Often these measures have been associated with the creation of new regional agencies and with the introduction of regional planning.

This current interest in regional development has come as a belated reaction to the wide regional disparities which have long characterized most Latin American nations. That such a response should have emerged at all is perhaps surprising. Its emergence at this time, however, is clearly related to the growth of national planning in the sixties and to the realization that recent development policies have magnified existing regional differentials in most Latin American nations. As a consequence of what has become known as the center-periphery mechanism, the dynamic urban centers have continued to grow at the expense of the slowly expanding rural periphery (Friedmann, 1966; Odell and Preston, 1973). Processes as diverse as industrial concentration, selective migration, the transfer of savings to cities from rural areas, and the failure of governments to spread infrastructure widely, have led to an increase in absolute income differentials in many countries (Gilbert, 1974a). In certain cases, "subsidization" of the center by the periphery has been so extreme that even relative income differentials have widened.

Naturally, reactions to these disparities have been very diverse. Many orthodox economists have interpreted the process of "subsidization" as part of the inequitable but highly necessary process of mobilizing the capital needed to finance economic "take-off" (Wingo, 1967; Johnson, 1958). Many Latin Americans and Marxists have argued that "subsidization" represents a further manifestation of the "dependency" relationship which is inevitably created under the system of monopoly capitalism (Sunkel, 1969; González Casanova, 1964-1965; Cotler, 1967-1968; Frank, 1967). The views of different Latin American governments have ranged between the two extremes, although in most cases they have tended toward the former view. Certainly, their traditional policies have reflected the view that little could be done to reduce the differentials or to weaken the processes leading to their perpetuation.

Through time, however, this attitude has changed and most now seem to feel that action should be taken to weaken the center-periphery mechanism. The regional policies which most of these governments have adopted, however, have rarely led to important modifications in national economic policy. The basic faith in urban-industrial growth, which has characterized development planning throughout Latin America, has continued to guide the planning of regional development. Regional programs, therefore, have rarely employed rural strategies and, even more rarely, redistribution measures. Regional development has normally been geared to traditional economic policies and has tried to do little more than decentralize existing forms of economic activity. Thus, the most common element in Latin American regional policy has been the attempt to disperse industry away from the largest urban centers. Even where governments have attempted more radical regional approaches, their unchanging developmental strategies have shone through clearly. In Brazil, for example, regional development has been pursued through strategies similar to those used in national policies. Large-scale projects aiming at the development of export products and the exploitation of natural resources have dominated the Amazon projects. The dispersal of capital-intensive industry from the Southeast has formed the basis of development efforts in the Northeast (Goodman, 1972; Hirschman, 1968). Solutions to the problems of the poorest regions, therefore, are being sought among existing development strategies. Rather than leading to a modification in national development strategies, regional policies have been based on industrial growth, export development and economic nationalism.

Similar attitudes have been evident in the Colombian experience. During the past nine years, Colombian governments have become aware that all regions of the country have not benefited equally from economic growth. Under Presidents

Lleras Restrepo and Pastrana Borrero, regional measures were introduced aimed at reducing economic concentration in the largest four cities (DNP, 1968-1970; DNP, 1971a; DNP, 1973). Deliberate efforts were made to disperse industry to the poorer regions, to improve infrastructure in the intermediate cities, to build rural development concentrations, and to extend local planning services. These measures showed a welcome change in the attitudes of Colombian governments toward the less prosperous regions. Clearly, however, their introduction did not herald a change in the basic philosophy underlying economic development planning. Despite the proposed establishment of rural development concentrations and other measures aimed at improving conditions in the rural areas, most of the regional programs were concerned with urban and industrial activities. Indeed, it can be argued that the policies reflect and accentuate the faith in urban and industrial growth which has been a feature of Colombian development during the past thirty years. To this extent, therefore, Colombia's regional program has been similar to that of most other Latin American nations.

Where the Colombian experience does differ, however, is in the recent espousal of the "Four Strategies" (DNP, 1972). This plan represents a change in Colombia's own development policy and indeed marks the first overt move by a Latin American government toward economic development *through* urban growth. The Four Strategies aim to accelerate investment in urban housing, to increase exports, to raise agricultural productivity, and to reduce existing income inequalities. It is, of course, the first of these strategies which is the novel part of the Plan, and the one which has turned a neutral attitude toward urbanization into an overt pro-urbanization strategy. Its object is to generate a higher rate of domestic savings, to direct these savings toward housing construction, and to create large-scale employment opportunities in the construction industry and in related sectors (Currie, 1971; DNP, 1972). The new savings are being stimulated by the offer of four percent interest over and above the rate of inflation.[1] The savings are channelled through five Savings and Housing Corporations (CAVIs) to potential house buyers. These borrowers are required to repay their loans in monthly installments adjusted to account for changes in the price index. Providing that sufficient borrowers can be found (it is already clear that the savings will be forthcoming), the Plan should boost the construction industry and, through the multiplier mechanism, the rest of the economy. Local industries producing construction materials such as bricks, glass, tiles, ceramics and wood will immediately benefit, and higher personal incomes should stimulate the demand for home-manufactured consumer goods such as textiles. Providing that national industries are able to increase production, neither inflation nor the balance of payments should pose problems. In addition, there should be positive incentives for agricultural development. Larger numbers of migrants will be attracted to the cities by the increased opportunities for employment. Out-migration will reduce pressure on the land, which together with increased credit provision will facilitate development of more efficient commercial producers.

The main appeal of the Plan is that it will overcome the twin problems holding back Colombian development: persistently high unemployment and recurrent balance of payments problems (Avromic, 1972; ILO, 1970). It is by no means a new idea, for Lauchlin Currie—the creator and chief advocate of the Plan—had presented its outlines to the nation as early as 1961 (Currie, 1961; 1963; 1965a, b; 1966; 1971). Its adoption by the Pastrana administration, in fact, was determined largely by the personal respect held for Currie by the President and by the head of the National Planning Office. What the Plan offered the new administration was intellectual appeal and a means of differentiating its economic policy from that of its predecessor. The Plan was greeted, however, with opposition from many quarters. It was seen as a source of inflation, as a tactic to divert attention from land reform, and as a means for generating profits for the private construction industry (Rosas et al., 1973). Its final adoption was secured only through a constitutional reform which allowed the government to bypass the legislative process and to introduce its economic programs by decree.

Since 1970, therefore, Colombia has tried to implement both a national urban policy and a new regional development program. The results of such a combination in a country where there is no primate city are, therefore, intriguing. If Colombia turns its back on regional balance and encourages the growth of a few major cities, the cause of regional development throughout Latin America may be set back for years. This is especially likely in view of the fact that several economists have recently argued that continued urban growth is desirable even in the case of the largest cities. Alonso (1971), Mera (1973), and Richardson (1973) have argued that most empirical evidence suggests that productivity in the largest centers is normally far higher than the diseconomies caused by increasing city size. In this context it would seem valuable to examine the Colombian policies and experience.

Four main areas will be examined in this paper. First, a brief review will be made of urban growth in Colombia since 1951. Second, the changing distribution of industry will be described and the processes underlying these changes examined. Third, the objectives and methods of Colombia's new urban and regional policies will be analyzed and their likely success assessed. Finally, the general philosophy and methods underlying Colombian regional development planning will be discussed in light of their possible application in other nations.

THE PATTERN OF URBAN GROWTH IN COLOMBIA SINCE 1951

It is well known that Colombia, like most other Latin American countries, has been experiencing a rapid process of urban development during the past thirty years (Camacho de Pinto, 1970; Cardona, 1970, 1971; Rodríguez, 1967;

Vernez, 1971). This rapid growth was reflected in the increase from 39.6 to 52.8 percent in the proportion of the population living in officially-defined urban settlements between 1951 and 1964. Even if a higher population threshold is considered urban, growth was extremely rapid. Between 1951 and 1964 the share of the nation's population living in localities which had more than 10,000 inhabitants increased from 25.8 to 36.8 percent (Gilbert, 1970).

Equally well known is that Colombia's urban growth has not featured the acute primacy characteristic of all Latin American countries except Brazil and Ecuador. In most of these nations, primacy has long been pronounced and has recently shown signs of worsening. In Peru, for example, Lima-Callao was eight times larger than Arequipa-Miraflores in 1940, but eleven times larger in 1972. In Chile, Santiago was four-and-a-half times larger than Valparaíso in 1940, but seven-and-a-half times larger twenty years later. In Venezuela, Caracas was not much more than twice as large as Maracaibo in 1936, but three times as large in 1971.

By comparison, the Colombian city system has remained extremely balanced and has long approximated what has become known as the rank-size distribution. In 1973, for example, it was close to the "ideal" distribution whereby the largest city was approximately twice the size of the second city, three times the size of the third and n times the size of the nth largest (Browning, 1958; Rosing, 1966; Zipf, 1941). It is clear, however, that there has been a trend since 1951 toward a long-term weakening of this pattern. Between 1951 and 1964, for example, the populations of the three largest cities all increased more rapidly than those of most other cities (see Table 1). Their combined share of the total population living in centers with more than 20,000 inhabitants grew from 45.9 percent in 1951 to 50.1 percent in 1964. Individually, Cali had the fourth, Bogotá the fifth and Medellín the eleventh fastest growth rates among this group of cities. Only three centers in the country managed to grow more rapidly than Cali, and all three were located in agricultural colonization areas and were growing from a small population base.

After 1964, further modifications occurred which promised to weaken the rank-size relationship in the longer term. Between 1964 and 1973, the principal feature of urban growth was the increasing dominance of Bogotá.[2] Both Cali and Medellín grew more slowly, and only six cities with more than 25,000 inhabitants managed to grow more rapidly than Bogotá—none of which had more than 100,000 inhabitants. And by comparison with the 1951-1964 period, when Bogotá, Cali and Medellín strengthened their positions over the rest and over Barranquilla, the experience since 1964 suggests that Bogotá may one day achieve a position of primacy. Bogotá's share of the total number of checks cashed in the three largest cities, for example, rose from 55.9 percent in 1951 to 61.2 percent by 1964 and 70.1 percent by 1971 (see Table 2). Similarly, there was a pronounced rise in the city's share of building construction, from 46.7 percent in 1953 to 71.3 percent in 1971. If further data available on a

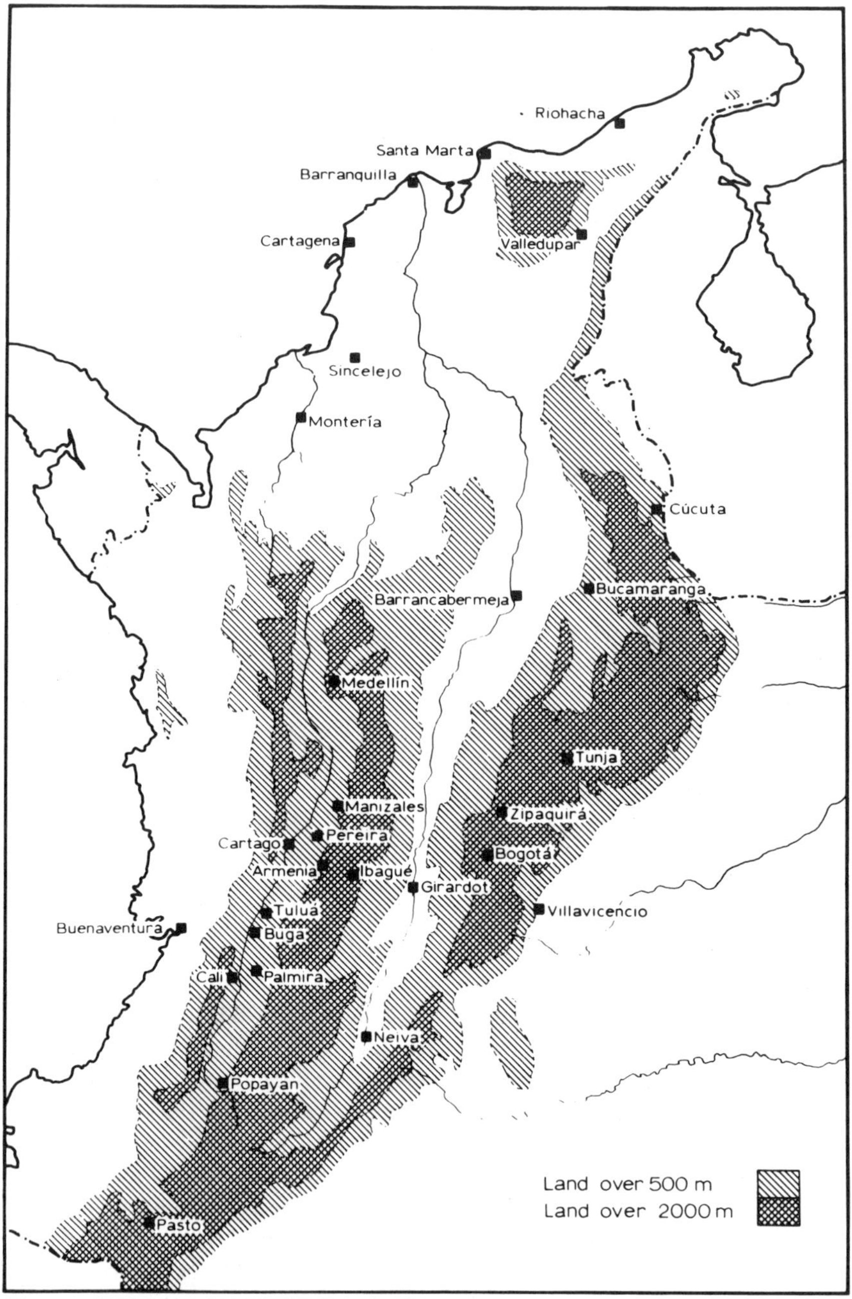

Figure 1: PHYSICAL STRUCTURE AND CITIES OF COLOMBIA

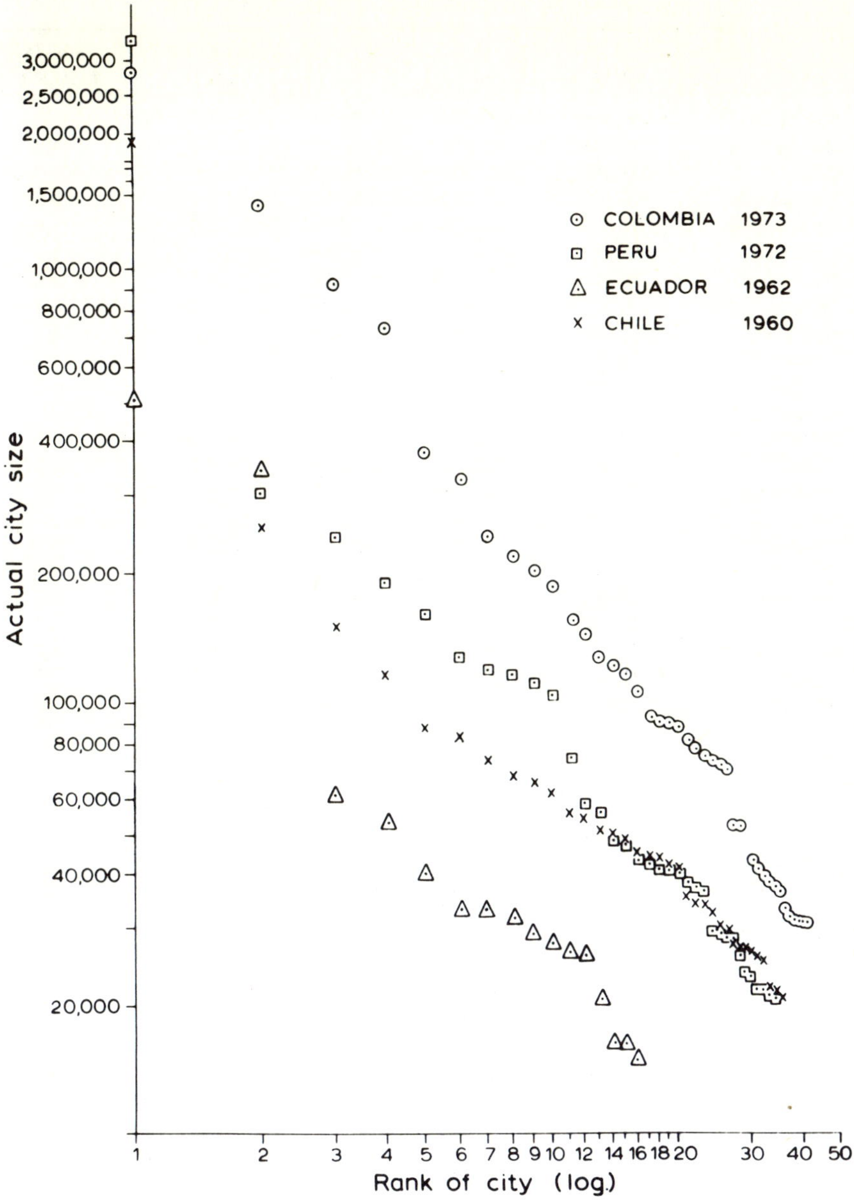

Figure 2: CITY SIZE HIERARCHIES IN SELECTED ANDEAN COUNTRIES

TABLE 1
GROWTH OF COLOMBIAN CITIES, 1951-1973

City	1951	1964	1973	Annual Change (%)	1964-1973 Change (%)
Bogotá	664,506	1,673,370	2,870,594	7.4	6.2
Medellín	397,738	948,025	1,410,154	6.9	4.5
Cali	245,568	633,485	926,264	7.6	4.3
Barranquilla	296,357	530,651	728,533	4.6	3.6
Bucaramanga	107,887	224,876	377,149	5.8	5.9
Cartagena	111,291	217,910	356,424	5.3	5.6
Pereira	89,675	179,133	245,214	5.5	3.6
Cúcuta	70,375	147,176	216,509	5.8	4.4
Manizales	92,030	195,542	204,024	6.0	0.5
Ibagúe	54,347	125,233	180,734	6.6	4.2
Armenia	72,805	155,364	158,388	6.0	0.2
Palmira	54,293	106,502	140,481	5.3	3.1
Santa Marta	37,005	89,161	126,719	7.0	4.0
Pasto	48,853	82,546	119,339	4.1	4.2
Buenaventura	35,087	70,079	115,770	5.5	5.7
Neiva	33,040	75,886	105,595	6.6	3.7
Valledupar	9,011	43,553	92,187	12.9	8.7
Villavicencio	17,126	45,277	90,211	7.8	8.0
Montería	23,682	70,531	89,552	6.8	2.7
Tuluá	28,715	56,539	86,736	5.3	4.9
Barrancabermeja	25,046	59,625	82,171	6.9	3.6
Popayán	31,866	58,500	77,669	4.8	3.2
Sincelejo	21,625	44,001	73,465	5.6	5.9
Girardot	35,665	78,599	71,964	6.3	1.0
Buga	32,016	65,535	71,016	5.7	0.9
Cartago	31,051	55,682	69,154	4.6	2.4
Sogamoso	14,122	34,960	51,474	7.2	4.4
Tunja	23,008	40,451	51,301	4.4	2.7
Ciénaga	24,358	47,719	43,048	5.3	1.1
Magangué	17,114	27,354	40,613	3.7	4.5
Tumaco	12,692	25,145	38,742	5.4	4.9
Ocaña	15,214	28,028	37,935	4.8	3.4
Chiquinquirá	10,143	16,926	37,504	4.0	9.2
Duitama	7,723	31,865	36,551	11.5	1.2
Aguachica	2,384	8,556	33,237	8.1	16.3
Espinal	9,389	22,791	31,838	7.1	3.8
Zipaquirá	12,708	22,648	31,267	4.5	3.7
Sevilla	17,210	26,757	31,143	3.5	1.7
La Dorada	14,577	26,168	30,995	4.6	1.9
Ipiales	11,569	23,320	30,871	5.5	3.2
Pamplona	16,396	25,072	28,911	3.3	1.6
Quibdó	9,013	19,989	27,318	6.3	3.2
Facatativá	13,479	20,742	27,238	3.4	3.1
Sabanalarga	13,982	20,254	27,110	2.9	3.3
Plato	8,039	13,364	26,985	4.0	8.1
Maicao	–	9,347	26,887	–	11.1
Fusasusagá	8,345	18,755	25,026	6.4	3.3

SOURCE: D.A.N.E., Censo Nacional de Población, 1951, 1964, 1973.

departmental basis are included, the same pattern is evident. Between 1964 and 1971, Cundinamarca's share of the total loans issued by the Central Mortgage Bank to the departments of Antioquia, Cundinamarca and Valle increased from 64.1 percent to 70.0 percent, and the department's share of total commercial bank loans increased from 55.6 to 62.9 percent. Similarly, Cundinamarca's share of all imports consumed in the three departments increased from 55.5 percent in 1951 to 63.7 percent in 1964 and 70.1 percent in 1969. In terms of industrial measures, Bogotá's dominance was less clear cut, but definitely greater than it had been in the early fifties. Between 1951 and 1971, Bogotá's share of the consumption of electricity by industry increased from 39.3 percent to 46.7 percent.[3]

In terms of measures of economic growth, therefore, Bogotá appears to have grown more rapidly than either Medellín or Cali between 1951 and 1964, and especially since 1964. Such a relative expansion, however, was not reflected in the provision of municipal services, with the exception of electricity. The length of roads in Cundinamarca, for example, did not increase relative to the other departments, nor did the proportion of subscribers to the municipal water system, nor the share of municipal expenditures. These data suggest, therefore, that while Bogotá was growing rapidly in economic terms, this growth had not resulted in major social advances for the city's population.

Industrial Development Since 1951

Since 1951, Colombia has experienced a period of rapid industrial expansion which has led to the manufacturing sector assuming a more important role in the national economy. Between 1953 and 1969, industrial value-added increased by 6.5 percent per annum in real terms, manufacturing employment increased from 199,116 to 326,826 (64.1 percent), and industry's share in the nation's gross internal product increased from 16.7 percent to 20.0 percent.[4] This rapid expansion had a pronounced effect on the geographical pattern of industrial activity.

The most important regional changes since 1953 were as follows: First, most new industrial employment was created in the metropolitan areas of Bogotá, Medellín, Cali and Barranquilla. In 1953, 74.3 percent of all manufacturing workers were employed by companies located in the four departments of Cundinamarca, Antioquia, Valle and Atlántico, a share which had risen to 82.8 percent by 1969 (see Table 3). Second, there was a tendency for employment in Cundinamarca to grow more rapidly during the 1953-1969 period than in any other department. This expansion was particularly marked during the late fifties and early sixties, becoming less accentuated after 1964.[5] Third, a corollary of the first trend was that growth in other parts of the country was very slow. The country's poorest departments experienced only a small increase in manufacturing workers (from 15,094 to 16,286), and suffered a relative decline in

TABLE 2

BOGOTA, MEDELLIN AND CALI: RELATIVE SHARES OF DIFFERENT ECONOMIC MEASURES, 1951-1971

	Bogotá			*Medellín*			*Cali*		
Variable	*1951*	*1964*	*1971*	*1951*	*1964*	*1971*	*1951*	*1964*	*1971*
Population	51.4	52.1	52.5[c]	29.7	28.4	27.7[c]	18.8	19.4	19.6[c]
Industrial electricity consumption	39.3[a]	38.6	46.7	50.0[a]	41.5	36.0	10.5[a]	19.8	17.3
Industrial employment	–	43.7	43.5[b]	–	35.7	35.5[b]	–	20.4	20.9[b]
Net generation of electricity	39.0	34.6	46.8	49.5	43.0	35.9	11.5	22.5	17.3
Bank deposits	69.4	68.8	–	18.4	16.4	–	12.1	14.6	–
Checks paid directly	55.9	61.2	70.1	27.1	23.3	17.3	16.9	15.3	12.5
Municipal costs (ordinary)	54.3	66.8	64.0	26.5	20.7	23.5	19.0	12.4	12.5
Subscribers to water system	47.5	51.0	50.6	31.3	26.9	26.9	21.1	22.0	22.4
Building construction (square meters)	46.7[a]	60.2	71.3	31.4[a]	19.2	17.7	21.7[a]	20.5	10.9
Arrivals at airport	52.8[a]	55.5	54.5	28.0[a]	27.1	27.1	19.3[a]	19.5	18.4
	Cundinamarca			*Antioquia*			*Valle del Cauca*		
Population	37.8	40.1	41.4[c]	36.5	35.2	34.6[c]	25.7	24.7	24.1[c]
Industrial workers	36.9[a]	42.5	43.0[b]	36.4[a]	33.3	33.7[b]	26.7[a]	24.2	23.4[b]
Commercial bank loans	–	55.6	62.9	–	22.2	19.2	–	22.0	17.7
Commercial bank loans to commerce	–	63.7	71.8	–	18.7	14.5	–	17.4	13.5
Commercial bank loans to industry	–	54.2	61.5	–	25.0	22.9	–	20.7	15.6
Loans of Banco Central Hipotecario	–	64.1	70.0	–	18.2	18.5	–	17.7	11.4
Imports (value)	55.5	63.6	70.0[b]	22.6	17.2	14.7[b]	21.9	19.1	15.3[b]
National and Departmental Roads	43.9	35.0	34.0	33.1	30.1	32.9	19.1	34.9	33.1

a. 1953 figures.

b. 1969 figures.

c. Estimate based on 1951-1964 trends.

SOURCE: Boletín Mensual de Estadística, various years; Revista del Banco de la República, various years.

their share of employment (from 7.6 to 5.0 percent). Other departments such as Caldas, Bolívar, Santander and Tolima, which contained small industrial concentrations in 1953, fared marginally better. Even so, their share of employment fell during the period from 18.0 to 12.2 percent.

The processes underlying these trends have been described at length elsewhere and can be explained in terms of changes in the structure of the manufacturing sector, in the general industrial environment, and in the Colombian economy as a whole since 1953 (Arango, 1970; DNP, 1971b; Gilbert, 1970; Manrique, 1970). The present analysis, therefore, will mention only the more important factors.

The different industrial structures which existed in each urban center in 1953 were undoubtedly a major factor leading to industrial concentration. Most of the smaller centers contained industrial sectors which were dominated by a number of traditional industries, notably drinks and foodstuffs. These industries tended to grow less rapidly on a national scale than other, newer sectors such as metals, machinery and electrical products. The growth of the smaller cities was handicapped as a result.[6] It should be noted, however, that Medellín suffered from a similar concentration of workers in a slowly expanding sector (textiles), but managed to grow rapidly despite this difficulty.[7]

Another disadvantage facing the smaller cities was that most of the country's largest and most efficient companies were located in the major industrial centers. Even when a smaller city had a well-diversified and dynamic industrial structure, therefore, individual plants tended to grow less rapidly than those in the larger cities. This difference in scale and efficiency was clearly revealed by the effects of transport improvements which took place in the 1950s. These improvements reduced the costs of transportation between the principal cities and enabled the most efficient plants to sell to markets previously supplied by local plants. As a result, the smaller and less efficient companies, especially those in the food, drinks and clothing industries, tended to close down or amalgamate with their larger competitors.

One factor which could potentially have helped the smaller centers was that most industrial growth after 1953 took place in new plants rather than in existing factories. Unfortunately, however, the largest industrial complexes were also in a superior position with respect to new plant establishment. The four largest centers could attract new companies more easily than the smaller centers because they could offer a pool of skilled labor, better infrastructure and ancillary services, as well as access to industrial markets and material supplies. The lack of infrastructure in itself was not a decisive factor against expansion, since up to the middle sixties both Barranquilla and Cali suffered from severe shortages of electricity. But in the absence of compensating advantages such as those available in Cali, deficiencies in electricity and other services was probably a critical factor.

Of equal importance to their ability to attract new companies was the larger

TABLE 3
MANUFACTURING EMPLOYMENT BY DEPARTMENT, 1953-1969

	Workers Employed				*Percent Change*			
Department	*1953*	*1958*	*1964*	*1969*	*1953-1969*	*1953-1958*	*1958-1964*	*1964-1969*
Antioquia	47,278	57,729	68,811	81,245	+3.4	+4.1	+3.6	+3.4
Atlántico	18,344	23,451	25,660	29,539	+3.0	+4.9	+2.1	+2.9
Bolívar	6,036	5,188	5,811	6,395	+0.4	–3.0	+2.3	+2.0
Boyacá	3,340	6,376	5,683	4,189	+1.4	+13.8	–1.9	–5.7
Caldas	12,134	11,737	13,123	17,230	+2.2	–0.7	+2.3	+5.6
Cauca	1,550	1,092	1,500	2,754	+3.7	–6.7	+6.6	+12.9
Córdoba	816	777	572	318	–5.7	–1.0	–5.0	–11.0
Cundinamarca	47,859	70,111	87,696	103,718	+5.1	+7.9	+4.6	+3.4
Huila	1,010	996	971	1,207	+1.1	–0.1	–0.4	+4.5
Magdalena	1,390	1,302	1,659	1,677	+1.2	–1.3	+5.0	+0.2
Narino	2,772	3,200	3,395	2,743	–0.1	+2.9	+1.2	–4.2
N. Santander	3,451	2,939	2,654	2,448	–2.2	–3.2	–3.6	–1.6
Santander	12,461	10,861	12,123	13,128	+0.3	–2.8	+2.2	+1.6
Tolima	5,181	3,158	3,024	2,919	–3.7	–9.5	–0.7	–0.9
Valle	34,729	37,221	50,045	56,366	+3.1	+1.4	+6.1	+2.0
Others	765	610	1,114	950	+1.4	–1.4	+3.8	–1.0
Total	199,116	236,748	283,841	326,826	+3.1	+3.9	+2.1	+2.9

SOURCE: Boletín Mensual de Estadística: Industria Manufacturera, 1969.

cities' ability to develop entrepreneurial talent from within their own ranks. In larger cities, such businessmen had privileged access to banks and other financial institutions. The major banks were based in the four main cities, and in March, 1972, 93.2 percent of their industrial loans went to Cundinamarca, Atlántico, Antioquia and Valle. Initially, too, the founding of new finance corporations favored Bogotá and Medellín, where the first two companies were established in the early sixties.[8]

The combination of all these factors led to the failure of smaller cities, and especially those with less than 150,000 inhabitants (1964), to attract new industries. Only where specific resource or locational advantages were available, as with the oil reserves near Barrancabermeja (population 59,625 in 1964) and the salt deposits at Zipaquirá (population 22,648), did new industries develop.

The previous factors do not wholly explain, however, why some of the larger second-rank cities such as Manizales, Bucaramanga, Cartagena or Pereira failed to grow as rapidly as the largest four cities. Probably the best explanation is that all of the latter had some additional advantage to offer over and above their size and industrial structure. Bogotá contained the largest urban population and the highest level of per capita income in the country and was the seat of the national government. Medellín had a major advantage in possessing an established industrial group who wished to maintain Antioquia's national position and who possessed sufficient initiative and capital to assure this end. Cali had a privileged location near the Pacific coast, had easy access to the main markets of the country, and was located in the nation's richest agricultural area. Lastly, Barranquilla was ideally located to supply the market on the Atlantic coast and through its port could attract a variety of export and import-based industries.

More difficult to explain is why, after 1953, Bogotá's expansion was so much more rapid than that of the other three cities. It would seem, however, that one factor was the increasing concentration of government agencies. Certainly, this view was reflected in the replies to a questionnaire of fifteen companies which had moved their general headquarters from Valle to Bogotá. Most of these companies claimed that they would have remained in Valle had they not been forced to ease the process of negotiations with the various branches of government.[9] The author also gained a similar impression from interviews in Valle. Several companies stated that negotiations over import licenses were one of the major reasons why managers from other cities travelled regularly to Bogotá, and why several companies had moved, or had considered moving, their plants or offices to that city.[10]

Unlike the transfer of established companies to Bogotá, which is a new tendency, there has long been a tendency for entrepreneurs from other areas to establish businesses in the capital. In a sociological study of the characteristics of the Bogotá manager, Lipman (1966) found that only 19 out of a sample of 36 industrial managers originated in the capital. The rest came from other areas of the country, notably from Antioquia and Valle. A similar tendency was found

TABLE 4
ORIGINS OF FOUNDERS OF COMPANIES IN COLOMBIA

City	*Founder From Same City as Location of Company*	*Founder From Another Colombian City*	*Founder First or Second Generation Immigrant*	*Foreign Corporations*	*Total*
Bogotá	30	8	35	15	88
Medellín	75	4	11	7	97
Cali	20	3	11	16	50
Barranquilla	10	4	34	8	56
Cartagena	15	1	7	2	25
Manizales	9	0	0	2	11
Pereira	16	1	1	3	21
Bucaramanga	25	3	0	2	30

SOURCE: See text.

by the author when he consulted a number of people in different cities about the origins of the founders of companies in those centers. The details of this listing are shown in Table 4, which underlines the fact that only Bogotá and, to a lesser extent, Barranquilla and Cartagena attracted entrepreneurs from other areas. In the case of Bogotá, accessibility to the government should certainly be regarded as a major factor behind this tendency.

The Role of Government in the Growth of Bogotá

Industrial development was only one factor in the growth of Bogotá. Although industrial employment in the city expanded rapidly between 1951 and 1964, the growth of employment in commerce and services was still faster. What this general expansion in the city reflected was the increasing tendency toward centralization in the Colombian economy. From the beginning of World War II, in fact, the growing size and complexity of the economy have helped the city's growth. In the business sector, there has been a tendency toward larger companies, more complex financial organizations, and the growth of a capital market. In the public sector, this tendency has been marked by the growth and increasing role of the national government.

The growing importance of the government in Colombia since 1940 is obvious. The government has gradually intervened in economic matters as diverse as labor relations, import controls, mortgages, transport development and tourism. In the social sphere, the government has become concerned with the expansion of health, education, sports and cultural facilities (Dix, 1967). In part, this expansion has been encouraged by the growing complexity of the economy and the need to intervene in it, in the interests of future growth and financial stability. The fluctuating price of coffee, for example, has encouraged close supervision of coffee marketing, the balance of payments and the development of new agricultural products. In turn, the supervision has encouraged the emergence of a political philosophy more favorable to intervention. Such an attitude was explicit in the formation of the National Planning Office in 1951, and has developed strongly since the creation of the National Front system in 1958 (Dix, 1967; Payne, 1968).

Increasing government involvement directly helped Bogotá's growth. First, it led to an expansion in the central government bureaucracy and thereby to greater employment in the city. Between 1952 and 1970, the share generated in the gross internal product by the government sector increased gradually from 4.9 to 6.9 percent.[11] And between 1955 and 1964, employment in all forms of government rose annually by 5.1 percent, compared to the annual growth in population of 3.2 percent. Second, the nature of government expansion was especially favorable to Bogotá, since the expenditures of the national government increased much more rapidly than those of local government. Table 5 shows that the costs of the national government rose from 62.7 percent of total government expenditures in 1951 to 70.7 percent in 1964 and 80.7 percent in 1970. Of major importance in this rapid expansion of central government was the growth of the inaptly named "decentralized agencies."[12] The expenditure of these agencies increased from 32.3 percent of total governmental expenditures in 1964 to 48.4 percent by 1970.

Third, Bogotá gained not only from the expansion of the national government bureaucracy but also from the increasing expenditures of local government. In particular, the growth of the Special District led to a major increase in the relative share of local government workers in the capital. Table 6 shows that the share of all municipal and departmental employees working in Bogotá and Cundinamarca increased from 10.4 percent in 1954, when the Special District was formed, to 17.7 percent in 1969.[13] The formation of the Special District, though, was not just important in expanding the local

TABLE 5
GROWTH OF GOVERNMENT, 1951-1970

	Public Expenditure					
	Million Pesos			*Percentages*		
	1951	*1964*	*1970*	*1951*	*1964*	*1970*
National government	–	4,706.0	15,020.7	–	38.4	32.3
Decentralized agencies	–	3,957.2	22,546.1	–	32.3	48.4
Total national government	690.5	8,663.2	37,566.8	62.7	70.7	80.7
Departmental government	233.6	1,624.7	3,234.8	21.2	13.3	7.0
Municipal government	176.8	1,968.3	5,735.3	16.1	16.1	12.3
Total	1,100.9	12,256.2	46,536.9	100.0	100.0	100.0

SOURCE: Boletín de la Dirección General del Presupuesto.

TABLE 6
DEPARTMENTAL AND MUNICIPAL EMPLOYMENT IN BOGOTA AND CUNDINAMARCA, 1954-1969

	1954	*1964*	*1969*
1. Departmental and municipal employees in Cundinamarca	7,223	11,579	14,012
2. Employees of the Special District	2,175	7,247	12,113
3. Sub-total	9,398	18,826	26,125
4. Departmental employees in country	49,427	65,806	88,830
5. Municipal employees in country	23,056	44,443	48,446
6. Sub-total	72,483	110,249	137,276
7. (3) / (6) X 100	13.0%	17.1%	19.0%

SOURCE: Boletín Mensual de Estadística.

bureaucracy. Its political importance, and especially that of its Mayor vis-à-vis the average city mayor or departmental governor, helped it gain many investments which might not have been approved in other areas.

Finally, but of equal importance, was the indirect attraction of the government on private companies. The influence of government negotiations on industrial location has already been noted, and there is every reason to believe that a similar tendency affected commercial and financial institutions. It is certain that this influence grew as a result of the increasingly interventionist role adopted by the government in recent years.

CURRENT REGIONAL DEVELOPMENT MEASURES

Before 1966, Colombian governments made few efforts to alter the regional distribution of employment, income or social welfare. Several autonomous regional corporations were created in different parts of the country, one free trade area and one frontier development zone were set up, and local planning offices were established in a handful of cities and departments. It was not until the Lleras Restrepo administration that a major change occurred in attitudes toward national and regional development planning. The personnel of the National Planning Office was strengthened, its responsibilities widened, and its planning functions linked to those of other government institutions. As a result of the Constitutional Reform of 1968, the national executive was able to implement certain economic policies without the approval of Congress. Regional development also began to command attention. The National Planning Department began a study in 1967, "The Regionalization Model," which was intended to define regional planning zones and to provide guidelines for "the efficient location of urban infrastructure and industrial investments" (DNP, 1969: 17). The "Model" is important as it has served as the basis for regional development planning ever since (DNP, 1971a, 1973).

The Model considered the regional disparities in the country, examined the infrastructure provided in the different urban areas, and defined the functional hinterlands of the country's major cities. To guide regional development planning, six levels of urban center were classified and the functions of each level were specified. Bogotá was considered to be of singular importance and was classified as the "National Metropolis." Next in importance were the three "Metropoli of Equilibrium," Medellín, Cali and Barranquilla, which it was hoped could act as counter-magnets to the dominance of Bogotá. To help them in this role, manufacturing complexes were to be developed and high-level urban services such as universities, central government regional offices, and finance corporations established. In addition, the efficiency of local government was to be raised by the merging of neighboring urban complexes into Metropolitan areas.

The third and fourth levels in the hierarchy consisted of cities with 30,000 to 200,000 inhabitants capable of supporting sustained economic growth. These "regional centers," which included Palmira, Ibagué, Manizales, Bucaramanga, Cartagena, Santa Marta and Cúcuta, would be encouraged to develop labor-intensive industries and to build the social and economic facilities they lacked. In the case of regional centers located in areas of high agricultural potential, a special effort was to be made to integrate industrial and agricultural production.

"Local centers" were also designated where it was felt agricultural development might be stimulated. These centers were to receive special assistance to develop artisan and small industrial activities, and in certain cases tourism. Local services were to be provided, the quality of which would depend on each center's distance from regional and metropolitan centers.

The strategy underlying the Model was clearly based on the concept of the "growth pole" (Kuklinski, 1972; Hansen, 1972). Industrial development was to be the main source of economic growth in the larger cities, with regional and local centers acting as commercial and service centers for the surrounding rural areas. Implicit in the strategy was the aim of raising agricultural productivity through the encouragement of commercial enterprises and through the colonization of new agricultural land. The Model did not conceive of a rural-based pattern of development, nor of a widespread land redistribution. Nor, it may be suspected, did it conceive of a development strategy such as that adopted after 1972. The Model was geared, therefore, to a gradual program of industrial, commercial and agricultural expansion. It assumed that major changes in economic and social policy would not occur, so it did not contemplate major changes in spatial organization. Within these limits it was of fundamental importance in policy formulation. During the Lleras and the Pastrana administrations several new agencies were established to implement the policy. Under Lleras, the Urban Development Finance Fund (FFDU) and the Industrial Finance Fund (FFI) were established, as well as regional planning agencies such as the Foundation for the Industrial Development of Santander (FUNDISER).

Under the Pastrana administration, many changes in credit provision and local administration were made, and further regional agencies established. The mere fact that two successive administrations followed the same policies is in itself a strong commendation of the Model since, even under the National Front system, such continuity has been the exception rather than the rule. Quite clearly, however, the Pastrana administration did accept the need for a reduction in income disparities. One of the main goals of the 1970-1973 Development Plan was the achievement of "greater participation and a fairer distribution of opportunities, income and wealth, thereby achieving a wider spread of the fruits of development to all members of society" (DNP, 1970b: 10). In the regional context this fairer distribution was to be achieved through the establishment of new planning agencies, through the continued decentralization of industrial credit, through local government reform, and through the dispersal of national government offices.

Industrial Decentralization

A key element in the new regional policies has been to decentralize industrial development by encouraging public lending in areas outside the major cities. New agencies have been set up to improve the availability of credit in the intermediate cities, and a number of existing public agencies have resolved to decentralize their patterns of lending. Among this latter group the most important have been the Institute for Industrial Development (IFI) and the Fund for Agricultural Industrial and Mining Credit (Caja Agraria).

Two important new institutions were also created to help decentralize lending. The Industrial Finance Fund was established in 1969 to provide funds for medium- and small-scale manufacturing enterprises. In addition, five Regional Funds for Social Capital were established January, 1973, to act as pension funds for all private companies with more than five employees. Among the functions of these Regional Funds were the creation of new economic activities, the encouragement of balanced regional progress, the increase of employment and the expansion of export industries (Ministerio de Desarrollo Económico, 1972-1973: Vol. II, 49). Funds were established in five zones based on the cities of Bogotá, Medellín, Cali, Barranquilla and Bucaramanga. In 1974, however, Congress declared the Regional Funds to be unconstitutional, and they have subsequently been abolished.

Industrial dispersal has also been encouraged by the creation of local industrial development corporations in each department. These Foundations for Industrial Development are charged with "identifying industrial investment opportunities and of carrying out feasibility studies for industrial projects and other similar promotional activities" (DNP, 1973: 33). The Foundations are mixed enterprises which are entitled to obtain funds from diverse sources, including industrial companies, finance corporations, autonomous state enterprises and local government. They cooperate with state institutes such as IFI and in certain cases, such as FUNDISER, are entitled to make direct investments. By late 1971, Foundations had been established in Caldas, Cartagena, Quindío, Risaralda, Santander, Tolima, and Valle, and three others were planned for Huila, Meta, and the Guajira.

A further incentive to industrial decentralization has been the creation of industrial free trade zones. The Barranquilla zone has existed since 1963, but new zones in Buenaventura and Palmaseca (Cali's Airport) were created in 1970. Similar zones have since been established in Bogotá and in Cúcuta on the Venezuelan border.

With respect to the efforts being made by existing organizations, the Ministry of Development has been at the forefront of the decentralization policies. During 1969, the ministry agreed to establish offices in each departmental capital and hoped to set a pattern for other ministries. As a further aid to decentralization, the ministry decreed that the head offices of industrial enterprises in which the state held a majority holding should be located in the regions where the enterprises function.

The Intermediate Cities Program

Part and parcel of the plan to decentralize industry has been the improvement of the economic services and social environment of the medium-sized cities. Without such improvements it was felt that industry would continue to locate in the major cities, and professional and skilled workers to leave their home areas. Since 1968, therefore, a number of measures have been introduced to provide local authorities with the means to improve their amenities.

The most important of these new sources of funds is the Fund for Urban Development (FFDU), which was created in 1968 to provide credit for municipal projects. The Fund is specifically designed to favor requests from cities with 30,000 to 350,000 inhabitants for projects concerned with road improvements, street paving, and the construction of market places, parks, drainage and water systems.[14] Other sources of credit were also made available, although their lending was not limited to the intermediate cities. The largest sources of funds were the Institute for Territorial Credit (ICT), the National Savings Fund (FNA), and the Corporations for Savings and Housing (CAVIs). The CAVIs were mainly designed for housing improvements.

Rural Concentrations

The largest regional disparities in Colombia are associated with the differences between rural and urban areas. In order to reduce these differences and in the hope of stimulating rises in agricultural productivity, various ministries are collaborating in the establishment of rural concentrations (DNP, 1973; González, 1973). These concentrations will contain a variety of agricultural, education, health and community-action services. Various agencies of the Ministry of Agriculture will be represented, such as INCORA (land reform), ICA (technical assistance), IDEMA (marketing) and the Caja Agraria (credit). Primary education will be provided up to the ninth grade in the concentrations themselves and up to the fifth grade in the surrounding *municipios.* Minimum hospital facilities will be available in the centers, together with professional medical services. Lastly, community-action services will be set up in an attempt to provide adult education and to generate channels for community participation.

The object of the program is to provide basic services in the rural areas. Rather than spreading facilities too widely, the concentrations will allow resources to be used effectively and will help retain professional workers in the rural areas by reducing feelings of social isolation and by providing reasonable support facilities. The concentrations are not intended to stop rural out-migration but to assist in the full exploitation of rural areas with higher-than-average social and economic potential. No attempt will be made to slow the migration process from areas of population pressure.

Fifty-four of these concentrations were planned for construction during 1973 and 1974. Their location has been determined on the basis of the economic and demographic characteristics of the rural areas. According to the National Planning Department, the kind of areas most likely to be selected are those which are experiencing rapid population and economic growth, those with high agricultural potential but with a low population density, and those where a large population exists without services. The program has, therefore, a mixture of social and economic goals.

Changes in Local Administration and Planning Institutions

A major plank in the regional development programs of both the Lleras Restrepo and Pastrana administrations was an attempt to improve the quality of public administration at the regional and local levels. Several measures were taken to achieve this, including restrictions on the growth of new municipios and departments, the creation of new local and departmental planning institutions, strengthening of the tax base, and the establishment of new regional development agencies. Some of these measures have been approved by Congress and are being implemented at the present time. Others are still enmeshed in the long legislative process and may never reach the statute book.

In order to strengthen the system of sub-national planning, a bill was introduced into Congress which required that regional planning agencies be established.[15] At the highest level, eight regional planning agencies would be created for the regions defined in the Regional Model. These eight regions would be under the control of Regional Development Committees consisting of the respective departmental governors, representatives of the major municipalities, and other local officials. The purpose of the committees would be to advise the national government on regional development plans, to coordinate and promote regional action by national and departmental bodies, and to report periodically to the National Planning Department and the Ministry of Economic Development on economic and social developments in the region (DNP, 1970a). Each committee would be assigned a technical secretariat. In addition to these regional committees, the individual departments and the larger cities would be required to establish their own planning offices. The smaller municipios would be included under the Plans prepared by the Departmental Planning Offices. Special provision is also made under the bill for planning in the largest cities. For those conurbations with more than 300,000 inhabitants which are centered on a municipio of 250,000 persons, and which are growing at more than 4.5 percent per annum, new metropolitan governments will be established. This measure is aimed at removing the problems created where the urban area spreads beyond the boundaries of a single municipio. Such a difficulty long ago occurred in Medellín, where several neighboring municipios form part of the metropolitan area. The separate municipal authorities have complicated the process of providing basic services such as water, drainage and electricity and have posed still more problems for planning. The new governments would be entitled to levy an "added value tax" and would be responsible for preparing and executing plans and programs for the physical, economic and social development of the urban region.

In addition to these proposed planning agencies, a number of distinct regional development organizations have been created. Since 1966 four new autonomous regional corporations have been established for the Chocó, Quindío, and Urabá regions, and for the cities of Manizales, Salamina and Aranzazu (1971). Like the older agencies (CVR and CAR), their major functions have been confined to infrastructural improvements such as electrification and water supply. The agency for Urabá is especially concerned with problems related to agricultural colonization and banana production. Its growing emphasis on agricultural projects was reflected in its transfer in 1968 from control by the Ministry of Development to the Ministry of Agriculture.

Autonomous Development Institutes have also been established in 10 departments by the departmental authorities. The forerunner of these institutes, the Institute for the Development of Antioquia (IDEA), was founded in 1964 and has been concerned with the provision of loans for education, water supply, electric energy, and so on, to the municipios of the department. It has also offered considerable technical assistance to the municipios, and now acts as a regional office of the Institute for Industrial Development. Most of the other departmental institutes have scarcely begun operations and have less embracing functions. Many of these institutes are likely to benefit from the provision of recent loans from the U.S. Agency for International Development.

AN EVALUATION OF THE REGIONAL PROGRAM

In discussing the likely success of the new regional program, two basic questions need to be considered. The first is to ask whether the different elements of the program are being implemented, since Latin American planning offers a multitude of examples of statutory programs that have never been implemented. The second question relates to the success of those elements which have been implemented.

The Decentralization of Lending

There is clear evidence that two government institutions have recently been following a policy of lending favorable to the less industrialized departments. Between October, 1966, and June, 1970, only 35.3 percent of IFI's loans went to companies in Antioquia, Cundinamarca or Valle. This represented a genuine pattern of decentralization when compared to the distribution of employment or value added, and indeed became more decentralized toward the end of the period. That IFI should have followed a decentralized lending pattern is, in part, a reflection of its traditional role of developing industries which will exploit the country's natural resources. It has been in this context, more than in the guise of decentralization, that the Institute has established companies in Boyacá (Paz del Río), the Guajira Peninsula (Manaure Salt Concession), and Buenaventura (Industria del Mangle). Since the early sixties, however, the Institute, and to some extent the Ministry of Development, have followed a definite policy of decentralization.

Another government fund, the Caja Agraria, has also been following a policy of decentralized lending. In December, 1972, only 32.8 percent of its outstanding loans were destined for the four main departments. Several other official agencies, however, have not followed a similar policy. In 1969, the Popular Finance Corporation (CFP) lent as much as 42 percent of its funds to Cundinamarca and another 38 percent to the other three main departments. In addition, the Industrial Finance Fund (FFI) and the Fund for Private Investments (FIP) also pursued a highly concentrated lending pattern. In 1971, 65.9 percent of FFI's loans were destined for Bogotá, and 26.2 percent for Antioquia, Atlántico and Valle. In the same year, 46.4 percent of FIP's loans went to Bogotá and 49.6 percent to the other three main departments.

In terms of implementation, therefore, there has been a measure of success in encouraging the state lending institutions to decentralize their pattern of loans. Even so, unless all state institutions follow such a policy the total effect may be limited. For, despite the fact that IFI's portfolio is much larger than those of other government funds and makes up an important proportion of all industrial lending, it cannot hope to bring about a pattern of decentralized industrial employment on its own.

This point is underlined by an examination of the results of IFI's lending policy. In terms of employment the local impact of the new IFI-backed industries has been limited. The main reason for this has been that most of IFI's investments have been directed to capital-intensive projects. A study by the National Planning Department concluded that this had been due to the fact that "IFI has not followed an employment policy. A few small, directly financed industries are labor-intensive, but they are a minority . . ." (DNP, 1971b: 188). In this respect IFI has experienced problems similar to those of SUDENE in northeast Brazil, where Goodman (1972) found that the net increase in employment from the 34/18 mechanism has been very limited. Unfortunately, the available data do not allow as detailed a calculation for Colombia as that for Brazil; but the DNP's indirect calculations do show that because "the credit is assessed largely without a selection criterion based on employment, . . . relatively few jobs have been created" (DNP, 1971b: 188). This problem has been aggravated by another difficulty common to the 34/18 program: the new industries' isolation from their main suppliers and markets. Due to this isolation, local linkages are limited and little is generated in the way of indirect employment or income within the surrounding regions. The decentralization program, therefore, has not been successful in creating new jobs, leading to the construction of new infrastructure, raising local salary levels, or increasing the participation of local capital in the industries.

The impact of the decentralization program has also been limited by IFI's tendency to invest in a few large-scale enterprises. This has meant that few companies have been established and few areas have benefited from the program. In fact, between October, 1966, and June, 1970, 44.5 percent of IFI's total loans and 65.5 percent of its loans destined for departments outside Antioquia, Cundinamarca and Valle, were concentrated in eight major projects. And since two of these eight projects, accounting for 27 percent of the funds, were located in Cartagena, it can be seen that decentralization was limited. Of these eight projects, in fact, only three can be said to have really fostered industrial decentralization: the salt concession in the Guajira, the rail-carriage works in Paipa (Boyacá), and the cement works in Toluviejo (Sucre). Again, this is an experience very similar to that of the SUDENE program in Brazil. In 1967, for example, 36 percent of the 34/18 investment was concentrated in the state of Bahia, 34 percent in Pernambuco, and 15 percent in Alagoas. In the same year it was estimated that these states had 27, 18 and 5 percent, respectively, of the Northeast's population (Goodman, 1972; Hirschman, 1968).

Infrastructural Development

Any assessment of the effect of infrastructural improvements in the intermediate cities must also take note of the short time the program has been operating. However, two features of the program are already clear. The first is that funds have been obtained for this program through two soft loans from the U.S. Agency for International Development. The second is that FFDU's first loans were marked by a pattern of concentration in the largest cities. In June, 1972, 14.2 percent of the FFDU loans were destined for Antioquia, 3.9 percent to Atlántico, 24.9 percent to Cundinamarca and 41.2 percent to Valle. While a number of intermediate cities are located in these departments, the fact is that only 15.9 percent of loans were going to the other 18 departments, where 17.2 percent of industrial employment was located in 1969. This pattern of lending does not conform to the claims of the DNP that the FFDU is designed to favor requests from the intermediate cities.

Even if the program eventually benefits the intermediate cities, however, infrastructural provision is not being related directly to the industrial development program. As such, although the new investment will provide employment in those cities and is likely to have a positive effect on the quality of life, it is not likely to affect the distribution of industry dramatically.

This situation could change, since IFI was given permission in 1968 to participate in the creation of industrial parks. Indeed, there has been interest in such parks since 1965, when a United Nations expert was sent to Colombia to advise the government on this matter. Since that time, however, the government has not established any industrial parks. Only two private parks have been established in Manizales and Sogomoso, with the possibility of another in Cali. Even if industrial parks are created in greater numbers, experience from other countries suggests that this will not ensure industrial decentralization. In countries such as Brazil, Mexico, Peru and Puerto Rico, the only successful parks have been those where some form of tax incentive has been available (Gilbert, 1974a).

Administrative Decentralization

The establishment of regional offices of the Ministry of Development is clearly an important step toward the decentralization of the government bureaucracy. So, too, is the utilization of different regional institutions such as IDEA and FUNDISER to help in the negotiation of regional credit. This kind of decentralization, however, will only be effective if the regional offices are permitted to make decisions and are not used merely for the "processing of requests." If they are not given some autonomy, and all major decisions continue to be made in Bogotá, then the procession of managers and local dignitaries travelling to the capital will also continue. In any case, the present situation is likely to persist, since other ministries are not creating similar branch offices. And since industrial managers often have to deal with a number of different government agencies, they will only cease travelling to Bogotá once all ministries operate semi-autonomous offices in the major cities. This point is underlined by a survey carried out by the Foundation for the Industrial

Development of Valle which included a list of the various offices of the government consulted most frequently by the group's members (DNP, 1971b). These offices included the Institute for Foreign Trade (INCOMEX), the Superintendencies for Prices and for Joint-Stock Companies, the National Tax Administration, and the Ministries of Agriculture, Health and Labor. Unless all these government authorities establish regional offices and delegate a measure of independence to them, therefore, the government's presence in Bogotá will continue to influence industrial managers in their location decisions.

Administrative Reform

As described above, a number of administrative reforms are included in the regional program. These reforms include the strengthening of regional, departmental, local and metropolitan planning, the creation of new autonomous regional corporations, the creation of mixed and private departmental development corporations, and control over the growth of new departments and municipios. The outcome of these reforms poses a number of questions.

First, the viability of a policy of decentralization based largely on a system of loan provision to local authorities must be questioned. The FFDU and other infrastructural lending institutions all depend on local authorities coming forward with well-conceived and self-financing municipal projects. In terms of efficiency and economy the virtues of such an approach are obvious. At the same time, the scheme guarantees that the richest and most sophisticated municipal administrations will have a major advantage in applying for loans. That this advantage is already making itself felt is suggested by the concentration of FFDU loans in 1972. It is also probable that this tendency will continue, since the sophisticated tax measures (such as valorization) which are required to finance many of the infrastructural projects are only now being adopted by the intermediate cities. The pattern of concentration is also likely to be assisted by the current vogue among lending institutions for feasibility and planning studies before loans can be approved. Again, there can be little criticism of such a stand in terms of efficiency; but implicit in it is a bias favoring the largest cities.

A second area of difficulty relates to the practice of establishing new agencies to carry out functions which could be performed by existing bodies, were the latter efficient. This practice has been common in Colombia for a number of years and has been one of the main forces leading to the creation of decentralized state corporations. The establishment of agencies in the education sector such as ICCE to build schools, ICOLPE to improve teaching methods, and ICFES to improve higher education, was clearly intended to counter the traditional inefficiency of the Ministry of Education. The philosophy has been that if existing institutions could not be reformed, new institutions should be created. The same philosophy has been apparent in the regional program with respect to the inefficiency of departmental authorities. As a result of this trend, a situation is developing at the local level where a multiplicity of agencies has evolved which overlap in functions and responsibility. The autonomous regional corporations are a good example of this process at work, for most of their functions clearly overlap with those of departmental and municipal authorities and with those of other decentralized agencies. While provision has frequently been made for one agency to perform a function in a particular area, this has not always been possible. With the continuing creation at the present time of regional planning committees, departmental development agencies, and mixed industrial development corporations, the administrative situation is clearly becoming highly complex. The situation may resolve itself with the systematic delegation of functions, and specifically with the further erosion of departmental and municipal authority. On the other hand, the very complexity of the situation may lead to duplication of effort, the creation of a planning and development bureaucracy, and to the waste of technical and professional manpower.

Third, if the new supra-departmental planning agencies are created there is a likelihood that their complex organization and multiple representation may result in little effective planning. There are already many examples of inefficient planning organizations in Colombia, especially at the municipal level. And while standards are constantly improving and much of the inefficiency can be explained by political factors, it is not at all clear what function these new agencies will play.

In summary, it is certain that most of the administrative reforms do represent an improvement on the existing system. This is especially true of the reforms affecting the municipios and the departments. The danger is, however, that in an effort to find a politically viable solution, too many regional institutions have been created.

The Rural Sector

The orientation of this chapter does not permit a detailed examination of the implications of the regional program for the rural sector. One comment should be made, however, about the functions and manner of operation of the autonomous regional corporations. This point concerns the degree to which the regional corporations are concerned with rural development.

The statutes of most of the corporations show that their main concern is with electricity generation and water control. Naturally, this directive is reflected in their budget allocations, an illustration of which is the budget of the Cauca Valley Corporation (see Table 7). Even when the corporations have carried out projects specifically concerned with agricultural development, this may have led to a deterioration in the living standards of the poorer groups in the regions. This is the view of Andrade Lleras (1963: 52), who has argued that "these corporations have served to accentuate the existing social disequilibria in the production. By that time, however, earnings from cotton planting had fallen from an average level of over 2,500 pesos per hectare to less than 1,000 pesos (these figures are subject to a wide range of variation in any crop year and include the rental value of the land as a cost).

As a result, cotton was harvested on less than one quarter of the total land cultivated in the Tierra Caliente in 1970 and only one-fifth of this area was reported to be sown by renters. But because of the continuing importance of cotton as one of Mexico's major export crops, government policy has dictated an increase in production in the coming years. The BNCE and two other government agricultural banks are expanding their lending operations; they financed an increase in the planted area of almost 50 percent for the 1971-1972 agricultural season in the Tierra Caliente. In this way, many of the private investors who also had large investments in ginning capacity continue to be assured of a supply of raw materials for their processing plants while not having to run the risk of low profits. The ejidatarios and other smaller planters are now being given the resources to cultivate their own lands, but only at a time when the profit rate has made it unattractive for others to do so.

Similar conditions prevail for the other principal commercial export crops in the region—melons and watermelons. Cultivation of these products is financed principally by the packing houses which have contracted to export to the United States; some of them are owned by foreigners. During the three-month harvest, the melon production of the Tierra Caliente is one of the principal sources of supply of the product in the United States. Although the prices of these fruits fluctuate much more than cotton, the profit squeeze caused by rising costs has not yet discouraged private interests from renting land and financing its cultivation.

In the case of both cotton and melons, as well as other crops in the zone, the intermediate stage of preparing the product for market—ginning or grading and packing—is more profitable than the growing of the crops. The BNCE has constructed facilities in order to bypass intermediaries who would be able to appropriate this profit for themselves, but its efforts have continually been thwarted by pressures from private interests who also want to enter into this lucrative field. Small groups of ejidatarios have been able to enter the melon-packing industry because of the low initial capital requirements and found that they were able to fully recoup their investments in less than three seasons, while employing their own members as workers and guaranteeing the best prices for their fruit. The high costs of building a cotton gin, however, precludes similar initiatives with that crop. It is likely that established packers will exert even greater pressures in the future to prevent the establishment of additional melon-packing houses in view of the lack of growth in the planted area and the danger such competition represents for their ability to fulfill export contracts.[4]

As mentioned above, the implicit division of responsibility between the

TABLE 7
INVESTMENT EXPENDITURE BY THE CAUCA VALLEY CORPORATION, 1955-1969

	1955-1963		*1964-1969*	
Category of Expenditure	*000 Pesos*	*%*	*000 Pesos*	*%*
Agriculture, livestock and forestry	75,861	18.5	143,261	18.6
Energy and fuel	321,260	78.5	580,595	75.5
Studies of economic development	8,180	2.0	33,608	4.4
Other	3,700	0.9	12,244	1.6

SOURCES: Posada and Posada (1966: Table VI.5); Boletín de la Dirección del Presupuesto, 1970.

regions in relation to the distribution and use of land and wealth." Whether or not this represents an extreme view, the basic philosophy of the corporations is clearly favorable to large-scale enterprises. And, given the emphasis of their budgets on electricity generation, it may be asked whether they should be labelled as development corporations at all.

Compatibility of the National and Regional Strategies

To be successful, a regional dispersal policy should normally satisfy one of two conditions. Either incentives for regional dispersal should be sufficiently strong that they can overcome all tendencies toward regional concentration in the economy, or they should be supported by the national development strategy. In the Colombian case it is likely that neither of these conditions is being met. The regional policies concentrate on the industrial sector, do little for the rural areas, and have been implemented only by certain government agencies. In addition, it can be argued that the Plan of the Four Strategies is likely to undermine the regional policy's real chances of success.

Expansion of the construction industry, as contemplated in the Development Plan, would seem to encourage continued concentration in the country's largest cities. First, if the distribution of loans under the new housing mortgage scheme reflects the past pattern of housing loans in the country, then most recipients of mortgages will be concentrated in the major cities. In the past, the lending policy of the Central Mortgage Bank (BCH) and of the commercial banks strongly favored housing construction in Bogotá. In 1971, for example, 46 percent of the loans of the Central Mortgage Bank went to Bogotá and its surrounding department. Similarly, 60 percent of commercial bank loans to the construction industry went to companies in the Bogotá area. It would seem unlikely that this well-established pattern will be reversed in the lending policy of the CAVIs.

Second, the impact of the housing boom on the manufacturing sector will be felt most strongly in industries producing construction items. The brick and cement industries are expected to gain approximately 56 percent of new manufacturing employment due to be created directly by the new housing and urban investments (Sarmiento, 1973).[16] And since most of the companies in these industries are located close to the main cities and sell primarily to local markets, the construction boom will mainly benefit factories near the largest centers. In addition, any expansion in wage-good industries such as textiles will clearly benefit the major centers, where those industries are concentrated. The effect of the Plan on industrial development in the poorer regions, therefore, is likely to be minimal.

Finally, the new Plan lays great stress on the non-manufacturing sectors. By contrast, the regional dispersal policies are concerned mainly with the distribution of manufacturing industry. As a result, it is unlikely that the general pattern of economic activity in the country will be affected greatly by the regional policies. Only if the housing boom is widely spread and related industries are established near the smaller urban centers will the two sets of policies be compatible. But if, as seems likely, the boom is concentrated in the largest centers, then the dispersal incentives are likely to appeal only to a limited range of industries. And if the boom in housing is seen to be the main growth sector in the economy, the location of new industrial activity is likely to follow the distribution of that growth sector.

Certain government planners have denied that the Four Strategies Plan will have this effect, and they may prove to be correct. At the same time, the recent introduction of certain ideas which complement the Plan does create doubt. The most important of these ideas concerns the need for city planning in the five largest cities. Between August, 1972, and January, 1974, the firm of Llewelyn-Davies, Weeks, Forestier-Walker, and Bor was employed to draw up an urban structure plan for Bogotá. Similar studies are now under way for the cities of Medellín, Cali, Barranquilla, and Bucaramanga. These studies are clearly being made now because a rapid expansion in the populations of these cities is expected. Every effort, therefore, is being made to limit the difficulties caused by traffic congestion, housing shortages and environmental pollution. The National Planning Department has recently produced a document suggesting that the establishment of urban sub-centers within the large cities may minimize external diseconomies of scale. And since this idea shows strong similarities to work previously carried out by Lauchlin Currie (Universidad Nacional, CID, 1969; DNP, 1974; Currie, 1965a, b; Sandilands, 1974), it is reasonable to infer that it is part and parcel of the grand urban strategy.

What these different points suggest is that the Pastrana government, while continuing the regional policies of its predecessor, was less than committed to regional dispersal. And, if it is accepted that "political will" is a major determinant of the success of regional policies, this conflict between national urban and regional development strategies cannot be seen as a good omen for the success of the latter.

CONCLUSION

Since 1967, two separate governments have introduced the first coherent set of regional development policies to be produced in Colombia. These policies seek to encourage the development of economic activities in the poorer areas of the nation, and are aimed at both the public and the private sectors. To encourage the dispersal of industry, efforts are being made to improve infrastructure in the intermediate cities, to widen the availability of financing in the smaller urban centers, and to partially decentralize government agencies. Various efforts are also being made to improve the quality of local and departmental government and to introduce a stronger planning element into regional development. Finally, efforts are being made to encourage development in rural areas, and areas with growth potential are being provided with infrastructure and services.

Although genuine improvements for the poorer regions are likely to result from the program, two questions must be posed about its likely outcome. First, are the present policies sufficiently strong to check the powerful economic social and political forces leading to spatial concentration? Second, is the strategy embraced in the program *relevant* to Colombia's regional problems, or indeed to those of other Latin American nations?

Unfortunately, it is only too easy to argue that the current regional program will fail to alter the present distribution of employment, income and economic activity in the country. The industrial incentives, for example, are very weak, especially when compared with those introduced in other countries. Unlike Brazil, Mexico and Puerto Rico, tax incentives for companies locating in the poorer regions have not been introduced. Recent governments have failed to establish industrial parks in the smaller cities, nor have they created disincentives to location in the largest cities. As a result, current policies are unlikely to counter the increasingly strong pressures on companies to locate in Bogotá.

Similarly, the modifications being made in the administrative system, while both sensible and necessary, will hardly lead to major changes in the spatial structure of the economy. The system of loans to local government tends to favor the most prosperous authorities which are in the best position to borrow funds. This also happens in Colombia with respect to the distribution of health and education funds, which are given to the departments roughly in proportion to the funds they themselves generate (Gilbert, 1974c). This works well for the large departments with high tax revenues but is clearly inadequate (and has to be partly supplemented) in the case of small departments lacking a strong tax base. If one of the objects of a dispersal policy is to help those poorer departments, certain problems will arise. In addition, the proposed regional planning agencies will create a new set of official and semi-official institutions, which can scarcely help the poorer regions. Colombia already possesses a great number of government agencies which overlap in function and which have too few funds to operate effectively. The designation of new regional agencies appears to reflect the continuing faith that new agencies will achieve something which the previous agencies could not. If the older agencies were abolished then little harm would be done. Invariably, however, both sets of agencies are expected to coexist and wallow in a confusion of different policies, strategies, and personalities.

Finally, the Colombian regional program suffers clearly from what I have called elsewhere (Gilbert, 1974a) a lack of political will. If the intention of a regional program is to bring about fundamental changes in regional structure, then it is not apparent in the design of the Colombian program. This lack of commitment became even clearer in 1972 when the Pastrana administration introduced its national urban strategy. Although the Four Strategies are clearly designed to bring positive changes to the Colombian economy, they are unlikely to directly help the cause of the poorer regions. The choice of economic priorities is, of course, the prerogative of the Colombian government; and it is their decision alone to encourage or discourage regional concentration. If, however, the government believed that urban concentration was the most effective development strategy, why adopt regional dispersal policies at all? And if they wish the regional program to benefit small towns and rural areas, their choice of policies does not reflect this desire.

The deficiencies of the Colombian regional program, however, should not be attributed wholly to the government's lack of political commitment to balanced regional development. In turn, the government has good grounds for arguing that the package of regional measures offered to them by the regional planning literature is confusing, vague and over-academic. Certainly, it is the brave planner who would claim that the literature on regional development offers a comprehensive set of programs to governments in less-developed nations. Even if judgment is restricted to individual measures and concepts, the situation hardly improves.

Take, for example, the literature on "growth poles"—an appropriate example, since the Colombian Regional Model owes much to this concept. The "growth pole" idea has diffused widely through the planning literature and now appears in many national development plans. Its underlying rationale is irrefutable. It is not possible to spread industry, services and infrastructure to all regions within a nation, so concentrations of economic activity must be developed where they will maximize economic development and social welfare. Unfortunately, beyond this preliminary agreement, the concept is ill-defined and is often used to mean whatever planners wish it to mean. Some writers use the terms "growth center" and "growth pole" interchangably, while others differ widely in their interpretations of the two terms (Darwent, 1969; Moseley, 1973a; Gilbert, 1974b). There is little agreement over the kinds of economic activities which should be established in these centers (Darwent, 1969). It is unclear through what mechanism "growth centers" are expected to generate development in the rural areas, and doubt is even being expressed in some quarters whether they can benefit such areas at all (Moseley, 1973a, b; Robinson and Salih, 1971; Gilbert, 1975).

Similar imprecision is apparent in most of the planning literature, whatever the subject under discussion. Do we really know whether large cities are more "efficient" than medium-sized cities, and are we certain that our present methods offer good ways of measuring urban costs and benefits (Mera, 1973; Richardson, 1973; Ternent, 1970)? Can we agree on the point beyond which regional income disparities are undesirable and actually begin to slow down economic growth? Can we suggest ways in which the poorest regions in a nation can develop without leading to the destruction of their cultures or the massive acceleration of out-migration? Certainly, the literature on many of these questions has become more informed and more specific through time. As a result, the quality of regional planning programs adopted in many Latin American countries has improved dramatically. Until it improves still further, however, it would be unfair to lay all the blame for ineffective regional programs on the national governments concerned.

NOTES

1. Decree 1728 of 12 August 1974 reduced the minimum annual interest payable on index-linked savings accounts from 5 to 4 percent. It also specified that the increase in the value of the *unidad de poder adquisitivo constante* (UPAC) would be limited to 20 percent beginning in September, 1974.

2. Figures taken from D.A.N.E., Tabulado Preliminar No. 2. These data differ from other provisional figures published in the Boletín Mensual de Estadística during 1974. Common to both sets of figures, however, is the faster growth of Bogotá.

3. This rapid increase was not reflected in the industrial employment figures, however, possibly because the data series ended in 1969 while the fastest period of growth in Bogotá's industrial electricity consumption occurred between 1969 and 1971 (25.7 percent in the two years).

4. Gross internal product at factor cost in market prices.

5. This tendency may have been misleading; see note 3.

6. Gilbert (1970) has used shift-share analysis to examine the importance of this growth factor.

7. Thirty-nine percent of the city's industrial employment in 1953 was in the textile sector. Even as late as 1965, the concentration of employment in this sector was very marked. This fact is reflected in the following indices of industrial diversification, listed in order of decreasing diversification: Cali (58.0), Bogotá (56.7), Barranquilla (49.6), Cartagena (48.5), Palmira (45.0), Bucaramanga (39.7), Medellín (38.6), Manizales (36.8), and Pereira (27.7).

8. The intermediate cities began to set up finance corporations in increasing numbers after 1967.

9. Study carried out by the Fundación para el Desarrollo Industrial del Valle del Cauca, and discussed in DNP (1971b).

10. Between October, 1967, and June, 1968, the author interviewed the managers of over 100 companies in all of the main Colombian cities. The results of the survey are presented in Gilbert (1970).

11. Gross internal product at factor cost in market prices.

12. The term "decentralized" relates to the semi-autonomous administrative position held by these agencies. It clearly does not apply to their locations.

13. The same tendency was apparent in Cali and Medellín.

14. The cost of the projects must be recouped through consumer charges or through valorization.

15. Introduced into Congress in 1967, but had still not become law by September, 1973.

16. According to Table III-3 in Sarmiento (1973), sectors 22-28 would obtain 4,887 out of a total of 8,764 new jobs in the manufacturing sector generated by 1 billion pesos additional demand in housing and 250 millions in urbanization.

REFERENCES

ALONSO, W. (1971) "The economics of urban size." Papers and Proceedings of the Regional Science Association 26: 67-83.

ANDRADE LLERAS, G. (1963) El papel de la planificación regional, departamental, local y de las corporaciones de fomento en Colombia como instrumentos del desarrollo. Bogotá: Escuela Superior de Administración Pública.

ARANGO, G. (1970) Informe sobre localización industrial. Asociación Nacional de Industriales, XXVI Asamblea General, Cartagena.

AVROMIC, D. [ed.] (1972) Economic Growth of Colombia: Problems and Prospects. Baltimore and London: Johns Hopkins University Press.

BROWNING, H. L. (1958) "Recent trends in Latin American urbanization." Annals of the American Association of Political and Social Science 316 (March): 111-120.

CAMACHO DE PINTO, T. (1970) Colombia: el proceso de urbanización y sus factores relacionados. Tunja: Ediciones "La Rana y El Aguila."

CARDONA, R. [ed.] (1971) Las migraciones internas. Bogotá: Asociación Colombiana de Facultades de Medicina.

--- (1970) Migración y desarrollo urbano. Bogotá: Asociación Colombiana de Facultades de Medicina.

--- and A. SIMMONS (1973) Apuntes sobre la llamada "crisis" en las grandes ciudades. Bogotá: Monografías de la Corporación Centro Regional de Población.

COTLER, J. (1967-1968) "The mechanics of internal domination and social change in Peru." Studies in Comparative International Development 3 (December).

CURRIE, L. (1971) "The exchange constraint on development: a partial solution to the problem." Economic Journal 81 (December): 886-903.

--- (1966) Accelerating Development: The Necessity and the Means. New York: McGraw-Hill.

--- (1965a) Operación Colombia. 2nd ed. Barranquilla: Cámara de Comercio.

--- (1965b) Una política urbana para los países en desarrollo. Bogotá: Ediciones Tercer Mundo.

--- (1963) Ensayos sobre planeación: introducción a una teoría de desarrollo conocida como "Operación Colombia." Bogotá: Ediciones Tercer Mundo.

--- (1961) "La 'Operación Colombia'." Diario Oficial (September).

DARWENT, D. F. (1969) "Growth poles and growth centers in regional planning: a review." Environment and Planning 1 (January): 5-32.

DIX, R. H. (1967) Colombia: The Political Dimensions of Change. New Haven: Yale University Press.

DNP [Departamento Nacional de Planeación] (1974) Ciudades dentro de la ciudad: la política urbana y el plan de desarrollo en Colombia. Bogotá.

--- (1973) La política nacional de distribución espacial de la población en Colombia. Bogotá.

--- (1972) Las cuatro estrategias. Bogotá.

--- (1971a) Plan de desarrollo: desarrollo regional. Bogotá.

--- (1971b) Bases para una política de descentralización industrial. Bogotá.

--- (1970a) "Política de desarrollo regional y urbano: modelo de regionalización." Revista de Planeación y Desarrollo 2 (October): 303-352.

--- (1970b) Plan de desarrollo, 1970-73. Bogotá.

--- (1969) Modelo de regionalización, IV: bases para una política regional en Colombia. Bogotá.

--- (1968-1970) Modelo de regionalización. 14 vols. Bogotá.

ECLA [Economic Commission on Latin America, United Nations] (1971) "Some regional development programs in Latin America linked to metropolitanization." Economic Bulletin for Latin America 16, 2: 57-90.

FRANK, A. G. (1967) Capitalism and Underdevelopment in Latin America: Historical Studies of Chile and Brazil. New York: Monthly Review Press.

FRIEDMANN, J. (1966) Regional Development Policy: A Case Study of Venezuela. Cambridge, Mass.: MIT Press.

GILBERT, A. G. (1975) "A note on the incidence of development in the vicinity of a growth center." Regional Studies 9 (June): forthcoming.

--- (1974a) Latin American Development: A Geographical Perspective. Harmondsworth, Middlesex: Penguin Books.

--- (1974b) "Growth poles: the instant solution to regional problems?" pp. 111-128 in R. S. Thoman (ed.) Proceedings of the Commission on Regional Aspects of Development of the International Geographical Union, Vol. 1: Methodology and Case Studies. Toronto: Allister Typesetting.

--- (1974c) "The spatial allocation of education and health facilities in a less-developed nation," pp. 307-342 in E. M. Helleiner and W. Stöhr (eds.) Proceedings of the Commission on Regional Aspects of Development of the International Geographical Union, Vol. 2: Spatial Aspects of the Development Process. Toronto: Allister Typesetting.

--- (1970) "Industrial growth in the spatial development of the Colombian economy between 1951 and 1964." Ph.D. dissertation. University of London.

GONZALEZ, G. A. (1973) La educación rural en Colombia: un programa de cambio social. Bogotá: Ministerio de Educación Nacional.

GONZALEZ CASANOVA, P. (1964-1965) "Internal colonialism and national development." Studies in Comparative International Development 1, 4: 27-37.

GOODMAN, D. E. (1972) "Industrial development in the Brazilian Northeast: an interim assessment of the tax credit scheme of Article 34/18," pp. 231-274 in R. J. Roett (ed.) Brazil in the Sixties. Nashville, Tenn.: Vanderbilt University Press.

HANSEN, N. M. [ed.] (1972) Growth Centers in Regional Economic Development. New York: Free Press.

HIRSCHMAN, A. O. (1968) "Industrial development in the Brazilian Northeast and the tax credit scheme of Article 34/18." Journal of Development Studies 5 (October): 1-28.

ILO [International Labour Office] (1970) Towards Full Employment. Geneva: ILO.

JOHNSON, H. G. (1958) "Planning and market in economic development." Pakistan Economic Journal 8.

KUKLINSKI, A. [ed.] (1972) Growth Poles and Growth Centers in Regional Planning. The Hague and Paris: Mouton.

LIPMAN, A. (1966) El empresario bogotano. Bogotá: Ediciones Tercer Mundo y Facultad de Sociología de la Universidad Nacional.

MANRIQUE, R. (1970) "Localización industrial y proceso de urbanización en Colombia." Boletín Mensual de Estadística 224 (March): 10-33.

MERA, K. (1973) "On urban agglomeration and economic efficiency." Economic Development and Cultural Change 21 (January): 309-324.

Ministerio de Desarrollo Económico (1972-1973) La política del Ministerio de Desarrollo, Tomos II y III. Bogotá.

MOSELEY, M. J. (1973a) "The impact of growth centers in rural regions, I: an analysis of spatial 'patterns' in Brittany." Regional Studies 7 (March): 77-94.

--- (1973b) "Growth centers: a shibboleth?" Area 5: 143-149.

ODELL, P. R. and D. A. PRESTON (1973) Economies and Societies in Latin America. London: Wiley.

PAYNE, J. L. (1968) Patterns of Conflict in Colombia. New Haven, Conn.: Yale University Press.

POSADA, A. J. and J. POSADA (1966) The C.V.C.: Challenge to Underdevelopment and Traditionalism. Bogotá: Tercer Mundo.

RICHARDSON, H. W. (1973) The Economics of Urban Size. Lexington, Mass., and Westmead, England: Saxon House and Lexington Books.

ROBINSON, G. and K. B. SALIH (1971) "The spread of development around Kuala Lumpur: a methodology for an exploratory test of some assumptions of the growth pole model." Regional Studies 5 (December): 303-314.

RODRIGUEZ, L. R. (1967) El desarrollo urbano en Colombia. Bogotá. Ediciones Universidad de los Andes.

ROSAS, L. E. et al. (1973) Controversia sobre el plan de desarrollo. Bogotá: Corporación para el Fomento de Investigaciones Económicas.

ROSING, K. E. (1966) "A rejection of the Zipf model (rank size rule) in relation to city size." Professional Geographer 18 (March): 75-81.

SANDILANDS, R. J. (1974) "Colombia: another miracle ahead?" BOLSA Review 8 (March): 142-146.

SARMIENTO, E. (1973) Aspectos cuantitativos del plan de desarrollo. Bogotá: Departamento Nacional de Planeación.

STOHR, W. (1972) "The state of the art: regional development programs in Latin America at the end of the 1960s," pp. 241-257 in G. Geisse and J. E. Hardoy (eds.) Latin American Urban Research, Vol. 2. Beverly Hills, Calif.: Sage Publications.

SUNKEL, O. (1969) "National development policy and external dependence in Latin America." Journal of Development Studies 6 (October): 23-48.

TERNENT, J.A.S. (1970) "Algunas consideraciones económicas sobre una política urbana para Colombia." Centro de Investigaciones para el Desarrollo, Documentos de Trabajo 2: 17-128.

Universidad Nacional, Centro de Investigaciones para el Desarrollo (1969) Alternativas para el desarrollo urbano de Bogotá D.E. Bogotá: Universidad Nacional.

UTRIA, R. D. (1972) "Regional structure in Latin American development," in G. Geisse and J. E. Hardoy (eds.) Latin American Urban Research, Vol. 2. Beverly Hills, Calif.: Sage Publications.

VERNEZ, G. (1971) "El proceso de urbanización de Colombia." Revista de la Sociedad Interamericana de Planificación 5 (September): 14-34.

WINGO, L. (1967) "Recent patterns of urbanization among Latin American countries." Urban Affairs Quarterly 2 (March): 81-110.

ZIPF, G. K. (1941) National Unity and Disunity. Bloomington, Ind.: Principia Press.

GLOSSARY OF ACRONYMS

CAVI–Corporation for Savings and Housing
DNP–National Planning Department
FFDU–Urban Development Finance Fund
FFI–Industrial Finance Fund
FIP–Fund for Private Investments
FNA–National Savings Fund
FUNDISER–Foundation for the Industrial Development of Santander
ICT–Institute for Territorial Credit
IDEA–Institute for the Development of Antioquia
IFI–Institute for Industrial Development
INCOMEX–Institute for Foreign Trade
INCORA–National Agrarian Reform Institute

DAVID BARKIN teaches Marxist political economy at the Universidad Autónoma Metropolitana in Mexico City and is a Research Associate at El Colegio de México. He received his doctorate from Yale University in 1966 and has done field research in Mexico, Chile, and Cuba. At present he is completing a study of Mexican economic development since 1940 and is continuing his research on the socialist experience in Cuba. He is coauthor (with Timothy King) of *Regional Economic Development: The River Basin Approach in Mexico* (Cambridge University Press, 1970); coeditor (with Nita Manitzas) of *Cuba: The Logic of the Revolution* (Warner Modular Publications, 1973); and editor of *Los beneficiarios del desarrollo regional* (Sep-Setentas, Mexico City, 1972). He has also published numerous articles on problems of regional development, education, income distribution, and problems of the transition to socialism in the countries where he has done fieldwork.

Chapter 12

REGIONAL DEVELOPMENT AND INTERREGIONAL EQUITY: A MEXICAN CASE STUDY

DAVID BARKIN

In this paper I focus on the effects of regional development on the national process of economic development in Mexico. I begin by describing a regional development program. After describing the setting and the nature of the program, I explore the reasons for the limited effect of this development in other sectors and on the possibility of an autonomous growth process. With this perspective, I examine the impact of the regional development effort on the structure of the labor force and the implications of these changes for labor force mobility and the national urbanization process. Finally, these points are drawn together in a discussion of the relationships between regional development, national development and equity.

The analysis reveals that in the case examined here–and in others in Mexico–regional development has led to the effective integration of an isolated geographic area into the national market economy. In the process independent farmers and craftspeople who managed to live at subsistence levels were not able to maintain their independence. The new economic structure requires capital, special technical skills and access to political influence in order to thrive. Most people are not permitted access to these resources or to political power and they become dependent on a privileged group who are, in the case of regional development examined here, predominantly people who came from outside the region and were part of the well-established financial groups in the national economy. As a result, the original inhabitants of the region often found themselves still living at subsistence–albeit a somewhat higher level consistent with the region's new status as part of the national economy–and without their former independence. They now depend on employment from these outside groups who have gained effective control over the land and the new commercial agricultural economy.

Regional development programs may lead to a significant rise in regional production and, in this case, to a very substantial financial return on the resources invested in public works. The increased production was an important contribution to the "national" development effort because the crops could be exported, and foreign exchange is one of the primary bottlenecks in Mexican development. The region also attracted a certain number of people who might otherwise have migrated to one of the metropolitan areas and further heightened social tensions and overcrowding. But, in the ultimate analysis, the program did not provide a basis for the continued growth of the region and the benefits from its production are systematically channeled into the vaults of the dominant economic groups who are benefiting from Mexico's "economic miracle" (see Barkin, 1971).

A REGIONAL DEVELOPMENT PROGRAM IN MEXICO

The setting for this analysis is one of the most successful of the regional development programs in Mexico, when measured by the traditional tools of public investment analysis. Concern for regional development has been professed in Mexico for at least one century, but the program examined in detail here dates from 1947, when a semi-autonomous governmental commission was established to exploit the water resources of the Tepalcatepec river basin.[1] The Tepalcatepec river basin is located in the states of Michoacán and Jalisco, about 200 miles west of Mexico City. Although by both international and Mexican standards the project is a small one, with a total investment during 20 years of less than U.S. $50 million and an area of only 7,000 square miles, the total population of the basin is currently about 600,000. The construction program included a series of dams, irrigation canals, roads and hydroelectric facilities. They were designed to utilize the spring-fed rivers, which could be inexpensively harnessed for both electricity and irrigation without the need for storage or flood-control dams. The facilities were in operation by the end of the 1950s, and since that time the construction program in the region has diminished greatly. In 1960, the Tepalcatepec River Commission was absorbed into the larger Balsas River Commission, which has jurisdiction over an area of 43,000 square miles in eight states and is now dedicating its attention and resources to other, less developed regions within the larger jurisdiction (see Cárdenas, 1972).

The region under discussion in this article is defined by the geographical scope of the activities of the Tepalcatepec Commission. The area includes subregions or zones that vary from very hot, arid, flat lands of the Tierra Caliente to the mountainous and rainy reaches of the Tierra Fría. Culturally speaking, the region is also quite diverse. In the lower, hot country, recent migrations have brought people from all parts of Mexico to settle in the area, and the population is similar to that in the remainder of the country: It is of mixed indigenous and Spanish descent with a high degree of integration into the national culture. In the higher parts of the region, much of the population still does not use Spanish as its principal means of communication; Purépecha (or Tarascan, as it is also known) is still the most common first language although an increasing number of people are bilingual and can converse comfortably in Spanish in the regional marketplaces.

Two cities in the region, Uruapan and Apatzingán, are important market centers and headquarters of the regional offices of the government agencies that have been participating in the development effort. Uruapan, located in the temperate zone between the hot and the cold zones, is the larger of the two (82,672 people). As is true for most secondary cities in Mexico, migration from rural areas, in this case from the surrounding mountainous areas, has swelled its population. Indians from the Tierra Fría mix with mestizos to exchange artisan and other regional products in the large market of this town. Apatzingán (44,819 people) is in the Tierra Caliente and has more than quintupled its population during the 20 years since the commission was set up, as a result of the large increase in agricultural production and employment induced by development of the region.

More than 60 percent of the Commission's investments during its first 20 years were in the Tierra Caliente. Although inhabited for centuries by groups of Tarascan and Nahua Indians, the Tierra Caliente was sparsely settled and its lands were largely uncultivated because of the lack of capital to develop their potential. At the turn of this century, Italian immigrants settled in the zone and constructed irrigation facilities to plant rice and lemon orchards and to raise livestock. They undertook the development of almost 64,000 hectares, which were subsequently expropriated in 1938 and converted into collective communities under the Mexican land reform program.[2]

After the expropriation, the workers took control of the haciendas formerly controlled by the Italians, and, with the help from government agricultural banks, they attempted to expand cultivation and plant new crops. With the construction of new irrigation facilities and the improvement of those already in the region, new communities were formed and large areas of land were brought under the plow. In addition, other infrastructure facilities were constructed which have had a dramatic effect on the Tierra Caliente. During two decades of government investment, the region's links with the rest of the country were developed from a primitive road system, serviceable only in dry weather, to include a first-class road network, airports and regular postal service. Schools, hospitals, and other public services were markedly improved, and the incidence of malaria and dysentery was greatly reduced with the improvement in sanitary conditions. Public health facilities also contributed to a decline in the mortality rate from 16 per thousand to 10 per thousand. These improvements have transformed the area into one in which standards for public services are only slightly below those prevalent in other rural areas closer to the center of the country.

Agricultural Development

The Tepalcatepec Commission devoted most of its energies and resources to agriculture. Between 1950 and 1970, the cultivated area in the Tierra Caliente increased by 2.5 times, while the irrigated area was expanded to almost six times the initial acreage (see Table 1). A slow shift from traditional subsistence crops to exportable commercial crops accompanied the expansion of the irrigated area. Cotton displaced maize as the principal crop, but rising costs have recently forced reductions in the planted area; melon acreage grew in importance. The techniques of production also changed and the value of production per acre more than trebled. The value of the agricultural product of the region increased

TABLE 1
AREA CULTIVATED IN THE TIERRA CALIENTE, MICHOACAN, MEXICO, 1950-1970

	Time Period				
	1949/50	*1954/55*	*1959/60*	*1964/65*	*1969/70*
Area under cultivation (000's of hectares)					
	42.3	63.3	105.7	109.5	107.7
Percentage of land in major crops:					
Beans	1.4	1.7	1.5	0.5	–[a]
Cotton	–[a]	0.8	11.3	38.4	28.5
Lemons	7.4	7.0	7.9	7.3	8.0
Maize	52.7	52.1	44.9	18.3	31.6
Melons	0.6	2.1	4.3	5.5	4.7
Rice	16.2	18.4	13.1	11.0	5.8
Sesame	18.6	12.6	10.1	11.0	14.2
Sugar cane	1.6	0.2	0.5	–[a]	–[a]
Watermelon	0.2	0.2	3.8	4.6	0.2
Others	1.3	4.9	2.6	3.4	7.0
Percentage of irrigated land					
	36.3	49.8	68.1	81.7	70.0[b]
Value of agricultural production (000's of 1960 pesos)					
	33,600		219,000		252,300[b]

a. Less than 0.05 percent.
b. Estimated.

SOURCES: For the period 1950-1965, Barkin and King (1970: ch. 4); for 1970, México, Secretaría de Agricultura y Ganadería, Departamento de Economía Agrícola.

more than sixfold when measured in constant prices. The changing composition of the crops on a larger irrigated area, combined with mechanization and better technology, help to explain the large increase in the value of the product.

Even by the most conservative standards of evaluating its profitability, the project yielded a 13 percent return on the government's capital investment (Barkin and King, 1970: 211-221). In addition to the sizable increase in agricultural production which this calculation measures (and other economic benefits which were not measured), the Commission's social investments improved the quality of the environment for people living in the region. By most standards of public investment evaluation, therefore, the investment program of the Tepalcatepec River Basin Commission was, from a national point of view, a wise use of resources. That is, the increase in income and other benefits generated by this investment program were greater than those which might have been expected had the funds been invested elsewhere in the country.

This traditional benefit-cost analysis, which presents so sanguine a view of the effect of the public investment program on the Tierra Caliente, should be qualified. By not including in the calculations the fact that income differences among people within the basin are now greater than they were in 1950 and that the benefit to the region from the project is different from that to the country, the calculations ignore some of the most important welfare issues raised by programs of this nature. Much of the profit from the agricultural production is directed, through the banking system and the investment process, to industrial development in wealthier parts of the country (cf. Barkin and King, 1970: 211-221); almost all hydroelectric power is exported to industrial areas; and the colder and higher parts of the basin which supply the water for the prosperity of the Tierra Caliente have remained virtually unchanged during the period.

The poverty that characterized the Tierra Caliente has been ameliorated but, as is shown below, not without causing large differentials in personal incomes for people in the area and leaving the highland parts of the basin with little improvement. The absence of government investments in these areas prevented the mobilization of capital and natural resources to provide additional sources of employment. In addition, the agricultural developments in the Tierra Caliente did not establish a base for further economic growth; once all the water available for irrigation was harnessed, there was little prospect for additional employment growth because industrial development was limited to the first stage of processing of agricultural products. Government policies did not encourage a process of self-sustained economic growth in the region, but, instead, provided inducements for the transfer of profits to other, more industrialized parts of the country.[3]

Financing of Agricultural Development

The investment program provided the basic infrastructure which made the Tierra Caliente an attractive place in which to make further investments in agriculture. As with many other public works projects in Mexico, it was implicitly assumed that private entrepreneurs and venture capital would take advantage of the lucrative opportunities provided by the Commission. The prompt and efficient exploitation of the irrigation and transport facilities by individual producers reacting to new productive opportunities was assumed almost as an article of faith.

This assumption is an important part of the underlying strategy for development in many capitalist countries. The role of government is often conceived of as explicitly facilitating and influencing the private decision-making process: Private investment is made more attractive, thereby stimulating additional private ventures. In this conception, the government is not expected to intervene in the direct production of goods and services for the marketplace, but rather to establish the best conditions possible for the operation of private enterprises which will produce these goods. Only when private enterprise is unwilling or cannot produce a certain product which the government deems essential will the public sector step in to produce the item. An important exception to this general description of private-public interaction is the reservation of certain key industries—such as electricity and petroleum in Mexico—for public sector production in the "national interest." Thus, in this type of model, governmental development expenditures are expected to stimulate additional and complementary private investments to increase the volume of goods available in the marketplace.

In the Tierra Caliente of Michoacán, it became apparent that the farmers did not anticipate the high profits that would be earned by modernizing agriculture, and, as a result, they did not respond as rapidly as might have been hoped. Even with the help of an agricultural experiment station, the process of converting a traditional agricultural economy into a modern commercial one was slow and often uncertain. Furthermore, several institutional and structural factors were responsible for a longer transitional period and a highly concentrated distribution of income in the region. Two of these, the high costs of production and the supply of agricultural credit, are examined at some length below.

All agricultural production in Mexico is conditioned by the land reform promulgated following the 1910 Revolution. Since that time, landless peasants have been granted parcels of land which they can farm; these parcels are organized into communities called *ejidos* and the peasants who live in them are *ejidatarios.* Although the ejidos were conceived of as units in which peasants would work and administer the land collectively, most ejidatarios do not work their lands collectively, but instead manage them as if they were private holdings. An important difference between ejidal and private land, however, is that the ejidatario has no legal right, except in special circumstances, to alienate the land in any form (through sale, mortgage, renting, or the like), and he or she must not let the land lie idle for more than two years if she or he wishes to retain his right to cultivate it. In spite of this proscription, some peasants find ways of renting or selling their rights to cultivate their land, when it is necessary to do so.

This situation is likely to occur when the introduction of irrigation permits the cultivation of commercial crops. Without the right to mortgage land, ejidatarios are often without recourse in their search for credit for their farming operations. Credit is necessary for the production of commercial crops because of the high costs. In the Tierra Caliente, the problem of costs was further heightened by the initial investments which were required to prepare the land for cultivation. Most of the best and most accessible land belonged to the ejidatarios; but it was covered with brush, small shrubs and rocks which had to be cleared to facilitate the use of machinery, which is almost indispensable for cotton production. This operation was very expensive and beyond the means of most ejidatarios and small private farmers.

Even after the land was prepared for mechanization, however, cotton planting was still an expensive process. The widespread practice of renting equipment with operators to do much of the work eliminated the need for most farmers to make large investments in machinery and made it possible to farm relatively small plots almost as efficiently as larger farms; it also provided another profitable investment outlet for those with capital or access to credit. Nevertheless, the costs of cultivating cotton are much greater than those for traditional crops because of mechanization and the need for increasing disease and pest control as the area under cultivation is expanded. These expenses have been steadily rising during the past several years.

From the cost side, therefore, both the high investment costs of preparing the land for cultivation and the money costs of renting equipment to work the land, using chemicals to control diseases and pests and to enhance fertility, and employing men to assist in all these tasks, presented sizable obstacles to the entry into cotton production of many people with sufficient and appropriate land.

The National Credit Bank for Ejidatarios (BNCE) was established in 1935 to help supply the necessary credit by providing unsecured short-term crop loans to finance ejidal agriculture. The bank began operating in the Tierra Caliente in the 1940s to finance production on the haciendas which were expropriated in 1938. In the main, it financed the production of traditional subsistence crops, although some rice planting and experiments with livestock were also funded. After the Tepalcatepec Commission was formed and irrigation water became relatively plentiful, the successful work of the local experiment station and some profitable private efforts with cotton induced the bank to finance cotton production on a limited scale. From the very beginning the resources of the bank were inadequate to provide credit for all the ejidatarios; private lenders were unwilling to lend to all those who would have liked to borrow because of the lack of security and experience with commercial crops on the part of most of the potential landholders who might have solicited credit.

The inability of BNCE to provide the necessary credit for ejidatarios to cultivate cotton is in sharp contrast to the rapid expansion of cotton acreage financed by private sources of credit who realized the attractiveness of the new crop. Not only did they finance the planting of the crop, but the private sector began to construct ginning mills to process the raw cotton in the region. It was usually the same financial groups which entered into both the construction of the processing facilities and the financing of cultivation or the actual cultivation through rental agreements.

The financing of the production of cotton was necessary to assure a minimum supply of the fiber for the ginning facilities and to meet their market obligations. At the instigation of a group of non-ejidal farmers, the bank constructed a ginning mill from used components in 1956 and built another one in the early 1960s; they increased the profits of ejidal and private users by transferring the very large profit from processing the fiber to the planters. Subsequent pressures from the other firms and inadequate financial resources limited the ability of BNCE to expand; eight other ginning mills were built by private groups.

Since private credit sources were willing to lend to large-scale operators, they actively searched for cultivated land, and many ejidatarios found it profitable to rent their land to others instead of planting traditional crops. Legal arrangements evolved to permit ejidatarios to rent to those who wanted to plant cotton, and by 1960 rental contracts became quite common in the region. The usual terms provided that the tenant would clear the land in lieu of paying rent and that he or she could use the land for two years. This was usually a sufficient period in which to realize an attractive return on the land-clearing operation. About 40,000 hectares were cleared in this way during five years.

Renting continued, however, beyond the two-year period because the ejidatarios still could not obtain the needed working capital. The local office of the Department of Agriculture estimated, on the basis of a survey, that in 1965 about 65 percent of the ejidal land planted in cotton was being rented to other ejidatarios or to private farmers ("investors," as they are called in the region). This system was tacitly permitted to continue, perhaps because the crops were among the most important export products of Mexico (Restrepo and Sánchez, 1969).

More recently, the renting of ejidal lands has declined substantially, along with a reduction in the total area planted in cotton, as cultivation costs continued to climb. Rising costs coincided, at an early stage, with the softening of the world market for cotton, and the government of Mexico was induced to eliminate export taxes on cotton. With the fall in the very high rates of profit received by the growers, an increasing disenchantment with cotton planting became noticeable in the region, especially on the part of the large cultivators who were heavily involved in the use of rented lands. Partially in response to this tendency and because of the importance of cotton to the balance-of-payments needs of Mexico, BNCE increased its financing of the cotton crop for ejidal

public and the private sectors of the economy, reflected in the lack of public resources to finance directly productive activities at crucial moments, prevented most of the small farmers and ejidatarios from planting cotton and other commercial crops on their own lands until the profit rates had declined substantially. For the profitable production of commercially saleable agricultural products, credit from some financial institution is essential; in the Tierra Caliente, the initial costs of land preparation were added to the normally high costs of production, which are continually climbing because of inadequate crop rotation and the absence of natural physical defenses against crop diseases and plagues. The dearth of agricultural credit and the biases against its distribution to the smaller and ejidal farmers set up a process of concentration of the means of production which compounds similar processes in other aspects of the agricultural economy in the Tepalcatepec river basin.

REGIONAL DEVELOPMENT AND INCOME CONCENTRATION

As noted above, there was a large increase in agricultural production in the Tierra Caliente, accompanied by an increase in the population and a concentration in the control of the land, which, in turn, facilitated the concentration of income. This section will examine the dynamics of this process of concentration and the possibilities of a change in the existing pattern of distribution.

The development pattern in the Tierra Caliente has made it possible for a small number of people to receive incomes above the regional average and to enjoy a very high standard of living. As previously mentioned, the importance of agricultural credit in commercial production permitted those with access to capital to obtain control over the best lands through rental agreements. These "investors" saw their enterprises grow rapidly and they became important employers of agricultural labor in the zone. Many ejidatarios and small farmers had the choice of working as agricultural laborers and receiving rent for their lands or planting their lands with traditional subsistence production which is much less profitable.

Others with capital and appropriate commercial contacts were able to get valuable franchises to supply agricultural inputs to the commercial farmers in the region or to open service enterprises which rent and repair equipment or provide technical and marketing assistance to the more successful farmers. These merchants prospered with the increasing use of farm machinery, including airplanes for spraying, and with the need for chemical products to control diseases and insects and to fertilize the intensively used lands. They are rarely adversely affected by the rising costs of production; on the contrary, the rising costs are due to an increased use of the products and services that they supply.

Many of the people financing both melon and cotton production in the region and others who established themselves in the various service industries associated with agricultural development are immigrants from the northern part of the country or from the United States. They brought their capital with them and were able to establish themselves during the first years of rapid growth independently of, or in close association with, one of the groups of monied interests directly involved in the financing of cultivation. These were usually people who had contacts from their regions of origin and who migrated to the Tierra Caliente specifically to set up these new businesses. They came with the financial resources, commercial connections and technical know-how necessary to begin immediately.

But most of the people in the Tierra Caliente are not fortunate enough to have sufficient capital to be able to participate in the lucrative parts of the service industry or to rent lands on which to plant commercial crops. In 1970 more than half (55 percent) of the agricultural labor force reported that they worked for others as their principal source of income; this figure does not include the substantial number of unpaid family members working principally on family lands, the large group of ejidatarios who work on other people's land for short periods during the year, or the seasonal workers who were censused as living elsewhere. Since most of these workers receive only minimal wages, these data suggest that a large proportion of the population in the zone is living at the subsistence level.

Even all of those who work their own lands are not able to plant them with commercial crops. The BNCE is currently supplying credit for planting cotton to only 33 of the 96 ejidos in the zone, and the irrigation system constructed by the River Commission is not large enough to supply water to all of their lands in every agricultural season. Some private farmers can obtain credit; but even among the private planters, there is a high degree of concentration of control in the hands of a few important planters and financiers. Private interests also often supplement the governmental irrigation system with investments in wells; such investments are usually beyond the financial ability of most ejidal communities.

It is ironic that as the official credit for planting cotton becomes more widely available, the profits from cotton growing are diminishing. This writer's suggestion that one way to attack the problem would be the enforcement of the legal proscription against renting and the extension of credit to ejidatarios now appears both dated and even misguided in light of the rapid rise of costs (Barkin, 1970). These measures might have been effective in redistributing income a decade earlier, but with the decline in profits, the private interests themselves have been encouraging such a redistribution of credit, which shifts the risks from the larger planters (who often are owners of the ginning mills) to the ejidatarios or to BNCE.

The general impression of the close proximity of poverty and affluence that strikes the visitor to the Tierra Caliente appears to be explicable in terms of a form of capitalist development which at first favored those who already possessed capital resources and/or technical and marketing know-how. These people migrated to the zone early in its development and collaborated with the official agencies to utilize more fully its agricultural potential. Their experience and access to capital facilitated the growth of the region, but closed the routes of access to most of the benefits from agricultural development for most of the ejidatarios and farmers in the zone. Commercial agricultural and service enterprises thrived on the growth of the area, but many persons were only able to enjoy the fruits of the project indirectly through the improvement of sanitary conditions and the greater availability of public services; the breach between the rich and the poor widened, and the system of social stratification in the region became more rigid.

REGIONAL DEVELOPMENT, MIGRATION, AND THE LABOR FORCE

Economic policy in Mexico is designed to encourage a high rate of industrial growth because it is supposed to be the key to greater social welfare (see Derossi, 1971). Regional development programs complement and support the national industrialization program; their potential redistributive impact only seems important in political declarations. In practice, regional development efforts in the Balsas region and in others like the Fuerte, Chontalpa, Papaloapan and others, have repeated the pattern suggested in the first parts of this article: Rapid growth in agricultural output with a subsequent stabilization at a higher level once cultivation could no longer be extended (Palerm, 1972).

Regional development is important to the policy makers, therefore, because it provides additional resources for national development: more exports, scarce raw materials, greater agricultural production and more investible capital (from profits). It is assumed—and sometimes stated explicitly—that these efforts will automatically improve the economic well-being of people living in these favored regions. Furthermore, by creating additional jobs in rural areas and especially in the agricultural sector, regional development programs can make the task of finding jobs for the burgeoning ranks of workers a little more manageable for national economic policy makers.

For investors, however, regional development is important because it provides another source of easy profits from investments which are often financed on attractive terms with government resources. Subsidized credit makes investment less costly and tax benefits help increase profit rates so that substantial profits are available for use in other areas. Since the principal motivation for investment is profits, expansion generally only continues as long as resources are available in the poor area. Once the initial impetus for development has been played out, the regions begin to stabilize at a new higher level but one which no longer plays a direct, continuing role in the nation's growth. To be sure, the region continues to help finance development in other areas by providing huge surpluses which the capitalists are able to extract from the highly profitable farming activities, but most of the people in an area like the Tierra Caliente continue to fulfill the role they played before development began–i.e., providing labor and living at levels materially below those prevailing in other parts of the country. Under present arrangements they are being exploited even more effectively because their labor power is being mobilized to produce cash crops for the national and international markets.

During the 1950-1970 period, agricultural development in the Tierra Caliente did attract many migrants in search of better economic opportunities, but this in-migration was substantially offset by out-migration from the upper reaches of the region. As a result, total population growth in the basin was slightly less than the natural rate of increase between 1950 and 1970. It is estimated that 39,000 people (or 0.5 percent of the population) left the region during the twenty-year period.[5]

The Tierra Caliente attracted some 32,000 people (in contrast to the estimated 71,000 who abandoned other parts of the basin), in addition to providing sufficient inducements to prevent the emigration of about 80,000 others who might have been expected to leave the Tierra Caliente had the government investment program not been undertaken. Approximately 12,000 more jobs were available in 1970 than might otherwise have existed without the investment program. Nevertheless, competition for the available employment opportunities increased markedly, due to in-migration as well as the rapid rate of natural population increase, which continued to rise in the Tierra Caliente as health conditions improved. For all these reasons, the Tepalcatepec development program has contributed less than might have been expected by project planners in 1947 to the reduction of migration to the overcrowded urban areas of central Mexico.[6]

As might be expected, the rapid population increase in the Tierra Caliente (from 68,405 to 195,680 between 1950 and 1970) was concentrated largely in the urban areas. In fact, some 29 percent of the total population increment resided in the zone's largest city, Apatzingán, in 1970. Several other urban areas also grew rapidly during this period, so that the zone's urban population (defined as people living in localities with more than 10,000 inhabitants) jumped from zero in 1950 to 30.5 percent in 1970. (Using the official Mexican census definition of urban population, i.e., those living in localities of 2,500 or more inhabitants, the zone's urban population climbed from 22.9 percent to 47 percent in the same period.) The villages, while still growing in absolute numbers, declined relatively in this period as many villagers sought work elsewhere in the zone (Barkin, 1972).

Conforming to this changing settlement pattern, the job structure was also altered. Many of the new migrants and the people within the zone left their village homes for the urban areas, where they were employed in the growing service sector. Sales people were growing in numbers as commerce expanded rapidly; service industries catering to the needs of an increasingly mechanized agricultural economy sprang up rapidly and the food trades also grew. All of these occupations help explain the rapid growth of Apatzingán and the transformation of another town, Nueva Italia, into an important urban center.

The particular nature of the agricultural development in the area led to significant changes in the agricultural labor force. First, there were the owners of the land. They could not afford to cultivate; they rented it out and worked as day-laborers on their own farms to support their families. Second, some others were brought into the zone to become ejidatarios on land recently rehabilitated and distributed under the agrarian reform. Although the latter was a widely heralded program, only 200 families from the Tierra Fría were given ejidal plots. Third, there was an influx of "unskilled" labor in search of employment–people who were unable to obtain even small ejidal plots or who were unable to survive on their subsistence-farming incomes. During the height of the growing season (4-6 months), poorly paid, hard manual labor was in demand. No housing was available and the peons, as they are called, slept in the fields or the portals of the nearby town and were preyed upon by small-scale merchants selling basic food items at very high prices. Finally, a small group of capitalists and skilled workers (agronomists, mechanics, machinery operators, managers and professional people) came to manage the transformation from subsistence to commercial agriculture. Most of them were Mexican nationals who came to the region to work but continued to live in the northern part of the country where commercial, irrigated farming had a long history.

A special category of workers was also recruited for the zone's labor force: the migrant harvest worker. Travelling in relatively large work gangs, they move from region to region in Mexico as crops mature in search of work. These people are generally paid on a piece-rate basis and earn substantially more than the normal wage because of their skill and the long hours they work during the short harvest season in each region. In the zone I studied, some were able to earn two and one-half times as much as the normal day rate, and most of the "professional" pickers were paid twice the going wage rate. In the heyday of the zone's prosperity almost 15,000 workers were recruited for up to three months and sent relatively large sums of money back to their families in the northern part of the country (Botey and Cantú, 1971).

These same processes moved agriculture, like other sectors of the economy in the Tierra Caliente, towards commercial production oriented to the national and international markets. People in the zone no longer were able to subsist on the basic crops they had once produced because price rises and more intensive cultivation required them to have more money for essentials and limited their ability to eke out an existence from the natural economy. Most peasants were unable to continue as independent farmers and by 1970 at least 55 percent of the people working in agriculture were wage laborers. The managers and other technical people who directed the economic transformation replaced the peasants in organizing production, even when the peasants were able to obtain loans from the BNCE to farm their own lands. In these cases, the ejidatarios did not have very much opportunity for decision-making, since the loans were made in kind and directed by "professionals" who established time-tables, set wage rates, and even dispensed living allowances for the farmers themselves.

This structure of job opportunities is instructive. The large pool of unemployed labor in Mexico is very responsive to the availability of new job opportunities—even when the wages offer bare subsistence. Workers flocked to the Tierra Caliente when they thought employment opportunities were available. The people within the region were able to find regular year-round jobs at the minimum wage; for the most part, however, they were unable to take advantage of the higher wages paid at the peak cultivation and harvest seasons because these were also peak work periods on their regular jobs. Thus, while job opportunities increased, the special relationship which the migrant labor force had with the commercial farmers from the northern part of the country meant that the privileged corps of migrant workers were able to get the best paying jobs.

For the Tierra Caliente, regional development has meant the full integration of the area's social and economic structure into the national economy. Subsistence production by independent farmers became increasingly uncommon and the labor force was proletarianized as commercial crops occupied an increasingly large proportion of the total cultivated area. By the mid-sixties, some twenty years after the public investment project was initially conceived, the region had stabilized with a new economic structure, in which the benefits were centralized in the hands of a small elite and the majority of the people—landowners and day workers alike—were living poorly and dependent on the capitalists for their livelihood. The tendency towards growing regional inequality was further strengthened by population movements and the incorporation of people into the wage labor system (cf. Albrechtsen and Murayama, 1972).

THE NATIONAL PERSPECTIVE

In the Tepalcatepec river basin, regional development has systematically benefited the affluent and the well-connected groups more than the people who have an original claim on the region's productive resources: These favored groups do not live in areas needing special regional development programs. This is true throughout Mexico, where inequalities on both a geographic and interpersonal level have been growing for decades. These inequalities are not surprising or even unexpected by government officials, who openly acknowledge their belief that increasing concentration of income facilitates the use of savings for investment, and carefully tailor policies which further encourage income concentration.[7] It is no wonder, then, that less than 1 percent of the manufacturing firms control almost two-thirds (64.3 percent) of all production, that six banking groups control almost three-quarters (72.9 percent) of all private banking resources, and that 3.3 percent of all farms produce more than one-half (55.3 percent) of all agricultural production. Mexico's political stability created an attractive environment for foreign investment, and the government's ability to keep wages for most workers from rising enabled the upper class, and many of the middle sectors, to develop a pattern of luxury consumption which necessitates foreign investment to help finance the large balance-of-payments deficits. In such a setting, foreign capital gained control of more than one-quarter (26.7 percent) of the 938 largest industrial enterprises, and this capital was concentrated in the dynamic, modern industries. This concentration, and the official blessings which have been bestowed upon it, may partially account for the rapid growth that Mexico has experienced during the past three decades (annually 7 percent in real terms), but it has come at the cost of increasing gaps between rich and poor, and especially between urban and rural dwellers. As suggested above, even when there has been a rapid increase in production in an agricultural region, the benefits have been highly concentrated in the hands of a relatively small group of people.

Although it is clear that the Tepalcatepec regional development project succeeded in achieving an acceptable rate of return on the governmental investment in the zone, it did not induce a self-sustaining process of regional growth. It did attract some migrants and contributed to the national development strategy. This program, however, constitutes only a small part of the U.S. $16 billion in federal government investments during the period under consideration. In sharp contrast to the limited decentralizing features of the program described in this paper, most government investments are placed in the richest parts of the country and further heighten the existing differences among the population.

During the 1958-1970 period, for example, the industrialized areas of Mexico City (including the state of Mexico) and Nuevo León received 30 percent of total public investment while five other "semi-industrialized" states accounted for another 20 percent of all public investment spending. When we add to this the 11 percent or so which went to large-scale irrigation projects during the twelve-year period, less than 40 percent of public investment was available for the 25 states in which the most impoverished people eke out their existence (México, 1964, 1970).

These investments are not haphazardly made. Governmental expenditure programs respond to the strong pressures for public support of private investment activity. The bulk of public funds were channeled into industrial projects; in fact during the 1952-1970 period only 23 percent of these funds were available for urban services, education, housing and health care. More than one-third (37 percent) of public investment was channeled directly into industry, while large irrigation projects absorbed some 11 percent of the investment budget. These funds were designed to promote a national policy of economic growth—and in large measure were successful in "Mexican" (i.e., capitalist class) terms: The gross national product continued to grow at about 7 percent per year in real terms.

These investments complemented other policies of deliberate government action to promote private investment activity. Industrialization was encouraged by a gradual closing of the borders to foreign imports, as manufacturers built assembly plants and other production facilities within the country. Agricultural output rose rapidly for a period, as new lands were place under cultivation and yields were raised substantially as a result of hybrid seeds and irrigation.

These official policy decisions in the industrial area led to a rapid growth of industrial production in the important urban centers. The metropolitan areas of Mexico City and Monterrey now account for more than one-half of all industrial output; this share has been growing during the past thirty years or so. It is no wonder that many job opportunities are also available in these cities (49 percent of all industrial employment in the country is located in these two metropolitan areas), and that they now account for more than one-third (37 percent) of the nation's urban population (Nacional Financiera and Comisión Económica para la América Latina, 1971: Table 33). These few statistics can only give a flavor of the degree of regional concentration of industrial activity in the country and the pressures for continuing migration to these centers.

Production is also concentrated within the agricultural sector. Of the 2.5 million farm units in Mexico in 1960, a bare 3.3 percent of them produced more than half of the total agricultural product (in value terms) and about 80 percent of the increase in agricultural product during the previous decade (Eckstein, 1968). While the data do not permit us to identify these units with precision, it is clear that these were the farms operating in the newly opened irrigation lands of north and north central Mexico. It is not surprising that these farms employ a disproportionately small share of agricultural labor in Mexico.

Further heightening the trend towards concentration is the seemingly irrational way in which policies which might be effective in stemming the concentration of income and population are implemented. The most notable of these is the agrarian reform, which might have been successful in slowing migration and stimulating regional development in the poorest parts of the country. The distribution of ejidal land to a large number of poor peasants was effective in stopping or braking a potentially large number of migrants to the cities. It did not do so, however, without seriously limiting the economic opportunities of those who failed to abandon the subsistence agricultural areas. The concentration of public investment in a few irrigation districts limited the impact of technological improvements in commercial agriculture. The nation needed the output and the government spent huge sums of money to promote agricultural development for the benefit of some 79,000 units, which were able to gain control of 42 percent of the cultivated land in spite of the agrarian reform. The concentration of income within agriculture today is greater than in the economy as a whole and the concentration of means of production within the sector is probably greater today than it was on the eve of the Revolution of 1910.

CONCLUSION

It might be asked if public policy could be effective in counteracting these concentrating tendencies of economic development. This must be the question behind the preoccupation of social scientists with urban growth, population movements and growing regional and personal inequality. To begin to develop a response I suggest that we must refer, once again, to the normal process of capitalist growth.

If the government interprets economic growth as requiring the continued unfettered expansion of private investment, as it does in Mexico, then public policy will be formulated to ensure high profit rates. Economic expansion, however, also tends to have the effect of providing each capitalist with more resources through reinvestment; success generally permits some capitalists to expand at the expense of others, creating a tendency towards centralization. The growing power of a limited number of entrepreneurs is enhanced by personalities and official policies which make it easier for established concerns to obtain credit and favorable treatment on matters requiring official action.

This concentrated power is also geographically circumscribed. While it is often true that investments must be made in "backward" areas or remote cities in order to take advantage of particular natural resources or abundant labor, the profits and the products themselves are brought back to the centers of economic wealth and political power. Economic expansion may take place wherever there are opportunities for investment which promise high rates of profit, but control over them resides in the financial centers.

Regional agricultural expansion does not necessarily provide the needed impetus for the development of other sectors within the area—nor does it necessarily create the basis for self-sustaining growth. This is not surprising in view of the development pattern described above. In the case of Tepalcatepec, the small groups that gained control of most of the increased production and organized the export of the crops had no special interest in the area itself, but rather moved their production facilities there to create a profit center, a place to generate profits which might be used freely for other investments elsewhere as part of their overall expansion process. It was not the products themselves that interested these people but the profits that were promised; they did not need to look beyond the readily available resources which the region exported and therefore characterized the area as one which offered no special advantages for the production of non-agricultural goods. Had the government been willing (or induced) to offer additional incentives (subsidies) to the capitalists, they might have been persuaded to continue increasing and diversifying their investments in the region. But the government did not do this, and the profits were transferred to other areas for reinvestment in projects offering further profit opportunities and greater access to other available subsidy programs.

This pattern is similar to the effects that foreign investment might have on a country in which the investors were unwilling to make additional investments to expand or diversify production. An important difference is that a region within a country cannot usually make special regulations about the conditions under which it will accept foreign (from outside the region) investment and the conditions for profit repatriation. Within a country the possibility of such transfers is virtually unlimited, except in very special circumstances. Certainly a given number of jobs are created, but the region's resources are exploited often at the expense of its ability to produce or even purchase from other regions the very goods it needs for survival. This process, sometimes called integration, leads to the increasing dependency of one region on others, without necessarily increasing the local people's ability to pay for the goods which they must import from other parts of the country. This is the process of uneven development referred to in the literature as the "backwash effect" or "internal colonialism."

The Mexican experience in this regard points to several clear lessons. The most important is that unless strong financial incentives are provided for industrial relocation, decentralization will be slow and halting at best—that is, government investment in infrastructure is insufficient. The growth of new industrial areas in Mexico has responded to several different factors, the least important of which are the official exhortations and meager subsidies offered to firms. The decisive factors were the expanding markets in rapidly growing secondary cities and the rising costs of doing business in the traditional urban-industrial centers. The secondary cities were growing because rural-urban migration and rapid rates of natural population growth led to very high rates of urban growth in many parts of the country. Moreover, rapid economic growth meant that large numbers of people were receiving sizable increases in their incomes in spite of the deteriorating distribution of income. The growing traffic snarl, the pollution, and the difficulty of obtaining skilled workers in the largest cities, along with a better integrated national transportation system and low labor costs (associated with lower living costs) in the secondary cities, started to have a telling effect on relative costs of production in the traditional urban centers.

Public policy has affected many of these factors, but not with the problem of regional development in mind. Rather, it aims to promote private investment generally. In the one case where public policy has been effective in influencing industrial location—in the border areas in northern Mexico—the success is due to differential labor costs between Mexico and the United States and the acquiescence of U.S. authorities.

A second lesson is that the normal operation of the competitive system—with official encouragement—leads to increasing intraregional concentration of wealth and encourages a growing inequality between town and country. This pattern inevitably leads to increased emigration from the rural areas with the beginning of industrialization. Policies to halt this tide should not be directed at the migrants themselves, who are only reacting to economic incentives beyond their control, but at the system which encourages continued industrial concentration.

This is the source of the contradiction between increasing wealth concentration and expressions of concern for equity. Control over ever-increasing amounts of capital is the objective of investment and seemingly leads to a deteriorating (or static, at best) income distribution. Limitations on the expansion of capital will have an immediate depressive effect on private investment. Restrictions on the use of capital will also lead to changes in the way in which business people behave and may affect economic growth negatively. But official attempts at control and regulation almost always are ineffective in the face of determined efforts by businessmen to circumvent them in the search for higher profits.

The forces demanding restraints on business or corrective legislation do not have much scope for action. Capitalists control the productive apparatus and they are, in the end, the source of authority and resources for state action. If the governmental process is one in which the competing demands of opposing social classes must be reconciled, this must be done in such a way as to placate the masses while assuring the capitalists continued hegemony for their profitable operations. Thus, there must be strong limits on the extent to which income can be redistributed and even narrower limits on the possibility of directly intervening in the way in which private business people make decisions about increasing profits.

Public policy, therefore, cannot be shaped solely to deal with inequities arising from the normal process of capitalist development. This would only be possible if private capital accumulation were not the "raison d'être" of development policies and the capitalist class were not the mainstay of political power in the society. These conditions do not obtain in present-day Mexico; thus policy can be designed only to mitigate some of the most oppressive side effects of concentration and centralization without threatening its basic premise. Often the government bureaucracy will have to struggle against some parts of the business community who do not have the foresight to realize that some restrictions are necessary for the continued growth of the economy. Conflicts also arise among the capitalists as to the best policies, because corrective actions often endanger small businesses more than better established, powerful enterprises.[8]

Public policy thus operates within narrow constraints. The distribution of income on a personal and geographic basis cannot be separated from the basic structure of ownership of productive facilities.[9] If redistributive mechanisms were confiscatory they would be unacceptable to the wealthy and powerful who dominate the political decision-making process. In Mexico, recent history suggests that not only are public policies not confiscatory but their redistributive impact is regressive—that is, resources are transferred from poor people and poor regions to the rich in the wealthier sections of the country. This is the only explanation for the continuing concentration of economic activity in the Mexico City and Monterrey metropolitan areas and the increasing concentration of personal income which is widely bemoaned in public pronouncements.

In sum, Mexico's approach to regional development is not one of inaction. Rather, regional development seems to be part of a deliberate strategy to speed the process of "national development." Public investments in poorer parts of the country are designed to mobilize underutilized resources to increase production in critical areas, e.g., agricultural products for export, as in the case examined above. To do this the areas selected for new investments experience a short period of rapid economic growth which attracts new migrants and upgrades living conditions somewhat. Traditional structures and control over resources are often eroded, and the people without access to capital or special privileges find themselves unprotected in the face of rapid change. They must adjust to a new level of subsistence while the fruits of their labor, land, and other natural resources are siphoned off in the name of national economic development.

Public policy further accelerates this process by encouraging continuing concentration and centralization of capital. A redistribution of industrial activity towards the poor parts of the country would, under present conditions, require an unlikely decision by the leading financial groups to relocate their centers of influence and power to these new areas. In the absence of such a decision, a government bent on encouraging economic development will necessarily have to encourage further growth in the centers where the industrialists themselves choose to invest. Only when the negative effects of continuing geographic concentration become too great for the capitalists themselves—in terms of falling profit rates—will there be changes in the location of economic activity and therefore of population. Such changes in the profit rate are not likely to occur dramatically as long as public policy continues to be strongly influenced by the very groups that benefit from the substantial subsidies to industrialization in present power centers. This is the normal and even necessary pattern for shaping development policies in a society whose economic expansion is based on private capital accumulation.

NOTES

1. For further details about the Mexican concern for regional development, see Barkin and King (1970: chs. 3, 4). For further information about the Tepalcatepec river basin and its regional development program, see chapters 5-7 in the same book. This section of the paper is drawn heavily from that material and was taken from Barkin (1973).

2. An account of the settling of the region and its subsequent development, written by the son of the original colonizer, may be found in Cusi (1969).

3. A number of Mexican scholars have noted this tendency toward interregional resource flows to the richer parts of the country. See, for example, Albrechtsen and Murayama (1972). It is also observed frequently that the policy of the Mexican government has systematically channeled resources into areas that contribute to overall national economic growth regardless of their impact on the distribution of income or regional balance. See Ortiz Mena (1969) and Palerm (1972) for more on this.

4. Effective pressures were applied within a year of the founding of these small packing houses by the larger privately owned groups. The large groups moved to limit the scope of the cooperative packers' operations and even threatened their very existence. In December, 1971, a series of articles in *Excélsior*—the most highly regarded newspaper in Mexico—clearly pointed out the problems that these small groups of farmers were facing.

5. For additional information and analysis of the migratory consequences of the regional development program, see Barkin (1972).

6. For further information on migratory patterns and problems in Mexico, see Cabrera (1970), Cornelius (1975), Muñoz et al. (1971), and Unikel (1971).

7. See, for example, Ortiz Mena (1969). There is an ample bibliography on the problems of income distribution in Mexico. See in particular Tello (1971) and Prieto Vázquez (1969). The most recent study, based on data gathered in 1968, is that of the Banco de México (1974).

8. See, for example, Kolko (1967) for an analysis of the interaction of business and government during the process of promoting economic development.

9. See Marx (1857) for further discussion of this very important point.

REFERENCES

ALBRECHTSEN, K. and D. MURAYAMA (1972) "Desarrollo desigual en México." Demografía y Economía 6 (January): 1-40.

Banco de México (1974) La distribución del ingreso en México. México, D.F.: Fondo de Cultura Económica.

BARKIN, D. (1973) "A case study of the beneficiaries of regional development." International Social Development Review 4: 84-94.

--- (1972) "The demographic impact of regional economic development." Growth and Change 3 (January): 15-22.

--- (1971) "La persistencia de la pobreza en México." Comercio Exterior (México) 21 (August): 667-674.

--- (1970) "Agricultural development in Mexico: a case study of income concentration." Social Research 37 (Summer): 306-320.

--- and T. KING (1970) Regional Economic Development: The River Basin Approach in Mexico. Cambridge, England: Cambridge University Press.

BOTEY, C. and R. CANTU (1971) "Los jornaleros migratorios: el caso específico de los pizcadores de Apatzingán." Unpublished study available at El Colegio de México, México, D.F.

CABRERA, G. (1970) "Migración interna," pp. 85-114 in La Dinámica de la población en México. México, D.F.: El Colegio de México.

CARDENAS, C. (1972) "Regional rural development: the Mexican Río Balsas Commission," pp. 143-150 in G. Geisse and J. E. Hardoy (eds.) Latin American Urban Research, Vol. II. Beverly Hills, Calif.: Sage Publications.

CORNELIUS, W. A. (1975) Politics and the Migrant Poor in Mexico City. Stanford, Calif.: Stanford University Press.

CUSI, E. (1969) Memorias de un colono. México, D.F.: Editorial Jus.

DEROSSI, F. (1971) The Mexican Entrepreneur. Paris: Organization for Economic Cooperation and Development.

ECKSTEIN, S. (1968) El marco macroeconómico del problema agrario mexicano. México, D.F.: Centro de Investigaciones Agrarias.

KOLKO, G. (1967) The Triumph of Conservatism. New York: Quadrangle.

MARX, K. (1857) Introduction to the Critique of Political Economy. Reprinted in editions edited by M. Dobb (New York: International Publishers, 1970) and M. Nicolaus (New York: Random House, 1974).

México, Secretaría de la Presidencia (1964, 1970) México: Inversión pública federal, 1925-1963, 1965-1970. México, D.F.: Secretaría de la Presidencia.

MUNOZ, H., O. DE OLIVIERA, and C. STERN (1971) "Categorías de migrantes y nativos y algunas de sus características socioeconómicas: comparación entre las ciudades de Monterrey y México." Revista Paraguaya de Sociología 8, 21 (May-August): 40-59.

Nacional Financiera and Comisión Económica para la América Latina (1971) La política industrial en el desarrollo económico de México. México, D.F.: Nacional Financiera.

ORTIZ MENA, A. (1969) "Stabilizing development: a decade of development strategy in Mexico." El Mercado de Valores (Mexico), Supplement to No. 44 (November 3).

PALERM, A. (1972) "Una crítica del desarrollo económico regional," pp. 13-62 in D. Barkin (ed.) Los beneficiarios del desarrollo regional. México, D.F.: Sep-Setentas.

PRIETO VAZQUEZ, J. (1969) "La distribución del ingreso en México." Comercio Exterior (Mexico) 19 (September): 686-696.

RESTREPO, I. and J. SANCHEZ (1969) "El arrendamiento de tierras ejidales: el caso de Apatzingán." Revista de México Agrario (Mexico) 3, 1: 37-58.

TELLO, C. (1971) "Notas para el análisis de la distribución del ingreso en México." El Trimestre Económico (Mexico) 150 (April): 629-657.

UNIKEL, L. (1971) "The process of urbanization in Mexico," pp. 247-302 in F. F. Rabinovitz and F. M. Trueblood (eds.) Latin American Urban Research, Vol. I. Beverly Hills, Calif.: Sage Publications.

EDUARDO E. LOZANO is Associate Professor of City and Regional Planning, and Assistant Chairman of the Department of City and Regional Planning, at Harvard University. Originally an Argentinian architect, he obtained a Ph.D. in City and Regional Planning at Harvard, and taught later at Princeton University. His two contributions to this volume are based on field research in Chile during the Allende period.

Chapter 13

THE REGIONAL STRATEGY OF "UNIDAD POPULAR" IN CHILE

EDUARDO E. LOZANO

When the Unidad Popular government took power in Chile in November, 1970, it promised to implement radical changes in the country's regional structure. Chile had been known for its long experience in regional planning, but the electoral victory of a leftist front suggested the strong possibility that a period of key changes would ensue.

Since regional policies often require a long implementation period, it may be impossible to ascertain the outcome of Unidad Popular policies, based only on two and a half years of experience. However, it is of considerable interest to analyze the views of Unidad Popular planners toward the regional policies of previous regimes and their proposals for the future. These are the principal objectives of the present chapter.

THE CHILEAN REGIONAL STRUCTURE BY 1970

Chile in 1970 exhibited characteristics typical of most Latin American countries at that time, including relatively rapid population growth (2.3 percent per year), relatively low per capita income (around $500 per year) which was growing rather slowly (1.5 percent per year), within a framework of an economy based on copper exports (Universidad de Chile, 1963). Chile's economic dependence on the copper mines was, and is, extremely high; a price change of

Author's Note: I wish to acknowledge with thanks the assistance of the Chilean Oficina de Planificación Nacional (ODEPLAN) in the preparation of this paper. The Program for Latin American Studies at Princeton provided the necessary financial support.

$0.15/lb. of exported copper was equivalent to the total annual foreign investment in the country (ODEPLAN, 1970).

This in no way should obscure the fact that Chile was among the most progressive countries in Latin America, in terms of literacy, political stability, and even average income. However, the social inequality typical of Latin American countries also afflicted Chile: the top 2 percent of Chilean families received 12.5 percent of the national income, while 30 percent of the families at the bottom of the social hierarchy received only 7.6 percent of the income. Blue-collar workers, who represented 45 percent of the labor force, earned only 21 percent of the income, while proprietors, renters and owners of business enterprises–constituting 5 percent of the labor force–earned 25 percent of the income (ODEPLAN, 1970).

Chile's regional structure also resembled in many ways that of other Latin American countries: concentrated urbanization, large-scale migration from rural areas and small towns, and increasing economic dominance of the few "modern" population centers over the depressed provinces. There was a strong tendency toward increased concentration of the nation's population in a few large urban centers, mainly the capital city of Santiago. During the 1960s, Santiago's population grew by 33 percent, as compared with a 26 percent increase in the total population of Chile. Santiago's share of the national population increased from 33 percent in 1960 to 34.6 percent in 1970 (ODEPLAN, 1970).

The phenomenon of concentrated urbanization was closely linked with that of internal migration. The rate of migration increased from an average of 5.2 percent per year in the 1940-1952 period to 7.4 percent per year in 1952-1960 (ODEPLAN, 1970).[1] The favored destinations were the larger cities; over three-quarters of all migrants settled in Santiago. As a result, one-third of the capital's population is of migrant origin, and about 70 percent of Santiago's squatters and slum dwellers are migrants (MINVU, n.d.). Apart from the Santiago metropolitan area, the only regions experiencing net in-migration were copper-rich Antofagasta and Valdivia-Osorno in the 1940s and Magallanes in the 1950s–all of them "boundary" regions.[2] An intra-regional analysis shows that the city of Concepción also has had net in-migration. In terms of the migrants themselves, almost 60 percent are practically illiterate. Though they are underpaid and there is a substantial level of underemployment, the degree of stability shown by the newcomers in their mostly low-skilled jobs is surprising. Significantly, 50 percent of the migrants were found to be unemployed in their place of origin, indicating the single most important factor behind migration.[3]

As a result of these processes, Chile had become a country with a few dominant urban centers, located in relatively dynamic regions, within a rather stagnant country. This regional "imbalance" is reflected in changes in the regional Gross Geographic Product and in the relative shares of various regions in the national GGP. Table 1 shows the "core" areas of growth: four regions with larger GGP indices than the country as a whole–Tarapaca, Antofagasta (both

TABLE 1
INDEX OF CHANGE IN REGIONAL GROSS GEOGRAPHIC PRODUCT, CHILE: 1960-1970 (1960 = 100)

Region	*1960*	*1967*	*1970*[a]	*Direction of Change (compared with country as a whole)*
Tarapaca	100	181	228	+
Antofagasta	100	145	181	+
Atacama-Coquimbo	100	135	130	–
Aconcagua-Valparaíso	100	118	120	–
Santiago Metropolitan Area	100	157	181	+
O'Higgins-Colchagua	100	131	169	+
Curico-Talca-Maule-Linares	100	120	137	–
Nuble-Concepción-Arauco-Bio Bio-Malleco	100	123	136	–
Cautín	100	107	100	–
Valdivia-Osorno	100	120	127	–
Llanquihue-Chiloé-Aysén	100	130	140	–
Magallanes	100	145	155	0
Chile	100	140	157	

a. Estimated.

SOURCE: ODEPLAN (1970).

mining regions), Santiago (the capital's metropolitan region) and O'Higgins-Colchagua (the coterminous fertile central valley to the south of Santiago). Since the GGP includes the earnings of foreign owners of factors of production, the two mining regions would show a lower national income index, leaving the central urban regions as the main national "core." On the other hand, eight out of the twelve regions show GGP indices lower than the country's, noticeably Cautín, which remained completely stagnant during the 1960-1970 period. (It is not surprising that Cautín has been a particularly restless region, where peasants have been organizing and invading rural land since 1970.)

This process of concentration has led to the growing dominance of the capital and its central valley and, to a lesser degree, of the mining regions, as shown in Table 2. Santiago increased its regional share in the national GGP from 40 percent in 1960 to 46 percent in 1970; the other three regions showing positive index changes varied only slightly, and even the regions with the next two largest cities, Aconcagua-Valparaíso and Nuble-Concepción, show a reduced share. Again, Cautín had the smallest and decreasing regional share in the country. It is important to note that the process of economic concentration appears to be more rapid than that of population concentration; Santiago's GGP share increased 6 percentage points in 1960-1970, but its population share increased only 1.6 percentage points.

TABLE 2
RELATIVE LEVEL OF REGIONAL PARTICIPATION IN CHILE'S GROSS GEOGRAPHIC PRODUCT (in percentages)

Region	*1960*	*1970*[a]	*Direction of Change*
Tarapaca	1.91	2.76	+
Antofagasta	6.32	7.24	+
Atacama-Coquimbo	5.22	4.30	–
Aconcagua-Valparaíso	11.90	9.10	–
Santiago Metropolitan Area	39.98	45.92	+
O'Higgins-Colchagua	5.64	6.06	+
Curico-Talca-Maule-Linares	5.05	4.41	–
Nuble-Concepción-Arauco-Bio Bio-Malleco	12.65	10.92	–
Cautín	2.69	1.72	–
Valdivia-Osorno	3.96	3.20	–
Llanquihue-Chiloé-Aysén	2.70	2.40	–
Magallanes	1.98	1.97	0
Chile	100.00	100.00	

a. Estimated.

SOURCE: ODEPLAN (1970).

THE REGIONAL PLANNING EXPERIENCE UNDER THE CHRISTIAN DEMOCRATS

The Christian Democrats, a reformist party which ruled between 1964-1970, took notice of the concentrated urbanization tendencies operating in Chile. Their response, heavily influenced by the "growth poles theory," was to postulate a range of deconcentration options. At one end they projected the historical trends which would have led, by 1975, to the concentration of 46.7 percent of the GGP in Santiago; the only other regions growing more rapidly than the country were the same ones indicated in Tables 1 and 2. At the other end, in the so-called "strong deconcentration" option, Santiago's share in the national GGP by 1975 would have been reduced to 43.3 percent, due to a channeling of investment to selected "growth poles" in Tarapaca, Antofagasta, Valparaíso-Aconcagua, O'Higgins-Colchagua, Bio-Bio, Los Lagos and Magallanes (ODEPLAN, 1970). The difference in results between the two extreme policy options was kept relatively small.

The Christian Democrats' published plans did not specify fully the advantages to be obtained by the deconcentration strategy, and they indicated only some of the roles of the growth poles, such as geographic specialization and absorption of rural migration. The disadvantages of concentration to be avoided were, mainly, the construction of costly urban infrastructure–subways, highways, and so on–in the larger cities to service the growing population, implying that those cities were near a threshold in their expansion.

However, a close examination reveals that the Christian Democrats did not follow the deconcentration strategies that they had proposed; in fact, there is evidence that official actions actually reinforced existing concentration trends. Table 3 presents data on public investment by regions, categorized as investment in productive sectors (agriculture, mining, industry) and in infrastructure (transportation, housing, utilities, education, health). During the 1965-1968 period only 26 percent of public investment was allocated to productive sectors, with the remainder going to infrastructure. This was consistent with the Christian Democrats' belief that the public sector should support and encourage the private sector, but should not attempt to replace it.

Also noteworthy is the fact that 33.9 percent of the total investment was located in the Santiago metropolitan area—a proportion equal to its population share. There are important differences in the allocation of investment between productive sectors and infrastructure. Santiago received a relatively minor share of investment in productive sectors (12.7 percent), ranking third among regions; but it received the bulk of the country's investment in infrastructure (41.9 percent)—a proportion close to the capital's share of national GGP. Specifically, the Santiago metropolitan area received 53.6 percent of the national investment in housing, 46.0 percent of the investment in electricity, gas and water, 36.6 percent of the investment in education, 27.9 percent of the investment in health, and 22.7 percent of the investment in transportation (ODEPLAN, 1970). This allocation might have led to two presumably undesired outcomes: the strengthening of incentives for the location of private economic activities in the capital, and the weakening of the competitive position of the provinces. Public investments were raising the level of physical and social infrastructure in Santiago, eliminating some metropolitan diseconomies (e.g., extended travel time, scarcity of utilities and housing, lack of skills), and helping the private sector to reap the advantages of scale economies and market concentration.

The apparent intent of the Christian Democrats' investment decisions was to support the location of private investment where "it wants to be," and at the same time, to implement a publicly-financed, mild deconcentration policy. Since a considerable part of the productive sector investment corresponded to agriculture and mining, efforts toward industrialization in the provinces must have been minor.

In terms of per capita investment, the Christian Democrats' regional policies benefited most noticeably two frontier regions with abundant natural resources (Magallanes, Tarapaca), and the regions where the three largest cities (Santiago, Valparaíso, Concepción) are located (see Table 4). The other regions rank considerably lower, and especially Cautín, the trouble-ridden agricultural region. Due to their large populations, the three urbanized regions managed to obtain 62 percent of the total investment.

The apparent gap between stated objectives and implemented plans was not being narrowed in time; on the contrary, every year resulted in increased

TABLE 3

ANNUAL PUBLIC INVESTMENT BY REGION (average for 1965-1968)

Region	*Productive Sectors*		*Infrastructure*		*Total*	
	Absolute[a]	*Relative*[b]	*Absolute*	*Relative*	*Absolute*	*Relative*
Tarapaca	30.8	6.2%	81.7	6.2%	112.5	6.2%
Antofagasta	7.9	1.6	34.2	2.6	42.1	2.3
Atacama-Coquimbo	30.9	6.2	50.8	3.8	81.7	4.5
Aconcagua-Valparaíso	53.6	10.7	133.2	10.0	186.8	10.2
Santiago Metropolitan Area	63.3	12.7	555.3	41.9	618.6	33.9
O'Higgins-Colchagua	33.7	6.7	44.6	3.4	78.3	4.3
Curico-Talca-Maule-Linares	44.0	8.8	45.6	3.4	89.6	4.9
Nuble-Concepción-Arauco-Bio Bio-Malleco	109.7	22.0	213.5	16.1	323.2	17.7
Cautín	12.7	2.5	32.7	2.5	45.4	2.5
Valdivia-Osorno	14.5	2.9	57.5	4.3	72.0	3.9
Llanquihue-Chiloé-Aysén	20.9	4.2	61.5	4.6	82.4	4.5
Magallanes	77.2	15.5	16.3	1.2	93.5	5.1
Total	499.2	100.0	1,326.9	100.0	1,826.1	100.0

a. In millions of escudos, 1965 value.

b. In percentages.

SOURCE: ODEPLAN (1970).

TABLE 4
ANNUAL PER CAPITA PUBLIC INVESTMENT BY REGION
(average for 1965-1968)

Region	*Absolute*[a]	*Index: Chile = 100*
Magallanes	960.0	486.6
Tarapaca	793.9	402.4
Llanquihue-Chiloé-Aysén	226.2	114.6
Nuble-Concepción-Arauco-Bio Bio-Malleco	204.6	103.7
Aconcagua-Valparaíso	199.3	101.0
Chile (average)	197.3	100.0
Santiago Metropolitan Area	194.2	98.4
Antofagasta	157.9	80.0
Atacama-Coquimbo	152.0	77.0
Valdivia-Osorno	148.1	75.1
O'Higgins-Colchagua	143.8	72.9
Curico-Talca	128.9	65.3
Cautín	104.6	53.0

a. In escudos, 1965 value.

SOURCE: ODEPLAN (1970).

dominance by the capital region, as shown in Table 5. Santiago improved its share of public investment from 31.2 percent in 1965 to 35.3 percent in 1968; in absolute figures the increase is considerable, from 495 million to 722 million *escudos* (in constant value). Other regions showing relative increases were, principally, two southern frontier regions (Llanquihue-Chiloé-Aysén and Magallanes) and the central valley regions coterminous with Santiago (O'Higgins-Colchagua). All other regions remained stable or showed relative decreases, and two—Atacama-Coquimbo and Aconcagua-Valparaíso, a large area between the northern mining district and the urbanized central valley—even showed absolute reductions in public investment.

In contrast to its short-range policies, that appeared to have supported the interests of private capital through the continuous concentration of public infrastructure in the capital, the Christian Democratic administration developed a myriad of public agencies with the responsibility of increasing the government's role in national development. These agencies included ODEPLAN (National Planning Office), CORVI (Housing Corporation), CORMU (Urban Renewal Corporation), and CORFO (Industrial Development Corporation); all were to be used later by Unidad Popular to implement its radical policies.

Evaluation of the Christian Democratic experience in regional planning is difficult due to the selective character of the data chosen to be published. As discussed below, the planners and officials of Unidad Popular were extremely critical; on the other hand, the planners who contributed to the Christian Democrat effort—both Chileans and Americans—are still supporting it. It is evident that there was, at some planning and administrative levels, an awareness

TABLE 5
PUBLIC INVESTMENT BY REGION, 1965-1968 (in percentages)

Region	*1965*	*1966*	*1967*	*1968*
Tarapaca	6.8	5.3	6.5	6.1
Antofagasta	2.1	2.0	2.6	2.4
Atacama-Coquimbo	6.0	4.5	3.7	3.9
Aconcagua-Valparaíso	12.0	11.4	9.5	8.6
Santiago Metropolitan Area	31.2	32.4	36.2	35.3
O'Higgins-Colchagua	2.8	3.4	6.2	4.6
Curico-Talca-Maule-Linares	5.6	4.7	4.4	5.0
Nuble-Concepción-Arauco-Bio Bio-Malleco	17.4	19.9	16.0	17.5
Cautín	2.6	2.6	2.6	2.2
Valdivia-Osorno	4.5	4.2	3.4	3.7
Llanquihue-Chiloé-Aysén	4.1	4.6	4.6	4.7
Magallanes	4.9	5.0	4.3	6.0
Total	100.0	100.0	100.0	100.0

SOURCE: ODEPLAN (1970).

of the regional concentration trends focused on the capital, coupled with general stagnation in the country, except for the foreign-controlled mining areas. It is also evident that strategies aimed at more egalitarian development were considered, although they were based more on ideology than on regional analysis, as would also happen under Unidad Popular.

On the other hand, it appears that the Christian Democrats lacked both the power and the will to depart from traditional "developmentalist" policies; as a result, the short-range objectives of the private capital—which are in conflict with a deconcentration approach—replaced the long-range public objectives of regional development. Thus, the Christian Democrats ended up contributing to the regional trends they criticized.

THE REGIONAL STRATEGY OF UNIDAD POPULAR

Six months after the government of Unidad Popular took power, the Ministry of Economics, the Ministry of Finances and ODEPLAN prepared a document (1971) that set forth the ideological bases of the 1971-1976 Development Plan. This document was focused on the specification of main objectives, which can be summarized as follows:

(a) Transformation of the economic structure of the country, defining the priorities of state and of nationalized enterprise, and the role of the small private enterprise.

(b) Agrarian reform, including a thorough presentation of planning criteria and of the alternatives for future organization of land and services.

(c) Economic development, stressing a reorientation of production to satisfy popular consumption needs, guaranteed employment, expropriation of foreign enterprise, decentralized growth, diversified exports, and anti-inflationary measures.

(d) Social objectives, including workers' participation in wage determination and in administration of pension and retirement funds, full and free health services, women's rights, education for people of all ages, and housing.

(e) National security, transforming the military into a more technical and socially integrated group, independent of class allegiance—an objective that was to be tragically unfulfilled.

Two months later, ODEPLAN prepared a more detailed document (1971) dealing specifically with criteria for the formulation of regional development policies in the 1971-1976 period. The regional policies were to be defined according to three main areas of change:

(a) Structural changes, involving the elimination of both the economic base and the political power of the old dominant classes through nationalization, agrarian reform, and creation of social-oriented industries.

(b) The expansion of the productive activities of the country, in response to increased consumer demand among the low-income sectors, abandoning the policy of import-substitution that is responsive only to the selective demand of higher income groups.

(c) The development of regional economies, as opposed to the draining of resources to the capital city and to an "asphyxiating centralization."

Ten basic regional development objectives were specified:

(a) Modification of regional economic structures according to new requirements of production and transportation.

(b) Decentralization of population growth and migration flows.

(c) Creation of new workplaces in each region.

(d) Mobilization of insufficiently utilized resources.

(e) Development of regional industries.

(f) Expansion of activities with high social productivity.

(g) Creation of social infrastructure, assuring workers' rights to health, education, recreation and housing.

(h) Stimulation of cultural development.

(i) Encouragement of workers' participation in planning, decision-making, administration and allocation of benefits resulting from the productive process.

(j) Fostering a harmonic regional development, with each region contributing according to its special characteristics.

This set of basic regional objectives has important political overtones, but it lacks technical precision. Some of the objectives are found in most plans of underdeveloped countries—such as decentralization (b), employment generation (c), resource mobilization (d), and industrial development (e). Other objectives are more uncommon, corresponding to the socialist orientation of Chile—structural changes (a), social productivity (f), social rights (g), and workers' participation (i). The last objective (j) could be interpreted in several ways due to the lack of a technical definition of "harmonic regional development."

The gap between political goals and technical precision was also related to an emerging conflict, that between the academic-advisory and the pragmatic-political roles, felt very strongly in Chile during 1971-1973. Each of the objectives described above represents, for the academician, a major research task, but to government officials, they represented accepted postulates that guided important day-to-day decisions. In the highly-charged political environment of Chile under Unidad Popular, there was little time for analytical thinking and, under pressure, the best one could hope for was to make a reasonable guess given the available data; for this reason, practical experience, intuition and ideological consistency were as important as theoretical or analytical skills.

The specification of regional objectives, agreed upon by the political structure, became an indispensable input to the planner and policy maker. It allowed rapid decisions and some certainty that the actions taken approximated a politically "good solution." It also assured that the collective path made up by many decisions was, roughly at least, coherent with the long-run goals set up for the country.

The 1971 ODEPLAN document outlining criteria for regional development policies concludes with a list of guidelines or directives for specific policies. The most important of these may be summarized as follows:

(a) Depressed areas must receive special attention.

(b) Programs of regional development must be integrated.

(c) Basic social services must be increased in population centers of all sizes.

(d) Investment in social infrastructure must be integrated with productive investment.

(e) Population centers must be linked with nearby available resources to promote economic development.

(f) Political and administrative units must be decentralized to encourage popular participation in the decision-making process.

(g) Urban growth must be oriented to the location of economic activities and to the harmonious development of the country.

(h) The growth of large metropolitan areas must be controlled, and the growth of medium-sized population centers must be encouraged.

(i) Priority must be given to areas that allow rapid economic growth.

(j) The dispersion of the rural population must be reduced, concentrating it in areas with the services necessary for living and productive activities.

This last guideline could have led to a breakthrough in the regional structure in Chile, and is one of the few cases in which a Latin American country would have attempted a radical reform of its isolated and backward peasantry. The other guidelines, however, are more conventional and even contradictory; there is a potential conflict between the efficiency-oriented guideline of assigning priority to the regions capable of generating more rapid growth (i) and the equity-oriented guideline supporting decentralization and encouragement of middle-sized towns (h). In this conflict we find summarized the regional policy dilemma faced by countries aiming at development with redistribution.

A brief analysis of the first regional policy documents drafted in Chile after 1970 clarifies the emerging characteristics of planning under Unidad Popular. Political and economic goals are accorded roughly equal importance; for instance, agrarian reform and nationalization of domestic capital are deemed necessary not only for economic (efficiency and equity) reasons, but also to reduce the old and new elites to a politically powerless position. Industrial production must be shifted to low-cost goods, not only to serve economic common sense, but also to encourage socio-cultural changes away from "consumerism." Even the ill-defined decentralization goal is justified as much by socio-political considerations as by economic ones.

While some regional objectives are clearly defined and justified, others are stated only in terms of opposition to previous policies. This reflects the extreme time pressure under which Unidad Popular planners operated, which led to the establishment of ideological guidelines as program or project criteria, as well as the lack of previous radical experiments in specific fields such as the issue of urban-industrial concentration versus decentralization.

The Implementation of Regional Policies[4]

Egalitarianism was the constant concern of Unidad Popular policy makers: One of their first actions was to standardize the "salario vital" (minimum wage) throughout the country to E° 840; before, it had varied from E° 630 in Santiago to E° 410 in Arauco.[5] Although there was awareness that the cost of living and access to services varied within the country, the aim was to impede the institutionalization of these differences and to effect a radical change in the availability and cost of social services. This policy immediately increased the attractiveness of the less-developed regions, where the cost of life is usually lower than in the "core" regions.

Agrarian reform was another key area of change. Using the available institutions and the existing laws, the speed of agrarian reform was greatly accelerated after Unidad Popular took power. During the six years of Christian Democratic administration only 1,000 large landholdings were expropriated; in contrast, during the first eight months of Unidad Popular government, over 1,150 such holdings were expropriated. It was expected that by mid-1973 the remaining 3,000 large landholdings would have been expropriated, ending the acquisition stage of the reform. Not everything went smoothly: The pressures built up among the peasantry often forced quicker action, leading in many cases to unauthorized *"tomas"* (takeovers) of land. The most restless region was Cautín, a rural area in the south of Chile, populated by impoverished Mapuche Indians. This region, as mentioned before, ranked last in per capita public investment during the past decade.

However, it was clear that agricultural policies alone would not do; in Cautín, for example, even allowing for the best and most intensive use of the agricultural land, there would have been at least 30,000 people without jobs. For this reason a dual strategy was adopted: First, in order to make full use of agricultural resources and to accelerate the redistribution of benefits to the peasants, the implementation of the agrarian reform had top priority; second, ODEPLAN was working to develop labor-intensive industries that used the natural resources of the provinces.

The agrarian reform would also have led to fundamental changes in the physical and social structure of rural areas, because of the new policy of "urbanization of the countryside." This was a revolutionary program, which had little similarity to "reforms" undertaken by othe Latin American regimes (e.g., Colombia, Chile before 1971). The existing rural pattern is one of dispersed huts, often located on the periphery of the large *"fundo"* to better guard it, sacrificing any possible advantages of concentration in terms of social interaction and services. Unidad Popular planned to cluster peasant families in agricultural villages, to be provided with social and economic services, and which would also be used to increase their political awareness and class consciousness. Every rural community would be assigned production targets and be encouraged to develop pride in its achievements.

One of the key elements of the Unidad Popular regional development plan was its stress on "decentralization." Among the first questions I asked of Chilean officials was whether this policy would not mean, in fact, an "inefficient" equalization of regional income through a redistribution of regional investment, at the cost of a reduction in the growth rate of national income. Their position was that the notion of "efficiency" had been understood mainly in regard to the private, capitalist enterprise, for which a continuation of the concentration trend is acknowledged to be beneficial. Private firms are oriented toward the satisfaction of the demands of middle- and upper-income groups; thus, the concentration of the elite markets in a few metropolitan areas is a highly beneficial factor. In contrast, the policy of Unidad Popular was to produce for large masses of people living throughout the country. Unidad Popular officials also pointed out that there has been no accounting of the indirect subsidy given by the public sector to private firms in the form of social and physical infrastructure and the absorption of the external dis-economies produced by the private economic activities. The concentration of people and economic activities in Santiago, for example, has forced the government to commit large sums to solve traffic congestion, environmental pollution, and social problems, all of which demand the maintenance of a high level of services. In contrast, the new policies were to redirect public investment and to create new infrastructure outside of the existing large centers.

Unidad Popular officials accepted the fact that, for some producers, transportation costs are decisive, and these firms have no choice but to locate in the large urban centers. There are many other firms, however, that are footloose, that is, for which location is of only minor importance, and that need not be concentrated in the capital. The assumption was that realistic cost/benefit analysis, with all social costs included, would change the locational decisions of many firms. The proclivity of private managers to live in large cities would be one of the main obstacles to be overcome.

At the core of the Unidad Popular regional development strategy was the notion that the economy of each province should be based on its native resources, hoping to achieve greater economic efficiency in the long run, and greater social equality immediately. Thus the two objectives of equity and growth were not, in their opinion, in conflict; on the contrary, in order to achieve growth, a fair distribution is a necessary precondition.

Up to 1970, the "growth poles" strategy constituted the undisputed formula for Chilean regional planning. Unidad Popular planners criticized the "growth poles" strategy strongly, stressing that the State's role was restricted to that of an observer, which only occasionally developed its own projects–and then following the same criteria as a private firm. Unidad Popular planners defined their regional strategy as "development of economically integrated areas." The development of "growth poles," according to them, was characterized by the concentration of investment in a few promising urban centers, in the hope that their influence would spread to the surrounding region. The result was that the growth centers drained the countryside and smaller towns of their resources, increasing their dependence. Instead, the new policies aimed at the recognition and planning of geographic areas as integrated wholes. The best way to clarify this is to present two examples of actual programs that were being implemented in the depressed provinces of Chiloé and Magallanes.

Chiloé is an isolated island in the southern part of the country, with a monoculture economy of potatoes, handicapped by long distances (and high transportation costs) to the large urban centers. As a result, its economy stagnated and the young population emigrated heavily. The proposed program involved the development of a productive complex combining a new cattle and dairy industry, feeding on potatoes and producing milk and butter, linked with a chemical industry using the rural production as input to manufacture dextrose and antibiotics. Dairy and chemical products are specialized enough to bear relatively high transportation costs. While this productive complex did not require a particularly large investment, it was expected to have a major developmental impact on the whole province. Rather than affecting only the main population center of the region, benefits of the investment would have been distributed throughout the island.

Magallanes is another depressed rural area in the South, afflicted by low income and high unemployment, which led to heavy out-migration to urban centers and to Argentina, where 300,000 Chileans work in the wool industry of Patagonia. Although Magallanes is very suitable for lamb and wool production and there was strong demand for wool in Chile, there were obstacles to developing this industry in the region. The main problem, according to Unidad Popular planners, was that the commercial monopolies in Santiago fixed prices according to their own interests, and small rural producers could not profitably enter the wool business. A few family-owned firms, which had control across the whole spectrum of financial, industrial and agricultural enterprises, were keeping this region underdeveloped and, even worse, the State was subsidizing those firms by absorbing the high social costs generated by their actions. The elimination of monopolistic controls would have permitted the development of the region, starting at the level of small rural producers.

No discussion of regional policies should conclude without mention of the issue of the copper mines, which are the backbone of the Chilean economy. They were originally owned by foreign firms, partially acquired by the Christian Democratic administration, and fully expropriated by the government of Unidad Popular in one of its first actions. The long-term consequences of expropriation would have been considerable, since the profits remitted abroad by foreign firms averaged around 60 percent per year during the 1960s.[6] Regionally, Unidad Popular planners expected that reinvestment and local development practices would have begun to benefit the copper-producing regions.

CONCLUSION

There were several important elements of the regional planning process in Chile under Unidad Popular which reflect the experimental path the country was following during this transitional period. Political goals, defined in clear ideological terms, had explicit priority in the planning process. Popular needs and participation became an integral part of this process; there was extensive involvement of grassroots organizations such as trade unions, peasant unions, and squatter settlement associations. Nationalism was strongly asserted. There was emphasis on finding Chile's own road to socialism, which meant that the experience of other countries was carefully filtered before being applied. What may be more important, experiences in non-socialist countries were seldom considered.

The technical level in the planning process was low. This was complicated by the belief of some officials that theoretical and analytical tools of regional planning developed in Western countries are applicable only in the capitalist environment, limiting unduly the possibilities of adapting knowledge generated in the United States and Western Europe. Programs were rather pragmatic and based on trial and error, while basic goals were ideologically defined: There was a constant search for paths to reach the desired goals, constrained by lack of experience, time and analytical capacity. On the other hand, there was no uncertainty about the general direction of change.

Planning was handicapped by lack of control over all branches of the government. Unidad Popular had only the executive power, while the legislative power was in the hands of the opposition and the judicial power was, traditionally, independent. Thus, all policies, regardless of their degree of radicalism, had to be based on previous legislation.

In summary, the experience of Chile under Unidad Popular constituted an important experiment in regional policy-making, in which unorthodox approaches to egalitarian development were being employed, providing potentially valuable lessons for the rest of Latin America.

NOTES

1. For further details on the historical development of internal migration in Chile, see Herrick (1965).

2. This classification of regions as "boundary" or "core" regions follows that of Friedmann (1973).

3. Unemployment in the place of origin was even higher for female migrants, reaching 65 percent (MINVU, n.d.).

4. This section is based on interviews with Chilean officials in several agencies, especially ODEPLAN, and on working documents of on-going projects.

5. The "salario vital," or minimum wage, equalled the minimum income necessary for an average-size family to live at the lowest acceptable level. Often, the wage/salary scale was measured in multiples of "salarios vitales."

6. Speech of President Salvador Allende to the United Nations General Assembly, 1972 Session.

REFERENCES

FRIEDMANN, J. (1973) Urbanization, Planning, and National Development. Beverly Hills, Calif.: Sage Publications.

HERRICK, B. H. (1965) Urban Migration and Economic Development in Chile. Cambridge, Mass.: MIT Press.

Ministerio de Economía, Ministerio de Hacienda, ODEPLAN (1971) Instrucciones para la preparación del proyecto de Plan 1971-76 y Plan Anual 1972. Santiago, Chile.

MINVU [Ministerio de la Vivienda y Urbanismo] (n.d.) Migraciones internas, marginalidad y desarrollo urbano. Santiago, Chile.

ODEPLAN [Oficina de Planificación Nacional] (1971) Antecedentes y criterios para la formulación de la política de desarrollo regional 1971-76. Santiago, Chile.

--- (1970) El desarrollo económico y social de Chile en la década 1970-1980. Santiago, Chile.

Universidad de Chile (1963) La economía de Chile en el período 1950-1963. Santiago, Chile: Instituto de Economía, Universidad de Chile.

NOTES

NOTES

NOTES

NOTES